Newbold and Rosenbloom have assembled a 'who's who' of U.S. scholars thinking big thoughts about public administration through the lens of the Constitution. This book is a must read for anyone who wants to understand the full story of American public administration.

Rosemary O'Leary, *University of Kansas*

Newbold and Rosenbloom have produced a volume that should be on the desk of every public administration professor and practitioner, and in the hands of every student. They and a distinguished group of contributors provide an intellectual and practical road map for refocusing the field – and the nation – on constitutional foundations and purposes in an era of institutional decay and political uncertainty. It is high time for us all to enroll in The Constitutional School.

Danny Balfour, *Grand Vallley State University*

This book is a must read for those who want to understand the Constitutional School of public administration. Written by two of the leading scholars who have popularized this approach, David Rosenbloom and Stephanie Newbold have assembled a first rate collection of essays and previous articles that lay bare the meaning and consequence of the Constitutional School for our role as teachers, scholars and practitioners of public administration.

Doug Morgan, *Portland State University*

Twentieth century government has been aptly characterized as an administrative state. The basic institutional arrangements have been designed by the Founding Fathers, but they are not set in stone. In fact, the present politicized debate about the relation between legislature, executive and judiciary, calls attention to the importance of state and administrative law in the study of public administration. This volume pulls together earlier published pieces with new introductions, and invites public administration scholars to more deeply investigate the role and meaning of constitutional and administrative law in this administrative state. Calibrating the balance between the three branches of government cannot be left to Members of Congress and Supreme Court Justices only. This volume is a call for more research into and teaching of constitutional and administrative law in the study of public administration. This constitutional school of thought is too important to ignore.

Jos C.N. Raadschelders, *Ohio State University*

The Constitutional School of American Public Administration

The growing Constitutional School of Public Administration has roots in *The Federalist Papers*, constitutional law, and the writings of several contemporary leaders and contributors in the field. It comprises a loose grouping of scholars who subscribe to the proposition that constitutions and the constitutional characteristics of a regime are key determinants of public administrative culture, institutions, organizations, personnel practices, budgetary and decision-making processes, commitment to the rule of law and human rights, and myriad aspects of overall behavior. Participants in Constitutional School research believe that the "big questions" in public administration cannot be answered without reference to constitutional designs, institutions, and regime values. This edited volume brings together many of the most prominent names in Constitutional School scholarship in an aim to make it more visible, accessible, and central to the field of public administration's pedagogy, scholarship, and intellectual development. It will be essential reading for scholars and students of public administration with an interest in constitutional law, administrative law, and political theory around the globe.

Stephanie P. Newbold is Director of the Master of Public Administration program at the School of Public Affairs and Administration and Associate Professor of Public Affairs and Administration at Rutgers University—Newark, USA.

David H. Rosenbloom is Distinguished Professor of Public Administration at American University, USA and serving as a Chinese Thousand Talents Program Professor at Renmin University of China for 2016–2019.

Public Administration and Public Policy
A Comprehensive Publication Program

Editor-in-Chief
David H. Rosenbloom
Distinguished Professor of Public Administration
American University, Washington, DC

Founding Editor
Jack Rabin

Logics of Legitimacy
Three traditions of public administration praxis
Margaret Stout

The Politics–Administration Dichotomy
Toward a constitutional perspective, second edition
Patrick Overeem

Managing Development in a Globalized World
Concepts, processes, institutions
Habib Zafarullah and Ahmed Shafiqul Huque

Cybersecurity
Public sector threats and responses
Kim J. Andreasson

Reinventing Local and Regional Economies
Gerald L. Gordon

Government Budgeting and Financial Management in Practice
Logics to make sense of ambiguity
Gerald J. Miller

Globalism and Comparative Public Administration
Jamil Jreisat

Procurement
edited by Khi V.Thai

The Constitutional School of American Public Administration
edited by Stephanie P. Newbold and David H. Rosenbloom

The Constitutional School of American Public Administration

Edited by
Stephanie P. Newbold and
David H. Rosenbloom

Routledge
Taylor & Francis Group
NEW YORK AND LONDON

First published 2017
by Routledge
711 Third Avenue, New York, NY 10017

and by Routledge
2 Park Square, Milton Park, Abingdon, Oxon OX14 4RN

Routledge is an imprint of the Taylor & Francis Group, an informa business

Library of Congress Cataloging in Publication Data
Names: Newbold, Stephanie P., 1979- editor. | Rosenbloom, David H., editor.
Title: The constitutional school of American public administration / edited by Stephanie P. Newbold and David H. Rosenbloom.
Description: New York, NY : Routledge, 2016. | Series: Public administration and public policy | Includes bibliographical references and index.
Identifiers: LCCN 2016020849| ISBN 9781466567252 (hardback : alk. paper) | ISBN 9781315438962 (ebook)
Subjects: LCSH: Public administration–United States–Philosophy. | Administrative law–United States. | Constitutional law–United States.
Classification: LCC JK421 .C6345 2016 | DDC 351.7301–dc23
LC record available at https://lccn.loc.gov/2016020849

ISBN: 978-1-4665-6725-2 (hbk)
ISBN: 978-1-315-43896-2 (ebk)

Typeset in Sabon
by Taylor & Francis Books

For Herbert J. Storing and John A. Rohr

Contents

List of Illustrations

Table

Box

Preface

> "The Constitution is the guide which I will never abandon."
>
> George Washington

The *Constitutional School of American Public Administration* is an edited volume that explores how the rule of law and democratic-constitutionalism serve as the intellectual, theoretical, and practical foundations of the American administrative state.

This work includes commentaries on previously published articles and two book chapters from scholars who not only support the Constitutional School but who are also willing to demonstrate how their work advances the mission and purpose of this school of thought.

Part I explains what the Constitutional School is and its relevance to democratic governance. We offer an earnest discussion of how the Constitutional School provides the normative basis for democratic governance in the 21st century, how it advances the field intellectually, and how its potential achievements improve the democratic-constitutional underpinnings of U.S. public administration. This analysis is followed by Stephanie Newbold's 2010 *Public Administration Review* article on the need to establish this school of thought within the field, which is the publication that serves as the foundation for each commentary in this volume.

Part II emphasizes the foundations of the Constitutional School and why it matters to U.S. Public Administration. First, David Rosenbloom provides commentary on the legacy of Herbert J. Storing and how his contribution to public administration thought adds to the intellectual depth of the Constitutional School. Next, Rosenbloom explains how the constitutional principle of separation of powers advances public administration theory and why this is important to the Constitutional School. Stephanie Newbold then explores John A. Rohr's analysis of executive power and how the continual ambiguity associated with how much power the American president has to exercise his constitutional duties and responsibilities to make sure the laws are faithfully executed causes confusion and tension within U.S. politics and administration. Finally, Newbold explores the Blacksburg Manifesto and its relevance and importance to the Constitutional School.

Part III focuses on issues and controversies that are currently shaping the Constitutional School. Michael Spicer considers the importance of regime values and neorepublican freedom on public administration. He supports John Rohr's position that there is no single authoritative interpretation of American life that public servants must adopt. Instead, what remains critical for the constitutional integrity of the field is that public servants have to make a moral commitment to put themselves in touch with the values of the American citizenry. Next, David Rosenbloom examines Theodore Lowi's work on legitimating public administration and discusses why Lowi's ideas run somewhat counter to the Constitutional School. This is especially true concerning the idea that independent administrative powers cannot be constitutionally legitimated. While recent U.S. Supreme Court opinions have weakened Lowi's position, his cautionary warning regarding the potential problems that may arise if we make public administration fully compatible with democratic-constitutional norms and values must be taken seriously. This effort can create instances where unforeseen and perhaps undesirable consequences may occur and supporters of the Constitutional School must learn to grapple with those challenges.

Next, Brian Cook examines his efforts to create a theory of the political constitution for the American administrative state. He challenges us to think about public administration with regard to separation of powers, political leadership, the control of faction, and the nature and health of the citizenry in an effort to advance constitutional theory and democratic governance. The final contribution in this section is from Stephanie Newbold who reengages her work with Larry Terry on the President's Committee on Administrative Management. This piece provides a prominent example that illustrates how the intellectual history of the field can shed new light on the importance of democratic-constitutionalism to the theoretical development and practical understanding of the administrative state.

Part IV focuses on the application of the Constitutional School to public administration theory and practice. First, David Rosenbloom argues for the adoption of democratic-constitutional impact statements and scorecards as a means to measure agency performance. This recommendation requires us to devote more attention to democratic-constitutional values that oftentimes are overlooked because of increased foci on creating more cost-effective and results-oriented government. Next, Norma Riccucci assesses the significance of New Federalism for the Constitutional School. She draws attention to how the Supreme Court of the United States has relied on this constitutional principle to shape the administrative state in its own image. Riccucci also makes the case for how the Court's decisions continue to influence the administrative state, all of which is an important aim of the Constitutional School. Third, Stefanie Linquist reexamines her work with Michael Bitzer on the importance of understanding private contractors' liability for constitutional violations. This has become an increasingly important topic in public administration because of greater emphasis on privatization and contracting out public goods and services. Educating private sector contractors on their potential liability for constitutional violations is one way the government maintains constitutional competence and helps to ensure that individual rights are better protected even if the public sector is outsourcing its services to third parties. Finally, Robert Roberts explores the consequences of the U.S. Supreme Court's decision in *Garcetti v. Ceballos* on public employee's freedom of speech. His analysis underscores previous arguments made in a 2007 *Public Administration Review* article and a 2009 *Review of Public Personnel Administration* article. He draws the Constitutional School's attention to the sharp divisions currently being debated in the U.S. Federal Courts of Appeal over the application of the *Garcetti* precedent. Roberts correctly points out that the U.S. Supreme Court will eventually have to reexamine *Garcetti* to establish the constitutional boundaries associated with public employees' freedom of speech more firmly.

In Part V of this work, Newbold and Rosenbloom offer concluding thoughts for how the Constitutional School relates to the field of U.S. public administration in its entirety and advances the democratic governance process.

We dedicate this work to Herbert J. Storing and John A. Rohr, two brilliant constitutional scholars who contributed greatly to the intellectual development and institutional advancement of American public administration. Storing was David and John's professor at the University of Chicago; Rohr was Stephanie's professor at Virginia Tech. Both were unapologetically committed to the democratic foundations of the American republic and to the constitutional legitimacy of the nation's administrative institutions. The Constitutional School is part of their legacy and this edited volume serves as a formative way to incorporate their ideas back into the field's contemporary discourse.

Stephanie P. Newbold
David H. Rosenbloom

Part I

Introduction to the Constitutional School of American Public Administration

1 Providing the Foundation for 21st Century Governance

The Constitutional School of U.S. Public Administration and Why it Matters

Stephanie P. Newbold and David H. Rosenbloom

Good government is dependent upon good administration. The framers of the American Constitution elaborated on this great theme throughout *The Federalist Papers* noting in the 68th entry, "The true test of a good government is its aptitude and tendency to produce a good administration" (Cooke, 1961, p. 461). The Constitution and the rule of law are the central legitimating forces that hold the American administrative state together. As the field of U.S. public administration has transitioned into one that focuses more on scientific enquiry, the application and reliance on quantitative analysis and statistical methods to determine governmental efficiency and effectiveness, the incorporation of business norms and practices into public sector management, and the contracting out of public goods and services to third party and private sector corporations, we find that there is less attention in the literature and in the field's doctoral education for how democratic norms and values work to conserve the constitutional integrity of the American state and its public institutions (Newbold & Rosenbloom, 2014).

In what many view as a modern classic, Ronald Moe and Robert Gilmour's (1995) article underscoring public administration's neglected appreciation for how the rule of law serves as the intellectual core of public sector governance is especially important for the institutional and intellectual integrity of the Constitutional School. Similarly, we believe that grounding public administration in the rule of law and constitutional tradition ensures better government and better administration. Moe and Gilmour challenged the field to focus more on the intersection between public law and public administration and less on trying to apply "glib aphorisms" from other disciplines in an effort to create "ersatz theory." In other words, applying ideas and theories from other intellectual disciplines to public administration just because they sound good is a faulty exercise, because too often what sounds impressive in theory only leads to disappointment and frustration in practice. The challenge of applying management theories from other disciplines to U.S. public administration is that our legitimacy, our heritage is grounded in the rule of law and democratic-constitutionalism. With the possible exception of political science, no other field in the social sciences can claim this legacy.

Every dimension of U.S. public administration—whether we are discussing management, policy, organization theory, ethics, or public affairs in general—has its foundation in public law and in the need for public managers to conserve and maintain democratic-constitutional norms and values (Terry, 2003; Newbold, 2010). The Constitutional School, therefore, is not simply a school of thought that promotes legal or constitutional conversation. Rather, it encourages scholars and practitioners to engage, discuss, examine, and advance theories and ideas that demonstrate how the Constitution, the rule of law, and democratic principles work to advance the governance process.

The Intellectual Foundation and Purpose of the Constitutional School

The Constitutional School, first named by Michael Spicer and Larry Terry in 1993, has its roots in *The Federalist Papers*, constitutional law, American government, and the writings of several contemporary leaders and contributors to the field of U.S. public administration many of whom contributed to this edited volume. Proponents of the Constitutional School maintain that the U.S. Constitution serves as the normative foundation for their analysis of public administration theory and practice (Newbold, 2010). The purpose of the Constitutional School is to create a school of thought that demonstrates how the dimensions of public administration theory and practice can and should be grounded in democratic-constitutional norms and values. We are working to underscore the idea that:

> law-based principles provide the necessary foundation for a growing and evolving administrative system. The principles not only protect the citizenry from an overbearing, arbitrary, and capricious use of government power, they permit substantial public involvement in the processes of developing rules and regulations.
>
> (Moe & Gilmour, 1995, p. 143)

What we know from the intellectual history of the field and from the more contemporary public administration literature is that there is a profound need for and a tremendous focus on topics and questions that address the robust connection between the maintenance and preservation of the rule of law and democratic-constitutionalism with public administration, public affairs, and public policy.

The Constitutional School is supported and sustained by a network of scholars who subscribe to the proposition that constitutions and the constitutional characteristics of a regime are determinants of public administrative institutions, organization, personnel practices, budgetary and decision-making processes, and the overall behavior associated with public sector governance. Together, we believe that the "big questions" in public administration cannot be answered without reference to governmental and legal institutions and regime values. Regime values, according to John Rohr (1989), are an integral component of public administration because they "refer to the values of that political entity that was brought into being by the ratification of the Constitution that created the present American republic" (p. 68). They represent the specific values and norms of behavior the government of the United States is responsible for safeguarding. These values, according to Rohr, are most prominently found in the opinions provided by the Supreme Court of the United States.

The effort to direct a broader and more in-depth conversation towards what types of regime values or public values should be advanced within the confines of American government provides the field of public administration with a distinctive normative opportunity to advance the constitutional integrity of the Union in a more precise and substantive way. We see this effort as one of the most significant contributions the Constitutional School makes to the theory and practice of American public administration.

What the Constitutional School Aims to Achieve

Supporters of the Constitutional School focus significant attention on seven key areas. First, we emphasize how the framing of the U.S. Constitution affects the development of public administration. This speaks to the importance of understanding the intellectual history of public administration and how we must develop a more comprehensive awareness for how the nation's constitutional heritage shapes contemporary political and administrative dynamics. Second, the constitutional principle of separation of powers is an instrumental component of the Constitutional School. Developing a broader understanding as to how the legislative, executive, and judicial branches not only check and balance each other's power but also how each branch works to shape the American administrative state in an image consistent with various economic, social, political, institutional, and legal norms and values is critical. Third, the Constitutional School is largely influenced by the governing principle of constitutional federalism. This underscores how federal, state, and local governments not only work together but also how they can challenge each other to determine which level of government will have the responsibility for creating, implementing, funding, and evaluating key public policies and governing initiatives.

Fourth, the effect of constitutional law on public administration has been profound. It has transformed the rights and responsibilities of the administrative state to the citizens it serves including the rights of individuals in their interactions with agencies and employees (Rosenbloom et al., 2004; Lee & Rosenbloom, 2005; Rosenbloom et al., 2010; Rosenbloom, 2014, 2015). Beginning with the 1982 U.S. Supreme Court case, *Harlow v. Fitzgerald* (457 U.S. 800) and the Court's contemporary application of 42 U.S.C. 1983 based constitutional tort law, public administrators at all levels of government in the United States are required to maintain constitutional competence

(Rosenbloom et al., 2004; Lee & Rosenbloom, 2005; Newbold, 2010). If a civil servant violates a citizen's constitutional rights of which a reasonable person would have known, the federal courts can hold him/her personally and professionally liable for tort violations. This judicially imposed responsibility on public servants further emphasizes the distinctiveness of the profession and how imperative it has become to connect public administration practice to constitutional law.

The Franklin D. Roosevelt administration represents the high noon of U.S. public administrative orthodoxy and the beginnings of the modern administrative state (Newbold & Rosenbloom, 2007). From this point in time to the present, the opinions of the Supreme Court have played a decisive role in shaping the scope of federal administration, the implementation of social programs, and the protection of individual rights. Judicial intervention into the governance process fundamentally changed the workings of the administrative state. The fifth aim of the Constitutional School thus encourages and supports more dialogue and discussion concerning how the Supreme Court's decision-making shapes American government, the administrative state, and the nation's democratic institutions.

To this point, the growth and development of administrative law has dramatically affected government and administration, which represents the sixth aim of the Constitutional School. Students of public administration cannot fully appreciate the art of running the Constitution if they do not understand rule-making, adjudication of agency decisions, and judicial review of agency decision-making. In the United States, for example, public policy is largely established through the rule-making process and rules help to determine the quality of American life. Empirical analysis illustrates this point best:

> From 1993 through 2013, federal agencies routinely promulgated roughly 3,500 to 4,000 rules per year, totaling 81,883. In 2013, agency final rules took up 24,690 pages in the *Federal Register*. On average, a law or rule was passed every 2.5 hours throughout the year, but rules outnumbered statutes by a ratio of 29 to 1. The gross cost of rules for the typical American family was almost $15,000, or 23 percent of their annual income.
>
> (Rosenbloom, 2015, p. 65)

The field is in need of more scholarly and practitioner-oriented discussions and analyses regarding how administrative law influences the practice of government and administration in the United States. The Constitutional School is the place that encourages this research and provides scholars with a contextual space to engage each other on the effects administrative law is having on the administrative state.

Finally, the Constitutional School explores how each of these six goals and governing principles work individually and collectively to advance the democratic governance process. These principles form the core of what this school of thought aims to achieve in the public administration literature and in the world of public administration practice. In the spirit of John Rohr's constitutional legacy, we are calling on scholars and practitioners as well as citizens to think of government, public administration, and governmental institutions in a way that works to secure our nation's regime values. This effort serves as one of the most valuable intellectual endeavors that aims to preserve a more perfect Union by working to secure justice, to safeguard domestic tranquility, to provide for the common defense, and to secure the blessings of liberty for ourselves and our posterity.

References

Cooke, J.E. 1961. *The Federalist*. Middletown, CT: Wesleyan University Press.

Lee, Y.S. & Rosenbloom, D.H. 2005. *A reasonable public servant: Constitutional foundations of administrative conduct in the United States*. Armonk, NY: M.E. Sharpe.

Moe, R.C. & Gilmour, R.S. 1995. Rediscovering principles of public administration: The neglected foundation of public law. *Public administration review* 55(2) March/April: 135–146.

Newbold, S.P. 2010. Toward a constitutional school for American public administration. *Public administration review* 70(4) July/August: 538–546.

Newbold, S.P. & Rosenbloom, D.H. 2007. Brownlow report retrospective. *Public administration review* 67(6) November/December: 1006–1058.

Newbold, S.P. & Rosenbloom, D.H. 2014. Rethinking doctoral education in the age of new democratic governance. In *New democratic governance and the search for legitimacy*, edited by Douglas Morgan & Brian Cook. Armonk, NY: M.E. Sharpe, pp. 284–298.

Rohr, J.A. 1989. *To run a constitution: The legitimacy of the American administrative state*. Lawrence: University Press of Kansas.

Rosenbloom, D.H. 2015. *Administrative law for public managers*. 2nd edn. Boulder, CO: Westview.

Rosenbloom, D.H. 2014. *Federal service and the Constitution: The development of the public employee relationship*. 2nd edn. Washington, DC: Georgetown University Press.

Rosenbloom, D.H., Carroll, J.D. & Carroll, J.D. 2004. *Constitutional competence for public managers: Cases and commentary*. Belmont, CA: Thompson-Wadsworth.

Rosenbloom, D.H., O'Leary, R. & Chanin, J. 2010. *Public administration and law*. 3rd edn. Boca Raton, FL: CRC Press.

Spicer, M.W. & Terry, L.D. 1993. Legitimacy, history, and logic: Public administration and the Constitution. *Public administration review* 53(3) pp. 239–246

Terry, L.D. 2003. *Leadership of public bureaucracies: The administrator as conservator*. 2nd edn. Armonk, NY: M.E. Sharpe.

Toward a Constitutional School for American Public Administration

Stephanie P. Newbold

From: *Public Administration Review* 70(4) July/August, 2010: 538–546.

Moving toward a Constitutional School for the field of public administration would improve the quality of scholarship associated with how to maintain and preserve core democratic-republican values embedded in the American constitutional tradition. Those of us who are part of establishing this movement define the Constitutional School as a group of public administration scholars and practitioners, joined in a loose confederation, characterized by an interest in the principles embodied in the U.S. Constitution as the basis for our research and practice.[1] We see the Constitution as *the* normative base for our scholarship, and it demands that we reemphasize and reestablish a greater commitment to how the rule of law pervades public administrative management in its entirety (Rosenbloom, 2002, 2003). Those associated with the Constitutional School would most likely still agree with Ronald Moe and Robert Gilmour's position, one they established 15 years ago: "Today, public administration has largely abandoned or forgotten its roots in public law—and has accepted, to varying degrees, the generic behavioral principles of management as taught in schools of business" (1995, p. 135).

The purpose of this article is to demonstrate in clear, articulate terms why constitutional tradition and rule of law should serve as the foundations of public administration scholarship in the United States. Without the acceptance of this norm, American public administration will find itself unable to embrace the intellectual underpinnings that legitimate the field in its entirety (Cook, 1996; P. Cooper, 1997, 2006; Lee & Rosenbloom, 2005; Moe and Gilmour, 1995; Rohr, 1986, 1998, 2002; Rosenbloom, 1971, 1983, 1987, 2003; Rosenbloom, Carroll & Carroll, 2000; Rosenbloom & Kravchuk, 2005; Rosenbloom & O'Leary, 1996; Spicer & Terry, 1993a, 1993b; Terry, 2003; Waldo, 1948; Wamsley et al., 1990). This movement provides three distinct ways to improve public administration scholarship: it emphasizes the intellectual and practical value of the Constitution to the American administrative state; it establishes a consistently used term that works to encourage a specific type of dialogue; and it helps demonstrate how the American Constitution pervades all areas of public administration scholarship and practice.

The Intellectual Origins of Moving toward a Constitutional School

Michael Spicer and Larry Terry first coined the term "Constitutional School" in their provocative forum on "Public Administration and the Constitution" for a 1993 issue of *Public Administration Review* (*PAR*). Several of us knew Terry quite well, and years after *PAR* published this manuscript, John Rohr and I asked him to expand on his understanding of this concept. Terry elaborated with great intellectual energy on this point and instructed us that it was Alexander Hamilton's position in *Federalist 27* that had inspired him to create this term. He was particularly influenced by Hamilton's idea that "[the people's] confidence in and obedience to a government will commonly be proportioned to the goodness or badness of its administration" (Cooke, 1961, p. 172). Creating a Constitutional School for American public administration, according to Terry, would allow more scholars *and* practitioners opportunities to determine whether the administration of our government was working to meet the citizenry's needs in responsible, efficient, effective, ethical, legal, and constitutional ways. Those who are part of moving toward a Constitutional School also want to encourage public administration scholars, practitioners, and students to pay more attention to what academics in other fields are publishing with regard to issues of constitutional significance. What we can learn from those who are writing on issues focusing on American constitutionalism holds the potential to legitimate the value that rule of law brings to the American administrative state even further.

Terry maintained that incorporating Hamilton's eighteenth-century argument into the intellectual framework and foundation for the Constitutional School was essential, because it provided the necessary theoretical basis to legitimate the contemporary value of this idea. In order for the public to maintain confidence in the integrity of administrative agencies, public servants must demonstrate constitutional competence, respect for the rule of law, and sound discretionary judgment in all aspects of their decision-making processes (Rohr, 1998; Rosenbloom, Carroll & Carroll, 2000; Terry, 2003). This way of thinking complements one of Terry's key arguments in support of administrative conservatorship:

> When public administrators take an oath to uphold the Constitution, they are making a moral commitment to the continuance of constitutional processes that encompass particular values, beliefs, and interests. This commitment is expressed in practical terms through their fidelity to duty in the administration of governmental institutions, including the values embodied in the Constitution.
>
> (2003, p. 28)

The American Constitution not only is vital to the preservation of the administrative state but also provides one of the most important sources of legitimacy for the field as a whole (Rohr, 1986).

David Rosenbloom (1971) has long examined the connection between the federal civil service and the American Constitution, a relationship, he argues, that is not only important but also undervalued within public administration. Rosenbloom's work helps legitimate the need for a Constitutional School, because it demonstrates how constitutional tradition and the rule of law characterize American public administration, especially with regard to the rights of civil servants and the conception of those rights in both theory and practice. In their review of Rosenbloom's work *Federal Service and the Constitution,* Charles Levine and Lloyd Nigro discuss an increasingly important aspect of federal public management:

> Rosenbloom documents an accelerating trend toward narrowing the gap between the political and legal rights of public employees and those of the general citizenry. While this trend liberalizes the public employment relationship, Rosenbloom worries about the implications of constitutional-legal equality for public employees and its potential impact on the role of public bureaucracies in our political system. He concludes that in the future the capacity of political officials to control the selection and behavior of employees will be reduced and that "the change will probably encourage an increase in the role that civil servants will play in the political arena."
>
> (Levine & Nigro, 1975, p. 100)

Two important U.S. Supreme Court cases provide clarification of Rosenbloom's excellent point. *Elrod v. Burns* (1976) and *Branti v. Finkel* (1980) dealt with the concept of patronage dismissals. Both focused on the constitutional question of whether newly elected officials could discharge previous non-civil service appointments made by outgoing administrations because they did not belong to the same political party. In both cases, the Supreme Court ruled in favor of the removed official. In reviewing the *Elrod* case, Rohr makes a keen observation: "The decision was a stunning illustration of the marked tendency in American constitutional law for individual rights to trump the claims of institutional interests—in this case the interest of political parties ... had traditionally been regarded as vital components of democratic government" (2002, p. 124). Rohr's reflection on *Branti* also illuminates another key area of constitutional concern for American public administration: "The ultimate inquiry is not whether the label 'policy maker' or 'confidential' fits a particular position; rather, the question is whether the hiring authority can demonstrate that party affiliation is an appropriate requirement for the effective performance of the public office involved" (2002, p. 127). Taken together, these two cases provide noteworthy examples of how public administration should incorporate issues of constitutional significance into an organized school of thought in an effort to inform scholars and practitioners about how the Constitution and the rule of law permeate public administration, public management, and the democratic governance process, especially in times of political and administrative transformation and change.

Rosemary O'Leary and Charles Wise provide another useful example that illustrates the value of moving toward a Constitutional School in their research on how judges and courts are "becoming increasingly active in their oversight of administrative agencies" because of the "new partnership that has emerged between judges and administrators" in recent years (1991, pp. 316, 317). The hope of a Constitutional School is that when scholars and practitioners write about and discuss issues of constitutional and legal significance, they will consider how this school of thought informs the field's institutional and intellectual heritage. Such efforts are precisely why Phillip Cooper argues that "[p]ublic law provides a foundation for administration and is essential to the infrastructure on which administrative institutions, and most other institutions of society for that matter, operate" (1997, p. 105). These types of unified perspectives could also serve as a useful attempt to bridge the theory–practice divide within the larger public administration community.

While *Federalist* doctrine provides the theoretical foundation for establishing a Constitutional School, the application of this approach has important, practical ramifications for the administrative state. For example, the recent, highly regarded supplemental issue of *Public Administration Review* (Volume 67, 2007) analyzing the government's response to Hurricane Katrina in 2005 would have provided an ideal forum for a supporter of the Constitutional School to discuss how Hamilton's observation in *Federalist No. 27* remains as relevant today as it was in 1787. In this issue of *PAR*, scholars and practitioners examine a number of important topics relating to the failed levee system, the government's emergency response plan, broad issues affecting public sector management and decision making, the consequences of economic status and race, and even federalism, especially for those most negatively affected in the Lower Ninth Ward. This collective analysis, as informative as it continues to be, overlooks the practical notion of what happens to the institutional integrity of a republican, constitutional regime that undermines the positive relationship between the administration of publicly funded disaster preparedness programs as well as emergency management mechanisms to respond to catastrophic natural disasters *and* the citizenry's confidence in their government to meet the needs of those most directly affected by extraordinary calamities outside their control. In a word, it substantiates Moe and Gilmour's observation that "public law is the under-appreciated 'cement' that binds the separated powers of the administrative state, ensures political and legal accountability of its officials, and restrains abuses of administrative discretion and conflicts of interest" (1995, p. 138).

Those who are part of the Constitutional School, as well as those who argue that public administration should focus more on how upholding the rule of law improves our continual efforts "to form a more perfect union," would have relished an opportunity to demonstrate that a government that fails to meet the needs of the citizenry, especially in times of crises, contradicts some of the most important themes that Publius advocated in *The Federalist*. Conserving democratic-republican values and the constitutional integrity of public administrative agencies that operate in a complex, separation of powers government is not an easy task, but it is a necessary one (Rainey, 2003; Shapiro, 1988).

On President Barack Obama's first day in office, he signed an executive order focusing on increased transparency and rule of law within the executive branch, particularly with regard to the Freedom of Information Act. This, he maintained, would be a hallmark of his administration. According to President Obama, "Public service is a privilege. It's not about advantaging yourself. It's not about advancing your friends or your corporate clients. It's not about advancing an ideological agenda or the special interests of any organization. Public service is simply and absolutely about advancing the interests of Americans" (*The Caucus*, 2009). The President's remarks invoked James Madison's great observation in *Federalist 51:* "The interest of the man must always be connected to the constitutional rights of the place" (Cooke, 1961, p. 349). Leaders of the American republic must live up to a higher notion of public virtue, and, in order to carry out Madison's expectation, public servants must maintain constitutional competence and a thorough recognition of how the rule of law and discretionary judgment affect the citizenry they serve so that the preservation of the nation's constitutional integrity is maintained. A careful examination of the historical evolution of American constitutional tradition demands no less.

A Government of the People, by the People, and for the People: How Establishing a Constitutional School Advances Democratic Governance

Proponents of the Constitutional School would likely champion the following observation by Charles Goodsell: "The quality of public service in the United States is vastly underrated. Our government's administrative agencies and those who work in them are commonly portrayed as inefficient, incompetent, and wasteful—and often uncivil and devious as well. This is simply not true" (2004, p. xi). Like the Progressive Era in the late nineteenth and early twentieth centuries (Goodnow, 1900; Wilson, 1887), the President's Committee on Administrative Management during the Franklin D. Roosevelt administration (1937), and the New Public Management movement of today (Considine, 2001; Loffler, 1997; Osborne & Gaebler, 1992; Peters 1992), administrative scholars and practitioners have long championed the need for government to work efficiently, effectively, and economically. In fact, Hamilton opens *Federalist 1* with the staunch assertion that the "unequivocal experience" under the Articles of Confederation led to the "inefficacy of the subsisting Foederal [*sic*] Government," and in order to secure the "existence of the Union," the majority of the states had to ratify the Constitution (Cooke, 1961, p. 3).

The field traditionally recognizes that these reform efforts attempted to apply efficient public administrative management strategies to the governing of the nation. But they also represented important historical, political, intellectual, and institutional opportunities to "reconcile traditional democratic institutions with the requirements of new administrative technology" (Fry & Raadschelders, 2008, 309). By means of contrast, scholars such as Terry Cooper (1991, 1994; Cooper & Wright 1992), Rosemary O'Leary (O'Leary & Wise, 1991, 2003), John Rohr (1986, 1998, 2002), David Rosenbloom (2002; Rosenbloom, Carroll & Carroll, 2000), Larry Terry (2003), Dwight Waldo (1948), Gary Wamsley et al. (1990), and Charles Wise (1998, 2001) have championed the notion that it is often just as important, and perhaps even more so, for government to implement public policies and rely on managerial techniques that demonstrate values associated with responsibility, representativeness, responsiveness, rule of law, and especially constitutional competence.

Yong Lee and David Rosenbloom (2005) present a useful distinction between utilitarian and instrumental values versus contractarian principles for public sector decision making that demonstrates where the Constitutional School could and should fit within the broader public administration literature. Lee and Rosenbloom maintain:

> Utilitarianism leads public administrators to judge the desirability of decisions and other actions in terms of cost-benefit ratios. Instrumentalism focuses on cost-effectiveness, that is, making government "work better and cost less." All modern administrative approaches to funding the public sector are based on some mix of utilitarian and instrumental thinking.
>
> (2005, p. 8)

By contrast, Lee and Rosenbloom point the field's attention to the differences between economically oriented public budgeting decision making and the need for American civil servants to apply constitutional competence so that they are able to protect the individual rights of citizens while simultaneously upholding the rule of law more efficiently and effectively:

> The contractarian judges do not have to consider how else public dollars headed for the jail may be used; the utilitarian-instrumental public budgeters routinely give short shrift to the rights of the prisoners. The reasonably competent public servant has to combine both perspectives: Within the framework of the discretion available to administrators, the rights of the detainees should be protected in the most cost-effective

> fashion. Individuals' constitutional rights, whether enumerated or nonenumerated, cannot easily be sacrificed for the greatest good of the greatest number.
>
> (2005, p. 8)

Their comparison of the utilitarian and contractarian perspectives is quite helpful in determining how establishing a Constitutional School could broaden our understanding for how the rule of law substantiates our democratic-republican regime in both theory and practice.

Joel Aberbach and Bert Rockman, in their 30-year analysis of the executive branch at the U.S. federal level, observe:

> A government of laws, as Americans often like to think theirs is, is a government thick with safeguards against the arbitrary or capricious use of power. Many of those safeguards also prevent administrators from responding in commonsense ways that might be regarded as responsive or adaptive.
>
> (2000, p. 14)

In the context of public administration reform movements and the examination of administrative management in general, their empirical observations illustrate some of the practical difficulties that can occur when governing in a separation of powers regime. Even so, we should not overlook the fact that when government works both efficiently *and* responsively, the citizenry's opinion of it usually increases (Barnard, [1938] 1968; Cooke, 1961; T. Cooper, 1991; Goodsell, 2004; Rosenbloom & Kravchuk, 2005; Selznick, 1957; Terry, 2003; Waldo, 1948; Wamsley et al., 1990). By contrast, when government leaders and administrative agencies fail to meet the needs of the citizenry, particularly during times of crises, as was the case in the early stages of the Great Depression and in the more recent response to the victims of Hurricane Katrina, citizen confidence in government naturally decreases.

Dwight Waldo, like Alexander Hamilton, was keenly aware of this dynamic, and he provided one of the most important, yet overlooked, observations about the relationship between efficiency and democracy within the American administrative state:

> A government that is *really* democratic is also an efficient government: it is sensitive to popular demand, it realizes popular will with intelligence, honesty, economy, and dispatch. Contrariwise, really efficient government is also democratic: it ministers to the real needs of the people it represents.
>
> (1948, p. 134)

Waldo's perspective largely comes from his comparison of the ideological differences between the American founders and the early twentieth-century administrative reformers who championed principles commonly associated with scientific management, one best way to organize, and economic efficiency.[2] However, it would be advantageous for twenty-first century American scholars and practitioners to think about Waldo's position regarding the need to connect democratic values with economic ones as a way to advance and improve the democratic governance process. In their timely reflection on Waldo's seminal work, David Rosenbloom and Howard McCurdy draw attention to this precise point: "True democracy represents the will of the people; true efficiency represents the selection of methods that are correct with respect to an unbiased standard, irrespective of what people desire" (2007, p. 204). Organization theorists, like some public administration scholars, have also examined the need to expand the general intellectual conceptualization of efficiency. In particular, Chester Barnard's classic work, *The Functions of the Executive*, provides a level of insight that illustrates important difficulties that often arise in any organizational environment when leaders fail to understand the concept of efficiency in multidimensional terms:

> To have an organization that lends prestige and secures the loyalty of desirable persons is a complex and difficult task in efficiency—in all-round efficiency, not one-sided efficiency. It is for these reasons that good organizations—commercial, governmental, military, academic, and others—will be observed to devote great attention and sometimes great expense of money to the non-economic inducements, because they are indispensable to fundamental efficiency, as well as to effectiveness in many cases.
>
> ([1938] 1968, p. 94)

Those who champion the need to move toward a Constitutional School do not argue that the only way to study and practice public administrative scholarship is through a constitutional lens. In a word, we want to draw attention to the value that studying American constitutional theory and the rule of law bring to the study and practice of public administration. In order to accomplish this objective, several dynamics must occur.

First, underscoring the importance of American constitutional theory to public administration demonstrates that the legitimacy of the administrative state is found only within the nation's constitutional heritage (Rohr, 1986). Second, developing a consistently used term that encourages discussion and debate on issues of constitutional and legal significance is a critical element of this intellectual endeavor. Third, we want to encourage scholars with expertise in areas such as public policy, organization theory, law, ethics, and public management to direct attention to how the Constitution permeates almost every intellectual dimension of public administration theory and practice. For example, Stephanie Newbold (2008) has initiated a discussion of how the constitutional principles of federalism and separation of powers e an excellent way to teach and study organization theory as it relates ıaging public sector organizations in the United States. Rosemary ◡ ʟeary and Charles Wise (2003) have discussed the role of the courts in shaping public management as well as the legal responsibilities of public institutions to the administrative state. In their discussion of the evolution of U.S. Supreme Court decisions from 1900 to 2000, O'Leary and Wise make a striking observation:

> As federal court supervision of public institutions has stretched over decades, the Supreme Court has seen the necessity of nudging the district courts toward ending their supervision of public institutions. As a result, the Court has begun to play a more directive role in indicating which considerations district judges should use when terminating judicial decrees in institution cases.
>
> (2003, p. 180)

The hope of a Constitutional School is to create and provide more opportunities for the emergence of this type of dialogue in our literature and at our conferences in order to demonstrate how this area of scholarship advances the field's understanding of the American Constitution and the rule of law and their direct and indirect relationships on the administrative state and its democratic institutions.

Gary Wamsley has often argued that public administrative agencies demonstrate how the United States represents an ever-democratizing constitutional republic.[3] According to Wamsley, the American state has not always lived up to the high standing moral principles espoused in its Declaration for Independence or in its Constitution, but public administration is the one entity of government we can look to that is constantly working to ensure that the normative values embedded within our constitutional heritage are conserved. Many examples exist throughout American history that support this argument, but here we will simply focus on one.

The Supreme Court's landmark 1954 decision in *Brown v. Board of Education of Topeka, Kansas*, which overturned *Plessey v. Ferguson* and made it unconstitutional to segregate public schools according to race, infuriated much of the Jim Crow South. The southern states' refusal to abide by the Court's decision forced President Dwight D. Eisenhower in 1957 to send the National Guard into Arkansas to ensure the safety of African American school-aged children who were entering all-white public schools for the first time. This example, as unfortunate and embarrassing as it is today, points to an important constitutional principle that Madison described in *Federalist 10*. It is always possible for a majority to infringe on the individual rights and constitutional protections of a minority. Indeed, as the American constitutional republic has grown and developed since its inception, the courts, especially the Supreme Court, have played an integral role in helping to preserve the individual rights and constitutional protections of minorities.

Administrative agencies, as a result, have also worked to implement many of the necessary policy changes, insisted on by the Court, in an attempt to conserve the nation's constitutional tradition and many of the core democratic principles equated with American republicanism.

Justice Stephen Breyer has publicly contended that the Court's ruling in *Brown* and President Eisenhower's subsequent decision to force much of the South to comply with the Court's opinion is a valuable example that illustrates why the Supreme Court should have the last word in matters of extraordinary constitutional significance. Breyer maintains this position not because the Court's rulings are always right, but because one branch of government must be insulated from politics[4] in order to carry out the will of the founders and to defend the constitutional rights of individuals and groups who *might* be discriminated against by an overbearing, oppressive majority.[5]

Rosenbloom (1987) has also focused the public administration community's attention to the idea that a "new partnership" has emerged between civil servants and the judiciary. He maintains that three distinct conditions exist, largely established by the courts, that enable this partnership to materialize:

> The declaration of new constitutional rights for individuals as they come into contact with public administration; efforts to use adjudication to obtain broad reforms of public institutions such as schools, mental health facilities, and prisons; and the Court's clarification that public administrators have qualified, but not absolute, immunity within the scope of their official duties.
>
> (1987, pp. 76–77)

Rosenbloom's analysis demonstrates the type of partnership that the courts maintain with public servants and the agencies in which they serve. This type of relationship builds on the nation's separation of powers system of government and provides insights into how the courts, like Congress (see Rosenbloom, 2002), play an active, participatory role in the administrative state. Scholars and practitioners interested in these types of institutional and constitutional changes are precisely the type of audience the Constitutional School hopes to attract.

Moving Toward a Constitutional School: A Bold, Much-Needed Addition to Public Administration Discourse

When Philip Selznick discussed the need to cultivate a political orientation for developing a more comprehensive understanding of institutional leadership, he also articulated a position that resonates with efforts to establish a Constitutional School: "The link between 'polity' and 'politics' must constantly be kept in mind" (1957, p. 61). The parallels between Selznick's argument and the case of the "Revolt at Justice," highlighted in Amy Gutmann and Dennis Thompson's edited volume on cases affecting ethics and politics, points to the need for public administration to pay greater attention to constitutional tradition and the rule of law. The "revolt" occurred when lawyers for the U.S. Justice Department refused to comply with the Richard M. Nixon administration's orders not to integrate public schools, as the High Court had ordered in 1954. Their acts of official disobedience illustrate an important example that highlights Selznick's observation regarding the need to distinguish between polity and politics. Gary Greenberg's personal description of this case is striking. The reasons why Greenberg and his colleagues did not merely resign their positions within the Justice Department are constitutionally intriguing and particularly insightful for the argument about why the Constitution should be at the center of American public administration theory and practice. As Greenberg recalls:

> While pledged by our oaths to support and defend the Constitution and bound by duty to follow our consciences and adhere to the law, we faced a situation in which the Administration had proposed to act in violation of the law. We knew that we could not remain silent, for silence, particularly in this Administration, is interpreted as support or acquiescence. Only through some form of protest could we live up to our obligations as lawyers and as officers of the United States ... For the duty to serve the law, to promote the administration of justice, to support and defend the Constitution is more than a negative command; it is more than a 'thou shalt not.' It is an affirmative duty to act in a manner that would best serve and promote those interests.
>
> (1997, p. 146)

Greenberg's actions reflect the very foundation of why the American Constitution serves as the theoretical and practical underpinning for the administrative state. It provides a grounding and a standard that cannot be rejected by those who follow its principles. We recognize and acknowledge many of the democratic defects associated with the Constitution (Levinson 2006), but we accept it nonetheless. For, as Publius concluded at the end of *Federalist 51,* "And happily for the *republican cause,* the practicable sphere may be carried out to a very great extent, by a judicious modification and mixture of the *federal principle*" (Cooke, 1961, p. 353).

Rosenbloom's (1983) analysis of the legal approach to public administration also provides an important intellectual foundation for the Constitutional School. His emphasis on procedural due process, individual substantive rights (as the Supreme Court has determined that the Fourteenth Amendment also incorporates the Bill of Rights), and how the American courts value equity and fairness when conflicts emerge between private parties and the government (Rosenbloom, 1983, p. 223) is quite helpful. The Constitutional School supports this type of argument because it demonstrates a way for the field to pay more active attention to how our government can and should secure the constitutional and individual rights of citizens. It places less emphasis on economic cost–benefit analyses and more attention on how government can work in responsible, representative, and responsive ways that uphold constitutional principles and the rule of law within the context of public sector decision making.

Contributors to the intellectual development of democratic theory, dating from the ancient Greeks to contemporary theorists such as Leo Strauss, Isaiah Berlin, and Sheldon Wolin, have consistently argued for the need to connect the study and practice of politics with higher values that are essential to the maintenance and preservation of democracy, including, but not limited to, fairness, justice, equality, freedom, individual rights, property, moral reasoning, and the use and misuse of discretionary judgment. Those interested in taking part in a movement toward a Constitutional School could make scholarly contributions to the literature that underscore where, when, and how a branch of government, an administrative agency, or a civil servant upholds democratic principles, as in the case of the "Revolt at Justice," and where, when, and how they might neglect them, as in the case of Hurricane Katrina. When members of the public administration community discuss, write, and teach issues that relate to ideas of constitutional significance and rule of law, a Constitutional School of thought provides an intellectual place and a framework for bringing these ideas to life in meaningful, lasting ways.

The Constitutional School for American public administration does not preference one constitutional perspective or idea over another; rather, we encourage and depend on different approaches, perspectives, and thoughts about how the American Constitution affects administrative theory and practice. Important examples already exist in our scholarly literature that support the position that this school of thought would improve the intellectual and institutional discourse regarding the relevance of American constitutional tradition to issues affecting contemporary public administrative management.

First, Herbert Storing's (1981) position that the Anti-Federalists were leading contributors to the ratification process of the proposed Constitution of 1787 is a significant addition to the history of public administration. His scholarship has improved the field's awareness of how the Constitution's opponents worked to improve the ratification process, because they were able to instruct Publius on certain weaknesses in his argument.[6] Although Storing never uses the term "Constitutional School," his scholarly work certainly makes him a contributor to the idea behind this intellectual movement because so much of his research focuses on the historical, political, institutional, and intellectual development of the American Constitution and the state it created. The field should take note that both John Rohr and David Rosenbloom were his students at the University of Chicago.

Second, O. C. McSwite's (1997) argument that the Federalists deceived the Anti-Federalists into ratifying a new governing document that did not represent their interests in the same way the Articles of Confederation protected individual and community rights is another highly contested point of view that is currently being debated in American administrative theory. Storing's and McSwite's perspectives could not be more different from one another in terms of their interpretation of the constitutional history of the United States. The fact that such dichotomous positions currently exist pertaining to the ratification process should continue to invoke meaningful, purposeful discussions and analyses by constitutional scholars and administrative historians as to the contemporary value that these positions bring to the intellectual practice of democratic governance and the study of public administration.

More recently, Sanford Levinson's (2006) questioning of where and how the American Constitution went wrong, and what the people can do to correct these deficiencies, provides another important argument that we would like to draw attention to in terms of demonstrating how this school could encourage the field to evaluate and debate the pervasiveness of the Constitution within our democratic republic. In this provocative and engaging work, Levinson maintains that the legislative process, Article II's creation of an all-too-powerful executive, lifetime appointments for Supreme Court justices, various forms of voting discrimination, and the difficulties that Article V imposes for amending the Constitution are undemocratic governing elements that permeate the American Constitution. These types of questions, irrespective of how one interprets Levinson's argument, are precisely the sort of discussion that the Constitutional School would like to initiate and promote in academic journals, at national conferences, and in graduate seminars. They demonstrate that perspectives on American constitutional theory are multidimensional and that we can all learn from engaging with ideas that might be the complete opposite of what we, as individual scholars, assert as fundamentally essential to the legal and constitutional foundations of the American state but are intellectually relevant all the same.

Another example is Supreme Court Justice Antonin Scalia's line of reasoning as to why the arguments made at the founding of the American republic continue to serve as a formative tool for interpreting the Constitution textually. While Scalia's interpretation of the Constitution is quite different from that of Breyer and many others, his distinctive, textualist approach to constitutional interpretation and legal reasoning provides another informative perspective for the Constitutional School of American public administration to discuss and learn from, to agree or disagree with, theoretically and practically. According to Scalia:

> I will consult the writings of some men who happened to be delegates to the Constitutional Convention—Hamilton's and Madison's writings in *The Federalist*, for example. I do so, however, not because they were Framers and therefore their intent is authoritative and must be the law;

> but rather because their writings, like those of other intelligent and informed people of the time, display how the text of the Constitution was practically understood. Thus I give equal weight to Jay's pieces in *The Federalist,* and to Jefferson's writings, even though neither of them was a Framer. What I look for in the Constitution is precisely what I look for in a statute: the original meaning of the text, not what the original draftsmen intended.
>
> (1997, p. 38)

While many within the legal community disagree with Scalia's form of constitutional interpretation, the purpose of the Constitutional School is not to defend or attack his legal reasoning. The point, rather, is to recognize that scholars, practitioners, lawyers, judges, justices, and others all have their own interpretive preferences of the rule of law. The Constitutional School hopes to embrace *all* interpretive perspectives as an inclusive means to encourage as many scholars and practitioners as possible to examine how the American Constitution permeates each area of public administration scholarship and practice. In a word, we could not agree more with the application of Thomas Jefferson's position when he established the University of Virginia: "[H]ere we are not afraid to follow truth wherever it may lead, nor tolerate any error so long as reason is left free to combat it."[7]

In their discussion of how to connect American constitutional tradition with the types of decision making that good and faithful civil servants make on a regular basis, Gary Wamsley and his colleagues argue:

> The public administrator takes an oath to uphold the Constitution of the United States—not the whims of the powerful. This oath initiates administrators into a community created by that Constitution and obliges them to know and support constitutional principles that affect their official spheres of public service.
>
> (1990, p. 47)

Those who were originally part of the Blacksburg School and those who are products of this educational and philosophical perspective continue to emphasize the idea that if American civil servants do not work to defend, protect, and preserve the Constitution, the republican structure of the nation's constitutional order and its institutional composition will be severely jeopardized (Rohr, 1986; Terry, 2003; Wamsley et al., 1990).

Such efforts have led Jeffrey Rosen (2006), a professor of law at George Washington University, to argue that the courts are the most democratic of the three branches of American government. He points to the vital role that the judiciary, especially the Supreme Court, plays in making decisions that affect race, the right to privacy, politics, and civil liberties. The theme he weaves together is particularly useful to the Constitutional School, because it provides another avenue to debate how the federal courts influence the democratic principles embedded in our republic. It also gives additional legitimacy to Wamsley's assertion that the field should pay more attention to the "ever-democratizing" dimension of American public administration.

Additionally, Robert Zinke points to another perspective on the role of the American Constitution in public administration:

> The Constitution establishes a rhetorical republic, where primary governmental activities consist of speaking, listening, and acting expressively and where national unity depends upon the commitment of citizens to learn about moral realities and to participate actively in conversations, debates, and expressive actions that make those realities manifest. This republic embraces a diversity of political and socioeconomic interests but allows no single voice to dominate public discussion.
>
> (1992, p. 145)

The purpose of a Constitutional School for American public administration is to encourage scholars and practitioners to continue to engage, debate, and write on issues that are significant to the constitutional heritage of the United States, its democratic institutions, and its administrative agencies, like the ones espoused by Rosen and Zinke. Those who are part of this movement hope that by discussing ideas that resonate with constitutional theory and the rule of law, the field will be encouraged to add more detailed examinations, like those already published by Rohr, Rosenbloom, O'Leary, Wise, Phillip Cooper, and Terry Cooper, among others, of how the law affects the administrative state. This, in turn, will provide for a more comprehensive understanding as to how the Constitution and the nation's legal system affects the maintenance and preservation of the American republic and its public organizations (Newbold, 2008).

In his latest book, *Active Liberty,* Justice Stephen Breyer expresses his views on the type of government that the American Constitution established and seems to embrace Rosen and Zinke's perspectives:

> I see the document as creating a coherent framework for a certain kind of government. Described generally, that government is democratic; it avoids concentration of too much power in too few hands; it protects personal liberty; it insists that the law respect each individual equally; and it acts only upon the basis of law itself.
>
> (2005, p. 8)

Whereas Terry looked back in time to *The Federalist* to demonstrate the need to move toward a Constitutional School, one could just as easily argue that Breyer's well-crafted analysis legitimates the need to establish this school of thought in strictly contemporary terms. Unlike France, for example, the American republic cannot exist without its Constitution, and if our state's institutional legitimacy is dependent on this governing document, so, too, are its administrative agencies (Rohr, 1995). Even the authors of the acclaimed President's Committee on Administrative Management report were perceptive enough to recognize that "bad management may spoil good purposes, and that without good management democracy itself cannot achieve its highest goals" (Brownlow, Merriam & Gulick, 1937, p. 4). Preserving the constitutional integrity of the administrative state not only was a goal of the founders of the republic, but also has been associated with every major movement for administrative change throughout the history of the United States, even those that were primarily concerned with improving the economic dimensions of efficiency and effectiveness.

Legitimating and moving toward a Constitutional School for American public administration will not only add to the intellectual history of the field, but also enhance our knowledge and understanding of how administrative scholars, civil servants, and state institutions work to conserve a particular type of democratic-republican order. As Moe and Gilmour correctly observe, public administration is:

> founded on the body of the Constitution and the Bill of Rights and articulated by a truly enormous body of statutory, regulatory, and case law to ensure continuance of a republican form of government and to protect the rights and freedoms of citizens at the hands of an all-powerful state.
>
> (1995, p. 135)

Moving toward a Constitutional School demonstrates the value of this scholarly perspective while also adding another important way to legitimate the intellectual and constitutional foundation of the American administrative state (Rohr, 1986, 2002; Rosenbloom, 2003).

Once the Constitutional Convention of 1787 concluded, a citizen approached Benjamin Franklin as he was exiting Independence Hall and asked, "Well, Doctor, what have we got?" Franklin responded succinctly, "A Republic, if you can keep it." Moving toward a Constitutional School for American public administration is one critically important way our field works "to keep it."

Notes

1 This movement was established by Rick Green, Karen Hult, Doug Morgan, Stephanie Newbold, John Rohr, and David Rosenbloom at the Annual Meeting of the Southern Political Science Association, held in January 2007, New Orleans, Louisiana.

2 Waldo argued that the American founders championed principles associated with limited, divided, and balanced government, whereas early nineteenth-century administrative democrats wanted it pulverized, dispersed, and vulgarized (see Chap. 8 of *The Administrative State*, especially, pp. 130–40).

3 Gary Wamsley, cofounder of the Center for Public Administration and Policy at Virginia Tech and editor of *Administration & Society,* makes this point in every course he teaches and every lecture he gives. He deduces this concept largely from Gibson Burrell and Gareth Morgan's *Sociological Paradigms and Organizational Analysis* (1979), in which those authors argue that the incommensurability of paradigms does not allow for the "incorporation of the less widely accepted approaches within the dominant functionalist paradigm" (p. 396).
4 This is a reference to the fact that federal judges are nominated by the president and confirmed by the Senate for a lifetime appointment.
5 See Justice Stephen Breyer's interview with CNN legal correspondent Jeffrey Toobin in the October 28, 2006 special *Broken Government: Judges on Trial.* For a less detailed analysis, see the chapter "A Serious Objection" in *Active Liberty* (2005).
6 Storing focused on the Anti-Federalists' concerns over the lack of a bill of rights in the proposed 1787 Constitution and the need for Publius to clarify his definition of representation and representative government in a federal separation of powers regime.
7 Thomas Jefferson to William Roscoe, from Monticello, 1820 (Lipscomb and Bergh, 1904, p. 303).

References

Aberbach, Joel D. & Bert A. Rockman. 2000. *In the Web of Politics: Three Decades of the U.S. Federal Executive.* Washington, DC: Brookings Institution Press.

Barnard, Chester I. [1938] 1968. *The Functions of the Executive.* Cambridge, MA: Harvard University Press.

Breyer, Stephen. 2005. *Active Liberty: Interpreting Our Democratic Constitution.* New York: Alfred A. Knopf.

Brownlow, Louis, Charles Merriam & Luther Gulick. 1937. *Administrative Management in the Government of the United States.* Washington, DC: President's Committee on Administrative Management.

Burrell, Gibson & Gareth Morgan. 1979. *Sociological Paradigms and Organizational Analysis: Elements of the Sociology of Corporate Life.* New York: Routledge.

The Caucus. 2009. President Obama's First Day. January 21. http://thecaucus.blogs.nytimes.com/2009/01/21/reporting-for-duty/ [accessed March 23, 2010].

Considine, Mark. 2001. *Enterprising States: The Public Management of Welfare-to-Work.* New York: Cambridge University Press.

Cook, Brian J. 1996. *Bureaucracy and Self-Government: Reconsidering the Role of Public Administration in American Politics.* Baltimore, MD: Johns Hopkins University Press.

Cooke, Jacob E., ed. 1961. *The Federalist.* Middletown, CT: Wesleyan University Press.

Cooper, Phillip J. 1997. Public Law as a Set of Tools for Management. In *Handbook of Public Law and Administration,* edited by Phillip J. Cooper & Chester A. Newland. San Francisco, CA: Jossey-Bass, pp. 104–119.

Cooper, Phillip J. 2006. *Public Law and Public Administration.* 4th edn. Belmont, CA: Thomson/Wadsworth.

Cooper, Terry L. 1991. *An Ethic of Citizenship for Public Administrators.* Englewood Cliffs, NJ: Prentice Hall.

Cooper, Terry L., ed. 1994. *Handbook of Administrative Ethics.* New York: Marcel Dekker.

Cooper, Terry L. & N. Dale Wright, eds. 1992. *Exemplary Public Administrators: Character and Leadership in Government*. San Francisco, CA: Jossey-Bass.

Fry, Brian R. & Jos C. N. Raadschelders. 2008. *Mastering Public Administration: From Max Weber to Dwight Waldo*. 2nd edn. Washington, DC: CQ Press.

Goodnow, Frank J. 1900. *Politics and Administration*. New York: Macmillan.

Goodsell, Charles T. 2004. *The Case for Bureaucracy: A Public Administration Polemic*. Washington, DC: CQ Press.

Greenberg, Gary J. 1997. Revolt at Justice. In *Ethics and Politics: Cases and Comments*, 3rd edn, edited by Amy Gutmann & Dennis Thompson. Chicago, IL: Nelson-Hall, pp. 143–151.

Lee, Yong S., with David H. Rosenbloom. 2005. *A Reasonable Public Servant: Constitutional Foundations of Administrative Conduct in the United States*. Armonk, NY: M. E. Sharpe.

Levine, Charles H. & Lloyd G. Nigro. 1975. The Public Personnel System: Can Judicial Administration and Manpower Management Coexist? *Public Administration Review* 35(1): 98–107.

Levinson, Sanford. 2006. *Our Undemocratic Constitution: Where the Constitution Goes Wrong*. New York: Oxford University Press.

Lipscomb, Andrew A. & Albert Ellery Bergh, eds. 1904. *The Writings of Thomas Jefferson*. Vol. 15. Washington, DC: Thomas Jefferson Association.

Loffler, Elke. 1997. *The Modernization of the Public Sector in an International Comparative Perspective: Implementation in Germany, Great Britain and the United States*. Speyer, Germany: Forschungsinstitut für Offentliche Verwaltung.

McSwite, O. C. 1997. *Legitimacy in Public Administration: A Discourse Analysis*. Thousand Oaks, CA: Sage Publications.

Moe, Ronald C. & Robert S. Gilmour. 1995. Rediscovering Principles of Public Administration: The Neglected Foundation of Public Law. *Public Administration Review* 55(2): 135–146.

Newbold, Stephanie P. 2008. Teaching Organization Theory from a Constitutional Perspective: A New Twist on an Old Flame. *Journal of Public Affairs Education* 14(2): 335–351.

O'Leary, Rosemary & Charles R. Wise. 1991. Public Managers, Judges, and Legislatures: Redefining the "New Partnership." *Public Administration Review* 51(4): 316–327.

O'Leary, Rosemary & Charles R. Wise. 2003. Breaking Up Is Hard to Do: The Dissolution of Judicial Supervision of Public Services. *Public Administration Review* 63(2): 177–191.

Osborne, David & Ted Gaebler. 1992. *Reinventing Government: How the Entrepreneurial Spirit Is Transforming the Public Sector*. Reading, MA: Addison-Wesley.

Peters, Tom. 1992. *Liberation Management: Necessary Disorganization for the Nanosecond Nineties*. New York: Alfred A. Knopf.

Rainey, Hal G. 2003. *Understanding and Managing Public Organizations*. 3rd edn. San Francisco, CA: Jossey-Bass.

Rohr, John A. 1986. *To Run a Constitution: The Legitimacy of the Administrative State*. Lawrence: University Press of Kansas.

Rohr, John A. 1995. *Founding Republics in France and America: A Study in Constitutional Governance*. Lawrence: University Press of Kansas.

Rohr, John A. 1998. *Public Service, Ethics, and Constitutional Practice*. Lawrence: University Press of Kansas.

Rohr, John A. 2002. *Civil Servants and their Constitutions*. Lawrence: University Press of Kansas.

Rosen, Jeffrey. 2006. *The Most Democratic Branch: How the Courts Serve America*. New York: Oxford University Press.

Rosenbloom, David H. 1971. *Federal Service and the Constitution: The Development of the Public Employment Relationship*. Ithaca, NY: Cornell University Press.

Rosenbloom, David H. 1983. Public Administrative Theory and the Separation of Powers. *Public Administration Review* 43(3): 219–227.

Rosenbloom, David H. 1987. Public Administrators and the Judiciary: The "New Partnership." *Public Administration Review* 47(1): 75–83.

Rosenbloom, David H. 2002. *Building a Legislative-Centered Public Administration: Congress and the Administrative State, 1946–1999*. Tuscaloosa: University of Alabama Press.

Rosenbloom, David H. 2003. *Administrative Law for Public Managers*. Boulder, CO: Westview Press.

Rosenbloom, David H., James D. Carroll & Jonathan D. Carroll. 2000. *Constitutional Competence for Public Managers: Cases and Commentary*. Itasca, IL: F. E. Peacock.

Rosenbloom, David H. & Robert S. Kravchuk. 2005. *Public Administration: Understanding Management, Politics, and Law in the Public Sector*. 6th edn. Boston, MA: McGraw-Hill.

Rosenbloom, David H. & Howard E. McCurdy, eds. 2007. *Revisiting Waldo's Administrative State: Consistency and Change in Public Administration*. Washington, DC: Georgetown University Press.

Rosenbloom, David H. & Rosemary O'Leary. 1996. *Public Administration and Law*. 2nd edn. New York: Marcel Dekker.

Scalia, Antonin. 1997. *A Matter of Interpretation: Federal Courts and the Law*. Princeton, NJ: Princeton University Press.

Selznick, Philip. 1957. *Leadership in Administration: A Sociological Interpretation*. Berkeley: University of California Press.

Shapiro, Martin. 1988. *Who Guards the Guardians? Judicial Control of Administration*. Athens: University of Georgia Press.

Spicer, Michael & Larry D. Terry. 1993a. Advancing the Dialogue: Legitimacy, the Founders, and the Contractarian Argument. *Public Administration Review* 53(3): 264–267.

Spicer, Michael & Larry D. Terry. 1993b. Legitimacy, History, and Logic: Public Administration and the Constitution. *Public Administration Review* 53(3): 239–246.

Storing, Herbert. 1981. *What the Anti-Federalists Were For*. Chicago, IL: University of Chicago Press.

Terry, Larry D. 2003. *Leadership of Public Bureaucracies: The Administrator as Conservator*. Armonk, NY: M. E. Sharpe.

Waldo, Dwight. 1948. *The Administrative State: A Study of the Political Theory of American Public Administration*. New York: Ronald Press.

Wamsley, Gary, et al., eds. 1990. *Refounding Public Administration*. Thousand Oaks, CA: Sage Publications.

Wilson, Woodrow. 1887. The Study of Administration. *Political Science Quarterly* 2(2): 197–222.

Wise, Charles R. 1998. Judicial Federalism: The Resurgence of the Supreme Court's Role in the Protection of State Sovereignty. *Public Administration Review* 58(2): 95–98.

Wise, Charles R. 2001. The Supreme Court's New Constitutional Federalism: Implications for Public Administration. *Public Administration Review* 61(3): 343–358.

Zinke, Robert C. 1992. American Constitutionalism in the Interconnected World: Administrative Responsibilities in a Rhetorical Republic. In *Public Management in an Interconnected World: Essays in the Minnowbrook Tradition*, edited by Mary Timney Bailey & Richard T. Mayer. New York: Greenwood Press, pp. 145–158.

Part II

Foundations

Why the Constitutional School Matters

2 Advancing the Intellectual History of U.S. Public Administration

Connecting Herbert Storing's Legacy to the Constitutional School

David H. Rosenbloom

As John A. Rohr noted in his Prologue to this selection, it is perplexing that the field of public administration has largely neglected Herbert J. Storing's work. Was Storing an anachronistic voice calling for nobility in and a central constitutional role for public administration at a time when "bureaucracy bashing" was becoming ever more prevalent? Alternatively, was he prescient in addressing the "big questions" of public administration before the field sought to define them in the 1990s? (Behn, 1995; Kerlin, 1996; see also Agranoff & McGuire, 2001; Denhardt, 2001). Or perhaps, his questions were too big for a field that since his day has increasingly turned its attention to narrower concerns (Durant & Rosenbloom, 2016). Or maybe still, it has taken decades for the Constitutional School of U.S. Public Administration, of which Storing was a founder, to develop into an identifiable intellectual current within the field. Whatever the reasons for Storing's relative obscurity today, we have included this analysis by Douglas Morgan, et al. in an effort to bring his big questions to the forefront of contemporary public administrative thought.

The Constitutional School focuses attention on the roles of public administration and public administrators in the U.S. constitutional regime. Storing was concerned both with "is" and with "ought" questions in this regard. His work helps clarify three enduring, but also contemporary issues in public administration: the relationship between politics and administration, the so-called identity crisis of public administration, and the normative bases of the field.

Politics and Administration

Analyzing or specifying the relationship between politics and administration has become a "perdurable" (Waldo, 1985) challenge for public administration. As the selection points out, this is in part because the nineteenth-century civil service reformers misspecified the problem by not distinguishing between partisan politics and politics involving matters of public policy, national interest, and statecraft. This misspecification is widely understood today. However, Storing adds to "politics" fundamental considerations regarding what can be called "regime principles," that is, how can public administration be not only compatible with the constitutional regime, but also strengthen it. For Storing, this was more than a matter of cost-effective administration, though that is not inconsequential. Public administration and those who carry it out can make fundamental contributions to the operation and success of the constitutional design. This premise underlays Storing's conceptual development of the "judicial model of administrative practice."

In addition to considering questions of civil service reform, a senior executive service, steering rather than rowing, and other ways to achieve cost-effectiveness, Storing's view is that public administration, as a field, should be analyzing such matters from systematic constitutional perspectives. Consider how hard-pressed one would be to find such considerations in the literature and prescriptions generated by the National Performance Review (NPR) of the 1990s and many other major reform proposals. In a regime designed to make ambition counteract ambition, reforms that strengthen presidential control over federal administration are almost certain to trigger counter-reforms by a Congress seeking to maintain its place in the separation of powers system of government. The rise of the New Deal–World War II presidency and Congress' effort to build a legislative-centered public administration in 1946 represents a formative example of how Madisonian ambition counteracts Madisonian ambition (Rosenbloom, 2000). Similarly, the NPR and President George W. Bush's unitary executive branch theory were partial responses to Congress's deep involvement in administrative decision-making conducted by the executive branch. In a word, Luther Gulick's preference for federal administration-based "unity of command," as manifested in the Final Report of the President's Committee on Administrative Management, could not succeed in the federal constitutional separation of powers system (Gulick, 1937; Rosenbloom, 2000, pp. 16–19).

The "Identity Crisis"

Although public administration is said to have a longstanding identity crisis, that crisis, if it is real, might be better considered a set of multifaceted sub-crises. Even then, it is not altogether clear why crisis or no crisis matters. As Raadschelders (2011, pp. 31–34) points out "identity crisis" is a "normal situation in most, perhaps all disciplines." The natural sciences, social sciences, and humanities are loaded with putative identity crises; sociology, comparative politics, international relations, management and business, economics, psychology, history, archeology, physics, and other disciplines can be said to have such crises. It seems to me there is a big, "So what?" hanging over concern with public administration's identity.

Many, however, find it perplexing that public administration has been characterized as art, science (social and design), profession, craft, the inter-disciplinary study of government, a discipline, a field of study, as well as a combination of management, politics, law, and more (Lynn, 1996; Berkley,

2004; Raadschelders, 2011; Rosenbloom, Kravchuk & Clerkin, 2015; see also Ostrom & Allen, 2007). Combining theory and practice contributes to definitional questions. Mentioning "public administration" to academics and practitioners outside the field often begets puzzlement as to what it is. Personally, I have found that explaining public administration as a body of thought directed toward building better bureaucrats and governmental management sufficiently conveys the essence of the "enterprise" (Waldo, 1980). Of course, some will be quick to ask, "What do you mean by 'better'?" and that is one of the several key areas in which Storing provides a cogent answer.

Storing urges us to look beyond techniques, processes, organizational and human resource designs, and other aspects of contemporary public administration dedicated to cost-effective applications and turn our attention to the more fundamental issues of how public administration can be constituted to fit and serve political regimes, primarily the U.S. constitutional one. This immediately reframes the way we conceptualize public administration. It emphasizes the importance of context, as Robert Dahl (1947) had urged before Storing, and roots it in applications central to the performance of political regimes.

In the U.S. case, viewing public administration in constitutional contexts also provides theoretical and analytical channels for expanding attention to constitutional and administrative law and integrating them more fully into the field. Rather than viewing law from the outside in, as more or less an interference with administrative management, Storing urges us to view it from the inside out, in terms of its fit with underlying regime principles. If the field were to follow Storing in this regard, our expertise might play a much greater role in informing the content of statutes and court decisions, thereby, potentially improving administrative performance in multiple respects. Even Woodrow Wilson (1887) conceded that "running a constitution" cannot be wholly divorced from framing, or at least continually reframing, one.

As it now stands, it is a fair question whether the field's emphasis on universal principles, derived scientifically or otherwise, best practices, and cost-effectiveness pose challenges to the bedrock constitutional principle of the rule of law. Storing urges us to develop greater theoretical depth in assessing the fundamentals of what public administration is and thereby potentially improve practice and constitutional government as a whole.

The Normative Bases of Public Administration

It is broadly claimed that U.S. public administration rests on three or four normative pillars. Wilson (1887) identified three as efficiency, economy, and effectiveness; Frederickson (1971), Svara and Brunet (2005), and the National Academy of Public Administration (Perry, 2005) add social equity as a fourth. Each includes serious operational limitations. Dimock (Lee, 2015, p. 6) and Waldo (1984, p. 193) ask "efficient for what?" Economy can conflict with efficiency depending on scale: the least expensive method or technology is not necessarily the most efficient. Effectiveness often eludes measurement and is multi-causal and time dependent. When falling short of Pareto optimality or improvement, effectiveness involves distributional concerns. Social equity lacks definitional clarity and, at least at present, has no means of weighing the value of its benefits to some in the groups helped by it against the burdens it thrusts on other members of those same groups (see Durant & Rosenbloom, 2016).

Some may view such weaknesses in the field's normative pillars as mere quibbles. Indeed, they may be relatively minor concerns relative to the far greater issues of what gives them primacy over other values such as representativeness, responsiveness, responsibility, constitutional integrity, individual rights, equal protection of the laws, civic republicanism, and so forth. Framed differently, following Victor Thompson's (1975) unhappily argued point, in our constitutional system of government, what gives academics and practitioners in public administration a warrant to identify the values that inform public administrative action? Shouldn't those values be based in constitutional provisions, statutes, court decisions, and directives by elected and politically appointed executives? Shouldn't the "profession of government" (Chapman, 1959)—public administration—be subordinate to government created by "We the People"? Although one can point to official mandates for the field's normative pillars, without much difficulty one can also find such mandates for the often countervailing values mentioned above. The Supreme Court has even gone so far as to say that "unworkability" does not provide a basis for circumventing constitutional process (*Immigration and Naturalization Service v. Chadha*, 1983, p. 959).

Storing's contention that public administration must be connected to constitutionalism writ large provides a foundation for value identification and supremacy in public administration. This was Rohr's point with respect to "regime values," but one could follow Storing as well in focusing on the founding period discourse between the Federalists and Anti-Federalists and major constitutional law cases that continue to frame the Constitution.

Storing's scholarship and theory-building was broad in scope, rich in detail, and complex. Neither the selection included in this volume nor these reflections can do more than scratch the surface of his potential contributions to the field of U.S. public administration and the Constitutional School. Readers are encouraged to seek out the works by Storing listed in the References in the selection and reflect on how they can contribute to their own thinking, understanding of public administration, research, scholarship, and where applicable, teaching.

References

Agranoff, R. & McGuire, M. 2001. "Big questions in public network management research," *Journal of public administration research and theory* 11(3): 295–326.

Behn, B. 1995. "The big questions of public management," *Public administration review* 55(4): 313–324.
Berkley, G. 2004. *The craft of public administration*, ninth edn. Boston, MA: McGraw-Hill.
Chapman, B. 1959. *The profession of government*. London: Allen and Unwin.
Dahl, R. 1947. "The science of public administration: Three problems," *Public administration review* 7(1): 1–11.
Denhardt, R. 2001. "The big questions of public administration education," *Public administration review* 61(5): 526–534.
Durant, R. & Rosenbloom, D. 2016. "The hollowing of American public administration," *American review of public administration*, doi: 10.1177/0275074015627218.
Frederickson, H. G. 1971. "Toward a new public administration," in *Classics of public administration*, seventh edn, Jay Shafritz & Albert Hyde, eds. Boston, MA: Wadsworth, 2012, pp. 294–305.
Gulick, L. 1937. "Notes on the theory of organization," in *Classics of public administration*, seventh edn, Jay Shafritz & Albert Hyde, eds. Boston, MA: Wadsworth, 2012, pp. 81–89.
Immigration and Naturalization Service v. Chadha. 1983. 462 U.S. 919.
Kerlin, J. 1996. "The big questions of public administration," *Public administration review* 56(5): 416–423.
Lee, M. 2015. "Colluding to create the American society for public administration and the consequent collateral damage," *Public Voices* 14(1): 2–27.
Lynn, L. 1996. *Public management as art, science, and profession*. Chatham, NJ: Chatham House.
Ostrom, V. & Allen, B. 2007. *The intellectual crisis in public administration*, third edn. Tuscaloosa, AL: University of Alabama Press.
Perry, S. 2005. "Social equity for the long haul." Doctoral dissertation, Virginia Polytechnic Institute and State University, Blacksburg, VA.
Raadschelders, J. 2011. *Public administration: The interdisciplinary study of government*. New York: Oxford University Press.
Rosenbloom, D. 2000. *Building a legislative-centered public administration: Congress and the administrative state, 1946–1999*. Tuscaloosa, AL: University of Alabama Press.
Rosenbloom, D., Kravchuk, R. & Clerkin, R. 2015. *Public administration: Understanding management, politics, and law in the public sector*, eighth edn. New York: McGraw-Hill.
Svara, J. & Brunet, J. 2005. "Social equity is a pillar of public administration," *Journal of public affairs education* 10(11): 253–258.
Thompson, V. 1975. *Without sympathy or enthusiasm: The problem of administrative compassion*. Tuscaloosa: University of Alabama Press.
Waldo, D. 1980. *The Enterprise of Public Administration*. Novato, CA: Chandler and Sharp Publishers.
Waldo, D. 1984. *The administrative state*, second edn. New York: Holmes & Meier.
Waldo, D. 1985. "The perdurability of the politics-administration dichotomy: Woodrow Wilson and the identity crisis in public administration," in *Politics and administration: Woodrow Wilson and American public administration*, J. Rabin and J. Bowman, eds. New York: Marcel Dekker, pp. 219–233.
Wilson, W. 1887. "The study of administration," in *Classics of public administration*, seventh edn, Jay Shafritz & Albert Hyde, eds. Boston, MA: Wadsworth, 2012, pp. 16–28.

Recovering, Restoring, and Renewing the Foundations of American Public Administration

The Contributions of Herbert J. Storing

Douglas F. Morgan, Kent A. Kirwan, John A. Rohr, David H. Rosenbloom and David Lewis Schaefer

From: *Public Administration Review* 70 (July/August, 2010): 621–633. Abridged.

Public administration continues to face an "identity crisis" that has been at the center of the discipline since its inception. The crisis turns on the following question: Are the animating principles of public administration to be discovered in the political foundations of a given regime, or are they to be found in more universal and transcendent principles of scientific management? The debate over the proper connection between politics and administration manifests itself today in numerous ways.

According to Dwight Waldo (1968, p. 5), it was Herbert Simon who created the discipline's "identity crisis" in public administration by destroying confidence in the validity of early administrative science. But Simon (1947) resolved that crisis by offering the prospect of a pure science of administration. Herbert J. Storing, by contrast, rejected the prospect of finding the identity of public administration in some kind of science. Instead, he outlined a resolution to the identity crisis by traveling back in time, beyond the field, to the American founding. In doing so, he reframed the identity crisis and transformed the study and practice of public administration into statecraft. Storing argued that the politics–administration dichotomy stems from the efforts of the American founders to create the conditions necessary for securing the long-term vitality of America's system of ordered liberty. Their efforts resulted in tensions between the administrative and political activities that are necessary to protect American democracy from the inherent dangers to which it is liable. In the process of illuminating the politics–administration dichotomy, Storing made four significant contributions to public administration theory:[1] (1) He reframed the politics–administration debate; (2) in doing so, he resolved the "identity crisis" in American public administration by stressing the central governing role of career administrators; (3) he introduced the "judicial approach" to administrative decision making and, in the process, restored prudential judgment as the centerpiece of administrative practice; and (4) through the height, depth, and breadth of his perspective, he revealed the vital importance of the bureaucracy, and not just its limitations. Correspondingly, he opened our minds to the nobility of the life of the civil servant by clarifying its potential for statesmanship. By sharing his vision, he enabled us all, teachers and practitioners of public administration alike, to better see what we are doing.

In this article, we will revisit Storing's contributions to the study and practice of public administration. We do so for two reasons. First, as former students, we believe Storing has received inadequate credit for and attention to the significant contributions he has made, largely because his teaching and writings were presented in collections of essays and compilations of writings rather than in a monograph format.[2] Second, we believe the unresolved debate over the proper role of administration in governing can benefit from Storing's insights.

Reframing the Politics–Administration Dichotomy: The Problem of American Democratic Governance

Storing regarded the politics–administration dichotomy as the unfortunate result of collective memory loss among both practitioners and students of American politics. The dichotomy did not originate with the writings of Woodrow Wilson and Frank Goodnow. Instead, it originated from the "problematic nature" of the American regime. "The preoccupation of Herbert Storing's professional life was the genesis and meaning of the American regime" (Cropsey, 1981, p. xv), which was to be found in the Federalist–Anti-Federalist debate. Both parties to the debate agreed that the purpose of government was to protect individual rights. They also agreed that liberty could not be assumed to result simply from the election of government officials by popular vote. For the Federalists, popular elections entailed the need for protections against majority tyranny and foolishness and the capacity for competent administration. For the Anti-Federalists, popular elections entailed the need to build in protections to ensure that elected officials would not become a ruling elite that used its power to advance its interests at the expense of protecting individual rights and preserving the local conditions necessary for these rights to thrive. For both the Federalists and Anti-Federalists, the purpose of democratic government was the protection of individual rights, but there was disagreement over *how* these rights could best be secured.

In his study of the founding, Storing identified four well-worn sources of danger to the health and survival of democratic governance: majority tyranny and foolishness, the loss of republican virtue, the abuse of power by government officials, and ineffective and inefficient administration. For Storing, each of these problems was foundational to understanding the nature of American politics and institutions and the role of administrators in the governance process.

Majority Tyranny: The Shays's Rebellion Problem

Storing was struck by the agreement between Federalists and Anti-Federalists that "[g]overnment by the people or, in practice, majority rule was not ... the very definition of free government, because it can lead to unjust deprivations of individual liberty" by a tyrannical majority (1981, 1: 40). So what is the best guarantor against majority tyranny? For the Federalists, it was a complex system of government that included reliance on a multiplicity of the numbers and kinds of factions generated by a large commercial republic, a system of representation, and a set of governing structures and processes that checked and balanced the exercise of governing powers. For the Anti-Federalists, liberty could be secured only by cultivating a set of republican virtues (further elaborated in the next section), which they believed would be eroded by the commercialism of a large republic.

In seeking to solve the majority tyranny problem, the Federalists promoted the virtues of a large commercial republic, which seemingly weakened the conditions needed for republican virtue and a politically vigilant and engaged citizenry.

Republican Virtue: The Engaged Citizen Problem

Storing's longest and perhaps most important labor of love during his relatively short life was the compilation of an authoritative seven-volume collection of Anti-Federalist writings. "The aim of the collection," he explained, "is to make available for the first time all of the substantial Anti-Federal writings in their complete original form and in an accurate text, together with appropriate annotation" accompanied by an introduction, providing "for the first time, in my judgment, a full and adequate account of the main lines, the principles and the grounds of the Anti-Federal position" (1981, 1: xix). He undertook this work because he believed that the Anti-Federalists had not received the credit they deserved for shaping the American Constitution. More importantly, he argued, the Constitution "did not settle *everything*; it did not finish the task of making the American polity. The political life of the community continues to be a dialogue, in which the Anti-Federalist concerns and principles still play an important part" (1981, 1: 3 [emphasis in original]). In short, Storing believed that "the Anti-Federalists may have something to teach" us (1981, 1: 4).

One of the most important teachings of the Anti-Federalists was the need to ground democratic governance in what Storing called "republican virtue" (1981, 1: 24, 73). Republican virtue consists of a set of political habits and dispositions that reflect a constant love of liberty. This love is cultivated by small, face-to-face government and the life exemplified by the yeoman farmer, which fosters the essential republican virtues of moderation, vigilance, industry, and thrift. Republican virtue contrasts with the virtue of the procedural republic, which emphasizes the importance of structures, processes, and formal rights to protect liberty (Kemmis, 1990, Chap. 2).

Storing's belief about the centrality of the Anti-Federalists to the American polity has obvious relevance to the increasing interest over the last three decades in America's communitarian roots (Etzioni, 1993; Kemmis, 1990; Putnam, 2000). Whether it is concern about the forces of globalization, reaction to the expanding powers of the national government, dismay at what appears to be excessive greed in the marketplace, or concern for the development of social capital, the nature and kind of citizen virtue needed to sustain democratic government is very much a part of our current political dialogue. In his introductory essay to the seven-volume compilation, Storing sympathetically summarized the Anti-Federalist "small republic" vision of self-government that could not be satisfied by simply protecting citizens from the abuses of rulers such as King George or becoming more efficient at performing government functions. Small democratic communities were important not simply because they provided better opportunities to maintain eternal vigilance over suspicious rulers; they also mattered because they produced policies and practices that were informed by local knowledge, and they provided processes that enabled citizens to acquire the knowledge and skills to be civically engaged in meaningful ways. To be so engaged enhances one's liberties and heightens the sense of self-interest rightly understood. The Anti-Federalists believed that a constitution that provides for a strong, professionalized central government and encourages the private pursuit of material gain tends to discourage civic engagement. Ultimately, this distracts the public from a proper vigilance over their liberties as well as from civic-mindedness more generally.

Abuse of Executive Power: The King George Problem

A recurring problem that Storing wrestled with in his teaching and scholarship was how power could be centralized without endangering the liberty of its citizens. His favorite text on the American presidency was Charles Thach's book *The Creation of the Presidency* (1969), to which he wrote a preface for the reprinted edition. Storing was especially interested in Thach's account of how the anti-tyrannical forces of the American Revolution resulted in the adoption of new state constitutions that concentrated governmental power in the popularly elected legislative branch (with New York as a notable exception), providing for a very weak executive branch (Thach 1969, Chap. 2). This weak-executive model was embodied in the Articles of Confederation, which resulted in a central government that was too weak to collect taxes and provision an army during the American Revolution, sowing the seeds for the model's own corrective in the Constitutional Convention of 1787.

Storing's concern for how executive power could be safely constructed was also at the center of his critique of Herbert Simon's administrative science. Storing argued that Simon's model of rationality and efficiency "takes its bearings from the goals of top management" (1962, p. 103), thus "radicalizing the claim for unity in administration." There are three reasons why Simon's model promotes centralization: (1) "the crucial and governing activity is development of the science itself, which can only occur (except derivatively) at the top"; (2) "gaps in the science make it necessary to resort to central authority to support the science"; and (3) "there remains a continuing need to enforce the rational design of the science" (Storing, 1980, p. 110). Storing's study of the American founding gave him pause about these centralizing tendencies. The reasons for centralizing have to be informed by the political ends that centralization is intended to serve, and once these ends are fully revealed, it is not so clear that centralization is the best means for achieving them. Centralization must be judged by whether it promotes the primary purpose of the American constitutional system: the preservation of individual liberty.

The Need for Energetic, Effective, and Efficient Government: The George Washington Problem

Storing recognized in his study of the founding debates that even the Anti-Federalist opponents of the Constitution favored a new kind of Union "to provide defense against foreign enemies, to promote and protect American commerce and to maintain order among the states" (1981, 1: 24). Storing observed that once the Anti-Federalists conceded the need for more power at the center, they "simply could not meet" the Federalist argument that sufficient powers needed to be given to the new government in order to ensure the achievement of its ends (1981, 1: 29). But Storing pointed out that the Anti-Federalists were right in warning that the desire for efficient government could easily fall prey to false concerns for the status and riches of the nation-state within the larger global order. "Indeed, the stress placed by the Federalists on national defense and a vigorous commercial polity often seems to mask a radical shift in direction from the protection of individual liberty to the pursuit of national riches and glory" (1981, 1: 30).

Storing's study of the American founding brought to light significant tensions among the prophylactics necessary to prevent democracy from succumbing to the inherent pitfalls of popular sovereignty. By giving all power to the people to prevent abuses by the King Georges of the world, democracy could succumb to a lack of power at the center to administer the powers of government with competence and efficiency (the Articles of Confederation problem). Or it could succumb to majority tyranny (the Shays's Rebellion problem), or to economic excess and lethargy (the engaged-citizen problem). From the perspective of the founding generation, the public interest was problematic because of the difficulty of addressing any one of the four major sources of danger to liberty without making the others worse. For example, creating a more consolidated government at the center with greater executive power to protect against external threats and the tyranny of the majority potentially endangers the liberty of citizens as a result of internal abuses of power by governing officials and limited civic engagement. Thus, an irreconcilable tension exists among the goals of competent government, responsiveness, preservation of minority rights, and civic engagement. For the Federalists, the danger of insufficient governmental power at the center and of majority tyranny outweighed the Anti-Federalists' concerns about excessive power at the center and the need to protect and cultivate the virtues of a small civic republic.

While Storing recognized that the need for administrative competence was one of the major reasons for creating a new Union, this competence was one among several different kinds of political expertise necessary to secure individual rights. From the founders' perspective, the administrative part of governance was a political activity, which Storing argued gives administrators "a reasonable and legitimate claim to share in rule" (1964b, p. 147). The political role played by administrators, however, was different from the political role played by elected members of the legislative body. "It is a distinction between broader and narrower political operations or between two levels of politics that emphasizes their connection and rejects a distinction between political and administrative *questions*" (Kirwan, 1981, p. 211 [emphasis in original]). By redefining the problem of democracy, Storing addressed the identity crisis in public administration and in the process carved out a central role for the bureaucracy and administrators in democratic governance.

Resolving the Public Administration Identity Crisis: The Role of Administrators in Democratic Governance

Herbert Storing propounded a pathbreaking reinterpretation of the role of the public administrator, at least at higher levels, as one of statesmanship. Prior to Storing's work, scholars had long recognized the insufficiency of the politics–administration dichotomy (as propounded by Woodrow Wilson and Frank Goodnow) as an empirical account of how government operates: civil servants inevitably exercise considerable discretion in their daily work, above and beyond the merely "technical" question of finding the most efficient means of carrying out the commands of their elected superiors. In fact, questions of means are never entirely separable from choices among ends. But scholars remained perplexed about how to legitimize this political role within a democracy, so as to offer meaningful guidance about how civil servants should go about their work, and hence to design an education that would best equip them to fulfill their duty.

The root cause of the failure of contemporary political science and public administration theory to provide an adequate account of the work of civil servants, as Storing observed in the last essay he wrote, "American Statesmanship: Old and New," was the tendency to reduce it "into two simple elements: populism, or radical democracy, and scientific management" (1980, p. 403). Because of their reluctance to distinguish, as the authors of *The Federalist* did, between the people's immediate wishes and their true interests, contemporary scholars saw no grounds to justify civil servants' partial autonomy from electoral direction except the claims of technical expertise (see Friedrich 1940). Only on the grounds of expertise or "scientific management" could the claim to administrative autonomy be upheld without offending the scholars' hyperdemocratic sensibilities. In this respect, public administration scholarship thus remained in thrall to the Wilsonian dichotomy. Because contemporary scholars had lost the founders' appreciation of democracy as a problem—a regime that, like all others, rests on a partisan principle that could destroy it if it is not institutionally moderated—they failed to appreciate the positive (and not merely technical) contribution that civil servants (not despite but because of their nonelected status) might make toward improving our system of government.

Storing's most fundamental criticism of contemporary academic approaches to public administration was articulated in his 1962 essay on Herbert Simon's purported "Science of Administration." In this essay Storing demonstrated the impossibility of substituting an evaluatively neutral science comprising universally valid rules of behavior for the administrator's practical judgment, in which questions of ends and means are inevitably intermixed. Subsequently, Storing set forth his account of the proper political role of the bureaucracy in three essays published in the mid-1960s: "The Problem of Big Government" (1963), "Political Parties and the Bureaucracy," (1964b), and "Leonard D. White and the Study of Public Administration" (1965).

In his essay on White, Storing showed how the work of a preeminent scholar of public administration gradually moved away from a belief in the uniformity of public and private administration, which could be perfected through a neutral science, toward an appreciation of the unique political character of public administration. At the same time, White's work exhibits a gradual renunciation of the Wilsonian assumption that it is possible to discover a set of rules for public administration that are valid for all governments alike—that is, without regard to differences among regimes. As Storing put it elsewhere, the impossibility of strictly separating politics from administration reflects the fact that "all interesting administrative questions are political questions" (1964b, p. 147). Precisely because "administration is the heart of modern government," as White stressed, requiring civil servants to exercise quasi-legislative and judicial functions (making and applying rules) as well as narrowly "executive" ones, the "age-old political and constitutional problems now present themselves as problems of (or in) public administration" (Storing, 1965, p. 48)—contrary to Wilson's claim that the fundamental constitutional problems had been "settled" and hence could be set aside. White's scholarly turn in his last years of research from pursuing administrative "science" to producing four volumes of history tracing the development of American public administration over the first century of the country's existence demonstrated a growing awareness that administrative systems both reflect and shape the political regimes that they serve.

To deny the possibility of severing politics from administration does not mean, however, that the civil servant is to be understood merely as a politician in the same sense as elected officials. The failure to conceive a political role other than that of the party or partisan politician was, in Storing's view, the crucial failing of the civil service reform movement, which aimed to cure the corruption of the spoils system by insulating the civil service from politics as such, not merely from partisanship. Storing stressed that the chief goal of the original reformers was not administrative efficiency but the elevation of the moral tone of the country as a whole. Reformers believed that treating public offices as spoils would encourage cynicism about government and spread an attitude of selfishness among the public at large. Without denying the reformers' achievement, Storing held that they "grossly oversimplified the problem of popular government." First of all, the idealism typified by George Curtis's forecast that turning elections into "a contest of principle" rather than "a fight for plunder" would make "the honest will of the people the actual government of the country" represented a forgetting of the founders' lesson that politics will always be guided in part by the pursuit of selfish interests, and that interest-based politics offers certain advantages in terms of moderation and stability over one based on unmitigated ideological conflict (Storing 1964b, p. 142; cf. the account of the advantages of "small" over "great" parties in Tocqueville, 2000, 1: ii; 2: 166–70). Second, the reformers' unqualified populism embodied a neglect of another key principle of the founding: the fact that popular majorities as well as "elites" may be prone to acts of injustice or folly—pointing toward the need to moderate pure majoritarianism no less than elitism (Storing 1980, 103).

Despite the deficiencies of their approach, Storing observed, the reformers left a lasting impression on the understanding of American government through their influence on the "second generation of reformer-political scientists" typified by Wilson and Goodnow, who "sought to state systematically the theory of government implicit in the reform movement and to elaborate ... its practical consequences." The model that emerged presented a quite different view of the problem of democratic governance from the view held by the founders. The legacy of this model can be seen in the demand for more "responsible" (i.e., ideologically coherent) parties as well as the scientific management movement (Storing, 1964b, pp. 143–44).

Storing's reform program for American public administration was informed by his understanding of the problematic nature of American democracy and the important role that the bureaucracy plays in fulfilling the purposes of democratic governance. In urging that higher civil servants and the bureaucracy as a whole be understood as practicing statesmanship, Storing was not inventing a role that they did not already perform, but trying to clarify the nature of their work so as to encourage them to perform it better. Storing was not blind to the defects of bureaucracy—its potential for inefficiency, indecision, and petty tyranny. But he maintained that "random carping or wholesale condemnation of the bureaucracy" served only to divert attention "from the need to nurture and strengthen its capacity for administrative statesmanship" (1963, pp. 84–85). These observations remain no less valid today.

Storing's teaching about the political role of public administrators as statesmen has special importance for the more than 87,500 local government jurisdictions in the United States. Nearly 75 percent of American cities today are governed by a council-manager form, with a part-time legislative body and a full-time professional manager (Adrian, 1999, p. 58). When originally created in the early 1900s, the council-manager system was intended to separate policy or politics from administration. Recent studies have documented that this "bright-line" distinction does not exist at the local government level, in large part because the city manager plays a "statesmanlike" role in facilitating both policy development and implementation (Nalbandian, 2000; Svara, 2001, 2006, 2008). In undertaking this role, managers must balance the competing needs for efficiency, responsiveness, community engagement, and the protection of individual rights (Morgan and Kass, 1993; Morgan et al., 2008, Chap. 3). These needs are pushed down even to the middle management layers of local government organizations (Morgan et al., 1996). Administrators are successful when they are able to play the role of the British civil servant in taking the initiative for problem solving without displacing the leadership role of elected officeholders. This requires "leading from behind," taking initiatory leadership without engaging in partisan political advocacy and, of course, looking "beyond immediate practical issues ... to understand the deeper ground on which they rest" (Storing, 1970, p. 9). Storing argued that playing this role requires the skills and temperament of a judge rather than those of a policy wonk or technical analyst.

Constitutional Law and the Judicial Model of Administrative Practice: Restoring Prudential Judgment to Administrative Work

Storing argued that the judicial model is the appropriate guide for understanding the nature of administrative rationality and judgment. This model was informed by two considerations. First, after undertaking an extensive examination of Herbert Simon's scientific model, Storing was convinced that the fact–value distinction on which it rested did not correspond to the reality of administrative practice, nor could it. Worse, the distinction was dangerously misleading, resulting in a failure to examine the ends of one's administrative actions. Second, the judicial model was informed by Storing's extensive understanding of American jurisprudence and the constitutional role that civil servants play in the modern administrative state through their responsibilities for implementation, rulemaking, and adjudication. Each of these influences will be elaborated more fully in the paragraphs that follow.

The Defects of the Positivist Science Model

Simon believed that the principles of modern science could improve public administration in much the same way that they had improved medicine. At the heart of the divide between common wisdom and science is Simon's separation of facts from values. Factual propositions, Simon argued, can be validated by determining their correspondence to the facts, while value propositions are validated through a process of intersubjective agreement. The values on which this agreement rests arise from the fiat of human will, not from any factual reality (Simon, 1957, p. 56). The earlier proponents of a distinct science of administration (Wilson, Taylor, Goodnow, and White) had argued that the separation between politics and administration turned on the difference between ends and means. Politics was concerned with determining ends, while administration was focused on how to best achieve these predetermined ends. While starting with the means–ends distinction, Simon ultimately abandoned it as an inadequate foundation for a science of administration.

Storing cited two reasons why Simon abandoned his predecessors' starting point. First, administrators are unable to separate the intermediate values that are imbedded in the subordinate means, which are part of the chain of means–ends causality (Storing, 1962, pp. 73–81). For example, the practice of using successive stages of employee discipline as a means of corrective action in human resource management is itself a value that may go beyond the instrumental goal of improving organizational efficiency and effectiveness. Giving employees a fair chance to improve may be a value that stands on a separate ground from the value of achieving results. The second reason for abandoning the means–ends distinction is Simon's recognition that, in practice, it is impossible for administrators literally to maximize the ends that are set by the political process. There is not enough time and money to calculate all of the possible alternatives to accomplish the policy goals established by that process. For that reason, Storing observed, Simon ultimately abandoned the economic model of "maximizing decisions" in his earlier work and substituted an organizational model of "satisficing" as the measure of administrative success (Storing, 1962, pp. 109–23). "Good enough" replaces the objective of maximizing the goals of a predetermined set of policy initiatives.

Storing concluded that Simon's attempt to replace common sense with a new science of administration is problematic because it rests on a flawed understanding of science. Science necessarily begins with a common sense understanding of the world, and the abandonment of this anchor would leave us without the ability to make rational choices about ends. Storing, therefore, stood Simon's approach on its head and thereby restored common sense as the necessary starting point for all governance work, making scientific knowledge subservient to knowledge about the ends of administrative activity.

Storing pointed out abundant examples in Simon's work of his reliance on practical opinions that are not validated by Simon's science. For example, Simon used phrases such as "correct decision-making," "rationality," "pure" values, "effective," "appropriate," "more final ends," "more final goals," and so on, without giving an account of how their meaning can be determined by and through his science (Storing, 1981, pp. 71–72). When Simon retreated to the ground of "satisficing" as the measure of administrative success, Storing pointed out, the term begs the question, What is good enough? and exhibits the subservience of Simon's notion of rationality "to nonrational preferences" (Storing, 1981, p. 71).

In addition to the incapacity of Simon's efforts to fashion a science of problem solving to replace prudential judgment, Storing pointed out that the adverse consequence of Simon's model of rationality is that it leaves us without any way of making rational choices about ends. Without a model of rationality that deals with the ends of human activity, we have no way of deciding what a problem is, and whether it is significant or urgent. "A decision about what is a problem, as distinct from a decision about how to solve a problem, is absolutely dependent on values" (Storing, 1981, p. 147).

Constitutional Law and the Judicial Model of Rationality[3]

As we have already pointed out, part of Storing's quarrel with some of the early founders of public administration was disagreement with their assumption that the great political questions of the day had been largely resolved in the United States by the Constitutional Convention and the end of slavery, thus leaving means-centered administrative questions as the major problems of the day (Wilson, 1887, p. 12). To the contrary, Storing argued that "age-old political and constitutional problems now present themselves as problems of (or in) public administration," and that "all interesting administrative questions are political questions" (1964b, p. 147). This argument reflected Storing's extensive study of administrative and constitutional law.

In many respects, Storing's attention to the linkage between the Constitution and public administration was unusual at the time. For the most part, as late as the 1960s, scholarly analysis of public administration and law was confined to administrative law, with some attention to major constitutional decisions handed down during the immediate postfounding period and the New Deal. The field's emphasis on administrative law was narrow, but understandable. It was not until the U.S. Supreme Court's decision in *Goldberg v. Kelly* (387 U.S. 254 [1970]), which applied constitutional due process to welfare benefits, that the rights revolution in U.S. constitutional law moved substantially beyond public personnel administration to broadly affect the administrative treatment of clients, customers, prisoners, public mental health patients, and individuals involved in street-level regulatory encounters. The rights revolution also made it easier for individuals to sue the government and its employees for the imposition of broad based institutional administrative reforms, financial compensation, and other relief.

Storing was deeply concerned with constitutional integrity. He closely analyzed the reasoning in relevant case decisions to assess their consistency with the Constitution's foundational principles. This approach often led him to focus on the allocation of constitutional powers between the executive and legislative branches of government.

In analyzing various conceptions of civil servants held in different historical periods, Storing looked to judicial decisions among other sources. For example, cases that held that a government job is a privilege to which no rights are attached supported a civil service based on partisanship, whereas those affirming Congress's and the state legislatures' power to prohibit civil servants from engaging in partisan activity supported the concept of neutrality.

Finally, Storing was concerned with the contest between individual liberty and national security, a theme that runs through the founding debates over the adoption of the U.S. Constitution. In terms of public administration issues in the 1950s and 1960s, this interest led Storing to focus extensively on the loyalty-security program for federal employees. He painstakingly analyzed the reasoning in key judicial decisions such as *Bailey v. Richardson* (182 F.2d 46 [1950]), *Joint Anti-Fascist Refugee Committee v. McGrath* (341 U.S. 123 [1951]), and *Keyishian v. Board of Regents* (385 U.S. 589 [1967]). Storing's textual-analytic approach sometimes revealed contradictions in a court's or an author's reasoning. When arguments were otherwise well reasoned, Storing viewed such contradictions as revealing the fault lines in broader controversies and point[ing] to areas where more thought was needed (though some issues inevitably remain intractable). Storing's interest in loyalty-security cases spun out into consideration of judicial doctrines affecting public administration, such as the doctrine of privilege, which came under heavy pressure in the 1950s and 1960s but did not fully crumble until the 1970s. What does it mean to say that a civil service job is a privilege? What would it mean to say it is a property right or interest? What are the effects of the middle position that there is no constitutional right to a civil service job, but civil servants retain some constitutional rights in the context of their public employment?

Taken together, Storing's teaching about the convergence and collision of constitutional law and public administration with respect to constitutional integrity, institutional development, the concept of a civil servant, and individual liberty versus national security set a theory-building and research agenda for many of his students. All of us probably pay great attention to the impact of major judicial decisions dealing with constitutional integrity and affecting public administration, such as *Bowsher v. Synar* (478 U.S. 714 [1986]) and *Morrison v. Olson* (487 U.S. 654 [1988]). In terms of institutional development, such as the scope of presidential power, *Hamdi v. Rumsfeld* (542 U.S. 507 [2004]) stands out along with theories such as those supporting claims by some presidents over the course of American history that the Constitution establishes a unitary executive branch. The concept of what a civil servant is or should be is also reflected in work on administrative ethics and issues posed by whistle-blowing and internal dissent in administrative organizations, such as those raised in *Garcetti v. Ceballos* (547 U.S. 410 [2006]). Individual liberty versus national security remains a strong concern in much of public administration theory, while the constitutional rights of public employees have become a major topic within public human resources management. Storing's effort to ground public administration theory and practice on the Constitution foreshadowed developments that will continue to have an enduring impact on the profession.

One of the important consequences of Storing's focus on the nexus between constitutional law and public administration was the development of the "judicial model" of administrative decision making. Storing was drawn to the way in which judges in appellate and common law settings have to make judgments that take facts into account while also considering principles that provide a moral standard, without prescribing a specific outcome.

For Storing's purposes, dissenting opinions were as important as majority decisions. In keeping with his view of the problematic nature of American democracy, he reminded students that the minority opinion of today may well become the majority opinion tomorrow. What was important to Storing in reviewing each judge's opinion was whether it was persuasive. Did it make sense? Was the reasoning compelling? Was it consistent with the purposes and intent of the Constitution? All of this was a way of teaching students what "judgment" meant as well as preparing them for the exercise of judgment in the their own teaching and practice. He was far less interested in the "doctrinal impact" of a case or vote than he was in the differing processes used by various judges to distill the ratio decidendi that connected moral principles to concrete facts.

Storing's call for using the judicial model as a guide to administrative practice foreshadowed a wide-ranging and growing critique of the positivist science decision-making model from critical theorists (Habermas, 1985), humanists (Hummel, 2007), feminists (Gilligan, 1993), and organizational theorists (Lipsky, 1980; Schön, 1984). As part of their critique, these theorists emphasized at least three forms of practical knowledge that can be acquired only through experience rather than through formal scientific analysis. These forms stand on a separate footing from the knowledge acquired through use of the scientific method (Jonsen & Toulmin, 1988; Vickers, 1965; Weick, 1979). In the world of administrative practice, these practical forms of knowledge often overshadow scientific knowledge as the most common bases for making judgments about policy development, implementation, and all matters related to the design and operation of public organizations.

There is, first, the prudential understanding that is acquired by undertaking an activity over a long period of time. The subtle nuances and complex interactions among materials, people, and settings acquired by master artisans and craftsman through a long period of "hands-on" experience exemplify this kind of tacit knowledge. Police officers, case managers, and city planners rely on it routinely to make decisions under conditions of limited resources, short time frames, significant uncertainty, and political conflicts that often make systematic analysis impossible.

A second kind of practical knowledge can be described as a "feel for the whole," and it is critically important for successful administrative practice. For public servants, knowledge of the whole tends to develop through experience in a variety of positions, and by moving to higher-level administrative roles that require an increasingly broad or "strategic" sense of their institution. As they do so, they become more aware of how their work forms part of the larger process of democratic governance. They develop a sense of proportion among priorities, and of balancing competing demands. They learn how to weave people and programs together and how to mobilize interests into new missions and institutional arrangements. Viewed in this way, knowledge of the whole is inseparable from managing change for the common good. It is what some call democratic statesmanship (Green, 1998).

Third, there is critical knowledge that gives skilled practitioners a sense of when things are not quite right, or do not add up. In these situations, their judgments often run against perceived facts and guiding principles. They also often run against the tide of opinion among colleagues, or in the general public, which invites conflict. The capacity to preserve and protect critical knowledge for the public benefit requires institutional safeguards such as secure tenure for key positions and careful staffing of critical workgroups to avoid problems with "groupthink" and related organizational pathologies. Critical knowledge represents a "sixth sense" for public servants who know that good administrative work cannot always follow prescribed formulas or seemingly convincing data.

These three types of practical knowledge contribute to the vital capacity for making judgments where other types of rational or systematic decision making fail because they are unable to connect facts to moral purposes. Storing's goal was not to denigrate scientific knowledge. Instead, he sought (1) to make the common knowledge acquired through experience and reflection central to successfully managing public affairs, and (2) to connect it to the larger moral purposes that this knowledge is intended to serve.

Conclusion: Restoring the Nobility of Public Service

Storing's intellectual agenda was guided by the desire to recover the foundational principles that would enable America's democratic system of government to thrive. His search for the meaning and implications of the American founding has produced three legacies that, taken together, restore the nobility of public service. First, his efforts to *recover* the founding principles have permanently reframed the debate about how we measure success in governing. Second, in the process of recovering the founding principles, Storing *restored* an important role for public administration and its agents in the governing process. Finally, Storing reminded us that the American democratic order can remain healthy only if its leaders and teachers of public service reach out to participate in an ongoing *renewal* process that connects current political issues to the underlying tensions inherent in American democratic governance.

The Task of Recovery: The Problematic Nature of American Democracy

Storing was singularly focused on the recovery of the problematic nature of the American democratic republic. In undertaking this recovery, Storing concluded that the prevailing views of the founding, whether they be liberal, conservative, elitist, or democratic (e.g., Beard, 1913; Brown, 1963; Elkins & McKitrick, 1962; Hartz, 1955; Hofstadter, 1948; Jensen, 1940; McDonald, 1958; Rossiter, 1953; Wood, 1973), failed to capture the full complexity of the problem that both the Federalists and Anti-Federalists were trying to solve. In revisiting the founding, Storing came to the conclusion that American democracy needed some unity in the executive, adequate opportunities for the expression of existing and emergent interests, wise leaders who had the motivation and discretion to use their judgment to promote the public interest, and vigilant and engaged citizens who cared deeply about democratic governance. Because there was no magic formula that would successfully and permanently reconcile these competing needs, it was important that each generation be prepared to continually reengage and rebalance such central political issues. Storing argued that the bureaucracy plays a central role in the success of this ongoing balancing process.

The Task of Restoration: The Bureaucracy's Role in Governance

Storing wanted to put responsibility for continually addressing the problem of American democratic governance on the doorstep of public administration. He rejected the notion that the bureaucracy can or should be limited to a simply subservient role, providing elected political officials with the benefit of narrow technical and neutral expertise. He argued that the bureaucracy was equally responsible for managing the problem of responsiveness, protecting against majority tyranny, and cultivating an engaged and vigilant citizenry. But in sharing responsibility for managing the ongoing problem of democratic governance, administrators needed to be armed with the kind of knowledge necessary to be successful. This knowledge is political in nature and requires the exercise of the kind of judgment found in a statesman.

The cultivation of the kind of judgment needed for a "closet statesmen" was reflected in Storing's approach as a teacher, as he moved from one set of texts to another, from *The Federalist*, to the writings of the Anti-Federalists, to the political writings of black Americans, to treatises on the U.S. Constitution (i.e., William W. Crosskey's history and analysis of the U.S. Constitution), to Supreme Court cases, to presidential papers, and always back again to the starting point of his agenda, the American founding. While the goal of reading these texts was to challenge the mind and recover important ideas written by thoughtful authors, it also set an example of what was required to be a good teacher and a good closet statesman. Here was a highly accomplished scholar at a top university who always worked hard—excessively, it sometimes seemed—to do his absolute best in the classroom. He was highly respected by students, and he respected them. For Storing, intellectual development was part of the larger process of character formation.

Storing observed in his study of the founding that while the framers believed in the importance of attracting the best individuals to public office, they failed to establish any mechanisms ensuring that this would happen on a consistent basis (Storing, 1981, 1: 73). Storing believed the establishment of a senior civil service would improve the overall quality of the American polity. To fulfill this function, however, civil servants had to be honest, upstanding, and committed to improving the civic culture and public morality.

Such concepts might seem old-fashioned—even archaic—in contemporary public administration writings, which see little that is special about civil service per se. Today, civil servants are largely viewed as interchangeable with private sector employees (including those working for nonprofits). "But for a handful of functions dealing with national security and criminal justice," remarked Paul Light, "it is not clear that there is a pure and inherently governmental function left today" (1999, pp. 9–10). With the blurring of the boundaries among the public, private, and nonprofit sectors, the role of the civil service has been significantly diminished. When this development is combined with the last three decades of criticism of the bureaucracy by the Reagan–Bush, Clinton–Gore and Bush–Cheney administrations, Storing would have been concerned about the long-term consequences for the quality of American democratic governance.

The Task of Renewal

Storing did not believe that recovering the founding principles by themselves and lodging shared responsibility for their stewardship in the bureaucracy was sufficient. These principles had to be connected to the realities of current political life. Principles held only as abstractions could not provide the energy and excitement for a renewal of public administration. Public administration is a clinical practice. As mentioned earlier in this essay, one of the proposed reforms that especially intrigued Storing was the creation of a senior civil service. But Storing was also mindful of the important role of education in this recovery and renewal process. "Unquestionably," Storing argued, "If our nation requires leadership, including administrative leadership, we had better give more and deeper consideration to the education of our leaders than we have done" (1963, p. 84).

While Storing did not set forth a curriculum for bureaucrats, the direction that such a curriculum might take is clear from his views on the role of administrators in governing and from his critique of the two accepted criteria of successful administrative work: technical competence and subservience to the popular will. Storing observed that "it is where these standards are unavailable, or contradictory, or insufficient that [an administrator] meets his most difficult and highest test" (1964a, p. 46). So what is the best way to educate administrators for the exercise of discretion, especially for the kind of political discretion characteristic of the closet statesmen? The answer for Storing might take a variety of forms. For example, Storing observed that the study of Supreme Court decisions "will sharpen and deepen the [bureaucrat's] practical grasp on the complex and sometimes ambiguous political principles that provide most of the ethical ground and substance of their work as American public administrators" (Rohr, 1978, p. vi). Because Storing was not a legal positivist, he believed that law constitutes "the normative horizon, or context, from which public administration must take its bearings." For Storing, the interpretation of law required reflection on the purposes of the law, and hence on questions of justice and right (Clor, 1980, p. 2). But the opportunity to reflect on justice and right was also provided for Storing by the writings of the Anti-Federalists and black Americans, a major reason he gave for assembling collections of their readings. One consequence of Storing's approach would be a greater focus in American schools of public administration on the thoughtful and critical study of constitutional law, political history, political theory, and political biography, at the expense of reducing the curricular role of generic courses that ignore the difference between public and private administration and the "systems science" approach, whether it be policy analysis, decision making, budgeting, personnel management, information management, or any number of other subjects.

An important opportunity for Storing to regenerate interest in public administration was provided by the civil rights movement of his day. The movement posed the question of how we can construct an enduring devotion to the principle of *e pluribus unum* without losing the identity of the parts. This was a central theme of his study of the founding, of constitutional law, and public administration. In the introduction to his collection of political writings by black Americans, Storing argued that social and political thought ought "to aim to help men find their way into broader and higher levels of significance." The aim should be, however, "not to abandon the narrower particular associations but rather by sustaining their integrity and exploring their implications, to enrich and elevate the whole community." Storing observed that W. E. B. Du Bois's writings raise basic questions about the foundations of American government and politics, and even about the accepted foundations of politics in the modern world (1970, pp. 11–12). In his preface to *What Country Have I?* Storing turns to Du Bois for guidance in identifying what is ultimately important in our work as teachers and scholars (1970, pp. vi–vii).

Du Bois described the African American as "a sort of seventh son, born with a veil, and gifted with second-sight in this American world ... . One ever feels his two-ness—an American, a Negro; two souls, two thoughts, two unreconciled strivings; two warring ideals in one dark body, whose dogged strength alone keeps it from being torn asunder." Storing observes that, "Du Bois knew that all men live within their veils of prejudice, convention and particularity, just as, at the same time, all thoughtful men reach out for a world beyond":

> I sit with Shakespeare and he winces not. Across the color line I move arm in arm with Balzac and Dumas, where smiling men and welcoming women glide in gilded halls. From the caves of evening that swing between the strong-limbed earth and the tracery of the stars, I summon Aristotle and Aurelius and what soul I will, and they come all graciously with no scorn nor condescension. So, wed with Truth, I dwell above the Veil.
>
> (1903, p. 109)

Storing cited Du Bois, first, because he stood "among the noteworthy makers and critics of the American regime," thus shedding light on our efforts to reconcile the political parts with the whole. But he praised Du Bois also because he stood among "those who seek to understand men and their relations with one another ... a teacher of all who aspire to wed Truth and dwell above the Veil" (Storing, 1970, pp. 11–12). Du Bois was an exemplar for Storing, both for what he taught us about living together as members of a common political community and for what he taught about being human. No less can be said of Storing's contributions as a teacher and as a scholar of public administration. The nobility of public service ultimately finds expression in the lives of men and women of noble character who devote their lives of service and teaching to balancing the tensions inherent in the foundations of America's system of democratic governance.

Notes

1 In preparing this article, we have drawn heavily from Kent Kirwan's (1981) earlier summary of Herbert Storing's contributions to public administration.

2 In summarizing Storing's teachings, we have drawn on the following sources: Storing (1962, 1963, 1964a, 1964b, 1970, 1980, 1981).

3 For an excellent extended discussion of the importance of the judicial model of reasoning to administrative practice, see Green (2002).

References

Adrian, Charles. 1999. Forms of Local Government in American History. In *Forms of Local Government: A Handbook on City, County, and Regional Options*, edited by Roger L. Kemp. Jefferson, NC: McFarland, pp. 47–62.

Beard, Charles A. 1913. *An Economic Interpretation of the Constitution of the United States.* New York: Macmillan.

Brown, Robert. E. 1963. *Reinterpretation of the Formation of the American Constitution.* Boston, MA: Boston University Press.

Clor, Harry. 1980. Herbert Storing. Commentary presented at the annual Meeting of the American Political Science Association on the panel "The Work of Herbert Storing."

Cropsey, Joseph. 1981. Foreword to *What the Anti-Federalists Were For: The Political Thought of the Opponents of the Constitution*, Vol. 1 of *The Complete Anti-Federalists.* ed. Herbert J. Storing. Chicago, IL: University of Chicago Press.

Crosskey, William W. 1980. *Politics and the Constitution in the History of the United States.* 3 vols. Chicago, IL: University of Chicago Press.

Du Bois, W. E. B. 1903. *The Souls of Black Folk.* Chicago, IL: A. C. McClurg.

Elkins, Stanley & Eric McKitrick. 1962. *The Founding Fathers: Young Men of the Revolution.* Washington, DC: American Historical Association.

Etzioni, Amitai. 1993. *The Spirit of Community: Rights, Responsibilities, and the Communitarian Agenda.* New York: Crown.

Friedrich, Carl J. 1940. Public Policy and the Nature of Administrative Responsibility. In *Public Policy*, edited by Carl J. Friedrich & E. S. Mason. Cambridge, MA: Harvard University Press, pp. 3–24.

Gilligan, Carol. 1993. *In a Different Voice: Psychological Theory and Women's Development.* Cambridge, MA: Harvard University Press.

Green, Richard. 1998. Impartiality and Administrative Statesmanship. In *Active Duty: Public Administration as Democratic Statesmanship*, edited by Peter Augustine Lawler, Robert Martin Schaefer & David Lewis Schaefer. Lanham, MD: Rowman & Littlefield, pp. 547–553.

Green, Richard. 2002. Common Law, Equity and American Public Administration. *American Review of Public Administration* 32(3): 263–294.

Habermas, Jürgen. 1985. *The Theory of Communicative Action.* Boston, MA: Beacon Press.

Hartz, Louis. 1955. *The Liberal Tradition in America: An Interpretation of American Political Thought since the Revolution.* New York: Harcourt, Brace.

Hofstadter, Richard. 1948. *The American Political Tradition and the Men Who Made It.* New York: Vintage.

Hummel, Ralph P. 2007. *The Bureaucratic Experience: The Post-Modern Challenge.* 5th edn. Armonk, NY: M. E. Sharpe.

Jensen, Merrill. 1940. *The Articles of Confederation: An Interpretation of the Social-Constitutional History of the American Revolution, 1774–1781.* Madison: University of Wisconsin Press.

Jonsen, Albert R. & Stephen Toulmin. 1988. *The Abuse of Casuistry: A History of Moral Reasoning.* Berkeley: University of California Press.

Kemmis, Daniel. 1990. *Community and the Politics of Place.* Norman: University of Oklahoma Press.

Kirwan, Kent A. 1981. Herbert J. Storing and the Study of Public Administration. *Political Science Reviewer* 11(2): 193–222.

Light, Paul C. 1999. *The True Size of Government*. Washington, DC: Brookings Institution.

Lipsky, Michael. 1980. *Street-Level Bureaucracy: The Dilemmas of the Individual in Public Services*. New York: Russell Sage Foundation

McDonald, Forrest. 1958. *We the People: The Economic Origins of the Constitution*. Chicago, IL: University of Chicago Press.

Morgan, Douglas F., Kelly G. Bacon, Ron Bunch, Charles D. Cameron & Robert Deis. 1996. What Middle Managers Do in Local Government: Stewardship of the Public Trust and Limits of Reinventing Government. *Public Administration Review* 56(4): 259–266.

Morgan, Douglas F., Richard Green, Craig W. Shinn & Kent S. Robinson. 2008. *Foundations of Public Service*. Armonk, NY: M. E. Sharpe.

Morgan, Douglas F. & Henry D. Kass. 1993. The American Odyssey of the Career Public Service: The Ethical Crises of Role Reversal. In *Ethics and Public Administration*, edited by H. George Frederickson. Armonk, NY: M. E. Sharpe, pp. 177–194.

Nalbandian, John. 2000. The City Manager as Political Leader: A Challenge to Professionalism? *Public Management* 82(3): 7–13.

Putnam, Robert D. 2000. *Bowling Alone: The Collapse and Revival of American Community*. New York: Simon & Schuster.

Rohr, John A. 1978. *Ethics for Bureaucrats*. New York: Marcel Dekker.

Rossiter, Clinton. 1953. *Seedtime of the Republic: The Origin of the American Tradition of Political Liberty*. New York: Harcourt.

Schön, Donald A. 1984. *The Reflective Practitioner: How Professionals Think In Action*. New York: Basic Books.

Simon, Herbert A. 1947. A Comment on "The Science of Public Administration." *Public Administration Review* 7(3): 200–203.

Simon, Herbert A. 1957. *Administrative Behavior: A Study of Decision Making Processes in Administrative Organizations*. 2nd edn. New York: Macmillan.

Storing, Herbert J. 1962. The Science of Administration: Herbert A. Simon. In *Essays on the Scientific Study of Politics*, edited by Herbert J. Storing. New York: Holt, Rinehart & Winston, pp. 63–150.

Storing, Herbert J. 1963. The Problem of Big Government. In *A Nation of States*, edited by Robert A. Goldwin. Chicago, IL: Rand McNally, pp. 65–86.

Storing, Herbert J. 1964a. The Crucial Link: Public Administration, Responsibility and the Public Interest. *Public Administration Review* 24(1): 39–46.

Storing, Herbert J. 1964b. Political Parties and the Bureaucracy. In *Political Parties U.S.A.*, edited by Robert A. Goldwin, 137–158. Chicago, IL: Rand McNally.

Storing, Herbert J. 1965. Leonard D. White and the Study of Public Administration. *Public Administration Review* 25(1): 38–51.

Storing, Herbert J. ed. 1970. *What Country Have I? Political Writings by Black Americans*. New York: St. Martin's Press.

Storing, Herbert J. 1980. American Statesmanship: Old and New. In *Bureaucrats, Policy Analysts, Statesmen: Who Leads?* edited by Robert A. Goldwin. Washington, DC: American Enterprise Institute, pp. 88–113.

Storing, Herbert J. 1981. *What the Anti-Federalists Were For: The Political Thought of the Opponents of the Constitution*. Vol. 1 of *The Complete Anti-Federalists*. Chicago, IL: University of Chicago Press.

Svara, James H. 2001. The Myth of the Dichotomy: Complementarity of Politics and Administration in the Past and Future of Public Administration. *Public Administration Review* 61(2): 176–183.

Svara, James H. 2006. The Search for Meaning in Political–Administrative Relations in Local Government. *International Journal of Public Administration* 29(12): 1065–1090.

Svara, James H. 2008. Beyond Dichotomy: Dwight Waldo and the Intertwined Politics–Administration Relationship. *Public Administration Review* 68(1): 43–52.

Taylor, Henry. [1836] 1998. *The Statesman*. Ed. David Lewis Schaefer & Roberta R. Schaefer. Westport, CT: Praeger.

Thach, Charles C. 1969. *The Creation of the Presidency: 1775–1789*. Baltimore, MD: Johns Hopkins University Press.

Tocqueville, Alexis de. 2000. *Democracy in America*. Trans. Harvey Mansfield & Delba Winthrop. Chicago, IL: University of Chicago Press.

Vickers, Geoffrey. 1965. *The Art of Judgment: A Study of Policy Making*. London: Chapman and Hall.

Waldo, Dwight. 1968. Scope of the Theory of Public Administration. In *Theory and Practice of Public Administration*, edited by James C. Charlesworth. Philadelphia, PA: American Academy of Political and Social Science, pp. 1–26.

Weick, Karl E. 1979. *The Social Psychology of Organizing*. 2nd edn. Reading, MA: Addison-Wesley.

Wilson, Woodrow. 1887. The Study of Administration. *Political Science Quarterly* 2(2): 197–222.

Wood, Gordon S. 1973. *The Confederation and The Constitution: The Critical Issue*. Boston, MA: Little, Brown.

3 Public Administration Theory, the Separation of Powers, and the Constitutional School

David H. Rosenbloom

On the thirtieth anniversary of the publication of "Public Administrative Theory and the Separation of Powers", the *American Review of Public Administration* published my invited essay, "Reflections on 'Public Administrative Theory and the Separation of Powers'" (Rosenbloom, 2013). In reflecting again here, I will review the main points I made there and add some additional thoughts.

First, the article should have defined "politics" more clearly. The term is intended in the Lasswellian sense of "who gets what, when, how" (Lasswell, 1950) as well as policymaking as treated in much of the bureaucratic politics and policy cycle literature. "Politics" in the article was not meant to focus attention on elections, electoral campaigns, partisanship, or intra-office and inter-agency turf and power contests.

Second, the most surprising feature of the original article has been its international impact. The article was conceived as a potentially relevant framework for connecting different approaches to U.S. public administrative theory and practice to the constitutional framework for the separation of powers. I then believed, as I do now, that the separation of powers is among the defining aspects of U.S. public administration. It gives three branches of government separate, yet overlapping, responsibilities for federal administration. As Lewis Meriam noted in 1939, "Under our system of divided powers, the executive branch of the national government is not exclusively controlled by the President, by the Congress, or by the courts. All three have a hand in controlling it, each from a different angle and each in a different way" (p. 131). The separation of powers also contributes to the difficulty of integrating or retrofitting the administrative state into the constitutional regime because the entire federal administrative component combines what the Constitution separates: legislation (e.g., agency rulemaking), execution, and adjudication. This combination of powers also exists in many individual agencies. Despite Alexander Hamilton's observation that public administration "comprehends all the operations of the body politic, whether legislative, executive, or judiciary" (Carey and McClellan, 2001, p. 374), the "collapsing" of the separation of powers into the executive branch and individual agencies presents a recurring challenge to legitimization of the administrative state (Freedman, 1978). Neither parliamentary nor authoritarian political systems resemble the U.S. in their organization of political functions and the history of separation of powers systems elsewhere, as in Latin America, is typically very different from our own. Nevertheless, the article's "three lenses" or "three perspectives" framework as further developed in the book-length version, *Public Administration: Understanding Management, Politics, and Law in the Public Sector*, is used and cited worldwide (Rosenbloom, 1986; Rosenbloom, Kravchuk & Clerkin, 2015). The book itself is a core text in Master of Public Administration programs not only in the U.S., but also throughout China and perhaps elsewhere.[1]

At least two factors heavily contribute to the framework's seemingly unlikely portability. First, despite the low status of public administration in the U.S. and incessant denunciation of "bureaucracy," academicians and political officials elsewhere consider the U.S. as a world-leading model to be understood, if not necessarily emulated. Second, and more important from the perspectives of public administration, management, politics and policymaking, and adjudication are major governmental functions everywhere regardless of how they are configured. Moreover, some of the values associated with these functions, such as cost-effectiveness for management, efficacy for policymaking, and fairness for adjudication are widely shared in aspiration, if not satisfactory realization. Disaggregating public administration into management, politics/policy, and law makes thinking about public administration and its implementation clearer and more manageable.

Third, the idea that values drive administrative organization, process, and behavior, how we think about individuals in administrative contexts, and cognition, while hardly new in 1983, may have played a role, however limited, in contributing to a resurgence of research on "public values" (Nabatchi, 2011). There was no mistaking the normative dimensions of public administration in the wake of Robert Dahl's famous article on "The Science of Public Administration: Three Problems" (1947). However, the controversy over New Public Administration values in the late 1960s and 1970s called greater attention to how putative core administrative values are anchored—in representative democracy, the Constitution, regime values, law, normative theory, in public administration as a profession, or otherwise (Thompson, 1975; Millett, 1976; Rohr, 1978; Rosenbloom, 1983; Marini, 1971).

The structural-functional approach taken in the article offers two perspectives on the contemporary study of public values. First, not all public values are core public administrative values. Some are "mission extrinsic" or "non-mission based" (Baehler, Liu & Rosenbloom, 2014; Piotrowski and Rosenbloom, 2002). That is, they underlie operations that agencies must perform, such as answering freedom of information requests, that do not support achieving most individual agencies' central purposes, core activities, *raison d'être*, and programs, or tap into their specialized competencies and technologies. The distinctions among public values; core public administrative values that inform organization, process, and behavior, program specific values, and mission extrinsic public values can be helpful in sorting out the current values research and literature. The functional approach to values; like constitutional and legal approaches to public administration, while perhaps too narrow for some theorists and researchers, provides a significant degree of anchoring.

Fourth, the question of "next steps" lingers. Fortunately, important theory building and research on moving the three perspectives framework forward is currently underway. Two of the most promising approaches are by Naomi Aoki and Yair Zalmanovitch. Aoki's article, "Let's Get Public Administration Right, But in What Sequence? Lessons from Japan and Singapore" (2015) raises major comparative administration questions: can regimes focus on management, politics and policymaking, and adjudication simultaneously, or does focusing on one or another function necessarily or beneficially precede addressing the other two, and under what conditions? Putting her analysis in U.S. historical context with reference to Herbert Kaufman's "Administrative Decentralization and Political Power" (1969), did developing the political dimensions of public administration necessarily have to precede building managerial political neutrality and competence? And, going beyond Kaufman, was regulatory policy and administration a prerequisite for the advent of administrative law (Rosenbloom, 2007)? Likewise, was the development of substantial social welfare policy implementation a prior condition for the emergence of the constitutional law dimensions of contemporary public administration? (Reich, 1964; Rosenbloom, O'Leary & Chanin, 2010).

Zalmanovitch's "Don't Reinvent the Wheel: The Search for an Identity for Public Administration" (2014) urges the field to stop offering up new putative paradigms, but rather to move forward with the three "pillars" delineated in "Public Administrative Theory and the Separation of Powers." In contrast to treating the three pillars individually, he asks us to "conceive of the identity of public administration as based on the mutual existence of and interaction among the three pillars. Each of the three addresses an essential function: what may be achieved (politics), how it may be attained (management), and under what strictures, limitations and rules (legality)" (2014, p. 6). Handling the pillars this way can generate a beneficial trialectic:

> Rather than hierarchically compartmentalizing the three pillars that lie at the heart of public administration, we should encourage their interaction. Whereas dichotomous dialectism plays one pillar off against another by substituting one for the other, trialectism promotes their simultaneous interrelations and coexistence. In such an environment, each pillar nurtures the other two, thereby facilitating the growth and development of an organic whole.
>
> (2014, p. 8)

The approaches advanced by Aoki and Zalmanovitch are theoretically and empirically promising. They speak to the potential comparative applicability of the Constitutional School's theoretical foundation to public administrative management in other countries, something that seems desirable, if not absolutely necessary, in today's globalized world and increasingly diverse public administration research community (Jreisat, 2012).

Finally, I cannot refrain from reflecting a bit on peer review. "Public Administrative Theory and the Separation of Powers" has been reprinted multiple times, including in editions three through eight of Shafritz and Hyde's *Classics of Public Administration* (2017). It is also widely cited in the public administration literature and listed among the 75 most influential articles published in *Public Administration Review* since its first issue in 1941.[2] Chet Newland, then *PAR*'s editor-in-chief, sent the manuscript to six reviewers. Five asked for minor revisions while one flatly recommended rejection. Fortunately, based on his own reading of the manuscript, Chet completely disregarded the outlier. However, after all these years, I am still dismayed that this reviewer ever got to be one, and speculate what might have happened if Chet had only sent it to two reviewers, the rejecter being one, and had not read it himself. In my experience, too often today, editors are excessively overwhelmed with submissions to give a careful reading to submitted manuscripts, and reviewers tend to push their own agendas. As something of a QED, I add that as author or coauthor, two of my articles have received leading journal "best article" awards. Both were invited and neither subjected to double blind peer review! I doubt that I am alone in wondering whether the poor quality of many peer reviews detracts from the overall development of public administration as a field of study.

Notes

1 To my knowledge, in addition to the U.S. and China, the book has had classroom use in Australia, Canada, Hong Kong, India, Indonesia, Iran, Israel, Kyrgyzstan, Lebanon, Malaysia, Nepal, the Netherlands, Norway, Pakistan, Portugal, Republic of Georgia, Romania, Singapore, South Africa, South Korea, Taiwan, Thailand, and Ukraine.

2 http://publicadministrationreview.org/full-list/ (accessed January 3, 2016).

References

Aoki, N. 2015. "Let's get public administration right, but in what sequence? Lessons from Japan and Singapore." *Public administration and development* 35(3): 206–218.

Baehler, K., Liu, C. & Rosenbloom, D.H. 2014. "Mission-extrinsic public values as an extension of regime values: Examples from the United States and the People's Republic of China." *Administration and Society* 46(2): 199–219.

Carey, G. & McClellan, J., eds. 2001. *The Federalist*. Indianapolis, IN: Liberty Fund.

Dahl, R. 1947. "The science of public administration: Three problems." *Public administration review* 7(1): 1–11.

Freedman, J. 1978. *Crisis and legitimacy: The administrative process and American government*. New York: Cambridge University Press.

Jreisat, J. 2012. *Globalism and comparative public administration*. Boca Raton, FL: CRC Press.

Kaufman, H. 1969. "Administrative decentralization and political power." *Public administration review* 29(1): 3–15.

Lasswell, H. 1950. *Politics: Who gets what, when, how*. New York: P. Smith.

Marini, F., ed. 1971. *Toward a new public administration: The Minnowbrook perspective*. Scranton, PA: Chandler.

Meriam, L. 1939. *Reorganization of the national government: Part I: An analysis of the problem*. Washington, DC: Brookings Institution.

Millett, J. 1976. "The Constitution and public administration." in R. Golembiewski, F. Gibson & G. Cornog, eds, *Public administration: Readings in institutions, processes, behavior, and policy*, third edn. Chicago, IL: Rand McNally, pp. 425–441.

Nabatchi, T. 2011. "Exploring the public values universe: Understanding values in public administration." The Maxwell School of Citizenship and Public Affairs, Syracuse University, Syracuse, NY: www.maxwell.syr.edu/uploadedFiles/conferences/pmrc/Files/Nabatchi%20_Exploring%20the%20Public%20Values%20Universe.pdf (accessed January 3, 2016; used with the author's permission).

Piotrowski, S. & Rosenbloom, D.H. 2002. "The problem of nonmission based values in results oriented public management: The case of freedom of information." *Public administration review* 62(6): 643–657.

Reich, C. 1964. "The new property." *Yale Law Journal* 73(5): 733–787.

Rohr, J. 1978. *Ethics for bureaucrats*. New York: Marcel Dekker.

Rosenbloom, D.H. 2013. "Reflections on public administrative theory and the separation of powers." *American review of public administration* 43(4): 381–396.

Rosenbloom, D.H. 2007. "Administrative law and regulation." in J. Rabin, W. B. Hildreth, and G. Miller, eds, *Handbook of public administration*, third edn. New York: Taylor & Francis, pp. 635–696.

Rosenbloom, D.H. 1986. *Public administration: Understanding management, politics, and law in the public sector*. New York: Random House.

Rosenbloom, D.H. 1983. *Public administration and law*. New York: Marcel Dekker.

Rosenbloom, D.H., Kravchuk, R.S. & Clerkin, R. 2015. *Public administration: Understanding management, politics, and law in the public sector*, eighth edn. New York: McGraw Hill.

Rosenbloom, D. H., O'Leary, R. & Chanin, J. 2010. *Public administration and law*, third edn. Boca Raton, FL: CRC Press.

Shafritz, J. & Hyde, A., eds. 2017. *Classics of public administration*, eighth edn. Boston, MA: Cengage.

Thompson, V. 1975. *Without sympathy or enthusiasm: The problem of administrative compassion*. Tuscaloosa, AL: University of Alabama Press.

Zalmanovitch, Y. 2014. "Don't reinvent the wheel: The search for an identity for public administration." *International review of administrative sciences*: available at https://www.researchgate.net/publication/265849842_Don%27t_reinvent_the_wheel_the_search_for_an_identity_for_public_administration (accessed January 3, 2016: doi: 10.1177/0020852314533456).

Public Administrative Theory and the Separation of Powers

David H. Rosenbloom

From: *Public Administration Review* 43 (May/June 1983): 219–227.

Introduction

It has been recognized for some time that the discipline of public administration is plagued by a weak or absent theoretical core. This has led some to conclude, along with Robert Parker,[1] that "there is really no such subject as 'public administration.' No science or art can be identified by this title, least of all any single skill or coherent intellectual discipline." Others, including Frederick C. Mosher,[2] have considered it a "resource," that public administration "is more an area of interest than a discipline," since this enables the field to draw upon a variety of disciplines. Still others, such as Herbert Kaufman[3] and James Q. Wilson,[4] have argued that public administration faces a serious and seemingly irresolvable problem in continually seeking to maximize the attainment of mutually incompatible values. The contention of this essay is that the central problem of contemporary public administrative theory is that it is derived from three disparate approaches to the basic question of what public administration is. Each of these approaches has a respected intellectual tradition, emphasizes different values, promotes different types of organizational structure, and views individuals in markedly distinct terms. These approaches are conveniently labeled "managerial," "political," and "legal." They have influenced one another over the years, and at some points they overlap. Yet, their primary influence on public administration has been to pull it in three separate directions. Furthermore, these directions tend to follow the pattern of the separation of powers established by the Constitution. Consequently, it is unlikely that the three approaches can be synthesized without violating values deeply ingrained in the United States political culture.[5]

The Managerial Approach to Public Administration

Origin and Values

In the United States, the managerial approach to public administration grew largely out of the civil service reform movement of the late 19th century. In the reformers' words, "What civil service reform demand[ed], [was] that the business part of the government shall be carried on in a sound businesslike manner."[6] The idea of "businesslike" public administration was most self-consciously and influentially discussed by Woodrow Wilson in his essay on "The Study of Administration."[7] There, Wilson considered public administration to be "a field of business" and consequently largely a managerial endeavor. He also set forth the three core values of the managerial approach to public administration: "It is the object of administrative study to discover, first, what government can properly and successfully do, and, secondly, how it can do these proper things with the utmost possible efficiency and at the least possible cost either of money or of energy."[8] Thus, public administration was to be geared toward the maximization of effectiveness, efficiency, and economy.

The managerial approach was strengthened by Frederick Taylor and the scientific management movement.[9] Taylorism sought to enshrine the values of efficiency and economy in a world view that promised to achieve harmony and affluence among mankind. Later, Leonard White's influential *Introduction to the Study of Public Administration*[10] asserted that "the study of administration should start from the base of management rather than the foundation of law, and is, therefore, more absorbed in the affairs of the American Management Association than in the decisions of the courts." When the managerial approach to public administration was at the pinnacle of its influence in the 1930s, it was widely held, along with Luther Gulick, that "efficiency" was "axiom number one in the value scale of administration" and that politics could not enter "the structure of administration without producing inefficiency."[11]

The essence of the managerial approach's values was captured by Simmons and Dvorin in the following terms:

> The "goodness" or "badness" of a particular organizational pattern was a mathematical relationship of "inputs" to "outputs." Where the latter was maximized and the former minimized, a moral "good" resulted. Virtue or "goodness" was therefore equated with the relationship of these two factors, that is, "efficiency," or "inefficiency." Mathematics was transformed into ethics.[12]

Organizational Structure

The managerial approach to public administration promotes organization essentially along the lines of Max Weber's ideal-type bureaucracy.[13] It the importance of functional specialization for efficiency. Hierarchy 'elied upon for effective coordination.[14] Programs and functions are :arly assigned to organizational units. Overlaps are to be minimized. s are to be classified into a rational scheme and pay scales are to be systematically derived in the interests of economy and motivating employees to be efficient. Selection of public administrators is to be made strictly on the basis of merit. They are to be politically neutral in their competence. Relationships among public administrators and public agencies are to be formalized in writing and, in all events, the public's business is to be administered in a smooth, orderly fashion.[15]

View of the Individual

The managerial approach to public administration promotes an impersonal view of individuals. This is true whether the individuals in question are the employees, clients, or the "victims"[16] of public administrative agencies. One need not go so far as Max Weber in considering "dehumanization" to be the "special virtue" of bureaucracy or to view the bureaucrat as a "cog" in an organizational machine over which he or she has virtually no control.[17] Yet there can be no doubt that a strong tendency of scientific management was to turn the individual worker into an appendage to a mechanized means of production. By 1920, this view of the employee was clearly embodied in the principles of position classification in the public sector: "The individual characteristics of an employee occupying a position should have no bearing on the classification of the position."[18] Indeed, the strong "position-orientation" of the managerial approach to public administration continues to diminish the importance of the individual employee to the overall organization.

Clients, too, have been "depersonalized" and turned into "cases" in an effort to promote the managerial values of efficiency, economy, and effectiveness. Ralph Hummel explains:

> At the intake level of the bureaucracy, individual personalities are converted into cases. Only if a person can qualify as a case, is he or she allowed treatment by the bureaucracy. More accurately, a bureaucracy is never set up to treat or deal with persons: it "processes" only "cases."[19]

"Victims" may be depersonalized to such an extent that they are considered sub-human, especially where physical force or coercion is employed as in mental health facilities and police functions.[20]

The human relations approach to organization theory and some contemporary views argue that reliance on impersonality tends to be counterproductive because it generates "bureaupathologies."[21] Nevertheless, the managerial approach's impersonal view of individuals is deeply ingrained and considered essential to the maximization of efficiency, economy, and effectiveness.

The Political Approach to Public Administration

Origins and Values

The political approach to public administration was perhaps most forcefully and succinctly stated by Wallace Sayre:

> Public administration is ultimately a problem in political theory: the fundamental problem in a democracy is responsibility to popular control; the responsibility and responsiveness of the administrative agencies and the bureaucracies to the elected officials (the chief executives, the legislators) is of central importance in a government based increasingly on the exercise of discretionary power by the agencies of administration.[22]

This approach grew out of the observation of some, such as Paul Appleby, that public administration during the New Deal and World War II was anything but devoid of politics.[23] Thus, unlike the origin of the managerial approach, which stressed what public administration ought to be, the political approach developed from an analysis of apparent empirical reality.

Once public administration is considered a political endeavor, emphasis is inevitably placed on a different set of values than those promoted by the managerial approach. "Efficiency," in particular, becomes highly suspect, as Justice Brandeis pointed out in dissent in *Myers v. United States* (1926):

> The doctrine of the separation of powers was adopted by the Convention of 1787, not to promote efficiency but to preclude the exercise of arbitrary power. The purpose was, not to avoid friction, but, by means of the inevitable friction incident to the distribution of governmental powers among three departments, to save the people from autocracy.[24]

Rather, the political approach to public administration stresses the values of representativeness, political responsiveness, and accountability through elected officials to the citizenry. These are viewed as crucial to the maintenance of constitutional democracy, especially in view of the rise of the contemporary administrative state, which may be likened unto "bureaucratic government."[25]

One can find many examples of governmental reforms aimed at maximizing the political values of representativeness, responsiveness, and accountability within public administration. For instance, the wide ranging academic controversy concerning the concept of "representative bureaucracy"[26] notwithstanding, the Federal Civil Service Reform Act of 1978 made it "the policy of the United States ... to provide a Federal workforce reflective of the Nation's diversity" by endeavoring "to achieve a work force from all segments of society."[27] The Federal Advisory Committee Act of 1972 sought to enhance responsiveness through the use of "representative" advisory committees.[28] Earlier, the poverty and model cities programs of the 1960s sought to use "citizen participation" as a means of promoting political responsiveness in administrative operations. The quest for responsiveness has also blended into attempts to promote the accountability of public administrators to political officials through a variety of measures including greater use of the General Accounting Office,[29] the creation of the federal Senior Executive Service, and structural changes such as the establishment of the Office of Management and Budget, the Office of Personnel Management, and the Congressional Budget Office. "Sunshine" provisions such as the Freedom of Information Act and "sunset" requirements are also examples of the attempt to promote political accountability. There is also a growing academic literature on the need to promote representativeness, responsiveness, and accountability in the modern administrative state.[30]

It is important to note that the values sought by the political approach to public administration are frequently in tension with those of the managerial approach. For instance, efficiency in the managerial sense is not necessarily served through sunshine regulations which can dissuade public administrators from taking some courses of action, though they may be the most efficient, and can divert time and resources from program implementation to the deliverance of information to outsiders. Consultation with advisory committees and "citizen participants" can be time consuming and costly. A socially representative public service may not be the most efficient one.[31] Nor is the intended shuffling of Senior Executive Servants from agency to agency likely to enhance efficiency in the managerial sense. Rather it is thought that by providing this cadre of top public administrators a wider variety of experience, they may come to define the public interest in more comprehensive terms and therefore become more responsive to the nation's overall political interests. Moreover, while various budgeting strategies and sunset provisions can promote economy in one sense, the amount of paperwork they generate and the extent to which they may require agencies to justify and argue on behalf of their programs and expenditures can become quite costly. Indeed, a quarter century ago, Marver Bernstein reported that "many officials complain that they must spend so much time preparing for appearing at Congressional hearings and in presenting their programs before the Bureau of the Budget and other bodies that it often leaves little time for directing the operations of their agencies."[32] Managerial effectiveness is difficult to gauge, of course, but federal managers have long complained that their effectiveness is hampered by the large congressional role in public administration and the need to consult continually with a variety of parties having a legitimate concern with their agencies' operations.[33]

Organizational Structure

Public administration organized around the political values of representativeness, responsiveness, and accountability also tends to be at odds with the managerial approach to organization. Rather than emphasizing clear lines of functional specialization, hierarchy, unity, and recruitment based on politically neutral administrative competence, the political approach stresses the extent and advantages of political pluralism within public administration. Thus, Harold Seidman argues that, "Executive branch structure is in fact a microcosm of our society. Inevitably it reflects the values, conflicts, and competing forces to be found in a pluralistic society. The ideal of a neatly symmetrical, frictionless organization structure is a dangerous illusion."[34] Norton Long makes a similar point:

> Agencies and bureaus more or less perforce are in the business of building, maintaining, and increasing their political support. They lead and in large part are led by the diverse groups whose influence sustains them. Frequently they lead and are themselves led in conflicting directions.[35]

Roger Davidson finds a political virtue where those imbued with the managerial approach might see disorder: "In many respects, the civil service represents the American people more comprehensively than does Congress."[36]

The basic concept behind pluralism within public administration is that since the administrative branch is a policy-making center of government, it must be structured to enable faction to counteract faction by providing political representation to a comprehensive variety of the organized political, economic, and social interests that are found in the society at large. To the extent that the political approach's organizational scheme is achieved, the structure comes to resemble a political party platform that promises something to almost everyone without establishing clear priorities for resolving conflicts among them. Agency becomes adversary of agency and the resolution of conflict is shifted to the legislature, the office of the chief executive, interagency committees, or the courts. Moreover, the number of bureaus and agencies tends to grow over time, partly in response to the political demands of organized interests for representation. This approach to administrative organization has been widely denounced as making government "unmanageable," "costly," and "inefficient,"[37] but, as Seidman argues, it persists because administrative organization is frequently viewed as a political question that heavily emphasizes political values.

View of the Individual

The political approach to public administration tends to view the individual as part of an aggregate group. It does not depersonalize the individual by turning him or her into a "case," as does the managerial approach, but rather identifies the individual's interests as being similar or identical to those of others considered to be within the same group or category. For example, affirmative action within the government service is aimed at specific social groups such as blacks and women without inquiry as to the particular circumstances of any individual member of these broad and diverse groups. Similarly, farmers growing the same crops and/or located in the same national geopolitical subdivisions are considered alike, despite individual differences among them. The same is true in any number of areas of public administration where public policies dealing with people are implemented. This is a tendency, of course, that fits the political culture well—politicians tend to think in terms of groups, e.g., the "black" vote, the "farm" vote, labor, and so forth. Indeed, this approach is so strong that some, such as David Truman,[38] consider it the main feature of government in the United States. Theodore Lowi argues that a central tenet of the contemporary American "public philosophy" is that "organized interests are homogeneous and easy to define, sometimes monolithic. Any 'duly elected' spokesman for any interest is taken as speaking in close approximation for each and every member."[39] In this view of the individual, then, personality exists, but it is conceptualized in collective terms.

The Legal Approach to Public Administration

Origin and Values

In the United States, the legal approach to public administration has historically been eclipsed by the other approaches, especially the managerial. Nevertheless, it has a venerable tradition and has recently emerged as a full-fledged vehicle for defining public administration. It is derived primarily from three inter-related sources. First is administrative law. As early as 1905, Frank Goodnow, a leading contributor to the development of public administrative theory generally, published a book entitled *The Principles of the Administrative Law of the United States*.[40] There he defined administrative law as "that part of the law which fixes the organization and determines the competence of the authorities which execute the law, and indicates to the individual remedies for the violation of his rights."[41] Others have found this broad conception of administrative law adequate for defining much of the work of public administrators and the nature of public agencies. For instance, Marshall Dimock writes:

> To the public administrator, law is something very positive and concrete. It is his authority. The term he customarily uses to describe it is "my mandate." It is "his" law, something he feels a proprietary interest in. It does three things: tells him what the legislature expects him to accomplish, fixes limits to his authority, and sets forth the substantive and procedural rights of the individual and group. Having a positive view of his mandate, the administrator considers himself both an interpreter and a builder. He is a builder because every time he applies old law to new situations he builds the law. Therefore law, like administration, is government in action.[42]

Taking a related view, Kenneth Davis argues that public agencies are best defined in terms of law: "An administrative agency is a governmental authority, other than a court and other than a legislative body, which affects the rights of private parties through either adjudication, rule-making, investigating, prosecuting, negotiating, settling, or informally acting."[43]

A second source of the legal approach has been the movement toward the "judicialization"[44] of public administration. Judicialization falls within the purview of Goodnow's definition of administrative law, but tends to concentrate heavily upon the establishment of procedures designed to safeguard individual rights. Dimock succinctly captures the essence of judicialization:

> Before the Administrative Procedure Act [1946] came into existence, decisions were made by the regular administrative staff, with the ultimate decision being entrusted to the head of the agency. Characteristically, it was a collective or institutional decision, each making his contribution and all checking each other. The decisions were made on the basis of statutory law, plus agency sublegislation, plus decided court cases. The system worked, and in most cases worked well. Then the idea arose of using "hearing examiners" in certain cases where hearings were long and technical, as in railroad cases coming under the Interstate Commerce Commission ... .
>
> When the Administrative Procedure Act ... was enacted, however, judicialization was speeded up, and now, like a spreading fog, it has become well-nigh universal. It began with hearing officers who were recruited by the U.S. Civil Service Commission and put in a pool, from which they were assigned to various agencies ... . [T]he idea of courtroom procedure was still further enlarged when Congress created the office of "Administrative Judge," this being one who operates inside the agency instead of outside it, as in the case of the European administrative courts.
>
> ... In actual practice ... the longer the system has been in existence, the more frequently the hearing examiner's recommended decision becomes the final decision.[45]

Thus, judicialization brings not only law but legal procedure as well to bear upon administrative decision making. Agencies begin to function more like courts and consequently legal values come to play a greater role in their activities.

Constitutional law provides a third source of the contemporary legal approach to public administration. Since the 1950s, the federal judiciary has virtually redefined the procedural, equal protection, and substantive rights and liberties of the citizenry vis-à-vis public administrators.[46] The old distinction between rights and privileges, which had largely made the Constitution irrelevant to individuals' claims with regard to the receipt of governmental benefits, met its demise. Concomitantly, there was a vast expansion in the requirement that public administrators afford constitutional procedural due process to the individuals upon whom they specifically acted. A new stringency was read into the Eighth Amendment's prohibition of cruel and unusual punishments. Wholly new rights, such as the right to treatment and habilitation, were created, if not fully ratified by the Supreme Court, for those confined to public mental health facilities. The right to equal protection was vastly strengthened and applied in a variety of administrative matters ranging from public personnel merit examinations to the operation of public schools and prisons.

The expansion of the constitutional rights of individuals vis-à-vis public administrators has been enforced primarily in two ways, both of which enhance the relevance of the legal approach to contemporary public administration. The courts have sought to force public administrators scrupulously to avoid violating individuals' constitutional rights by reducing public officials' once absolute immunity from civil suits for damages to a qualified immunity.[47] With some exceptions, public administrators are now liable for damages if they "knew or reasonably should have known" that an action taken abridged someone's constitutional rights.[48] In the Supreme Court's view, this approach "in addition to compensating victims, serves a deterrent purpose"[49] that "should create an incentive for officials who may harbor doubts about the lawfulness of their intended actions to err on the side of protecting citizens' constitutional rights."[50] Consequently, the concept of administrative competence is expanded to include reasonable knowledge of constitutional law. In addition, in suits challenging the constitutionality or legality of public institutions such as schools, prisons, and mental health facilities, the courts have frequently decreed on-going relief requiring institutional reforms that place the judges in the role of "partner"[51] with public administrators. Indeed, in some instances judges clearly become supervisors of vast administrative undertakings.

The legal approach to public administration embodies three central values. One is procedural due process. It has long been recognized that this value cannot be confined to any single set of requirements or standards.[52] Rather, the term stands for the value of fundamental fairness and is viewed as requiring procedures designed to protect individuals from malicious, arbitrary, capricious, or unconstitutional harm at the hands of the government. A second value concerns individual substantive rights as embodied in evolving interpretations of the Bill of Rights and the Fourteenth Amendment. In general, the judiciary views the maximization of individual rights and liberties as a positive good and necessary feature of the United States political system. Breaches of these rights may be tolerated by the courts when, on balance, some essential governmental function requires their abridgment. However, the usual presumption is against the government in such circumstances and, consequently, judicial doctrines place a heavy burden on official administrative action that infringes upon the substantive constitutional rights of individuals.[53] Third, the judiciary values equity, a concept that like due process is subject to varying interpretation. However, in terms of public administration in general, equity stands for the value of fairness in the result of conflicts between private parties and the government. It militates against arbitrary or invidious treatment of individuals, encompasses much of the constitutional requirement of equal protection, and enables the courts to fashion relief for individuals whose constitutional rights have been violated by administrative action.

One of the major features of the values of the legal approach to public administration is the downgrading of the cost/benefit reasoning associated with the managerial approach. The judiciary is not oblivious to the costs of its decisions, but its central focus tends to be on the nature of the individual's rights, rather than on the costs to society of securing those rights. This is especially evident in cases involving the reform of public institutions. As one court said, "inadequate resources can never be an adequate justification for the state's depriving any person of his constitutional rights."[54]

Organizational Structure

As suggested in the discussion of judicialization, the preferred structure of the legal approach to public administration is one that will maximize the use of adversary procedure. The full-fledged judicial trial is the archetypical model of this structure. In terms of public administration, however, it is generally modified to allow greater flexibility in the discovery of facts. Juries are not used and hearing examiners often play a more active role in bringing out relevant information. Although this structure is often associated with regulatory commissions, its general presence within public administration should not be underestimated. For example, it is heavily relied upon in contemporary public personnel management, especially in the areas of adverse actions, equal employment opportunity, and labor relations.[55] It is also common in instances where governmental benefits, such as welfare or public school education, are being withheld or withdrawn from individuals.[56] The precise structure varies from context to context, but the common element running through it is the independence and impartiality of the hearing examiner. As Dimock points out, to a large extent this independence undermines the managerial approach's reliance on hierarchy. Hearing examiners stand outside administrative hierarchies in an important sense. Although they can be told what to do, that is, which cases to hear, they cannot be told how to rule or decide. Moreover, for all intents and purposes, their rulings may be binding upon public agencies. This may introduce serious limitations on administrative coordination as the hearing examiner's interpretation of law and agency rules may differ from that of the agency's managerial hierarchy. Dimock summarizes the impact of the adjudicatory structure as follows:

> The hearing officers and administrative judges are on a different payroll. Moreover, unlike other officials in his department or agency, the executive is expressly forbidden to fire, discipline, or even communicate

> with the administrative judge except under very special circumstances, which usually means when the judge submits his proposed order. Under the new system, the judge is isolated in the same manner as a judicial judge, for fear that improper influence will be brought to bear upon him.[57]

To a considerable extent, therefore, this model is at odds with all the values embodied in the other two approaches: It militates against efficiency, economy, managerial effectiveness, representativeness, responsiveness, and political accountability. It is intended, rather, to afford maximum protection of the rights of private parties against illegal, unconstitutional, or invidious administrative action.

View of the Individual

The legal approach's emphasis on procedural due process, substantive rights, and equity leads it to consider the individual as a unique person in a unique set of circumstances. The notion that every person is entitled to a "day in court" is appropriate here. The adversary procedure is designed to enable an individual to explain his or her unique and particular circumstances, thinking, motivations, and so forth to the governmental decision maker. Moreover, a decision may turn precisely upon such considerations, which become part of the "merits" of the case. There are some outstanding examples of this in the realm of public administration. For instance, in *Cleveland Board of Education v. LaFleur* (1974)[58] the Supreme Court ruled that before a mandatory maternity leave could be imposed upon a pregnant public school teacher, she was entitled to an individualized medical determination of her fitness to continue on the job. In *Wyatt v. Stickney* (1971),[59] a federal district court required that an individual treatment plan be developed for each person involuntarily confined to Alabama's public mental health facilities. Emphasis on the individual *qua* individual does not, of course, preclude the aggregation of individuals into broader groups, as in the case of class action suits. However, while such a suit may be desirable to obtain widespread change, it does not diminish the legal approach's concern with the rights of specific individuals.

The Separation of Powers

Reflection upon these opposing approaches to public administration suggests that they cannot be synthesized for the simple reason that they are an integral part of a political culture that emphasizes the separation of powers rather than integrated political action. Thus, it is largely true that each of these approaches is associated with the values embodied in a different branch of government. The managerial approach is most closely associated with the executive. The presidency has taken on a vast number of roles and

functions, but a major feature of its constitutional power is t
that the laws are faithfully executed. This is largely the r
mentation, which is the focus of the managerial approach'
public administration. The political approach, by contrast, is mo..
associated with legislative concerns. It views public administrators as supplementary law makers and policy makers generally. Hence its emphasis on representativeness, responsiveness, and accountability. The legal approach is very closely related to the judiciary in its concern with individual rights, adversary procedure, and equity.

As Justice Brandeis pointed out, the founders' purpose in creating the constitutional branches was not simply to facilitate efficiency, coordination, and a smooth functioning of government generally. The purpose was also to create a system that would give each branch a motive and a means for preventing abuses or misguided action by another. This would prevent the "accumulation of all powers, legislative, executive, and judiciary, in the same hands," which, as Madison wrote in *Federalist* #47, the founders considered to be "the very definition of tyranny." But the separation of powers would also create a tendency toward inaction. Not only would each branch check the others, but a system of checks and balances would also serve as a check on popular political passions. Thus, the terms of office and the constituencies of members of the House of Representatives and the Senate differ from each other and from those of the president. The judiciary, being appointive, has no constituency *per se* and serves at good behavior, subject to removal by impeachment. Changing the staffing of the government as a whole, therefore, is something that can be accomplished only gradually. Altering its policy initiatives and directions drastically requires widespread consensus among the citizenry. Importantly, some actions of the legislature, such as approving treaties, over-riding vetoes, and proposing constitutional amendments, require extraordinary majorities. This can enable a political minority to protect itself from a majority passion.[60] Overall, the government was designed to be responsive slowly to relatively long-term public demands and to require the development of relatively broad agreement among the electorate prior to taking action.

This model of government has not seemed well-suited to public policy aimed at widespread penetration of the economic and social life of the political community. It is weighted in favor of inertia and inflexibility. In answer to this problem, during the past century or so, the United States developed a large administrative apparatus to facilitate specialized, positive, and flexible governmental action.[61] This phenomenon is commonly referred to as the "rise of the administrative state" and is hardly confined to the United States.[62] However, in this country it represents an effort to reduce the inertial qualities of the system of separation of powers. In essence, all three governmental functions have been collapsed into the administrative branch. Thus, public administrators make rules (legislation), implement these rules (an executive function), and adjudicate questions concerning their application and execution (a judicial function). The collapsing of the separation of powers has been well recognized. As Justice White wrote in *Buckley v. Valeo* (1976), "There is no doubt that the development of the administrative agency in response to modern legislative and administrative need has placed severe strain on the separation-of-powers principle in its pristine formulation."[63] This strain has also contributed to a "crisis of legitimacy"[64] in public administration because the accumulation of legislative, executive, and judicial functions in administrative agencies runs counter to the deeply ingrained desire within the political culture for a system of checks and balances.

In a very real fashion, however, a system of checks and balances has devolved to the administrative branch along with the three governmental functions. Thus, as has been argued in this essay, the values associated with each function have been transmuted into distinctive theoretical approaches toward public administration. These approaches have different origins, stress different values and structural arrangements, and view individuals in remarkably different ways. This is precisely because each stresses a different function of public administration. Consequently, although there may be room for greater synthesis of these approaches, seeking to unify theory by allowing one approach to drive out the others would promote public bureaucracy in the most invidious sense of the term. Rather, the task is to develop a distinctive theoretical core suitable to the political culture by building around the need to maintain values, organizational structures, and perspectives on the individual that tend to check and balance each other.

Precisely how such theory may be derived is, of course, not immediately evident or predictable. However, a few ideas come to mind. First, public administrative theorists must recognize the validity and utility of each of the approaches discussed here. Perhaps others can be added in the future, but the legitimacy of each of these is beyond question. Consequently, a definition of the field of public administration must include a consideration of managerial, political, and legal approaches. Second, it is necessary to recognize that each approach may be more or less relevant to different agencies, administrative functions, and policy areas. For example, regulation stresses adjudication and, consequently, probably should not be organized primarily according to the managerial or political approaches. Likewise, overhead operations most clearly fall within the purview of the managerial approach. Distributive policy *may* be best organized according to the political approach. Much more thought and research must be devoted to these matters before any firm conclusions can be reached. But clearly it is an administrative fallacy to try to treat all agencies and programs under a universal standard. This is one reason why the much vaunted "rational" budgeting techniques of PPBS[65] and ZBB[66] failed.[67] Third, as heretical as it will sound to some, public administrative theory must make greater use of political theory. As is argued here, the separation of powers goes well beyond the issues of legislative delegation and agency subdelegation—it reaches to the core of the leading theories of public administration. Finally, attention must be paid to the practical wisdom of the public administrative practitioners whose action is circumscribed by internal considerations of checks, balances, and administrative and political pressures generally. Individual public administrators are often called upon to integrate the three approaches to public administration and much can be learned from their experience.

Notes

1 Robert Parker, "The End of Public Administration," *Public Administration Review* 34 (June 1965): p. 99; quoted in Richard Stillman, *Public Administration: Concepts and Cases* (Boston, MA: Houghton, Mifflin, 1976), p. 3.
2 Frederick C. Mosher, "Research in Public Administration," *Public Administration Review* 16 (Summer 1956): 177; Stillman, *Public Administration*, p. 3.
3 Herbert Kaufman, "Emerging Conflicts in the Doctrines of Public Administration," *American Political Science Review* 50 (December 1956): 1057–1073.
4 James Q. Wilson, "The Bureaucracy Problem," The Public Interest, Vol. 6 (Winter 1976): 3–9.
5 See Gabriel Almond and Sidney Verba, *The Civic Culture* (Boston, MA: Little, Brown, 1965), whose findings provide a useful outline of the values forming the core of the U.S. political culture.
6 Carl Schurz, *The Necessity and Progress of Civil Service Reform* (Washington, DC: Good Government, 1894), p. 3.
7 Woodrow Wilson, "The Study of Administration," *Political Science Quarterly* 56 (December 1941): 481–506 (originally copyrighted in 1887).
8 Ibid., p. 481.
9 Frederick Taylor, *The Principles of Scientific Management* (New York: Harper and Bros., 1911).
10 Leonard D. White, *Introduction to the Study of Public Administration* (New York: Macmillan, 1926), pp. vii–viii. See also Herbert J. Storing, "Leonard D. White and the Study of Public Administration," *Public Administration Review* 25 (March 1965): 38–51.
11 *Papers on the Science of Administration*, ed. by Luther Gulick and L. Urwick (New York: Institute of Public Administration, 1937), pp. 192.
12 Robert Simmons and Eugene Dvorin, *Public Administration* (Port Washington, NY: Alfred Publishing, 1977), p. 217.
13 Max Weber, *From Max Weber: Essays in Sociology*, translated and ed. by H. H. Gerth and C. W. Mills (New York: Oxford University Press, 1958), pp. 196–244.
14 Peter Blau and Marshall Meyer, *Bureaucracy in Modern Society*, second ed. (New York: Random House, 1971), esp. p. 8. See also Victor Thompson, *Modern Organization* (New York: Knopf, 1961), pp. 58–80.
15 See Harold Seidman, *Politics, Position, and Power* (New York: Oxford University Press, 1970), Chapter 1.
16 See Eugene Lewis, *American Politics in a Bureaucratic Age: Citizens, Constituents, Clients, and Victims* (Cambridge, MA: Winthrop, 1977).
17 Weber, *Essays in Sociology*, p. 228.
18 Jay Shafritz, et al., *Personnel Management in Government* (New York: Marcel Dekker, 1978), p. 94.
19 Ralph Hummel, *The Bureaucratic Experience* (New York: St. Martin's, 1977), pp. 24–25.
20 See Erving Goffman, *Asylums* (Garden City, NY: Doubleday, 1961), esp. pp. 1–24; *Halderman v. Pennhurst State School*, 244 F. Supp. 1295 (1977); *Holt v. Sarver*,

304 F. Supp. 362 (1970); John Hersey, *The Algiers Motel Incident* (New York: Knopf, 1968).

21 See Amitai Etzioni, *Modern Organizations* (Englewood Cliffs, NJ: Prentice Hall, 1964), chapter 4, for a brief, cogent description of the human relations approach. Victor Thompson, *Modern Organization*, discusses bureaupathology at pp. 152–177.

22 Wallace Sayre, "Premises of Public Administration: Past and Emerging," in Jay Shafritz and Albert Hyde, eds, *Classics of Public Administration* (Oak Park, IL: Moore, 1978), p. 201. Dwight Waldo, *The Administrative State* (New York: Ronald Press, 1948), demonstrates how the basic value choices of managerial public administration are ultimately statements of political preference.

23 Paul Appleby, *Policy and Administration* (University, AL: University of Alabama Press, 1949); see also Theodore Lowi, *The End of Liberalism* (New York: W.W. Norton, 1969).

24 *Myers v. U.S.*, 272 U.S. 52, 293 (1926).

25 David Nachmias and David H. Rosenbloom, *Bureaucratic Government, U.S.A.* (New York: St. Martin's, 1980).

26 The literature here is too vast to cite in its entirety. See Samuel Krislov and David H. Rosenbloom, *Representative Bureaucracy and the American Political System* (New York: Praeger, 1981) for a recent discussion.

27 PL 95–454, sect. 3 and sect. 2301 (b) (1). See also *Givhan v. Western Line Consolidated School District*, 99 S. Ct. 693 [439 U.S. 410] (1979), which enunciates constitutional conditions permitting a public employee to act as a "representative" within a public administrative structure.

28 PL 92–463.

29 See William Keefe and Morris Ogul, *The American Legislative Process*, fourth ed. (Englewood Cliffs, N.J.: Prentice-Hall, 1977), p. 407.

30 See Frederick Mosher, *Democracy and the Public Service* (New York: Oxford University Press, 1968); Ralph Hummel, *The Bureaucratic Experience*; Morris Janowitz, Deil Wright, and William Delany, *Public Administration and the Public* (Westport, CT: Greenwood, 1977); Lowi, *End of Liberalism*; William Morrow, *Public Administration* (New York: Random House, 1975); and Bruce Smith and James D. Carroll, eds, *Improving the Accountability and Performance of Government* (Washington, DC: Brookings, 1982).

31 This was an implicit assumption of the 19th-century civil service reformers, who argued that "as the functions of government grow in extent, importance and complexity, the necessity grows of their being administered not only with honesty, but also with trained ability and knowledge," Carl Schurz, *Congress and the Spoils System* (New York: George Peck, 1895), p. 4. See Harry Kranz, *The Participatory Bureaucracy* (Lexington, MA: Lexington Books, 1976); and Samuel Krislov, *Representative Bureaucracy* (Englewood Cliffs, NJ: Prentice-Hall, 1974) for discussions of social representativeness and efficiency.

32 Marver Bernstein, *The Job of the Federal Executive* (Washington, DC: Brookings, 1958), p. 30.

33 Ibid., pp. 26–37. See also Herbert Kaufman, *The Administrative Behavior of Federal Bureau Chiefs* (Washington, DC: Brookings, 1981), esp. Chapter 2.

34 Seidman, *Politics, Position, and Power*, p. 13.

35 Norton Long, "Power and Administration," in Francis Rourke, ed., *Bureaucratic Power in National Politics* (Boston, MA: Little, Brown, 1965), p. 18.

36 Roger Davidson, "Congress and the Executive: The Race for Representation," in A. DeGrazia, ed., *Congress: The First Branch of Government* (New York: Anchor, 1967), p. 383.

37 See Seidman, *Politics, Position, and Power*, Chapter 1.

38 David Truman, *The Governmental Process* (New York: Knopf, 1951); see also Arthur Bentley, *The Process of Government* (Chicago, IL: University of Chicago, 1908).
39 Lowi, *End of Liberalism*, p. 71. See also Grant McConnell, *Private Power and American Democracy* (New York: Knopf, 1966), Chapters 4 and 5.
40 Frank Goodnow, *The Principles of the Administrative Law of the United States* (New York: G.P. Putnam's Sons, 1905).
41 Ibid., p. 17.
42 Marshall Dimock, *Law and Dynamic Administration* (New York: Praeger, 1980), p. 31.
43 Kenneth Davis, *Administrative Law and Government* (St. Paul: West, 1975), p. 6.
44 Dimock, *Law and Dynamic Administration*, Chapter 10.
45 Ibid., p. 113. According to Charles Dullea, "Development of the Personnel Program for Administrative Law Judges," *Administrative Law Review* 25 (Winter 1973), pp. 41–47, the title "Administrative Law Judge" was created by the U.S. Civil Service Commission.
46 The case law and literature are too voluminous to cite. See David H. Rosenbloom, *Public Administration and Law: Bench v. Bureau in the United States* (New York: Marcel Dekker, 1983).
47 See *Scheuer v. Rhodes*, 416 U.S. 322 (1974). See also Rosenbloom, *Public Administration and Law*, Chapter 6.
48 *Wood v. Strickland*, 420 U.S. 308, 322 (1975); *Harlow v. Fitzgerald*, 457 U.S. 800 (1982).
49 *Carlson v. Green*, 446 U.S. 14, 21 (1980).
50 David Bazelon, "The Impact of the Courts on Public Administration," *Indiana Law Journal* 52 (1976): 101–110.
51 Abram Chayes, "The Role of the Judge in Public Law Litigation," *Harvard Law Review* 89 (1976): 1281–1316; Roger Cramton, "Judicial Lawmaking in the Leviathan State," *Public Administration Review* 36 (September/October 1976): 551–555.
52 *Hannah v. Larche*, 363 U.S. 420 (1960).
53 See for instance, *Branti v. Finkel*, 445 U.S. 507, 518 (1980), which requires the public employer to "demonstrate that party affiliation is an appropriate requirement for the effective performance of the public office involved" when making a patronage dismissal.
54 *Hamilton v. Love*, 328 F. Supp. 1182, 1194 (1971).
55 See Robert Vaughn, *The Spoiled System* (New York: Charterhouse, 1975); Richard A. Merrill, "Procedure for Adverse Actions Against Federal Employees," *Virginia Law Review* 59 (1973), pp. 196–287.
56 *Goldberg v. Kelly*, 397 U.S. 254 (1970); *Goss v. Lopez*, 419 U.S.
57 Dimock, *Law and Dynamic Administration*, p. 114. 565 (1975).
58 414 U.S. 632 (1974). Argued and decided with *Cohen v. Chesterfield Co. School Board*.
59 *Wyatt v. Stickney*, 325 F. Supp. 781 (1971); 334 F. Supp. 387 (1972).
60 See *Federalist* #10.
61 See Peter Woll, *American Bureaucracy*, second ed. (New York: Norton, 1977). Woll is among several scholars with a constitutional focus who argue cogently that the administrative process is far more flexible than government according to the original constitutional scheme could be. See also, Davis, *Administrative Law and Government*. James O. Freedman, *Crisis and Legitimacy* (New York: Cambridge University Press, 1978), Chapter 2, provides a brief description of the rise of the contemporary administrative state and the tension between its operation and the founders' concept of the separation of powers.

62 Henry Jacoby, *The Bureaucratization of the World* (Berkeley: University of California Press, 1978).
63 *Buckley v. Valeo*, 424 U.S. 1, 280–281 (1976).
64 Freedman, *Crisis and Legitimacy.*
65 Planning, programming and budgeting system.
66 Zero based budgeting.
67 Allen Schick, "A Death in the Bureaucracy," *Public Administration Review*, Vol. 33 (March/April 1973): 146–156; "Budgeting Expert Calls Carter Plan 'Disaster,'" *Houston Post*, April 8, 1977, p. 14A, quotes Peter Phyrr, originator of zero based budgeting, as calling the federal effort to institute ZBB all-at-once "absolute folly."

4 Legitimating the American Administrative State Constitutionally

John A. Rohr's Lasting Influence to the Field of U.S. Public Administration

Stephanie P. Newbold

John A. Rohr's scholarship fundamentally changed the intellectual landscape of public administration theory and practice (Newbold, 2012; Newbold & Rosenbloom, 2014). Over the course of his distinguished career, he demonstrated empirically how the American Constitution legitimated the field of public administration (Rohr, 1986, 1998, 2002). Rohr's efforts to ground all dimensions of administrative theory and practice in constitutional tradition ultimately laid the intellectual foundation for the establishment of a Constitutional School of U.S. public administration. In reflecting on the value the Constitution brings to the American state and why a normatively oriented constitutional approach to public administration adds to the institutional integrity of the field, Rohr astutely observed:

> The normative theory proposed is intended to encourage administrators and the public to think about administrative behavior in constitutional norms ... By grounding our thinking about public administration in the Constitution, we can transform erstwhile lackeys, leakers, obstructionists, and whistle-blowers into administrative statesmen.
>
> (1998, p. 89)

The lasting legacy of Rohr's intellectual contribution to the field extends far beyond his published works. He heralded in a new era of discourse that demanded the field's immediate attention. He championed the position that the American Constitution matters to the institutional, intellectual, and managerial legitimacy of U.S. public administration (Rohr, 1986, 1989, 1998, 2001). The field, according to Rohr, undermined its own credibility by not embracing its constitutional origins as the starting point for examining how the American framers, the nation's constitutional tradition, and Supreme Court opinions established the foundation by which to examine all dimensions of public administrative management (Newbold, 2012; Rohr, 1986, 1989). Rohr's institutional leadership within the field and his commitment to the constitutional integrity of the administrative state represents one of the finest examples of how a scholar can use his ideas to encourage academics and practitioners to rely more on democratic-constitutional norms and values to advance the good of the state and the people it serves.

Almost all of John Rohr's published work supports the establishment of a Constitutional School of American Public Administration so the challenge here was to select an article that serves this effort best. In this publication, "Public Administration, Executive Power, and Constitutional Confusion," Rohr illustrates exactly what the Constitutional School champions in terms of relying on the constitutional tradition of the nation to explain contemporary issues affecting public administration (Newbold, 2010). He begins by examining the ambiguity associated with whether the American framers intended to create a powerful executive with strong decision-making authority or whether the American framers intended to establish a weak executive whose powers only extend to executing what Congress legislates into law. Rohr draws attention to the contemporary relevance of this distinction because it directly relates to how much power resides within U.S. public administration at the federal level of government. A strong executive whose power is both granted and implied will have greater authority over the direction of the administrative state than a weak executive who serves merely as an executor of legislative will.

One of the most useful tools Rohr relied on throughout his collective scholarship was illustrating how opinions made by the Supreme Court of the United States work to shape the administrative state. He relied on both affirming and dissenting opinions to illustrate how conflicting constitutional arguments provide illuminating analysis for understanding how the Court works to shape the administrative state in its own image. In this article, Rohr begins by examining the 1926 case, *Myers v. United States*, which sought to determine whether the U.S. President could remove an officer with a fixed term of office before that officer's term expired. Rohr was quick to critique Chief Justice Taft's majority opinion that afforded the President unconstrained power to remove executive officers for whom he or a predecessor had appointed with the advice and consent of the Senate. Rohr's analysis of Taft's decision not only speaks to why students of American public administration should be guided by decisions made by the High Court but also why constitutional foundations are critical to the institutional integrity of the field:

> The fundamental flaw in *Myers* is that Chief Justice Taft treated the executive branch of government as though it were a managerial enterprise instead of a political institution in which the Congress will always have a legitimate interest, an interest that was bound to grow along with the rise and development of the modern administrative state.
>
> (Rohr, 1989, p. 112)

Rohr was far more persuaded by Justice Brandeis's dissenting opinion. Unlike Taft, Brandeis interpreted the decision of 1789 in a much narrower context and argued that Congress did not preclude the Senate from having a role in the removal of certain executive branch officers.

Rohr's comparison of Taft's argument with Brandeis' exemplifies how debates at the founding period still affect the process of American government. By analyzing the *Myers* case in such a way as to demonstrate the flaws associated with Taft's affirming opinion and the strengths associated with Brandeis' dissenting opinion, Rohr not only advances the mission and purpose of the Constitutional School but also provides a concrete example of how the Court works to shape the functions of the administrative state in its own constitutional image.

Similarly, Rohr compared Chief Justice Rehnquist's affirming opinion in *Morrison v. Olsen* with Justice Scalia's lone dissent. In this case, the Court examined the constitutionality of specific appointment and removal provisions for the independent counsel. The majority held that the independent counsel was an inferior officer and as such Congress could confer her appointment in a judicial panel and not with the entire advice and consent of the Senate. Furthermore, Rehnquist held that because the independent counsel was an inferior officer, the President could not remove her from office. Scalia, by contrast, argued that the position of independent counsel was not an inferior officer, because the duties associated with this job are exclusively executive. "It is now," according to Scalia, "open season upon the President's removal power for all executive officers" (Rohr, 1989, p. 114). One of the fundamental problems this case created, as Scalia astutely pointed out, was that it assumed that members of the executive branch do not serve at the pleasure of the President; rather, they are subordinate to Congress and the federal courts (Newbold, 2008).

When Rohr concluded his first comparative analysis of the constitutional history of France with that of the United States, he made the following observation regarding the significance of the American Constitution:

> The Constitution is absolutely essential for our life together as a people organized in civic friendship for action in history. This is why it is so natural for us to require our civil servants to pledge their allegiance to our Constitution. So important is our Constitution to us that we depart from our customary abhorrence of compulsory political orthodoxy in order to be sure that anyone who exercises any sort of government authority shares our most cherished beliefs.
>
> (1995, p. 270)

The American Constitution is at the center of American public administration. It legitimates the field in theory and practice. The purpose of the Constitutional School is "to demonstrate in clear, articulate terms why constitutional tradition and rule of law should serve as the foundations of public administration scholarship in the United States" (Newbold, 2010, p. 538). John Rohr's scholarship embraces this goal in totality.

References

Newbold, S.P. 2008. Teaching organization theory from a constitutional perspective: A new twist on an old flame. *Journal of public affairs education* 14(3): 335–351.

Newbold, S.P. 2010. Toward a Constitutional School for U.S. public administration. *Public administration review* 70(4): 538–546.

Newbold, S.P. 2012. A good and faithful servant: John Rohr's contribution to the intellectual, constitutional, and professional advancement of Public Administration. A forum honoring the contributions of John A. Rohr to Public Administration. *Administrative Theory and Praxis* 34(4) December: 623–628.

Newbold, S.P. & Rosenbloom, D.H. 2014. Honoring the intellectual contributions and legacy of John A. Rohr to public administration theory and practice. Symposium co-editor & contributor. *Administration and society* 46(2) March: 128–130.

Rohr, J.A. 1986. *To run a constitution: The legitimacy of the administrative state.* Lawrence: University Press of Kansas.

Rohr, J.A. 1989. Public administration, executive power, and constitutional confusion. *Public administration review* 49(2): 108–115.

Rohr, J.A. 1995. *Founding republics in France and America: A study in constitutional governance.* Lawrence: University Press of Kansas.

Rohr, J.A. 1998. *Public service, ethics, and constitutional practice.* Lawrence: University of Kansas Press.

Rohr, J.A. 2002. *Civil servants and their constitutions.* Lawrence: University of Kansas Press.

Public Administration, Executive Pow and Constitutional Confusion

John A. Rohr

From: *Public Administration Review* 49:2, Special Issue 1989): 108–114. Abridged.

The Founding Period

At the time of the founding of the Republic, the ambiguity that engulfed the executive was due as much to political expectations as to etymology and usage. The framers of the U.S. Constitution wanted a strong executive for two incompatible reasons. The sad administrative experience under the Articles of Confederation taught them the need for an independent executive whose legal existence would be liberated from the committees of the Continental Congress. This line of argument anticipated that of the Civil Service Reformers who would appear a century later. It was an argument grounded in concern for governmental efficiency. The executive was to be independent in order to enable him (or them—the single executive was quite controversial) to carry out the will of the Congress more efficiently. This theme, arising from the colonial experience, favored an independent executive, but not an executive that was equal to the legislature. This is the origin of the clerkship side of the presidency.

Some framers of the Constitution also wanted an independent executive to check the legislative excesses that they saw in many of the states. If they were about to establish a real government at the national level, there would be need for an authentic legislature with powers far greater than those of the hapless Continental Congress. Steps would have to be taken to keep this new national legislature from oppressing the people and disregarding their rights. To this end an independent executive was an indispensable means. He or they would vindicate the rights of the citizens and would maintain a watchful vigilance against the "excesses of democracy," that notorious failing of all popular governments. This political sentiment grounds the theme of President as leader.

Not surprisingly, these ambiguities in language and political expectations found their way into the text of the Constitution itself. The first sentence of Article II provides that "The executive power shall be vested in a President of the United States." This language contrasts markedly with the opening words of Article I: "All legislative powers herein granted shall be vested in a Congress of the United States, which shall consist of a Senate and House of Representatives." Champions of a strong executive have always emphasized the absence of the qualifying words "herein granted" in Article II. This absence, they maintain, means that *the* executive power (presumably all of it) is vested in the President. Congress possesses all those legislative powers that are granted in the Constitution itself, but it does not possess all legislative power. That is, there are many areas of life in which Congress may not legislate. It may legislate only in those areas in which the Constitution permits it to do so. To be sure, Congress possesses all legislative powers in the sense that other institutions created by the Constitution have no explicit authorization to legislate. But the legislative powers of Congress are confined to the written document.

The practical import of these exegetical niceties is that they serve as a launching pad for a constitutional argument in support of *inherent* executive powers that are not confined by the text of the Constitution. This argument sees in the executive power clause a positive grant of power to the President to do whatever any political executive can do. Activist Presidents, like Jackson, Lincoln, and Theodore Roosevelt, made skillful use of this argument.

Critics of presidential power have responded in a variety of ways. One line of argument admits that the President does indeed possess all executive power without qualification, but it maintains that this does not justify the far-reaching conclusions of presidential apologists. What is executive power, they ask. It is simply the power to execute law. The President may only execute that which the Congress has legislated. It was perfectly logical for the framers to omit the "herein granted" qualification from the grant of the executive power to the President, because, having provided that the Congress has only those legislative powers "herein granted," there was no need to repeat the same language in the article establishing the executive. Executive power cannot outstrip legislative power, for there would be nothing for the executive to execute. He can only execute what the Congress can legislate. Hence the limitations on the scope of congressional power necessarily encumber the executive power of the President as well.

This argument is reinforced by explicit constitutional grants of power to the President to command the armed forces of the nation, to grant reprieves and pardons, to share in the power to make treaties and to appoint officers, to convene either or both houses of Congress, to receive ambassadors, and so forth. The fact that these powers are explicitly granted in the Constitution undercuts the argument that the executive power clause confers inherent executive powers on the President. If the executive power clause did this, what would be the purpose of spelling out all these other powers, which are traditionally associated with the executive? These additional powers would all be redundant. They could all be found in the teeming womb of the executive power clause. Clearly, the argument goes, the framers intended that the "executive power" clause should give the President nothing more than the power to execute laws passed by Congress. Whatever other powers he might possess are explicitly stated in Article II. The President has no powers other than the sum of the powers resulting from these two sources.

Another argument against the presence of inherent executive power in Article II is drawn from the opening words of Article III: "The judicial power of the United States, shall be vested in one supreme court, and in such inferior courts as the Congress may from time to time ordain and establish." Critics of presidential power highlight the contrast between Article II which vests only "the executive power" and Article III which vests "the judicial power *of the United States*" (emphasis added). It is the judiciary, not the executive, that enjoys inherent power. There is a judicial power of the United States, the argument runs, and this is the power to apply common law.[1] The grant of this inherent power is signaled by the explicit mention of a judicial power *of the United States*. It is a power that inheres in the judicial system of any nation influenced by the English legal tradition. Article II significantly omits any mention of an executive power "of the United States." Had the framers of the Constitution wished to confer such inherent executive power on the President, they would have used the sort of language they adopted when they created the judiciary.

A final textual response to the expansive view of presidential power is based on sections 2, 3, and 4 of Article II. Here the argument differs from the considerations, just discussed. The previous arguments conceded that the executive power clause does indeed grant complete executive power to the President. Having made this concession, the thrust of the previous arguments was to limit the scope of executive power by confining the meaning of the word to executing the will of the Congress and thereby to deny any additional, inherent powers to the President. The argument here maintains that other sections of Article II cannot be reconciled with the claim that the executive power clause gives *all* executive power to the President—no matter how narrowly one defines executive power.

The most important constitutional clause in support of this position states that the President "shall take care that the laws be faithfully executed, and shall commission all the officers of the United States." This language makes it rather clear that the President himself is not to execute the laws, but is to see to it that others do so; and to assist him in doing just this, the Constitution empowers the President to commission officers. These constitutional provisions are followed immediately by the impeachment clauses which clearly describe the President as a legally accountable officer who "presides" (as a *President* should) over an executive establishment that carries out the laws mandated by Congress. This is the textual basis for the clerkship view of the presidency. It is reinforced by the explicit constitutional provision for "executive departments," each of which will be headed by a single "principal officer."

ɔnstitutional language casts a shadow over the interpretation of the power clause that maintains that the framers meant to give the power (i.e., all of it) to the President alone. Surely a constitutional ..... for a principal officer in each of several executive departments implies that these high officials hold some sort of executive power in their own right. But if they hold any executive power at all, the President cannot hold all of it.

These considerations will suffice to support the point that at the time of the founding of the Republic, there was considerable ambiguity and confusion over the precise nature of executive power. This ambiguity and confusion came from the word "executive" itself and, perhaps more importantly, from the framers' conflicting expectations of a strong and independent executive. Not surprisingly, this ambiguity and confusion spilled over into the text of the Constitution itself and there found a permanent home for the irreconcilable themes of the President as leader on the one hand and clerk on the other. Public administration has established its constitutional dwelling place in this uneasy household whose bewildered inmates have brought forth anomalies, enigmas, and contradictions in their own image and likeness.

The President's Removal Power

Article II provides several ways in which federal officers may be appointed; but, except for the impeachment clause, it is silent on how they may be removed. This constitutional silence prompted an important debate during the first Congress. The debate occurred when the House of Representatives was establishing the Department of Foreign Affairs, the original name for the Department of State. There was no doubt that the Secretary of Foreign Affairs should be appointed by the President with the advice and consent of the Senate, but considerable doubt existed about how he should be removed from office. There were four distinct answers to this question, each of which involved an interpretation of the Constitution. One group maintained that the Constitution vests this power in the President alone. A second group said it was vested in the President and the Senate together—this had been the position of Publius in *Federalist* #77. A third said that Congress had the constitutional authority to vest this power in the President alone or in the President and the Senate together. A fourth group, much smaller than the other three, held that impeachment was the only constitutionally permissible method of removal.[2]

The argument was exceedingly complex and was highlighted by brilliant parliamentary maneuvers by the proponents of the position that the Constitution itself vests the removal of officers in the President alone. The debate consumed over five legislative days in which members of the House participated in three roll-call votes. The upshot of the debate was that the President emerged with the authority to remove the Secretary of Foreign Affairs without interference from the Senate. This outcome was called "the decision of 1789." It was a decision of monumental political significance. The President's power to remove the head of an executive department was at the heart of the most important constitutional crisis of Andrew Jackson's presidency and, even more significantly, at the heart of the effort to impeach President Andrew Johnson. To the present day it remains a crucial element in presidential control over the public administration.

Despite the overwhelming importance of the issue, the Supreme Court of the United States did not get around to addressing it until 1926 in *Myers v. United States*.[3] Myers was a postmaster first class in Oregon who had been appointed by President Wilson in July 1917. He was appointed pursuant to an 1876 statute that provided that postmasters "shall be appointed and may be removed by the President with the advice and consent of the Senate, and shall hold their offices for four years unless sooner removed or suspended according to law." In February 1920, long before the expiration of his four-year term, Myers was removed from office by the postmaster general acting under direction from the President. Although the Senate had consented to Myers's appointment, it did not consent to his removal. Myers therefore maintained that his removal was not "according to law" and brought suit for the salary due him for the remainder of his term.

Myers's efforts were in vain. Chief Justice Taft, writing for a six-member majority, held that "the provision of the law of 1876, by which the unrestricted power of removal is denied to the President, is in violation of the Constitution, and invalid." Taft's opinion was a remarkable paean to the need for strong managerial powers in the hands of the President. It was the sort of opinion that could only have been written by an erstwhile President turned Chief Justice. In the course of his opinion, the Chief Justice relied heavily on "the decision of 1789" as an authoritative declaration of the true meaning of the Constitution by a Congress that included a good number of the framers of the Constitution. In appealing to the action of the first Congress, Chief Justice Taft gave too little attention to the fact that in 1789 Congress was debating the President's removal powers over a Secretary of Foreign Affairs, the closest of the President's advisers in an area that is distinctly presidential. The contrast with an Oregonian postmaster could hardly have been greater. In addition, the *Myers* case raised the question of whether the President could remove an officer with a fixed term of office before the expiration of the term, a matter that simply was not at issue in the decision of 1789. These important factual differences between the decision of 1789 and the *Myers* case prompted Justice Holmes to complain in dissent that Taft's arguments "seem to me spider's webs inadequate to control the dominant facts."

The most startling aspect of Taft's opinion was his confident assertion that the historical record unequivocally supported his sweeping view of presidential removal powers. "[T]here is not the slightest doubt," said the Chief Justice, "after an examination of the record, that the vote [the decision of 1789] was, and was intended to be, a legislative declaration that the power to remove officers appointed by the President and the Senate is vested in the President alone." The Chief Justice overstated his case; the record is simply not this clear. Justice Brandeis gave a much more precise account of the 1789 debate, when he argued in his dissenting opinion that it "did not involve a decision of the question whether Congress could confer upon the Senate the right, and impose the duty, to participate in removals." In 1876 Congress did address this question and decided that it could confer this right and duty upon the Senate. It was the constitutionality of the 1876 decision that was before the Court in *Myers,* and this question, Brandeis maintained, could not be settled by appeals to the decision of 1789.

With characteristic precision, Brandeis showed that the decision of 1789 involved "merely the decision that the Senate does not, in the absence of a legislative grant thereof, have the right to share in the removal of an officer appointed with its consent; and that the president has, in the absence of restrictive legislation, the constitutional power of removal without such consent." Thus, for Brandeis, the decision of 1789 upholds the central role of Congress in the removal process. If Congress says nothing by law, the President alone may remove an officer whom he has appointed with the advice and consent of the Senate. For Brandeis, the decision of 1789 did not preclude Congress from providing by law that the Senate must concur in the removal of certain officers. The exercise of such power by Congress could be justified by the explicit constitutional authorization for Congress to make all laws "which shall be necessary and proper for carrying into execution the ... powers vested by the Constitution in the Government of the United States, or in any Department or Officer thereof." The President is an officer of the United States who is empowered to take care that the laws are faithfully executed. A congressional requirement for senatorial approval of a presidential decision to remove an officer like a postmaster might well be considered a necessary and proper means of assuring that the President does take care that the laws are faithfully executed.

Brandeis's interpretation of the decision of 1789 is more accurate than that of Chief Justice Taft.[4] Nevertheless, it is Taft's opinion that is the law of the land. As Edward Corwin has remarked, "what a judge cannot *prove* he can still *decide.*"[5] And Chief Justice Taft decided that, as a matter of constitutional law, the President has unfettered power to remove executive officers whom he or a previous President has appointed with the advice and consent of the Senate. This legal rule cried out for further clarification of just what is meant by an executive officer.

The clarification was not long in coming. Early in his first presidential term, President Franklin Roosevelt removed Federal Trade Commissioner Humphrey from office several years before his seven-year tenure had expired. The statute creating the commission and fixing its members' terms at seven years further provided that commissioners could be removed before the expiration of their terms only for cause. Humphrey had given no cause for removal. Clearly, Roosevelt's action was based on his belief that under the *Myers* decision the statutory restrictions on his removal powers were unconstitutional. Humphrey did not see it that way, and he sued for the salary due him for the remaining years in his term of office. In a unanimous decision the U.S. Supreme Court supported Humphrey's claim.[6]

In his opinion for the Court, Justice Sutherland distinguished *Myers* on the grounds that that case and the decision of 1789 involved officers whose functions were "purely executive," whereas federal trade commissioners exercise authority that is only quasi-legislative and quasi-judicial. Sutherland maintained that because of these functions, Humphrey was "an officer who occupies no place in the executive department and who exercises no part of the executive power vested by the Constitution in the President." He further maintained that when the Federal Trade Commission exercises an executive function, the power it exercises is not "executive power in the constitutional sense." Whatever action it takes, "it does so in the discharge and effectuation of its quasi-legislative or quasi-judicial powers or as an agency of the legislative or judicial departments of the government."

This was an astounding line of reasoning. It is difficult to comprehend the distinction between "executive power in the constitutional sense" and some other form of executive power. No less puzzling is the meaning of Sutherland's statement that the Federal Trade Commission is "an agency of the legislative *or* judicial departments of the government" (emphasis added). Sutherland seems to put the commission on a constitutional shuttle between the courts and the Congress depending on whether it happens to be exercising quasi-legislative or quasi-judicial authority. The shuttle, however, must not stop at the executive branch of government—or at least at that branch that exercises "executive power in the constitutional sense." Sutherland's strange language led one commentator to wonder just where the trade commissioner belongs in the Court's constitutional cosmology: "[I]s he, forsooth, in the uncomfortable halfway situation of Mohamet's coffin, suspended twixt Heaven and Earth?"[7]

The heart of the problem is that Sutherland accepted that portion of *Myers* that forbade Congress from limiting the President's constitutional power to remove executive officers appointed by the President with the advice and consent of the Senate. Having made this concession, Sutherland had a strong incentive to remove the "executive" label from any officer he believed might be rightfully protected by the Congress from an unfettered presidential power to remove. The *Humphrey* case gave the Court a chance to admit its error in *Myers* and simply to overrule that unhappy precedent. Unfortunately, the Court closed its eyes to the light at the end of the *Humphrey* tunnel. Instead, it ran in circles after an illusory executive power that is something other than "executive power in the constitutional sense." This will-of-the-wisp has as its sorry progeny the mindless chatter heard over the past half-century about the bureaucracy as a "headless fourth branch of government." Since there are only three constitutional branches of government, fourth branch rhetoric attacks the constitutional legitimacy of administrative institutions.

The problem is not confined to the so-called "independent regulatory commissions," like the Federal Trade Commission. The logic of Sutherland's opinion focuses on the function of an agency, not on its place in the *U.S. Government Organization Manual.* Under Sutherland's reasoning, it would seem that any officer who exercises quasi-legislative or quasi-judicial power could be described as one who "occupies no place in the executive department and who exercises no part of the executive power vested by the Constitution in the President." This would include those officers in the executive departments who exercise rule-making and adjudicatory powers.[8] Perhaps such officers should be exempt from presidential removal; this is especially true for those exercising quasi-judicial functions. It makes no sense, however, to say that such officers do not exercise "executive power in the constitutional sense." If the *Humphrey* Court had overruled *Myers,* it could have avoided the need to use such bizarre language. Had *Myers* been overruled, Congress could have resumed its traditional powers to limit the President's power to remove some officers and to give the President a free hand in removing others. The Congress could do this on an *ad hoc* basis that would consider the particular function of each officer without any constitutional legerdemain about purely executive officers as opposed to those whose duties are quasi-this or quasi-that. The fundamental flaw in *Myers* is that Chief Justice Taft treated the executive branch of government as though it were a managerial enterprise instead of a political institution in which the Congress will always have a legitimate interest, an interest that was bound to grow along with the rise and development of the modern administrative state.

Independent Counsel/Special Prosecutor

Quite recently, the perennial confusion over executive power took a new twist in a Supreme Court decision that resolved the volatile issue of the constitutionality of the office of independent counsel created by the Ethics in Government Act of 1978.[9] Popularly known as "special prosecutors," the independent counsels are appointed by three-judge panels to investigate alleged wrong-doings by high-ranking officials in the executive branch of government. The origin of the independent counsel can be traced to the messy constitutional problems that arose during the Watergate scandal. One of these problems centered on how Special Prosecutor Leon Jaworski, who was presumably an "inferior officer" in the executive branch of government, could defy the wishes of President Nixon, his executive superior, in his relentless (and successful) campaign to force the President to surrender the famous tapes that sealed his doom. The Supreme Court's unanimous ruling in *United States v. Nixon* failed to give an adequate response to this argument; an argument that was urged with the zeal worthy of a better cause by Nixon's brilliant attorney, James St. Clair.

A salient aspect of the problem was the absence of a clear statutory basis for the position and powers of the special prosecutor. The Congress addressed this problem in the Ethics in Government Act of 1978. Under this act, the Attorney General is required to conduct a preliminary investigation of plausible charges against high-ranking officials. After 90 days, he is to report the results of his investigation to a three-judge panel that is called the "special division," a division of the U.S. Court of Appeals for the District of Columbia. The three judges are appointed by the Chief Justice of the United States to serve for a term of two years. If the Attorney General finds "reasonable grounds to believe that further investigation or prosecution is warranted," he must ask the special division to appoint an independent counsel and to define the limits of the counsel's prosecutorial jurisdiction. The statute goes into considerable detail to describe the relationship between the independent counsel and the Department of Justice; but, for purposes here, the most important points are that the independent counsel is appointed by a three-judge panel and can be removed only by impeachment or "by the personal action of the Attorney General and only for good cause, physical incapacity, or any other condition that substantially impairs the performance of such independent counsel's duties."

The policy objectives behind the independent counsel legislation were quite clear. Congress wanted to avoid any repetition of the "Saturday night massacre" of the Watergate era. It was important that the independent counsel should be truly independent. To ensure that this would be the case, Congress provided that the appointment should be made by a judicial panel and that removal could be effected only for cause.

Not surprisingly, these provisions were challenged on constitutional grounds. In the case that reached the Supreme Court, *Morrison v. Olson,* a former Assistant Attorney General, Theodore Olson, was under investigation by independent counsel Alexia Morrison on charges of having given false and misleading testimony to a congressional subcommittee in 1983 and of having wrongfully withheld certain documents from the House Judiciary Committee at that time. In the course of the investigation, Morrison caused a grand jury to issue subpoenas to Olson and two others who refused to comply on the grounds that the legislation creating Morrison's office was unconstitutional. This refusal led to the litigation that eventually reached the Supreme Court.

In a 7–1 decision, Chief Justice Rehnquist upheld the constitutionality of the unusual appointment and removal provisions for the independent prosecutor. The appointment argument was straightforward. The second section of Article II provides that appointments to federal offices are to be made by the President with the advice and consent of the Senate. The same section then adds the following qualification: "but the Congress may by law vest the Appointment of such inferior Officers, as they think proper, in the President alone, in the Courts of Law, or in the Heads of Departments." The Chief Justice maintained that the independent counsel was an inferior officer and, therefore, that Congress could rightfully vest her appointment in a judicial panel. In a long and vigorous dissent, Justice Scalia argued that the independent counsel was not an inferior officer and, therefore, Congress could not vest her appointment in "the Courts of Law."

Underlying the technical issues concerning the meaning of the term "inferior Officer" was a deeper separation of powers question that became clearer as Rehnquist and Scalia presented their conflicting arguments on the constitutionality of the statutory provision that the independent counsel could be removed only for cause—i.e., she could not be removed at the pleasure of the President or of the Attorney General acting on behalf of the President. This issue beat a path back to the *Myers* and *Humphrey* cases. Scalia maintained that "the prosecution of crimes is a quintessentially executive function." Prosecutors, he said, are "the virtual embodiment of the power to 'take care that the laws be faithfully executed'" and therefore should be subject to the broad presidential removal powers announced in *Myers*.

Chief Justice Rehnquist disagreed and, in so doing, gave a new and very restrictive interpretation of *Myers*—an interpretation of considerable importance for public administration professionals. He maintained that "the only issue actually decided in *Myers* was that 'the President had power to remove a postmaster of the first class, without the advice and consent of the Senate as required by act of Congress.'" He then acknowledged that the *Humphrey* court had distinguished the case before it from *Myers* on the grounds that a federal trade commissioner exercised quasi-legislative and quasi-judicial authority, as opposed to the purely executive functions of a postmaster first class. According to the *Humphrey* court, this distinction justified the congressional action that imposed a "for good cause" limitation on the President's power to remove a trade commissioner.

Having rehearsed this history, the Chief Justice then made the following, startling comment: but our present considered view is that the determination of whether the Constitution allows Congress to impose a "good cause"-type restriction on the President's power to remove an official cannot be made to turn on whether or not that official is classified as "purely executive." The analysis contained in our removal cases is designed not to define rigid categories of those officials who may or may not be removed at will by the President, but to ensure that Congress does not interfere with the President's exercise of the "executive power" and his constitutionally appointed duty to "take care that the laws be faithfully executed" under Article II.

The Chief Justice went on to explain that in this and in future removal cases the Court will not focus exclusively or even primarily on the sorts of functions that an officer performs. To be sure, the Chief Justice acknowledged that an analysis of the functions performed would not be "irrelevant." "But the real question is whether the removal restrictions are of such a nature that they impede the President's ability to perform his constitutional duty, and the functions of the officials in question must be analyzed in that light."

This is new constitutional doctrine. In dissent, Justice Scalia stated (correctly, I believe) that the *Humphrey* case "is swept into the dustbin of repudiated constitutional principle." Although Scalia recognized some of the problems in the *Humphrey* opinion, he found the loose standard announced by the Chief Justice far worse. He surmised that the new standard would be "an open invitation to Congress to experiment." The experiments would test just how far the Congress could go in protecting purely executive officers from dismissal at the pleasure of the President without impeding "the President's ability to perform his constitutional duty." He conjectured that under this standard, the Congress could provide that an "Assistant Secretary of State, with responsibility for one very narrow area of foreign policy," might be removed "only pursuant to certain carefully designed restrictions." Or the Congress might offer similar protection to an Assistant Secretary of Defense for Procurement. Ominously, Scalia brooded:

> The possibilities are endless, and the Court does not understand what the separation of powers, what "[a]mbition counteract[ing] ambition," *Federalist No. 51* ... , is all about if it does not expect Congress to try them. As far as I can discern from the Court's opinion, it is now open season upon the President's removal power for all executive officers, with not even the superficially principled restriction of *Humphrey's Executor* as cover.[10]

The public administration community will greet Scalia's predictions with greater equanimity than does the dissenting justice. One might well doubt that the Congress will follow through with the bold experiments Scalia fears. If the Congress were to do so, however, it might not be simply to celebrate the new "open season upon the President's removal power." Congress just might take such actions to encourage administrative professionalism in high-ranking executive officers and to protect them from punitive political reprisals from Presidents who prefer ideological subservience to sound administration. Then it would be the duty of the executives themselves to see to it that the President's rightful place in the constitutional balance of powers is preserved. It would be their responsibility as practitioners of the art and science of public administration to be sure that their protected positions against mischievous presidential whim did not weaken the President's capacity to "take care that the laws be faithfully executed."

Notes

1 George Anastaplo, "The United States Constitution of 1787: A Commentary," *Loyola University of Chicago Law Journal* 18 (Fall 1986): 129–139.

2 I discuss the removal question in more detail in a forthcoming monograph, *The President and the Public Administration* (Washington, DC: American Historical Association).

3 272 U.S. 52 (1926).

4 For an extended argument in support of this assertion, see my monograph referenced in note 2. For a good counter argument, see Peter L. Schultz, "The Constitution, the Presidency, and the Rule of Law," in *University of Kentucky Law*

Journal 76, no. 1 (1987–88), pp. 1–14; and "Separation of Powers and Presidential Prerogative: The Case of *Myers v. U.S.* Reconsidered," in Gary L. McDowell, ed., *Taking the Constitution Seriously* (Dubuque: Kerdall-Hunt, 1981), pp. 220–231.

5 Edward S. Corwin, *The President's Removal Power Under the Constitution* (New York: National Municipal League, 1927: repr., Ithaca, NY: Cornell University Press, 1981), p. 339.

6 *Humphrey's Executor v. U.S.*, 295 U.S. 602 (1935). Humphrey himself died after Roosevelt removed him; hence the title of the case.

7 Edward S. Corwin, *The President: Office and the Powers, 1787–1984*, 5th ed. (New York: New York University Press, 1984), p. 108.

8 This interpretation follows Corwin, *The President*, p. 108. *Morrison v. Olson*, 108 S. Ct. 2597 (1988).

9 *Morrison v. Olson*, 108 S. Ct. 2597 (1988).

10 418 U.S. 683 (1974).

5 Revolutionary Then, Revolutionary Now

How the Blacksburg Manifesto Enriches the Foundations of the Constitutional School

Stephanie P. Newbold

Refounding Public Administration (Wamsley et al., 1990) was a pioneering publication in the field of U.S. public administration. It was one of the early efforts that challenged Herbert Simon's theory of bounded rationality and the implications of underscoring the study and practice of public administration based largely from the application of New Public Management theories, public choice theory, behavioralism, and logical positivism. The first chapter in this book, Public Administration and the Governance Process: Shifting the Political Dialogue, is commonly referred to as the Blacksburg Manifesto because its authors, Gary Wamsley, Charles Goodsell, John Rohr, Camilla Stivers, Orion White, and James Wolf, were part of the Center for Public Administration and Policy at Virginia Tech located in Blacksburg. The Manifesto called for a normative approach to the study and practice of public administration and was one of the first major publications in the latter part of the twentieth century that explicitly defended the bureaucracy. Wamsley and his colleagues made the case that U.S. public administration served as a core institutional component of American government and worked to advance democratic governance.

The four themes of the Blacksburg Manifesto complement the aims of the Constitutional School because each points to the importance of grounding all facets of public administration in the rule of law and democratic-constitutionalism. First, the agency perspective maintains that we should understand the responsibilities of public sector agencies with a fuller appreciation for how they benefit society at large. It also serves to promote and direct the public interest in a manner that emphasizes the historical, institutional, political, and constitutional underpinnings for how public issues and public policies affect the citizenry. Secondly, the Blacksburg perspective emphasizes the public interest, which Wamsley argues is a multi-dimensional approach to solving public problems. It seeks to incorporate a long-range perspective into deliberation on matters affecting public sector governance. This specific method for advancing the public interest attempts to consider all positions in the decision-making process, especially when competing demands are at stake. Public administrators, therefore, make the most informed decisions when they acquire as much information as possible.

John Rohr's (1986) influence on the Blacksburg school of thought was profound. The third theme of the Manifesto relates specifically to Rohr's argument that the constitutional heritage of the United States legitimates the administrative state in word and deed. Grounding the American administrative state in the constitutional foundations of the nation provides *the* normative framework that enables the field of public administration to promote democratic governance and in doing so advance the broadest possible public interest (Wamsley et al., 1990). This analysis represents the core of the Constitutional School. It speaks to how the constitutional foundation of the nation provides the foundation to examine, to understand, and to underscore the most central dynamics of the democratic governance process.

The final theme of the Manifesto focuses on the role of the public administrator, which is a position that demands the utmost professionalism (Wamsley et al., 1990; Green et al., 1993). Professionalism in public administration underscores the expectation that civil servants be competent in their job responsibilities, service-oriented, able to define the public interest in the broadest possible manner, conserve the nation's constitutional heritage, and be able to uphold the oath of office (Wamsley et al., 1990; Green et al., 1993; Terry, 2003). These professional expectations help to distinguish public administration from other professions and other forms of administration (Green et al., 1993).

The Constitutional School embraces this framework because of its emphasis on the democratic-constitutional requirements associated with public service and public administration. The Constitutional School works to draw attention for how the democratic-constitutional responsibilities of public sector governance work to differentiate the sectors from each other. This effort runs deep within the public administration literature to include Graham Allison's (1979) explanation for why public and private management are alike in all the unimportant respects; Ronald Moe's (1987) analysis regarding the limits of privatization; and Larry Terry's (2005) argument for how the application of private sector norms and values work to thin public administrative institutions and subsequently create a hollow state incapable of governing according to constitutional expectations.

Like Larry Terry, I am a product of the Blacksburg school of thought. John Rohr was my major professor and dissertation chair and Gary Wamsley served as one of my most trusted academic and professional advisors throughout my time at Virginia Tech. One of the most profound lessons of my graduate education was Wamsley's explanation regarding the contemporary relevance of the Manifesto. The field, according to Wamsley, is constantly changing because the needs of the citizenry are always shifting. The Refounding effort, perhaps more than any other piece of literature written since Dwight Waldo's (1948) classic treatise *The Administrative State*, recognizes this reality. Throughout Wamsley's pedagogical career, he emphasized the insightful point that the U.S. represents an ever democratizing-constitutional republic. The nation and its administrative institutions have not always embraced democratic values in its individual and collective decision-making, but the administrative state is the one entity in American life that is constantly working to get right what we previously got wrong. It works to become more representative of the citizens and individuals who make up this great country not less. The expansion of the public administration literature to include ideas and research that support representative bureaucracy, diversity, cultural competency, and social equity legitimates this point in a very substantial way.

The Blacksburg Manifesto and the Constitutional School advance the same message. Both challenge scholars and practitioners to seek a broader, more comprehensive understanding of the field, one that maintains that the legitimacy of the American administrative state can be found only within its democratic-constitutional heritage (Rohr, 1986; Wamsley et al, 1990; Moe & Gilmour, 1995; Newbold, 2010). Moving the Constitutional School forward into contemporary public administration dialogue is the most prominent and meaningful way we can carry on the legacy of its earliest champions. I am assuredly confident that if John Rohr and Larry Terry were still with us they would be most pleased with this effort.

References

Allison, G.T. 1979. Proceedings of the public management research conference. Washington, DC Office of Personnel Management. OPM document 127-153-1, pp. 27–38.

Green, R.T., Keller, L.F. & Wamsley, G.L. 1993. Reconstituting a profession for American public administration. *Public administration review* 53: 516–524.

Moe, R.C. 1987. Exploring the limits of privatization. *Public administration review* 47(6): 453–460.

Moe, R.C. & Gilmour, R.S. 1995. Rediscovering principles of public administration: The neglected foundation of public law. *Public administration review* 55(2) March/April: 135–146.

Newbold, S.P. 2010. Toward a Constitutional School for American public administration. *Public administration review* 70(4) July/August: 538–546.

Rohr, J.A. 1989. *To run a constitution: The legitimacy of the American Administrative state*. Lawrence: University Press of Kansas.

Terry, L.D. 2003. *Leadership of public bureaucracies: The administrator as conservator*. 2nd edn. Armonk, NY: M.E. Sharpe.

Terry, L.D. 2005. The thinning of administrative institutions in the hollow state. *Administration and society* 37(4): 426–444.

Waldo, D. 1948. *The administrative state: A study in the political theory of American public administration*. New York: Ronald Press.

Wamsley, G.L., Bacher, R.N., Goodsell, C.T., Kronenberg, P.S., Rohr, J.A., Stivers, C.M., White, O.F. & Wolf, J.F. 1990. *Refounding public administration*. Thousand Oaks, CA: Sage.

Public Administration and the Governance Process

Shifting the Political Dialogue

Gary L. Wamsley, Charles T. Goodsell, John A. Rohr, Camilla M. Stivers, Orion F. White and James F. Wolf[1]

From: *Refounding Public Administration*. 1990. Sage.

Nearly a century has passed since the appearance of Woodrow Wilson's essay "The Study of Public Administration." Some of what he wrote seems to have a disturbingly prophetic quality. For example:

> The weightier debates of constitutional principle are even yet by no means concluded; but they are no longer of more immediate practical moment than questions of administration. It is getting harder to *run* a constitution than to frame one.[2]

If those words have such a disturbing quality today it is doubtless because they have proven so painfully true for us as the twentieth century draws to a close. We have accomplished administrative wonders since Wilson penned those words: dug a canal connecting the world's great oceans; organized, equipped, and deployed millions of men and women to win two global wars; saved from collapse and altered the nature of the American political economy by massive administrative intervention during the Great Depression; organized scientists and workers in a secret and desperate race with Nazi Germany to develop a nuclear weapon; we built an interstate highway system of unmatched size and capacity; we have put together hundreds of organizations both public and private involving thousands of scientists and engineers and billions of dollars to place American footprints on the moon. The list could and should go on and on. Yet despite these and many other accomplishments, it "gets harder to run a constitution." All our administrative accomplishments do not add to, and some wonder if in fact administration even contributes to, the stable and effective functioning of our political system. The essence, we believe, of what Wilson meant by "running a constitution" is a public administration that *does* result in the stable and effective functioning of our political system in a way that steadily improves the quality of our lives and expands both equity and opportunity.

The problem then lies not simply in a lack of organizing and managerial skills, though we still have plenty of room for improvement. Rather it goes beyond, to the problem of governing a modern republic with a commi to freedom and justice on the one hand and a commitment to a cor mixture of capitalism and state intervention on the other. Several co dictory pressures are thus generated. The commitment to freedom and justice creates pressures for equity but commitment to state capitalism creates a counter pressure for economic and social differentiation. The requirements of maintaining a vigorous economy in an increasingly competitive world and of maintaining worldpower status in an increasingly dangerous environment create pressures for a rational, comprehensive, planning and policy process while our historical and constitutional tradition is based on fractionated power, overlapping jurisdictions, and disjointed incrementalism. The problems of public administration in America result from the difficulty of governing effectively such a political system; hence the difficulties of governing such a political system are not the result of, or caused by, public administration.

Rowland Egger sums up American history in a way that places our governance problem and the problems of bureaucracy in perspective. He points out that America has experienced four great social revolutions. The first was the revolution for independence, which set in motion forces of social change only partially crystallized and reflected in the great compromises of the Constitution; the second was the Jacksonian era, which marked our changed conceptions of who was entitled to participate in republican government; the third was the Civil War, which redefined the nature of the federal Union and further altered our definition of citizenship by making it national in character. There is, however, a fourth social revolution that is still in progress according to Egger. It began with the New Deal's response to the Great Depression and was given further impetus by the Civil Rights Movement now augmented by the Women's Movement. This revolution is in the process of redefining our concepts of justice and equity and our expectations of government's role in our efforts to find a uniquely American definition for these abstract concepts.

If this is a meaningful synopsis of our history then it becomes understandable, though no less lamentable, that America's public administration is caught in the eye of recurrent political storms: reviled by some because it does too much in pursuit of equity and justice, and by others who perceive it as doing too little. Both ends of the political spectrum have seen it at times as the ominous instrument of their opponent's will. Not only has it been forced to bear the opprobrium of being seen as the "opponent's instrument," but it has also become the scapegoat for the general problems of what Theodore Lowi has aptly labeled "interest group liberalism": the parochialization of the public interest, the fragmentation and erosion of public purpose and the centrifugal pressures that have franchised pieces of public authority to policy subsystems. Although American public administration is not without blame for some of these maladies, it has as often as not been victim rather than perpetrator, "compliant with" rather than "cause of," and, indeed, it can be argued that it has often served as the strongest available counterweight to these disturbing tendencies.

Be that as it may, political leaders have increasingly used "bureaucracy" as an epithet. Presidents of both parties have made attacks on it the centerpieces of their campaigns, only to find that this tactic, so useful in getting elected, becomes a self-inflicted wound in the subsequent struggle to govern. The gap between our system's need for effective governance and the capacity of our elected officials to provide it widens at an alarming rate.

Government and the American Dialogue

Much of the denigration of bureaucracy has been a natural outgrowth of our politics. Jacksonian democracy was heavily freighted with negativism toward government because new groups wanted both access to it and control of it. Even though the Progressive movement ran counter to this, the residual negativism has been amplified by contemporary conservatism and by political actors from all parts of the spectrum who are frustrated by the problems that derive from interest group liberalism but that are blamed on government or, synonymously, bureaucracy. Thus our political culture has come to include a pernicious mythology concerning the public sector and public administrators which needs to be corrected before the American dialogue can enter a new and meaningful phase. Items:

Most clients of bureaucracy are not dissatisfied; in fact the vast majority of them are very pleased with the services and treatment received.

The rate of productivity increase in the public sector is not clearly lower than the private sector; it is probably higher overall.

The federal government has not grown in number of employees since the early 1950s. The bureaucracy is not a monolith; it is composed of many small and diverse bureaus and offices.

Public agencies stimulate and implement change; resistance to change is no more endemic to the organizations in the public sector than to the private.

Studies have shown that the private sector is more top-heavy with administrative personnel than the public sector.

Waste and inefficiency are no more prevalent in the public sector than the private; but in the former it is seen as waste of the taxpayers money while in the latter we fail to see that it is passed on to us in the prices we pay as consumers.

But our purpose is neither to bury bureaucracy nor to praise it; rather we hope to take a step toward reconceptualizing it as The Public Administration. *Bureaucracy* in its technical sense refers to a form of social organization that is not confined to the public sector. We carry no brief for any particular organizational form. Our focus is on the *functions* of government agencies and not on how they might be organized. Thus we speak of "The

Public Administration" as an institution of government rather than of bureaucracy as an organizational form.

We see no way of arresting the pathologies of our political system and coming to grips with the sizeable problems of our nation's political economy without a new way of thinking about, speaking of, and acting toward The Public Administration. This will not be a sufficient condition for the challenges we face, but it will assuredly be a necessary one.

There must be, then, a significant change in both the content and breadth of the American Dialogue. This dialogue juxtaposes, on the one hand, ideas associated with broadening and deepening personal liberty and, on the other, ideas associated with social equity, public order, fiscal soundness, and capital accumulation. Inevitable tension between these two sets of ideas has meant that disagreement about the nature and role of government has always been central to that dialogue, though it has worn different masks at different times. During the last half-century the disagreement has become particularly acute as we have sought to redefine liberty and equity while carrying out our fourth social revolution.

We have been socialized, for complex reasons that have to do with the nature of capitalism, to fail to see this as the core issue of the dialogue. Nonetheless the great national debates of our history have as often as not involved questions about the nature and role of "government" in the struggle between democracy and order. Today we feel it is imperative that an important shift take place in the dialogue. Our political rhetoric and symbols have become too far divorced from reality and the conditions we face. We cannot preserve and revitalize American industry and our natural resources in the face of increasing global interdependence nor improve the quality of our lives, if our public dialogue is focused on whether or not government has any role in these matters or on how to reduce its role, while the reality of our world, our behavior, and our actions is of necessity trying to grapple with questions of "How?" and "What form is most effective?"

As Dwight Waldo reminds us, only in America did we create such rhetorical and symbolic disjuncture between the concepts of "good government" and "good management". In the rest of the Occident there is a profound and natural linkage resulting from legal concepts and institutions rooted in Roman law. Americans sharply attenuated that linkage when they revolted against the British monarchy and then, a century later, "invented" what Waldo calls "selfconscious administration," which strove to be "scientific" with empirically discoverable and generally applicable principles. We believe that attenuation and rediscovery were and are far more impressive in our rhetoric than in actual fact. This is not to say they were less important for being rhetorical; indeed they may be more important for that very reason. One point, however, is that the nature and role of public administration were never far from the center of America's public dialogue; they were only camouflaged as questions about "government" rather than "public administration." Beginning with the Articles of Confederation and continuing down to this day, we have been arguing about liberty and order and the nature and role of "government" in the pulling and hauling between these polar abstractions. From the suppression of Shays's Revolt and the Whiskey Rebellion, the assumption of the states' debts by the national government, the building of post roads, the national roads, the granting of land by the government to railroads and canal companies, the Northwest Ordinance (which dedicated land in each territory to support public schools), through the Interstate Commerce Act, down to current debates over the sale of government-developed communication satellites to private enterprise, in all these we have been engaged in a national struggle to define the nature and role of "government" in the perilous evolution of some kind of ordered liberty. We must therefore refocus the American dialogue from questions about the nature and role of "government" to questions about the nature and role of "public administration." This would be a subtle but crucial shift in the American dialogue from questions of "whether" there should be a role for The Public Administration to questions of "what form?" that role should take.

Finally, as part of an effort to shift the American dialogue, we need to assert that The Public Administration, with the managerial skills which lie at its core and its experience in applying those skills in a political context, is, despite its problems, a major social asset. As a major social asset it should be subjected to constructive criticism but not diminished, denigrated, or decapitalized lightly or for short-run partisan advantage. There may well be a direct relationship between the attacks on The Public Administration and the erosion of civic morality evidenced in behavior ranging from corruption and tax evasion to vandalism and littering. Those who attack The Public Administration for partisan advantage are no friends of the Republic; indeed they inflict considerable harm on the body politic. Similarly, those engaged in decapitalizing and disassembling administrative capacity should recognize that subsequent ruling groups (some of them of their own political persuasion), and all citizens will have to pay the price of such foolish disinvestment. Though The Public Administration needs many improvements and alterations, the need for administrative capacity will only increase, not diminish. One of the major political economic questions confronting the American political system, one that needs to be at the center of a refocused American dialogue is: which (not whether) government intentions and actions should be pursued through the public sector, that is, be a part of The Public Administration and therefore have its authority and legitimacy behind them while at the same time being subject to its constraints.

The Public Administration's Distinctive Character

The Public Administration is, of course, centered on the executive branch but includes segments of all branches of government to the extent that they relate to the constitutional mandate of the executive: the faithful execution of the laws through our multileveled governmental system. Our position is pointedly historical and includes not only those things we might point to with pride, like the Hatch Act, but also those of which we are justly ashamed, like the Teapot Dome Scandal.

The Public Administration is distinctive in character. It has at its core generic management technologies that comprise its "administrative capacity." These are a vital part of its expertise and they closely resemble the technologies of management in the private sector. But Wallace Sayre puts it aptly when he says that business and public administration are alike in all *un-important* respects. For The Public Administration is more than generic management. It is the administration of public affairs in a political context. As Carl Friedrich noted a half-century ago, administration is the core of modern government; it is an application of state power for what we hope are moral and humane ends, but always with the possibility of being used otherwise. Since governance entails the state's rewarding and depriving in the name of society as a whole, and since politics is the art of gaining acceptance for those allocations, administration is an inextricable part of both governance and politics.

Because of its role in rewarding and depriving, redistributing, distributing and regulating, and because it is the only set of institutions that can rightfully coerce to achieve society's ends, it is seldom viewed dispassionately. Rather it is, as Murray Edelman reminds us, an object against which the people displace fears, hopes, and anxieties. The Public Administration is inescapably fundamental to this displacement and therein lies its distinctive character. Its part in governance and the resultant political context means that: (1) the Public Administrator must engage not in a struggle for markets and profits but in a struggle with other actors in the political and governmental processes for jurisdiction, legitimacy, and resources; (2) those persons with whom he or she must interact possess distinctive perceptions, expectations, and levels of efficacy toward The Public Administration (e.g., the differences between consumers and citizens or suppliers and interest groups are profound); and (3) the requisite skills, foci of attention, and perceived tasks of The Public Administration differ markedly from private-sector management. These differences are so great that a manager successful in one sector will not be as successful in the other without considerable adaptiveness. To the degree that we lose sight of that distinction, to the same degree do we lose our vision of what The Public Administration is or can be.

The Public Administration is also self-consciously derived from, and focused upon, what we shall call an Agency Perspective. By agencies we mean those institutions that have grown up in the executive branches at all levels and that are the instruments of action in pursuit of the public interest. A better understanding of the distinctiveness of The Public Administration must be built upon a greater appreciation of the institutional histories of agencies—their histories in a broad contextual sense—the history of an agency's political economy.

We feel this is appropriate and necessary because many of these agencies are repositories of, and their staffs are trustees of, specialized knowledge, historical experience, time-tested wisdom, and most importantly, some degree of consensus as to the public interest relevant to a particular societal function. Indeed the persons staffing these agencies have been charged with acting in the public interest and in executing the popular will in ways that sustain and nurture legitimacy for generations. The Agency Perspective is thus based on many years of struggle within the larger political system and the more limited governance process to achieve and enact some kind of consensus over specific aspects of public policy. Surely this unique task and experience is worth far more than we have been willing to acknowledge up until now.

That is not to say that the agencies have not been misdirected or misused by others or that they have not operated at times in self-serving ways. Indeed, as acknowledged earlier, agencies have contributed at times to the centrifugal pressures in American government, and in some respects they may have aided those who aimed to reduce their legitimate sphere, by neglecting substantive relationships with the ultimate source of legitimacy in governance, that is, the citizenry. But the dangers of parochialism are endemic to all organizations and they are, in the final analysis, perversions of the Agency Perspective. The Agency Perspective is intended only to serve public administrators as a "center of gravity" or a "gyroscope" as they go about their duties. On this solid foundation they must build a concern for broader public principles and values; in other words, a concern for the public interest.

As Max Weber pointed out, bureaucracy can be used for good or evil; how it is used depends on the human beings who staff it and direct it. Fortunately, over the grand sweep of American history, with exception made perhaps for the period between the election of Jackson and the passage of the Pendleton Act, agencies have for the most part been staffed by persons who have taken seriously the task of faithfully executing the popular will and the public interest. Although some have no doubt been concerned with a broader public interest, most have viewed that task through the lens of their agency and assumed, like the rest of us, that the broader public interest would emerge from the governance process as a whole. The point is that few groups in our society have been given as demanding a task as executing the public interest from any perspective. That task and the special skills and knowledge acquired by The Public Administration in performing it are worth far more than our present political dialogue allows.

Political elites have failed for self-serving reasons to credit agencies and those who staff them with distinctive characteristics and legitimacy, therefore the public at large, cut off from the realities of administrative practice, has also failed to credit them. Most lamentably, The Public Administration has been too timid in pressing its rightful claims to legitimacy of which the Agency Perspective is the basic foundation, and too hesitant about building the sense of trust among citizens that would justify such claims.

Most recently we have also allowed The Public Administration to be diminished by the headlong rush to adopt a policy or program perspective with an excessive focus on output without balancing it by concern for the public good. The two are often erroneously assumed to be synonymous, when in fact they are not. An agency can produce outputs inimicable to the long-range public interest; as well as short-run "results" that can have devastating effects on its infrastructure and capabilities and, most importantly, the future public good. A park service, for example, can process a larger number of visitors through facilities that it is overloading and allowing to decay through lack of maintenance. It is therefore possible for an agency to be "responsive" to immediate pressures while simultaneously being irresponsible with regard to the public interest. One of the characteristics of the Agency Perspective and of The Public Administration therefore should be a prudent and reasoned attention to agency performance, one in which consideration is given both to the short *and* long-run consequences, qualitative as well as quantitative measures; and one which rejects "the bottom line" as a slogan antithetical to good public administration.

Although public policy analysis and program evaluations used wisely can be valuable in carrying out the public business and in demonstrating agency performance, they are not ends in themselves, and simplistic use and clever abuse must be constantly guarded against. In executive agencies these techniques make sense only when viewed as part of the ongoing processes of administration. Policy analysis, program evaluation, and decision sciences when applied within executive agencies should be subordinated to an agency perspective and to core management process. Too often the former have been allowed to intrude upon this perspective and these processes and have been detrimental to good public administration and inconsistent with their own aims.

A particularly corrosive influence on the Agency Perspective came from humanistic psychology and a variety of cultural dynamics during the 1960s. We refer to the denigration of the role of authority in the administrative process and management relationships. The adolescent texture of the 1960s' cultural upheaval wore heavily on our traditional concepts of authority within agencies. Now, in cooler retrospect, it is time to correct the misconceptions that arose from the debate of the traditionalists and the humanists in organization theory on this issue.

We need to note, first, that the traditional point of view was incorrect to the extent that it sought to base obedience to authority purely on the principle of deference and depicted the use of managerial authority as a tool by which managers could improve performance (the "shape up or ship out" position). This perspective was correct, however, in depicting the human situation as one requiring authority to check our sometimes capricious tendencies. In particular, the traditional view is correct in seeing that encounter with authority is an essential and positive part of the maturation process, not only in adolescence but throughout life; and for superiors and subordinates alike.

By the same token, the humanists were incorrect in carrying their attack on authority to the point of denying that it plays a needed role in institutional life—implying that it can thereby be replaced completely by processes of participation. They were, however, providing a helpful corrective to the traditional view by their call for more openness in the use of authority and for the establishment of a greater degree of mutual confidence in organizations.

What we can distill from this debate is the idea that authority is not as useful as feedback and other "humanistic" communication devices for improving performance in administration, but it is essential for dealing effectively with the intractable problem of compliance on issues wherein reasonable persons can disagree. It is these issues of compliance on which hinge both the personal development of managers and the people they manage, as well as the effectiveness of agencies in implementing public policies and programs. In sum, the message here is that the vitality of the Agency Perspective, the health of The Public Administration, and the self-concept of the Public Administrator hinge upon our return to a fuller appreciation of the positive role of authority in administration. This appreciation, in essence a form of trust, will develop among citizens to the extent that administrators communicate the realities of administrative practice so that citizens can understand them, and ultimately acknowledge the legitimacy of administrative authority.

The distinctive Agency Perspective is one that deserves greater legitimacy than it has received from our political culture. The very nature of the role the Agency plays in governance leads it inevitably to develop a distinctive perspective on the public interest. The Public Administration which rests upon the Agency Perspective as a foundation thus has an historic, covenantal, organic, and constitutional legitimacy that needs illumination. Many agencies at all levels of our political system have been with us from our genesis as a nation; some are even suggested in the text of the Constitution.

The distinctive nature of The Public Administration lies in the fact that it is a part of the governance process, that it is administration in a political context and competence directed *toward the public interest*. This sets it apart from management in business and provides the basis for a truly distinctive claim to status that has been too long ignored. The claim ought to rest, however, on more than competence to manage in a political context. It must also rest on a claim of competence in the maintenance of (1) the Agency Perspective; (2) the broadest possible public interest; and (3) the constitutional governance process.

The "public interest" has, of course, long been derided, particularly by social scientists, as a meaningless concept at best, a mask for arrogant despotism at worst. But setting aside for a moment the difficulties of defining its contents precisely, it is ironic that many social scientists prefer to be concerned with behavior but ignore the fact that the concept has a day-to-day, commonsensical, practical salience for the behavior of hundreds of thousands of Public Administrators. Caught as they are in the struggle of conflicting interests—sometimes as interpreters, other times as decision makers, and even at times as victims—they understand intuitively that the containment if not the resolution of that conflict is rooted in some notion of the public interest even though some may use the concept cynically or self-servingly. It is therefore a concrete, living, behavioral reality in spite of our problems in defining its specific content.[3]

The approach traditionally imposed for defining the concept has, however, led us astray by making a definition impossible. This approach has been to ask, "What is the public interest in terms of the *content* of given policy situations?" This question may never be answered. But, by shifting our perspective from specific content to an *ideal* and a *process,* and the emphasis from a search for certainty to recognition of the problematic nature of the public interest, the problem is no longer insoluble. In this vein, the "public interest" refers to a combination of several habits of mind in making decisions and making policy: attempting to deal with the *multiple* ramifications of an issue rather than a select few; seeking to incorporate the *long-range* view into deliberations, to balance a natural tendency toward excessive concern with short-term results; considering *competing* demands and requirements of affected individuals and groups, not one position; proceeding equipped with *more* knowledge and information rather than less; and recognizing that to say that the "public interest" is problematic is not to say it is meaningless.

Although this type of definition will not satisfy those who have been accustomed to posing the issue in substantive and finite terms, an ideal and process-defined norm is not that unusual—either as practical guidepost or positive symbol. The democrat endorses majoritarianism; the civil libertarian extols due process; lawyers cherish an adversarial legal process. We recommend approaching, if not defining, the public interest in the same spirit. Even the strongest opponent of the public interest concept, the economic conservative, is committed to an ideal and process-oriented norm, the competitive market.

Because this definition does not provide us with given policy or option answers, it invites the charge that the Public Administrator who lays claim to protecting the public interest is merely insisting on his agency's definition of what is "right." Such misplaced absoluteness constantly occurs on the part of public administrators as well as others. All must recognize the subjective elements in any conclusion as to which choice is "right," and indeed that "certainty" about the public interest is a dubious and perhaps dangerous posture. (Many of those involved in the Watergate Affair were certain that the public interest was embodied in the president's position.) At the same time, it can be said that all decision criteria are ultimately matters of agreement among relevant individuals. The key to the legitimacy of any criterion, including the public interest, is not whether it is subjective but whether all those who have a stake in the matter at hand have had the opportunity to share in defining it.

Although we feel that a commitment to a public interest viewed as an ideal, a process, and a habit of mind is the soundest ground for the concept, we would not preclude others. For example, the search in a positivist tradition for the specific content of the public interest has blinded us to another possible approach regarding its nature. It can be argued that we have already learned, believe, and know a good deal about what the public interest is *not*. Defining something negatively may be unsettling for those of us educated in contemporary social science, but it is commonplace in our everyday lives and in such diverse fields as theology and developmental psychology. In theology, for example, the transcendent is often undefinable and is therefore discussed in terms of what it is not. And in what may be a meaningful analog for The Public Administration and the public interest, Rollo May suggests that the human capacity to say and mean "no" is the most significant first statement of self-discovery—that is, knowing what we are not must, of necessity, occur well before knowing what we are.[4] Thus although we ought to continue to define the public interest in terms of a process, the pursuit of a positive but ever-problematic public interest could conceivably begin by explicating it negatively. We know, for example, that racism is not in the public interest. We may well debate what constitutes a manifestation of racism, but even on that issue we already have considerable definition in statutes, administrative regulations, and court interpretations. We probably have even more consensus on what constitutes racism than we realize; it is simply not well explicated. Starting with the negative as a means of explicating the public interest may yield more insight than a positivist approach has admitted thus far.

In speaking about The Public Administration's distinctive relationship to the "public interest" we thus wish to remain open to the idea that its content, however elusive and problematic, might yet to some degree be definable. But more important we think is the point that although the content of the public interest remains problematic, when an institutionalized tradition and support system exist to nurture a process *emphasizing* the relatively comprehensive, long-term, deliberative, and informed efforts essential *to the search for* the public interest, the chances increase that action will follow in accord with these values. Whatever the weaknesses of The Public Administration, it provides more of an institutionalized tradition of this kind than other elements of society or other actors in the political process, certainly more than political parties, interest groups, or mass media. Surely The Public Administration does not "know" the content of the public interest; but it is in a relatively good position to nurture the kind of process essential for its ongoing pursuit, particularly when it takes the enlarged view of the process that encompasses efforts to render faithful interpretations of the interests of all relevant stakeholders, including citizens at large.

The practical and beneficial consequence for The Public Administration of accepting the public interest as ever problematic may be a perspective that fosters: (1) tentative steps and experimental action rather than our typical "solutions" for this or "wars" on that; (2) curiosity and dialogue about ends as well as means; (3) individuals and institutions that "learn" as well as respond; (4) humility and skepticism about "grand designs"; (5) greater awareness of the unique responsibility and potential contribution of each individual to a national dialogue about the public interest; and (6) a greater attentiveness to the words of public discourse.[5]

Recognition of the distinctive character of The Public Administration can also be greatly enhanced if its academic community comes to a new and important point of resolution and clarity in the venerable question of whether or not there is a politics–administration dichotomy. First we must acknowledge that public administration theory detoured sharply into an intellectual cul-de-sac when some of us followed Herbert Simon's attempt to establish a fact–value dichotomy. We also erred in following too closely the organizational sociologists in their narrower quest to understand complex organizations. Both efforts led us astray from the important debate over a politics–administration dichotomy that had been carried on by Wilson, Goodnow, Gaus, White, Appleby, Waldo, and others. Our temporary obsession with behavioralism and our attempts to stay in step with political science, which was in the heat of its own behavioral fad, delayed moving on to a clearer resolution of the politics–administration dichotomy. Organizational sociology and business administration were never interested in questions of governance, and political science drifted farther and farther from such concerns and pulled public administration with it.

The path to a point of clarity on the dichotomy rests on grasping that the distinction between the two phenomena must be understood on three different levels. First we need to recognize that at the highest level, speaking descriptively and conceptually, there is no dichotomy. Public administration at this level of abstraction is an integral part of the governance and political processes. We need to comprehend this point as the beginning of our understanding of The Public Administration's role in the political system and the governance process. But in establishing that point over several decades, we have lost sight of the fact that at a second level of meaning (again speaking descriptively), at a less abstract level of behavior and action, there is, and always has been, if not a dichotomy, at least a considerable distinction. Persons in the governance and political processes seek to make and maintain a distinction between roles, behavior, situations, and phenomena that are political and those that are administrative. Sometimes the distinction is made self-servingly or even cynically; but it is made nonetheless. To ignore it is to ignore behavioral and empirical reality, and to do that is to thwart description and understanding of the behavioral phenomena we label public administration.

Finally, at a third level of meaning, if we speak prescriptively and normatively to those persons involved in ruling and governing, we feel we should acknowledge, elucidate, and extend the distinction between politics and administration. We need help distinguishing between political and administrative roles and to better understand and elaborate between political and administrative roles and better understand and elaborate upon the distinction between ruling and governing. That distinction, at this third level of meaning, is crucial if The Public Administration is to be accepted, not least by the public at large, as a legitimate and valued part of the political process in general and the governance process more particularly.

The emergence of judges as legitimate and valued actors and institutions in the governance process ("of" but not "in" politics) can serve as an analog. In the evolution of the English political system judges began as agents of the king, traveling the realm settling disputes in his name. Their work might best be looked upon as an early form of nation building. Their reputation for fairness fixed in the public mind a well-founded belief in the superiority of royal justice over the justice administered in the courts of the barons. These royal judges developed the common law—a law that was common throughout the realm and of a higher quality than the particularistic law of the feudal manors. Eventually, however, these royal officers developed distinctive symbols, ritual, language, a way of reasoning, and a claim to expertise and legitimacy that gave them a stature and role distinct from the king's—one that would lead them to use the law and their claim to be its legitimate interpreters to stand in opposition (but a loyal opposition) to the king. This development was taken even further on this side of the Atlantic when Chief Justice Marshall's adroit handling of *Marbury v. Madison* established the basis of the Supreme Court's claim to judicial review of the constitutionality of acts of Congress.

Like the judicial system, The Public Administration needs to assert but also to be granted, its propriety and legitimacy as an institution. It should assert the value of the Agency Perspective in effective functioning of the political system, the value and legitimacy of the Public Administrator as an actor in the governing process, and the distinctiveness and worth of his or her role-competence directed to the maintenance of the Agency Perspective, the broadest possible understanding of public interest, and the constitutional governance process. If this is done, and done far more successfully than it has been to date, it is conceivable that civilian Public Administrators, like judges before them or like their military colleagues today, could question a directive of their political superiors and have the question regarded as a sober second thought rather than an act of bureaucratic sabotage. When that can happen in The Public Administration, the Public Administrator, and our political system will have come of age. It may be, however, that just as the judicial agents of the king developed reputation by going out among the people and visibly demonstrated the superiority of their practice, The Public Administration's assertion of legitimacy will need to be founded on more direct linkages with the people, in order win their trust.

The Public Administration and Capitalism

In *The Administrative State,* Dwight Waldo questioned whether the rationalistic mentality reflected in the literature of public administration to that point could sufficiently comprehend what he called the "imponderable emotional substructure" of society. His point seems to have been that this aspect of social life had to be adequately understood if general social health were to be ensured. We wish to address this question in its current form in the United States, though we feel that our suggestion might have more general implications.

In our view social health, as with individual health, depends critically upon the existence of a reflexive relationship between the emotional substructure or unconscious and the conscious side of the human process. This reflexive relationship requires on the one hand a relative openness to the designs of the unconscious that emerge in ambition, pursuit of personal agendas, risk, and adventure.

On the other hand, it also requires that these designs of the unconscious be juxtaposed with collective needs and concerns and with needs for introspection, judgment, and moral reasoning applied to matters affecting others beyond the expression and gratification of selfish impulse. In the case of the United States, it seems that capitalism as an institutional form has well provided for one half of the reflexivity equation. The genius of the market is that it can so quickly and easily give expression to emergent needs, tendencies, and tastes that are constantly forming and seeking vent in the collective unconscious. It is this aspect of capitalism that leads advocates of laissez-faire to equate (and to some degree correctly so) capitalism with freedom. In this sense at least, suppression of the emotional substructure is hardly a problem in capitalist society. Growth and development, stemming from unconscious impulses whether economic, social, or psychological, can take place relatively unimpeded for most of our people with the exception perhaps of a disturbingly persistent "underclass."

But capitalism has been notably less successful in providing the other side of the reflexivity equation. The marketplace can so facilitate the expression of the unconscious or emotional substructure that it can overwhelm the conscious side of society. As wants are expressed and satisfied with increasing speed and facility, a point can be reached where new wants are created by the process itself. Gratification divorced from content and substance becomes the motivating orientation of individuals and eventually of society itself. When this happens, societal bearings are lost, points of reference, both moral and practical, become obscure, and public standards that are essential for the exercise of collective human discretion and judgment fail us. Hence, the market is a necessary but insufficient device for maintaining our social well-being. Public authority, expressed through stable institutions of The Public Administration, is essential as a cooling, containing, and directing foil to the capitalist marketplace. Such institutions, indeed, must represent the collective consciousness of our society and serve as the vehicle for our efforts to bring to bear reason, and moral judgment on both our problems and the design of our future. Capitalism in our case has been helpful in releasing the energy required to move our societal ship. It cannot by itself, however, give it adequate navigation. We must look to The Public Administration, under the captaincy of our political institutions, for this.

The Public Administration and the Constitution

Our political rhetoric and symbols are badly out of synchronization with our "enacted constitution" or at least with a Federalist interpretation of it. For that interpretation encouraged and anticipated The Public Administration. Unfortunately existing public administration theory is distressingly weak on this point and members of The Public Administration have themselves forgotten or failed to grasp it. Instead they have sought simply to emphasize their nonpartisan instrumentalism and to emulate management practices of business. Valuable though a claim of nonpartisan instrumentalism was in the emergence of The Public Administration at the turn of the century, it is neither well-grounded in the Constitution nor adequate to the role demands of the late twentieth century. The Constitution to some extent explicitly and to a greater extent implicitly and through historic practice has assigned a more demanding and significant role to The Public Administration. We have all known since our first civics class that our Constitution is designed to preserve freedom by dividing power, but we do not always connect that profound truth with our circumstances as public administrators. It means, of course, that in the never-ending battle between the chief executive, the legislature, and the courts, The Public Administration is a "free-fire zone" and that the Public Administrators serve as targets of opportunity for the combatants.

When we assert that the Constitution, or at least a Federalist interpretation of it, anticipated The Public Administration, do we mean that the framers thought of it in the bleak metaphors of war used above? Assuredly not. With the possible exception of Hamilton at his most prescient, they did not foresee The Public Administration of today any more than they could have foreseen the myriad changes in other institutions that have come to pass. But the history of the earliest days of the Republic (and indeed the actions of some of the framers themselves) show that as soon as the constitutional drama began to unfold, the Public Administrators were the persons in no-man's land who were left with ambiguities and a discretion that was viewed, on the one hand, as a threat to them (and to others) and, on the other, as a challenging opportunity to keep the constitutional process from becoming a stalemate in which the public interest would be the ultimate casualty.

In dealing with its constitutionally derived ambiguity and discretion The Public Administration must always act within the constraints imposed by its origin in covenant, a covenant manifested in the Constitution, t Service Reform tradition, and historic experience. The word cove sacral overtones that are not altogether inappropriate for our purp its secular usage preserves its fundamental sense of a solemn agre obligations between parties, and that would seem to capture what The Public Administration was, is, and ought to be: a solemn agreement between the Public Administrator and the citizens he or she serves; an agreement to serve the public with competence directed toward the public interest and the maintenance of a democratic process of governance; competence constrained by the vitality of the constitutional heritage, the law, and our common history as a people. The Public Administration therefore should look to the past as prologue to the great public dialogue that inspirits a free society. The Constitution should thus be viewed not as "The Word" but as "The Living Word."

The Public Administration should be neither monolithic nor homogeneous. It must assume a rich diversity of perspectives born of differentiation and specialization and ought to welcome constructive criticism from within and without. Differing perspectives ought to be granted a legitimacy, that is, they ought not to be judged as *ipso facto* self-serving, but as a part of the constitutional heritage of robust public dialogue. In this respect The Public Administration is an analog to the pluralism of the larger political process with all the attendant assets and liabilities plus one: the opportunity and the moral obligation to strive explicitly to achieve the broadest possible public interest, something theories of pluralism trust to an invisible hand. Thus the conflict among the differing perspectives of The Public Administration is a valuable part of the creative tension so essential to a healthy American dialogue.

If The Public Administration asserts and accepts its moral authority and rightful claim to be a constitutionally legitimate participant in the governance process, it can contribute to the correction of a major defect in the Constitution: its unsatisfactory resolution of the problem of representation. This problem was the centerpiece of George Mason's brilliant argument against ratification and was a source of embarrassment to such staunch Federalists as Washington and Hamilton. Both friends and foes of the Constitution wondered how the 65 members of the House would represent more than three million people. Today we ask how 435 members can represent a nation of more than 246 million people. Pluralist theory and the bureaucratic-politics school of thought have tried to suggest that the competition of interest groups is the best assurance of representation of all the people and that the public interest emerges as the vector sum of all interest group pressures. Although such a claim is not without merit, it has never been convincingly demonstrated and has been subjected to devastating criticism. It remains all too painfully clear that not all citizens and interests are represented by interest groups.

In light of this constitutional defect, The Public Administration as an institution of government has as valid a claim to being representative of the people both in a sociological and functional sense as a federal judge appointed for life, freshman congressman narrowly elected by a small percentage of the citizens in southeast Nebraska or a senator from Rhode Island. For that matter The Public Administration may be as representative of the people as a whole as a president elected by a coalition of voting blocs and interest groups claiming victory based on less than 51 percent of the popular vote and 29.9 percent of the eligible voters, which in turn is approximately 19 percent of the total populace. Political commentators have erred in looking for representation from elected officials alone.

It is time for us to advance the proposition that the popular will does not reside solely in elected officials but in a constitutional order that envisions a remarkable variety of legitimate titles to participate in governance. The Public Administration, created by statutes based on this constitutional order, holds one of these titles. Its role, therefore, is not to cower before a sovereign legislative assembly or a sovereign elected executive. Our tradition and our constitution know no such sovereign. Rather the task of The Public Administration is to share in governing wisely and well the *constitutional order* that the framers of the Constitution intended as an expression of the will of the people who alone are sovereign.

The Public Administration and the Public Administrator

We have spoken at length of The Public Administration—we now wish to speak more specifically of how it relates to our ideas about the Public Administrator.

As a critical first point, we need to remind ourselves that the Public Administrator takes an oath to uphold the Constitution of the United States—not the whims of the powerful. This oath initiates administrators into a community created by that Constitution and obliges them to know and support constitutional principles that affect their official spheres of public service. When law empowers rather than commands, that is, when it confers discretion upon administrators instead of issuing specific orders to them, the administrators' oath obliges them to exercise their discretion in a manner that is informed and guided by broad constitutional values as well as more immediate, short-term considerations.

Much has been said in recent years on the development of professionalism in the public administration and its meaning. What is important from the point of view of this essay is not so much whether the Public Administrator is or is not a member of a profession, or whether he or she has achieved a right to claim professional status. Rather, what is important is that the Public Administrator acts in a professional manner in the sense of a concern for the development of competence and standards, an orientation toward service, and a set of values that regards the broadest possible definition of the public interest as a real although problematic trust, and, above all, which holds the maintenance of the constitutional order as a fundamental duty. To act in a professional manner, for the Public Administrator, is to use expertise and competence toward these ends.

The more significant perspective on professionalism is thus to see the Public Administrator as a trustee and a legitimate and significant participant in the governance process of society.

As a trustee the Public Administrator must strive to look beyond both the political pressures of the day and a degrading self-image of mere instrumentalism. He or she should strive for a role that is "critically conscious": purposive in pursuit of the public interest and in maintaining the democratic governance process but disciplined by the rule of law and constitutional tradition of limited government; and conscious of the need at times to prudently accommodate powerful forces that may represent a temporary retreat from, or pause in, pursuit of the broadest possible definition of the public interest. Progress toward both the agency perspective and the broader public interest may not always be steady or forward.

The Public Administrator, however, must be steadfast and persistent, heeding Hamlet's advice to "play to the judicious few," rather than the vociferous many or the powerful few, to play to the long-term public interest rather than the most immediate and powerful pressures. And we need to remind ourselves that the "judicious few" need not be a small, closed, elite group. It has no preordained limits to its size. It is after all, an article of democratic faith—or at least an object of democratic hope—that the judicious few might become the judicious many. It is the duty of the Public Administrator to work to expand the ranks of the judicious few—by stimulating reasoned debate on the meaning of the public interest and by taking advantage of opportunities to facilitate substantive involvement by citizens in the governance process. The judicious few will only become the judicious many when more of the people develop the practical wisdom that is the essence of politics. This wisdom is best learned in the course of public-sphere activity itself. As the success of numerous publicly funded programs run by citizens attests, the administrative state is neither too big nor too complex for meaningful citizen involvement.

In large measure, it is the bureaucrat's faith in technical expertise and in the possibility of comprehensive solutions that makes him or her hesitant to turn to citizens. But the uncertainty and complexity of modern-day governance demand not comprehensiveness but tentative strategies, social interaction, and frequent feedback and adjustment. From this perspective, the postindustrial administrative state is *not only inconsistent* with involvement by citizens, *but it positively discourages it.*

Much has also been written about making the bureaucrat responsive and responsible. The Public Administrator must indeed act responsibly, and this means being responsive to constitutionally and legally valid orders that are specific. Responsiveness also means being attuned to the clientele that are served. The responsiveness of the Public Administrator to either elected officials or clients should not, however, be "seismographic" nor that of a "hired lackey," nor even that of a "faithful servant," for it must be more in order to be responsible in the highest sense of that word. Nor should it be the responsiveness of an artful dodger working between and among the forces resulting from interest group pressures, for it must be more than that. Rather the Public Administrator can only be responsible if his or her responsiveness is that of a trustee of that special perspective shaped by the agency's point of view, a public interest perspective and fidelity to the constitutional heritage.

This means that the responsiveness called for is one that conforms to the Public Administrator's ultimate responsibility, which like that of all governmental officers is to the constitutional order and the democratic governance process. This means that in their role as trustees the Public Administrators may have to incline their agencies' responsiveness toward the president at one point and toward Congress at another, or at other times toward the courts or interest groups that are likely to serve the long-term public interest as the agency sees it. Less often, it may mean that the Public Administrators must act on behalf of a public interest defined more broadly than the Agency Perspective, or on rare occasions they may have to act on behalf of the maintenance of the democratic governance process. This means, in essence, that the Public Administrators may have to play the role of balance wheel in the constitutional order, using their statutory powers and professional expertise to favor whichever participant in the constitutional process needs their help at a given time in history to preserve the purposes of the Constitution itself.

Inevitably some will view The Public Administration merely as a means to status and power and some will pervert their duty into a sinecure. In spite of the inevitable human frailties of a few, despite its erosion by careerism and the fragmenting pressures of specialization, and in spite of its current detractors, The Public Administration has been, and remains, a vocation given meaning in the service of a "cause." In the everyday words of public administration, this cause is characterized as being a "civil servant," "career executive," or "public employee." With a self-conscious shift in the American dialogue we feel that the sense of a calling will grow and flourish in The Public Administration and Public Administrators as never before—more will live "for" it as a "cause" and fewer "off" it from less noble impulses.

Certainly the founders of the Republic viewed public service as a "calling" and as a trusteeship; so did the idealistic reformers who came later in our history: the Populists, the Progressives, and the New Dealers. If we have not yet lost that vision, it is certainly in grave peril.

Much of our loss of transcendent vision has been brought on by our concern for professional status. We have paid a heavy price for adopting too slavishly the trappings of science believed essential to a claim of expertise. A focus on the *means* of governance—as in management science, systems analysis, PPBS, and program evaluation—is important to a claim of expertise. But when we focus on these means to the exclusion of claims of transcendent purposes and moral commitment to community building, or of enhancement of freedom and the improvement of the quality of citizens' lives, we erode the legitimacy of The Public Administration and reduce the Public Administrator to just one more profession or interest group. We have let our vision slip from transcendent purposes and moral commitment to a narrow focus on the application of "value neutral" instrumentalism. It has cost us and the nation dearly.

The code of behavior of the Public Administrator must be broadened to include approaches to practice that will support this transcendent commitment. First, as we have said, administrators must seek to expand opportunities for direct citizen involvement in governance, so that citizens develop the practical wisdom that is the ultimate basis of trust in administrative good faith. Also, administrators must develop personal reflexivity, that is, consciousness of their own values and assumptions and how they affect daily decision making. Such consciousness will enable them to become critical of established institutional practices that inhibit the expansion of freedom and justice, and work toward change where it is possible. Finally, administrators, must be able to give reasons for what they do.

Though established practices may frequently preclude direct dialogue with relevant stakeholders, it is the administrator's responsibility to consider who all these stakeholders may be, what their concerns are, and what reasons he or she would give for a decisive action if dialogue were possible.

The Public Administrator must assume that the human condition can be improved though never perfected. He or she should work for the amelioration of societal problems without expecting quick, cheap, or permanent solutions. The Public Administrator should work with the knowledge that some problems can best be alleviated by outcomes of the market or the use of market-like devices whereas others can best be met by some form of state intervention. Although Public Administrators must be responsive to ideological or party-based views of elected officials on social problems, they must also provide them with sound analysis and feasible options based on their special competence. The Public Administrator should thus be both an analyst and an educator but *not* a philosopher-king or mandarin. He or she must work for the long-term education of elected officials, other actors in the governance process, and citizens at large on matters of public interest, and assume that this will often be a thankless and arduous task.

The Public Administrator should be committed to (1) praxis, critically conscious action or pursuit of goals; and (2) reflectiveness, thoughtful and critical assessment of action taken, in order to learn from experience. Both praxis and reflectiveness are essential to a role that directs its competence toward the kind of transcendent purposes we have outlined. They are also essential to more specific, day-to-day goals of serving the public with grace and dignity, of respecting the public while at the same time respecting one's self and one's peers.

Conclusion

Whether or not the Public Administrator and The Public Administration are living up to the prescriptive ideals we have outlined is a question that must be repeatedly asked and answered as honestly as possible. There are inherent problems and pathologies that we deny or ignore at our peril. Thus, those of us in the academic community associated with The Public Administration have a special task that goes beyond producing the necessary skills and expertise in new members or even helping instill the transcendent purpose. It is the special task of constructive and friendly criticism. It requires caring enough to be critical in a constructive way.

We also have a special responsibility to play a leading role in refocusing the American dialogue, a duty all too neglected of late by most of us. Accordingly we hope this paper will serve in a small way to initiate the desperately needed refocus of the American dialogue, a change essential if we are successfully to conclude Egger's fourth revolution to redefine equity and justice. Seeking to redefine equity and justice in a system that remains in large part capitalistic, which derives much of its momentum from that part, and which has considerable socioeconomic differentiation as both a consequence and catalyst, will be as great a challenge as any democratic society has ever faced. If we are to have any chance of meeting that challenge, our political dialogue must shift from "whether" there ought to be a public administration to what the role of The Public Administration and the Public Administrator should be in the governance of the Republic—as it enters its third and perhaps most perilous century.

Notes

1 The co-authors of this paper bear equal responsibility for the ideas it contains and with one exception are listed alphabetically. Wamsley's name appears first simply because he was assigned the role of faithful scribe.

Camilla Stivers was not one of the authors of theory in the original manuscript that received considerable circulation. As one of our students she criticized the original manuscript because we failed to consider the crucial role citizens should play in The Public Administration and in the shift of our political dialogue. The list of persons whose ideas we have drawn upon is too long to present here, but surely it would begin and end with the names of Dwight Waldo and Norton Long. We decided the best way to deal with the criticism was to include her as co-author and to become her students in this matter.

We wish to thank our many colleagues who provided criticism and encouragement. Particularly helpful were the comments of Phillip Cooper, Bayard Catron, Linda Wolf, Fred Thayer, Philip Schorr, and Eugene Lewis. The faults that remain belong to us; they did all they could to save us. Obviously we are drawing on the thoughts of many other persons in the intellectual community associated with public administration. With a few exceptions noted below, however, we have chosen not to use notes. We do not intend this to be an academic paper but a statement (a manifesto?) that we hope will encourage dialogue.

2 Wilson, Woodrow. "The study of Public Administration," *Political Science Quarterly* 2(2) June 1887: 197–222.

3 We are especially indebted to Professor Bayard Catron for this point. Indeed, most of the words of the foregoing three sentences are his. We could do little to improve on them. Source: correspondence with the authors.
4 Our thanks to Linda Wolf for this point. Correspondence with the authors.
5 Ibid.

Part III

Issues and Controversies Shaping the Constitutional School

6 Reflections on John Rohr's "Regime Values," Neorepublican Freedom, and Public Administration

Michael W. Spicer

Over three decades ago, John Rohr (1976) argued that, in thinking about public administration ethics, public administrators should consult what he termed our "regime values." Important among these, for him, are our values of freedom, property, and equality. However, Rohr also acknowledged that the meaning of these values was never precise and always contestable and that they could only be understood by examining the way in which we have historically argued about them. It was, for this reason, Rohr argued, that the best way to understand our regime values was to examine the decisions of the U.S. Supreme Court. He noted how "in studying Supreme Court opinions, the bureaucrat will be exposed to many conflicting interpretations of American values" (p. 404), and how "concurring and dissenting opinions offer the bureaucrat alternative ways of looking at the same problem and thereby help him to avoid the danger of accepting dogmatic assertions uncritically" (p. 403).

Rohr's views reflect an essentially pluralist view of ethics and point to the limitations and dangers of monistic approaches that seek to ground public administration ethics on the pursuit of any single regime value or, for that matter, any single understanding of the meaning of that value. As an illustration of how things can go awry in such monistic approaches, this essay will examine critically the neorepublican conception of freedom as non-domination that has been advanced recently by political theorists such as Richard Pettit (1999) and Quentin Skinner (1998). It is argued, consistent with Rohr's views, that this single-minded conception of freedom can deflect attention away from the conflicts in values or conceptions of the good, including conflicts among our conceptions of freedom, that seem to characterize our moral and political experience.

Neorepublican Freedom

Neorepublicanism has been defined as the "attempt by current political scientists, philosophers, historians, lawyers, and others to draw on a classical republican tradition in the development of an attractive public philosophy intended for contemporary purposes" (Lovett & Pettit, 2009, p. 11). These writers see themselves as drawing upon a tradition of republican thought within European history that, in their view, has its origins in the neo-roman political ideas of Renaissance Italy, most notably the writings of Machiavelli, and that also helped shape English, as well as American republican political thinking and practice. Central to neorepublicanism is the notion that freedom should be thought of as an absence of domination by others or an absence of dependence upon others, as opposed to simply an absence of interference by others or what has often been called negative freedom. Under the neorepublican conception of freedom, to be free is to be "a person without a master or *dominus* … one who does not live under the arbitrary will or domination of others" (p. 12). This was the vision of freedom, according to Skinner, that was advanced by opponents of royal prerogative in seventeenth-century England, who held that you need not "suffer … overt coercion in order to forfeit your civil liberty" (1998, p. 69) and who recognized that "to live in a condition of dependence is in itself a source and a form of constraint" because "as soon as you recognize that you are living in such a condition, this will serve in itself to constrain you from exercising a number of your civil rights" (p. 84).

As Pettit notes, this idea of freedom as the absence of domination by or dependence upon others can be seen as responding to the grievance of "having to live in a manner that leaves you vulnerable to some ill that the other is in a position arbitrarily to impose" (1999, pp. 4–5). It is the type of grievance, for example:

> expressed by the wife who finds herself in a position where her husband can beat her at will, and without any possibility of redress; by the employee who dare not raise a complaint against an employer … by the debtor who has to depend on the grace of the moneylender, or the bank official, for avoiding utter destitution and ruin; and by the welfare dependant who finds that they are vulnerable to the caprice of a counter clerk for whether or not their children will receive meal vouchers.
>
> (1999, pp. 4–5)

In emphasizing the potential for non-interference with a person's actions by others, rather than actual interference, neorepublicans seem, in some respects, to advance a more expansive or broader notion of freedom than advocates of negative freedom. However, in other respects, their notion of freedom is notably narrower. In particular, many neorepublicans argue that interference with the actions of persons need not actually constrain their freedom provided it is carried out in a manner that is "non-arbitrary." In particular, they note that interference need not reduce freedom so long as it is "forced to track the interests and ideas of the person suffering the interference" or "at least forced to track the relevant ones" (Pettit, 1999, p. 55). From this perspective while:

> laws may impose taxation on all, coerce all with the threat of punishment for disobedience, and impose penalties on those who in fact disobey, ... such interferences will not be arbitrary if they are formed in accordance with the will of the subjects and framed so as to protect those subjects from domination from others.
>
> (Lovett & Pettit, 2009, p. 16)

Neorepublicans believe their idea of freedom as the absence of domination rather than interference by others lends support to a substantial role for government in limiting the domination of citizens by private individuals or organizations. This role includes, in their view, providing citizens "a reasonably prosperous economic life ... a sustainable [physical] environment ... a decent system of education and information," as well as "security on social and medical fronts" (Lovett & Pettit, 2009, p. 20). Moreover, neorepublicans see government as having a special responsibility to "guard the economically and socially vulnerable against domination" (p. 21). They believe that government should attend to the "special needs of empowerment that certain members of the society might have: for example, women, workers, and minorities" (p. 20).

Despite this apparently robust and energetic role for the state, neorepublicans do not worry that a state, constituted in this fashion, would ever become "too powerful and intrusive" because, in their view, "self-limitation is built right into the neorepublican ideal" (Lovett & Pettit, 2009, p. 22). In this regard, neorepublicans generally support the types of constitutional protections for citizens favored, not just by republicans, but by liberals and others, protections such as the separation of powers and the rule of law. However, they also favor an active citizenry, strongly motivated by republican ideals, arguing that "widespread enjoyment of republican freedom is most likely to be optimized" where "citizens are committed to that ideal, and each is willing to do his or her part in realizing it" (p. 23). Furthermore, they look to what they term a "contestatory" form of democracy to check the discretionary power of public officials. As they see it, citizens should have "not only electoral rights but also the effective opportunity to contest the decisions of their representatives" (p. 25). This requires, in their view, that "relevant decision-makers," including legislators, courts, and bureaucrats, "present reasons for their resolutions" and that these resolutions be "subject to open public debate" (p. 25).

The Limits of Neorepublicanism

While this idea of freedom as the absence of domination rather than as the absence of interference is attractive, it is nonetheless problematic in that it fails to take proper account of our experience of value conflict or value pluralism. Neorepublicans treat freedom from domination not simply as an important value, but elevate it as "a single paramount value" (Lovett &

Pettit, 2009, p. 18), a value that can and should be, to use their words, the "supreme ideal for the state" (Pettit, 1999, p. 9). A particular problem here is the neorepublican claim that government coercion of citizens need not reduce and, in fact, can actually promote their freedom so long as such coercion is carried out in a "non-arbitrary" manner. Rather than seeking to justify the loss of individual freedom entailed by government coercion in terms of other important values, neorepublicans appear to want to deny altogether the importance if not the reality of any loss of freedom at all, provided that such government coercion is not arbitrary. In doing so, they appear to deny any legitimacy or respect at all to that felt sense of loss that ordinary citizens experience in their own lives when they find themselves deprived of their negative freedom, however justifiably, in the pursuit of other important values. As Charles Larmore has argued, "ceasing to live at the mercy of powerful individuals" may well be, as neorepublicans such as Pettit claim, "of far greater moment than simply living unobstructed by others," but, even if this were true, "freedom from interference is not nothing" (2001, p. 234). In this respect, neorepublicans overlook Isaiah Berlin's important insight that where clashes between different kinds of freedom occur, "it is better to face this uncomfortable fact than to ignore it" or to "attribute it to some deficiency on our part" (1969, p. l).

Furthermore, the extensive role for government in the protection of freedom from domination apparently sanctioned by neorepublicans is itself potentially dangerous to the value of freedom. This is because of the sheer ubiquity of power relations, or instances where somebody might possibly dominate somebody else, which must exist within any complex society. In the world we ordinarily experience, there is, after all, always somebody who has the capacity or power to interfere in our actions in an arbitrary fashion, even if they normally choose not to exercise that power. As Geoffrey Brennan and Loren Lomasky put it,

> To live among other people is to be vulnerable to arbitrary encroachment by muggers, thieves, road-raging motorists, and jealous lovers. Telemarketers interrupt quiet evenings at home, proselytizing brethren knock on one's door to proffer salvation, and spam artists fill up email boxes.
>
> (2006, p. 243)

Given this ubiquity of opportunities for possible interference in our lives by others, to argue that government should engage in the pursuit of freedom as non-domination without regard to our other values and that it should attempt somehow to regulate all relationships in all cases where others might possibly interfere with our actions, even if they do not do so or even are unlikely to do so, would seem to invite the creation of an overbearing and intrusive state that would itself likely seriously encroach upon freedom in the sense that we normally understand the word. Marilyn Friedman

(2008), a feminist philosopher, recognizes this when she argues that "any state that uses its power to suppress all the various capacities that people have for dominating each other would be acting so pervasively in people's lives that it would amount to a totalitarian police state" (p. 251). Moreover, an overly zealous pursuit of neorepublican freedom is not only potentially dangerous to our other conceptions of freedom. It can also undermine the positive role that relationships of dependency on others sometimes play in our lives. As Friedman reminds us:

> Dependency relations are necessary throughout human life ... Any caretaker, who has some power greater than that of the one for whom she cares and whose needs she meets, also ... has the capacity to interfere in that someone's life without regard to the latter's interests or ideas. The capacity to clean someone's wound is also the capacity to infect it. The capacity to help someone climb the stairs is also the capacity to throw her down the stairs. An excess of power relative to another seems ... to be a necessary feature of relationships in which some people care for and meet the needs of others.
>
> (2008, p. 251)

Defending dependency, in this way, of course, is not to romanticize it; nor is it to downplay the cruelty and damage that may result from exploitative human relationships. It is simply to point out that dependency on others can, sometimes, have a positive value for human beings and that this value must inevitably sometimes come into conflict with that of freedom where freedom is thought of as the absence of such dependency.

Implications

In short, while freedom from domination may well be a worthwhile value for public officials to pursue, to treat such freedom, as neorepublicans urge, as a "supreme ideal for the state" is to neglect other important human values. In this regard, perhaps the most useful idea advanced by neorepublicanisn is not so much any particular conception of freedom but rather its emphasis on contestation, an idea also advanced by more traditional republicans such as Machiavelli. This is because political contestation can help to protect not only freedom of individuals and groups from domination by others, but also other kinds of freedoms, including freedom from interference by others as well as the plurality of other values or conceptions of the good that human beings seem to hold important. While political contestation can never guarantee the protection of these values, where there is political contestation, government leaders and the public officials who serve them are more likely to be more responsive to a broader range of these values and more sensitive to the conflicts that inevitably occur between them.

The foregoing argument lends support to Rohr's skepticism regarding any attempt to derive an "operational understanding of the public interest derived from some common metaphysical premise" (1976, p. 404). It also lends support to his view that in seeking guidance for public administration from our Constitution, we should look to "the *argument* of the founding, rather than its outcome" (Rohr, 1986, p. 9). By examining the Constitution, not as some sort of monistic blueprint for administrative action, but rather as an ongoing contestation over the meaning and weight that we attach to different regime values, we can resist the temptation to overemphasize some of these values at the expense of others. This provides a valuable intellectual dimension to the advancement of a Constitutional School of American public administration, and in doing so, we can come to appreciate better Rohr's view that "there is no one 'authoritative' interpretation of the American experience that all bureaucrats must adopt. What is important is that they accept the moral obligation to put themselves in touch with the values of the American people" (1976, p. 404).

References

Berlin, I. 1969. *Four essays on liberty*. New York: Oxford University Press.

Brennan, G. & Lomasky, L. 2006. Against reviving republicanism. *Politics, philosophy, and economics* 5: 221–252.

Friedman, M. 2008. Pettit's civic republicanism and male domination. In C. Laborde & John Maynor (eds), *Republicanism and political theory*. Malden, MA: Blackwell, pp. 246–268.

Larmore, C. 2001. A critique of Philip Pettit's republicanism. *Philosophical issues* 11: 229–243.

Lovett, F. & Pettit, P. 2009. Neorepublicanism: A normative and institutional research program. *Annual review of political science* 12: 11–29.

Pettit, P. 1999. *Republicanism a theory of freedom and government*. Oxford: Oxford University Press.

Rohr, J.A. 1976. The study of ethics in the P.A. curriculum. *Public administration review* 36: 398–406.

Rohr, J.A. 1986. *To run a constitution*. Lawrence, Kansas: University Press of Kansas.

Skinner, Q. 1998. *Liberty before liberalism*. Cambridge: Cambridge University Press.

Legitimacy, History, and Logic

Public Administration and the Constitution

Michael W. Spicer and Larry D. Terry

From: *Public Administration Review* 53:3 (1993): 230–246.

The bureaucrat bashing of both the Carter and Reagan administrations, as well as the national celebration commemorating the bicentennial of the U.S. Constitution, created an avalanche of scholarly activity within the public administration community. Much of this scholarship focused on defending administrative institutions of government against attacks perpetrated by a coalition of antibureaucratic forces (Farazmand, 1989; Rourke, 1987). A defense was mounted on two fronts. On one front, writers went to great lengths to document and publicize the adverse effects of these attacks on administrative agencies (i.e., Lane and Wolf, 1990, Chap. 1; Wolf, 1987; Wildavsky, 1988; Rosen, 1986 and 1983). On the other front, scholars of the Constitutional School of public administration (most notably John Rohr and his colleagues at Blacksburg) have fought to change the perception that the modern administrative state lacked constitutional legitimacy by linking it to the founding of the American Republic (Rohr, 1986; Wamsley et al., 1990; Cook, 1992). Although strategies on both fronts have enjoyed a measure of success, we are especially interested in the Constitutional School because of its widening influence in American public administration.

The purpose of this article is to argue that the Constitutional School is vulnerable to attacks because of the Idealists' method of historical explanation used by many scholars to explain the intentions and actions of the founding fathers. This method poses a problem for the Constitutional School because it fosters a romanticized view of the founders, which in turn raises questions about their conduct and character. Such questions, especially those relating to the issue of slavery, weaken the force of the argument offered by Constitutional School scholars. We contend that one need not rely solely on a purely historical approach to legitimate the administrative state in terms of constitutional principles. Other approaches may serve our purposes and deserve serious consideration as well. We argue that an active public administration may also be grounded in the logic of a constitution in general that pertains to the checking of power. This approach transcends history and the unfortunate moral legacy of the founders.

We begin by discussing the Idealists' method of historical explanation in order to show that Constitutional School scholars use this method to explain the intent and actions of the founders. We identify a problem with this method and argue that it perpetuates a distorted image of the founders. We then discuss the central logic of a constitution to see how this might provide a role for public administration. We believe that the logic of a constitution is about restraining power and that an active role for public administration may be justified provided it serves this purpose.

Historical Explanation by Method of Empathetic Understanding

Philosophers of history have invested a great deal of intellectual energy debating what they call historical explanation. This highly specialized area of scholarly inquiry is concerned with the philosophical analysis of methods used to explain, as well as interpret, events and human actions in history. Philosophers focus their attention on the question: What logical criteria must a historical explanation meet if it is to be an adequate one? (Weingartner, 1967). An influential group of philosophers known as the Idealists argue that the adequacy of a historical explanation should be judged by the extent to which it provides a satisfactory understanding of human acts.[1] In a rejection of the positivistic notion of historical explanation the Idealists assert that historians must seek to understand the motives, intentions and, in turn, the character of persons involved in the events they want to explain. According to the Idealists, such an understanding can only be acquired by the method of empathy. This method of empathetic understanding requires that historians imagine themselves in the place of the person involved in the event; try to "realize as completely as possible the circumstances under which they acted, and the motives that influenced their actions" (Hempel, 1953, p. 352). William Dray, an articulate spokesman for the Idealists, describes the method this way:

> To understand human action, ... it is necessary for the inquirer somehow to discover its "thought-side;" it is not sufficient merely to know the pattern of overt behavior. The historian must *penetrate* behind appearances, achieve *insight* into the situation, identify himself sympathetically with the protagonist, *project* himself imaginatively into the situation. He must *relive, re-enact, re-think, re-experience* the hopes, fears, plans, desires, views, intentions, etc., of those he seeks to understand.
>
> (1957, p. 119 [emphasis in original])

A consensus exists among philosophers of history that empathetic understanding is the method of choice for many historians as well as laypersons. A close examination of the writings of prominent Constitutional School scholars suggests that they rely on this method. It is difficult to say with any degree of certainty that Constitutional School scholars consciously follow the Idealists' method of empathetic understanding. We can say, however, that the method used by many scholars fits the description of what the Idealists do. The work of John A. Rohr (1986) is illustrative.

Rohr (1986) states at the outset that his purpose is to "legitimate the administrative state in terms of constitutional principles" (p. ix). In building his case, Rohr constructs an elegant case for legitimacy based on the "great public argument of 1787/88" (p. 9). Drawing on the writings of both Federalists and Anti-Federalists, Rohr argues that the blending of powers in administrative agencies is not inconsistent with the founders' notion of a separation of powers. He further argues that the administrative state performs a balancing role originally intended for the U.S. Senate and also serves as a remedy to the limits on representation provided by the House of Representatives.

It is apparent to the careful reader that Rohr uses the Idealists' method of empathetic understanding to explain the actions and intentions of the founders. In fact, Rohr alerts us of his intentions when he says:

> In examining the founding arguments for hints of what we call the administrative state, I will look to Publius and others to determine (1) what it was they wanted from the new Constitution and (2) what they thought they were providing. Conversely, the writings and speeches of the Anti-Federalist will tell us what they feared from the new Constitution and what they thought they were getting … . These arguments are important for determining the intent of the framers for specific parts of the Constitution.
>
> (1986, p. 10)

In a detailed analysis of the writings of the Federalists, Anti-Federalists and the text of the Constitution, Rohr employs a narrative storytelling style to discover the thought-side of the founders. Throughout the book, he makes a point of telling the reader what the founders had in mind. He tries to realize as completely as possible the circumstances under which they acted, and the motives which influenced their actions. Moreover, Rohr seeks to rethink the hopes, fears, desires, and intentions of the men who participated in the founding.

Although the Idealists' method of empathetic understanding used by Rohr and other constitutional scholars has proven its explanatory value, this method is not immune from criticism (White, 1965, Chap. 1; Hempel, 1953; Fischer, 1970, Chap. 7). Particularly important from our perspective is the criticism that empathetic understanding fosters an incomplete and romantic view of historical figures. David H. Fischer (1970, p. 199) criticizes historical writers for portraying historical figures as infallible, calculated individuals who possessed (or should have possessed) superior intellectual and intuitive powers. Historical figures are said to have known and understood precisely the motives and intentions governing their actions as well as the future consequences of such actions. It is an understatement to say that this view of human behavior expects too much and explains too little. Fischer (1970) points out that scholars concerned with the founding of the American Republic often commit the historians' fallacy[2] when attempting to explain the motive and intentions of the founders:

> There are many historians who have committed the historians' fallacy by celebrating the *celebration* of the founders. Marvin Meyers ... came close to interpreting John Adams in such a way that Adams recognized himself to be a Founding Father with the clarity that we possess in retrospect. Mr. Meyers suggests that Adams had a clear and accurate sense of the way in which the republic would develop after its founding and that both of these insights were intertwined in his motivational patterns and ideological responses. It is as if the American revolutionary slogan were "Liberty, Equality, Paternity" and the Fathers of the Republic were driven by a sense of fatherhood and by an accurate premonition of the career of their republican child.
>
> (Gellhorn, 1986, p. 211 [emphasis added])

Fischer's observations are instructive as they direct attention to a flaw in the writings of Constitutional School scholars. If one accepts Fischer's arguments, then it is possible to conclude that Constitutional School scholars have also committed the historians' fallacy by fostering a romanticized view of the founding fathers. For example, Rohr writes of the "sanctity" and "moral vitality" of the founding period. In doing so, the founders, by virtue of their authorship of the Constitution, are portrayed as noble men who possessed superior minds, characters, morals, and ideals. This romanticized view of the Constitution and the founders is understandable. As Kristol (1987) has noted, the Constitution, along with the flag and Declaration of Independence, enjoy an almost sacramental status in the eyes of citizens. Kristol argues that "there is a spirit of the Constitution, enveloping the text and transforming it in a covenanting document, a pillar of the American civil religion" (p. 5). Similarly, Rohr (1986) states that "the Constitution is more than a legal document: it is a covenant as well as a contract" (p. x).

The romanticized view of the founders is problematic and makes the Constitutional School vulnerable to attack because it ignores their conduct and character. Nowhere is this problem perhaps more apparent than with respect to the issue of slavery.

John Hope Franklin (1989), the distinguished American historian, has argued that the founders were "frail, fallible human beings, and—at the time—utterly indifferent to the great causes they claim to serve" (p. 160). Franklin reminds us that the founders "created a tragically flawed revolutionary document and a constitution that did not bestow the blessings of liberty" on all of the American people (p. 161). He suggests that the romantic view of the framers advanced by many writers ignores the fact that the "founding fathers made serious mistakes that have greatly affected the course of our national history from that time to the present" (p. 154). In expressing his objections to the romanticization of the founders, Franklin states:

> We may admire them for many things: their courage and bravery in the military struggle against Britain; their imaginative creativity in forging a new instrument of government; their matchless service to a cause that captured the imagination of people around the world. This does not follow, however, that we should admire them for betraying the ideals to which they gave lip service, for speaking eloquently at one moment for the brotherhood of man and in the next moment denying it to their black brothers who fought by their side in their darkest hour of peril, and for degrading the human spirit by equating five black men with three white men or equating a black man with a horse!
>
> (1989, pp. 160–161)

Herbert J. Storing (1986), the distinguished scholar who has written extensively in the area of American political thought, constitutional law, and public administration, is critical of Franklin's harsh reference to the founders' seemingly hypocritical stance on slavery. Storing concedes that the founders compromised on slavery and allowed the evil to enter the Constitution through the back door. As Storing sees it, this accommodation does not indicate that the founders sanctioned or willingly gave their moral approval of slavery. Storing states that:

> [i]n their accommodation to slavery, the founders limited and confined it and carefully withheld any indication of moral approval, while they built a Union that they thought was the greatest instrument of human liberty ever made, that they thought would lead and did in fact lead to the extinction of Negro slavery.
>
> (1986, p. 224)

In a direct attack on Franklin's argument, Storing continues:

> I think that Professor Franklin is wrong when he says that "they [the founders] simply would not or could not see how ridiculous their position was." They saw it all right, and they saw better than their critics how difficult it was to extricate themselves from that position in a reasonably equitable way. But they saw, too, a deeper irony: these masters knew they were writing the texts in which their slaves would learn their rights.
>
> (1986, p. 224)

Storing also argues that the problem is not that the founders "betrayed their principles," as Franklin and others contend. Rather, the "problem lies ... in the principles themselves, namely, the principles relating to individual rights" (p. 224).

This is not the time or place to engage in a lengthy discourse on whether the founders were hypocrites or not, for to do so would lead us astray from the task at hand. It is sufficient to say that the founders' conduct with respect to the issue of slavery cannot be easily dismissed, as a congeries of different scholars have pointed out (Loury, 1987; Roche, 1961). This poses a problem for the Constitutional School. It may be argued that the Thirteenth and Fourteenth Amendments have superseded the founders' ideas about slavery and the rights of African-Americans so that the founders' intent is no longer part of the constitutional heritage. Nonetheless, those who rely solely on the founders' work to support a constitutional vision of government or public administration remain vulnerable to the charge of romanticization. If we are to buttress the argument for a legitimate and active public administration anchored in constitutional principles, we need to continue searching for methods that will allow us to separate the quality of the constitutional argument from the character and conduct of the founders.

The Logic of a Constitution

An alternative approach is to make explicit the central logic of a constitution in general and see to what extent the constitutional argument of the founders reflects that logic. Implications of the logic can then be derived. This approach differs from that taken by the Constitutional School, which draws on a variety of arguments made by the founders to legitimize public administration. This article seeks to go beyond the founders' arguments to develop a logic of constitutions in general that can stand apart from those arguments and to see if this logic can be used to legitimize public administration. Whereas the Constitutional School seeks simply to develop an argument about the constitutional role of public administration that is consistent with arguments made by the founders, our approach seeks to examine the role of public administration in light of the logic or purpose of a constitution. In short, we seek to explain the logic rather than the history of constitutions.

When we refer to the logic of a constitution, we mean the reason or reasons why a community of rational individuals would agree in the first place to develop a constitution to guide their political order at all. To the extent that interpretations of the founders' writings are consistent with the logic of a constitution, based on agreement among rational individuals, then their significance as a basis for normative analysis is surely enhanced. Agreement or consensus among rational individuals, after all, provides an important criterion for normative analysis. Certainly, if it is not possible to interpret the founders' writings in the context of such a logic, then the normative significance of these writings becomes far less clear.

In order to see why rational individuals might agree to develop a constitution, it is important to define what is meant here by a constitution. A constitution, for purposes of this analysis, can be defined as a set of rules that govern the formulation and administration of public policies. In other words, a constitution sets the rules of the game for the public policy process. As such, constitutional rules may be written or unwritten. What is crucial is that participants in the policy process agree to be bound by such rules. The effect of constitutional rules is to limit the discretionary power available to government officials. Some constitutional rules may simply prohibit or block government officials from taking certain policy options. For example, the Bill of Rights prohibits the government from taking certain actions against citizens. In other cases, constitutional rules may make it more difficult to pursue certain policy options by requiring assent from a number of different groups of political leaders. Such rules limit discretionary power by providing in essence a number of potential veto points in the policy process. Constitutional rules providing for a separation of powers or a federal structure of government are examples.

To ask why rational individuals would agree to develop a constitution, then, is to ask why they would agree to limit the discretionary power of government officials. The reason advanced by contractarian economists such as James Buchanan and Gordon Tullock (1962) is that government officials can be expected to pursue their own economic self-interest, even when it is at the expense of citizens (see also Brennan and Buchanan, 1985). As a result, when individuals cede coercive powers to government to obtain certain public goods, they will recognize that government officials may have an incentive to use such powers to exploit them. In other words, they will recognize that the activities of government are both a source of potential value and a source of potential exploitation and, therefore, seek some limits on government power. This exploitation may take such forms as oppressive taxation, expropriation, discrimination in the provision of government services, or political violence.

Furthermore, the electoral process will not be seen as providing an adequate check on discretionary power. According to contractarian economists, majority rule does not prevent exploitation but merely changes its form. In particular, majority rule provides an incentive for groups in society to form majority coalitions that can then use government to secure benefits for themselves while shifting costs to minorities. As a result, rational individuals will see the necessity for constitutional rules beyond those providing for elections and will seek to limit the discretionary power of even a democratically elected government.

The notion that actors in the political process pursue their own economic interests is controversial among scholars in political science and public administration. However, it should be noted that, even if rational individuals expected that government officials would typically not pursue their economic interests at the expense of citizens, they might still desire constitutional rules as a form of insurance against at least the risk of an exploitative government; a government which potentially could destroy both their property and lives. Furthermore, when individual policy preferences are diverse, even the presence of public spiritedness in the policy process does not provide an adequate check on public power. Ideological and religious groups, for example, may seek to use government to impose their vision of a good society on others who disagree with them and so impose costs upon them. Indeed, an argument can be made that, in fact, zealotry may be more likely to lead to exploitative government than the pursuit of economic self-interest (Finer, 1941).

A further related reason why rational individuals might agree to develop a constitution is that they will recognize that, because of uncertainty regarding the effects of public policies, even a government which shares their policy preferences may make errors that lead them to bear unanticipated costs. Uncertainty regarding the effects of public policy is particularly important for policies that seek to change or modify private behavior. Examples here include monetary and fiscal policies designed to promote economic growth or educational programs that seek to improve the economic conditions of poorer individuals. As a result of uncertainty, constitutional rules which check discretionary power may be viewed as a desirable means of limiting the costs arising from policy errors.

The notion that rules may be developed as a means of coping with uncertainty has been advanced by Friedrich Hayek (1973). According to Hayek, rules governing human conduct are "adaptations to the impossibility of anyone taking conscious account of all the particular facts which enter into the order of a society" (p. 13). They serve an evolutionary function in helping communities survive in the face of uncertainty. Ronald Heiner (1983) has made this point more formally in examining the origins of predictable behavior. According to Heiner's model, individuals rely on rules because of uncertainty produced by a gap between their competence and the difficulty of problems to be solved. It is rational for an individual to depart from a rule-governed behavior only when the expected gain from selecting a correct action at that time exceeds the expected loss from selecting an incorrect action. The higher the degree of uncertainty, the less likely this is to be true and the more likely is the individual to rely on the rule. Heiner, interestingly enough, recognizes the constitutional implications of his theory and defines constitutionalism as "the design of rule mechanisms to restrict the flexibility of government to react to whatever influences might prompt it to engage in vulnerable activities" (p. 586).

Rational individuals will agree to develop a constitution because they wish to limit the discretionary power available to government officials. A set of constitutional rules, by checking discretionary power, limits the costs which government can impose on individuals, either as a result of exploitative policies or as a result of policy errors inevitable in an environment of uncertainty. Although the foregoing stresses the potential costs that government can impose on its citizens, this should not be taken as an endorsement of a laissez-faire state or a night-watchman form of government. On the contrary, the development of appropriate rules on discretionary power by government officials would be expected to lead rational individuals to endorse a much larger scope of government activity in terms of functions than would be the case in the absence of such rules. Indeed, in the absence of rules on government power, rational individuals might never cede any coercive power to government.

The Logic and the Founders

Whatever the motives and intents of the founders, it is not difficult to find arguments made by them which are at least consistent with the logic of a constitution as developed here. James Madison's argument for the Union was based on the notion that an extended republic would make it more difficult for various factions in society to use majority rule to exploit citizens. As Madison noted:

> Extend the sphere, and you take in a greater variety of parties and interests; you make it less probable that a majority of the whole will have a common motive to invade the rights of other citizens; or if such a common motive exists, it will be more difficult for all who feel it to discover their strength, and to act in unison with each other.
>
> (Wills, 1987, p. 48)

Madison's argument for a stronger central government is based on its role in checking the abuse of discretionary power by majority factions in state legislatures. At the same time, he also argued for a separation of powers as a means of checking the power of majority interests at the federal level. Separation of powers is desirable, according to Madison, because "ambition must be made to counteract ambition." Madison's constitution is designed to overcome the "defect of better motives" by providing for "opposite and rival interests" (Wills, 1987, p. 263).

Although Alexander Hamilton is frequently portrayed as a proponent of both a strong federal government and a strong executive, his arguments also reflect a concern with the need to check political power. Hamilton noted that a "spirit of faction which is apt to mingle its poison in the deliberations of all bodies of men will often hurry the persons of whom they are composed into improprieties and excesses, for which they would blush in a private capacity" (Wills, 1987, pp. 72–73). Hamilton's argument for a strong executive is based upon his assessment of the dangers of unrestrained legislative power. He argued that an energetic executive was essential to "the protection of property against those irregular and high-handed combinations, which sometimes interrupt the ordinary course of justice" and to "the security of liberty against the enterprise and assaults of ambition, of faction and of anarchy" (Wills, 1987, p. 355). Finally, Hamilton justified his argument for an executive veto on the grounds that "the injury which may possibly be done by defeating a few good laws will be amply compensated by the advantage of preventing a few bad ones" (Wills, 1987, p. 373).

This concern with the need to check political power was echoed by the Anti-Federalists. They differed with the Federalists in arguing that the Constitution would not provide an adequate check on federal government power, not with the need to check power. Brutus, in his critique of federal legislative power, warned that "power lodged in the hands of rulers to be used at their discretion, is almost always exercised to the oppression of the people, and the aggrandizement of themselves" and that "powerful checks" were necessary to prevent the abuse of political power (Ketcham, 1986, p. 331). Similarly, Cato noted that "rulers in all governments will erect an interest separate from the ruled, which will have a tendency to enslave them" (Ketcham, 1986, p. 324).

Public Administration and the Checking of Power

The emphasis here on the role of a constitution in checking the abuse of political power is well known among political scientists, who may even wonder why it is necessary to dwell on it here. However, the checking role of the U.S. Constitution, while acknowledged, has not always been stressed in recent writings by public administration scholars. John Rohr (1986), for example, argues that too much emphasis has been placed on the founders' fear of governmental abuse of power and that it is necessary to neutralize this aspect of the framers' argument if "we are to legitimate the administrative state" (p. 7). Rohr's argument on the separation of powers reflects his desire to justify the exercise of executive, legislative, and judicial power by administrative agencies rather than a concern with the abuse of power. Indeed, while he argues that public administration fulfills a role originally intended for the Senate, Rohr does not seem to view this role primarily as one of checking power, noting that "neither a Senate nor a bureaucracy that resists popular whim is a likely candidate for plaudits today" (p. 39). Also, David Hart (1989), in seeking a constitutional basis for his philosophy of civic humanism, argues that the founders set a model for governance "that relied heavily upon virtue, intelligence and persuasion" (p. 104). He acknowledges but clearly deemphasizes the founders' arguments concerning human fallibility and the need to check power.

Whereas some public administration writers have deemphasized the Constitution's role in checking power, others have been critical of it and have viewed it as a hindrance to the development of a strong and legitimate administrative state. Woodrow Wilson (1956), for example, saw the separation of powers as a constitutional defect that impeded effective government action. He argued that "the federal government lacks strength because its powers are divided, lacks promptness because its authorities are multiplied, lacks wieldiness because its processes are roundabout, lacks efficiency because its responsibility is indistinct and its action without competent direction" (p. 206). More recently, Lynton Caldwell (1976) has suggested that our constitutional heritage may be inadequate in light of the contemporary challenges facing government. According to Caldwell, "It has not been the excess of power but defect of responsibility that has most threatened the national welfare" (p. 487). Richard Stillman is perhaps one of the sharpest critics of the constitutional emphasis on checking power. He argues against the notion that the state must be "chained and immobilized to the ancient verities of the Founding Fathers" and cautions against "clinging to antiquated republican solutions for contemporary governance" (Stillman, 1989, p. 83). He sees the Constitution as producing a "stateless" government directed towards preventing the corruption of public power. According to Stillman (1990), such statelessness impedes effective government action by "permitting delays, stalemates, cross-purposes in actions, and inefficiency" (p. 165). He also suggests that our preference for statelessness unduly restricts our thinking realistically about public administration and its importance to public welfare.

Public administration writers have either tended to deemphasize the role of the Constitution in checking discretionary power or have been critical of it. The foregoing may raise doubts about the possibility of providing constitutional legitimacy for public administration. However, the notion that focusing on checking discretionary power is somehow inconsistent with an active and energetic public administration is by no means self-evident.

Toward Legitimacy

If it is accepted that the logic of a constitution is about restraining discretionary power, then an active role for public administration may be justified provided it serves that purpose. It follows, then, that administrative discretion may be justified on the constitutional grounds that it sometimes enables public administrators to modify, delay, or resist the directives of political leaders in a lawful manner. Such a role may initially strike some as elitist or undemocratic. It is, however, quite consistent with the logic of a constitution as we have interpreted it. If checks on the power of political leaders are justified because even leaders are prone to human weaknesses, then there is no *a priori* reason why such checks should not include the exercise of significant administrative discretion. As the provider of public services to citizens, public bureaucracies can determine the character of government to a significant extent. They can be the instrument by which government serves or burdens citizens. Administrative discretion, then, can be useful in helping limit the discretion of political leaders to impose costs on citizens.

This does not mean that administrators should ignore specific directives issued by elected leaders. Neither does it rule out a generally cooperative relationship between elected leaders and administrators. Rational individuals would never agree to constitutional rules that produced a runaway bureaucracy. However, the logic of a constitution does suggest that public administrators are empowered to raise questions with elected leaders, to try to persuade them to sometimes change course and to interpret directives in a manner, which permits them to limit the abuse of power by elected officials.

The notion that public administrators should use their discretion to resist particular directives of political leaders is by no means novel. George Frederickson (1971) and other writers in *Toward a New Public Administration* have expressed concerns about public administration being used as an instrument of repression. Similarly, Frederickson and Hart (1985), in discussing the ethics of administrative behavior, point to the resistance of Danish civil servants to their Nazi leaders during the German occupation as an example of the type of bureaucratic heroism that they would like to see in the United States. At one point, they ask, "But would there not have been real drama if American local government officials had simply refused to discriminate against black people in the 1950s" (p. 549). Although Frederickson and Hart's vision of public administration is perhaps more revolutionary than the one we present, seeming sometimes perhaps to condone even actions outside the law, their notion of public administration as a check on the abuse of political power is consistent with the logic of a constitution as discussed here.

Consistent with the logic of a constitution, however, the exercise of administrative discretion must itself be subject to limits. After all, while administrative discretion may serve as a check on the discretionary power of elected leaders, it too is subject to abuse and error and, therefore, rational individuals would see limits as desirable. Administrative discretion may be checked by the development of bureaucratic rules and procedures, or red tape, which reduce the ability of public administrators to treat citizens in an arbitrary fashion and to enrich themselves at the expense of citizens. Administrative discretion may also be checked to some degree by the power of political leaders to withhold funds from bureaucracies for certain activities. The point is that, while a case can be made for administrative discretion on constitutional grounds, it is a case for constrained discretion. Even the late Ludwig von Mises (1944), a strong critic of both bureaucracy and government intervention, interestingly enough, conceded that administrative discretion need not be a problem provided that it is exercised according to rules that limit arbitrary action by administrators and provided that elected leaders maintain budgetary control.

The foregoing argument is not entirely inconsistent with those made by the Constitutional School. Rohr's notion that public administrators should choose between political masters can be defended on the grounds that it permits administrators to resist harmful policies of political leaders while at the same time restraining them from simply ignoring the directives of political leaders. Similarly, Rohr's advocacy of a representative bureaucracy can be justified on the grounds that such a bureaucracy is more likely to resist exploitative policies imposed on any particular group. The difference is that the argument advanced here is grounded explicitly in the logic of a constitution in checking discretionary power. As such, it may provide an alternative means of legitimizing public administration.

Summary and Conclusion

This article has argued that the reliance of the Constitutional School on the Idealists' method of historical explanation inevitably leads it to promote an overly romantic view of the Constitution and of the founders. This means that its attempts to legitimate public administration on constitutional grounds are inherently vulnerable to questions about the conduct and character of the founders. We have suggested here that an alternative approach may be to embrace the central logic of a constitution that discretionary power should be checked. Such an embrace need not rule out an active and important role for public administration within the Constitution. Rather, public administration, according to this view, becomes a crucial check on the misuse of power by elected leaders.

It must be conceded that the constitutional role for public administration presented here may be insufficiently heroic and inspiring for some tastes. It is, however, consistent with the logic of a constitution and, as such, may at least serve as a legitimate benchmark for defining the minimum essentials of an active role for public administration that can gain support from a variety of ideological perspectives. Regardless of our views of government, many might concede that public administration, at a minimum, can play a potentially useful role in limiting misuse of power by elected officials.

Notes

1 Philosophers classified as Idealists and their works include: Collingwood, 1946; and Dray, 1957.

2 Fischer (1970) uses the term fallacy to denote "false organizing assumptions and false procedures." According to Fischer, "A fallacy is not merely an error itself but a way of falling in error. It consists in false reasoning, often from factual premises, so that false conclusions are generated" (p. xvii).

References

Brennan, Geoffrey & James Buchanan, 1985. *The Reason of Rules.* Cambridge: Cambridge University Press.

Buchanan, James & Gordon Tullock, 1962. *The Calculus of Consent.* Ann Arbor: University of Michigan Press.

Caldwell, Lynton, 1976. "Novus Ordo Seclorum: The Heritage of American Public Administration." *Public Administration Review* 36: 476–488.

Collingwood, Robin G., 1946. *The Idea of History.* Oxford: Clarendon Press.

Cook, Brian J., 1992. "The Representative Function of Bureaucracy: Public Administration in a Constitutive Perspective." *Administration & Society* 23, pp. 403–429.

Dray, William, 1957. *Laws and Explanation in History*. Oxford: Oxford University Press.

Farazmand, Ali, 1989. "Crisis in the U.S. Administrative State." *Administration and Society* 21: 173–179.

Finer, Herman, 1941. "Administrative Responsibility in Democratic Government." *Public Administration Review* 1: 335–350.

Fischer, David H., 1970. *Historians' Fallacies: Toward a Logic of Historical Thought*. New York: Harper and Row.

Franklin, John Hope, 1989. "The Moral Legacy of the Founding Fathers." In *Race and History: Selected Essays 1938–1988*. Baton Rouge: Louisiana State University Press, pp. 153–162.

Frederickson, George, 1971. "Toward a New Public Administration." In Frank Marini, ed., *Toward a New Public Administration*. Scranton, PA: Chandler Publishing, pp. 309–331.

Frederickson, George & David Hart, 1985. "The Public Service and the Patriotism of Benevolence." *Public Administration Review* 45: 547–553.

Gellhorn, Martha, 1986. *The Face of War*. New York: Atlantic Monthly Press.

Hart, David, 1989. "A Partnership in Virtue Among All Citizens: The Public Service and Civic Humanism." *Public Administration Review* 49: 101–114.

Hayek, Friedrich, 1973. *Law, Legislation and Liberty, Volume 1: Rules and Order*. Chicago, IL: University of Chicago Press.

Heiner, Ronald, 1983. "The Origin of Predictable Behavior." *American Economic Review* 73: 560–595.

Hempel, Carl G., 1953. "The Function of General Laws in History." In Herbert Feigl & Wilfred Sellers, eds, *Readings in Philosophical Analysis*. New York: Appleton-Century-Crofts.

Ketcham, Ralph, ed., 1986. *The Anti-Federalist Papers and the Constitutional Convention Debates*. New York: Mentor Books.

Kristol, Irving, 1987. "The Spirit of '87." *The Public Interest*, no. 86): 3–9.

Lane, Larry M. & James F. Wolf, 1990. *The Human Resource Crisis in the Public Sector*. New York: Quorum Books.

Loury, Glen C., 1987. "Matters of Color: Blacks and the Constitutional Order." *The Public Interest*, no. 86): 109–123.

Roche, John P., 1961. "The Founding Fathers: A Reform Caucus in Action." *American Political Science Review* 55: 799–816.

Rohr, John A., 1986. *To Run a Constitution: The Legitimacy of The Administrative State*. Lawrence, KS: The University of Kansas Press.

Rosen, Bernard, 1983. "Effective Continuity of U.S. Government Operations in Jeopardy." *Public Administration Review* 43: 383–392.

Rosen, Bernard, 1986. "Crises in the U.S. Civil Service." *Public Administration Review* 46: 195–215.

Rourke, Francis E., 1987. "Bureaucracy in the American Constitutional Order." *Political Science Quarterly* 102: 217–232.

Stillman, Richard, II, 1989. "Ostrom on the Federalist Reconsidered." *Public Administration Review* 49: 82–84.

Stillman, Richard, II, 1990. "The Peculiar Stateless Origins of American Public Administration and Consequences for Government Today." *Public Administration Review* 50: 156–167.

Storing, Herbert J., 1986. "Slavery and the Moral Foundation of the American Republic." In Robert H. Horwitz, ed., *The Moral Foundations of the American Republic*. Charlottesville: University Press of Virginia, pp. 313–332.

von Mises, Ludwig, 1944. *Bureaucracy*. New York: Yale Press.

Wamsley, Gary L., Charles T. Goodsell, John A. Rohr, Philip S. Kronenburg, Orion F. White, Camilla M. Stivers & Robert N. Bacher, 1990. *Refounding Public Administration*. Newbury Park, CA: Sage Publications.

Weingartner, Rudolph, 1967. "Historical Explanation." In Paul Edwards, ed., *The Encyclopedia of Philosophy*. New York: Macmillan, pp. 7–12.

White, Morton, 1965. *Foundation of Historical Knowledge*. New York: Harper and Row.

Wildavsky, Aaron, 1988. "Ubiquitous Anomie: Public Service in an Era of Ideological Dissensus." *Public Administration Review* 48: 753–755.

Wills, Garry, ed., 1987. *The Federalist Papers by Alexander Hamilton, James Madison and John Jay*. New York. Bantam Books.

Wilson, Woodrow, 1956. *Congressional Government*. New York: Meridian Books.

Wolf, James, 1987. "Disinvesting in the Administrative Capacity for Public Action." *International Journal of Public Administration* 10: 209–234.

7 Theodore Lowi's Cautionary Note for the Constitutional School

David H. Rosenbloom

Professor Theodore J. Lowi is a leading mid-20th to early 21st-century political scientist whose book, *The End of Liberalism* (1969), provided a powerful critique of the treatment of pluralism in then contemporary political science. It promoted a substantial rethinking of the operation and role of public administration in the national political system. Lowi's basic argument was that Congress had increasingly delegated its legislative power to federal agencies without clear standards for interpretation and implementation in violation of the "intelligible principle" doctrine established in *J.W. Hampton, Jr. & Company v. United States* (1928) and reinforced in *Schechter Poultry Corporation v. United States* (1935). In consequence, because politics in the U.S. flows to the point of policymaking, interest groups turned their lobbying efforts to obtain favorable governmental treatment from Congress to administrative agencies. Moreover, rather than agencies serving as neutral umpires of the public interest in the classical, though deeply flawed, pluralist model, they became captives and spokespersons for the interest groups whose policy objectives fell within their jurisdictions. In return, interest groups provided political support for these agencies and their policies.

The second edition of *The End of Liberalism* (1979) bore the subtitle, "The Second Republic of the United States." In Lowi's view, a major problem with interest group liberalism was that it shifted policymaking to an unelected and self-interested component of government, public agencies, or collectively "the bureaucracy." Lowi's prescription for righting the constitutional design of legislative supremacy was "juridical democracy," which entailed curtailing standardless delegations of legislative power to the agencies and thereby reasserting the rule of law and the rule by law, in place of what had become government by administrative discretion.

Lowi's prescription deviates from the thrust of the Constitutional School of American Public Administration by essentially contending that independent administrative power cannot be constitutionally legitimated and that the constitutional design demands legislative supremacy, not the equivalent of lawmaking by unelected career public administrators and their politically appointed bosses. Taken to its fullest conclusion, Lowi's contention negates the idea that broad policymaking discretion by public administration can be made compatible with U.S. democratic-constitutionalism by subordinating public agencies to generic administrative law statutes, such as the Administrative Procedure Act of 1946, the Freedom of Information Act of 1966, the Government in the Sunshine Act of 1976, and related statutes. Neither can the government's administrative component be legitimized through representative bureaucracy or public and stakeholder participatory and representational approaches, such as manifested in the Federal Advisory Committee Act of 1972. Ultimately, the Constitution is premised on legislative supremacy and while the separation of powers places some limitations on congressional power, public administrative independence is not among them.

A common critique of Lowi's position is that given the scope of the contemporary federal government, broad administrative discretion is unavoidable, necessary, and in some respects even highly desirable. This is especially true when one considers the vast regulatory functions and other policy outputs associated with the administration of the federal government. For example, which is better positioned to set standards for clean air, water, and environmental sustainability: Congress or the Environmental Protection Agency? Which is better positioned to set standards for food and drug safety: Congress or the Food and Drug Administration? Even returning to the "intelligible principle doctrine" may be infeasible because clear intelligible principles often negate congressional majority support for legislation. That is why statutes are laced with such terms as "to the extent feasible," "in the public interest," "as necessary or convenient," "expedient," "fair," "adequate," "equitable," "practicable," "reasonable," and "advisable." Furthermore, as Morris Fiorina (1977) has argued, it can be in the electoral interests of members of Congress to avoid controversial policy choices by deliberately shifting them to the agencies.

Contrary to Lowi's view, since its decision in *Chevron v. Natural Resources Defense Council* (1984), the Supreme Court has embraced the rule that when Congress has not clearly spoken to the meaning of key terms in statutes, the agencies are institutionally free to adopt any reasonable interpretation of them. As the Court explained in *City of Arlington, Texas v. Federal Communications Commission*:

> *Chevron* is rooted in a background presumption of congressional intent: namely, "that Congress, when it left ambiguity in a statute" administered by an agency, "understood that the ambiguity would be resolved, first and foremost, by the agency, and desired the agency (rather than the courts) to possess whatever degree of discretion the ambiguity allows." ... *Chevron* thus provides a stable background rule against which Congress can legislate: Statutory ambiguities will be resolved, within the bounds of reasonable interpretation, not by the courts but by the administering agency. ... Congress knows to speak in plain terms when it wishes to circumscribe, and in capacious terms when it wishes to enlarge, agency discretion.
>
> (2013, p. 1868)

Chevron may be part of the "derangement" of "our three-branch legal theories" brought on by the rise of the administrative state, as referred to by Supreme Court Justice Robert Jackson in *Federal Trade Commission v. Ruberoid* (1952, p. 487) and contested by Lowi. However, it appears that constitutional accommodation of the administrative state has made rejecting the "second republic" in favor of a return to the first or developing something new highly unlikely.

In an oblique way, the Court's decision in *Zivotofsky v. Kerry* (2015) further weakens Lowi's hard stance on legislative supremacy in our increasingly globalized world. There, the Court held that the president's constitutional power to recognize foreign governments is essentially plenary and exclusive. The Court's expansive words upheld the "exclusive power of the President to control recognition determinations, including formal statements by the Executive Branch acknowledging the legitimacy of a state or government and its territorial bounds" (*Zivotofsky v. Kerry*, 2015, p. 2096).

Nevertheless, Lowi's critique of a main thrust of the Constitutional School of American Public Administration sounds a cautionary note. Let us not assume that the administrative state can be made fully compatible with U.S. democratic-constitutionalism or that our efforts to make it so will succeed without unforeseen and undesirable consequences. Neither "bureaucratic government" (Nachmias & Rosenbloom, 1980) nor the aggrandized presidency that has accompanied it has solved the problem of legitimizing the administrative state.

On a personal note, I have taken the liberty of reflecting on Lowi's "disturbed dissent" because having had many conversations with him on the question of retrofitting the administrative state into the constitutional regime I can expand on his written work. Lowi was a favorite professor at the University of Chicago in the late 1960s when John Rohr, Peri Arnold, Douglas Morgan, and I were among the doctoral students most interested in public administration. While I was teaching at Syracuse University's Maxwell School of Citizenship and Public Affairs (1978–1990) and Lowi was at Cornell, I generally got together with him at least once a year or so and the conversations almost naturally turned toward the themes discussed here. For Ted, the idea that the unelected administrative branch (if he was willing to concede that it was indeed a branch) could be democratic was largely a nonstarter. Its independence was anathema to the constitutional design for legislative supremacy. Juridical democracy was not a panacea for all the derangement associated with the administrative state, but it was the most promising immediate step toward restoring the constitutional design.

References

Chevron v. Natural Resources Defense Council. 1984. 467 U.S. 837.
City of Arlington, Texas v. Federal Communications Commission. 2013. 133 S. Ct. 1863.
Federal Trade Commission v. Ruberoid. 1952. 343 U.S. 470.

Fiorina, M. 1977. *Congress: Keystone of the Washington Establishment*. New Haven, CT: Yale University Press.

J.W. Hampton, Jr. & Company v. United States. 1928. 276 U.S. 394.

Lowi, T.J. 1969. *The End of Liberalism*. New York: W.W. Norton.

Lowi, T.J. 1979. *The End of Liberalism: The Second Republic of the United States*. New York: W.W. Norton.

Nachmias, D. & Rosenbloom, D.H. 1980. *Bureaucratic Government USA*. New York: St. Martin's Press.

Schechter Poultry Corporation v. United States. 1935. 295 U.S. 495.

Zivotofsky v. Kerry. 2015. 135 S. Ct. 2076.

Legitimizing Public Administration

A Disturbed Dissent

Theodore J. Lowi

From: *Public Administration Review* 53:3 (May/June 1993): 261–264. Abridged.

Efforts to legitimize public administration go back a long way. In the past decade or so, these efforts have turned toward legitimizing public administration as a separately constituted institution of government.

Legitimizing public administration is something every regime has to do. The Federalists probably saw administration legitimized as long as "a few good men" were in place to make a few good decisions. The Jacksonians had a theory of legitimate administration that was, in fact, a general theory of government within which administration was legitimized. In effect, government should not only be small within a strict construction of the Constitution, it should never be involved in any activity that is beyond the ability of the common person to administer. What the critics eventually called the "spoils system" was actually a quite sustainable and logical argument that administration was legitimate as long as it was consistent with democracy, and it was consistent with democracy as long as it was accessible to the common person. Rotation of officials in public office according to which political party was victorious could be considered a simple and logical application of the principles of democracy, especially party democracy.

"Meritocracy" was the late 19th-century middle-class answer to the highly successful legitimizing theories of the Jacksonian Democracy. What is interesting about the merit argument for a legitimate public administration is not merit itself but the associated principle of neutrality. Administrators, according to the old axiom, were to be "on tap but not on top." They could be entrusted with the great powers and responsibilities of government not merely because they were trained in their craft and would spend a lifetime in the agency dealing with the problems of that agency, but because they added to their professionalism and training a willingness to subordinate their abilities to the wishes of the elected officials. "The neutral civil servant" was the key to legitimacy, not the professionalism by itself. This made meritocracy logically compatible with legislative supremacy, which is the core of the American Constitution.

Thus, through the 19th century and well into the 20th century, several theories were aimed at legitimizing public administration. The purpose of each was to flesh out a more general ideology or theory of state consonant with the party or regime that was in power during a particular epoch. Yet, except perhaps for the Federalists—and their view may have been the only one possible for the founding epoch—the theories legitimizing public administration kept well within the original position of the Constitution, which, to repeat, was legislative supremacy. It does not take an idealized or romanticized view of the founders to appreciate the fact that all of the powers of the national government are contained in the first article, which deals with the legislative branch.

How much constitutional reasoning, and how strong an assumption of rationality and of contract does it take to recognize that Congress was the recipient and therefore the source of all the powers of the national government? As John Rohr correctly puts it in his essay, powers have to come first and limitations have to follow. Rohr does not, however, draw the proper conclusion from this any more than do [Michael] Spicer and [Larry] Terry. Powers are in Article I, Section 8 and limitations follow in Section 9—and in Articles II and III. Of equal importance—and of greater relevance to the issues here—is the provision for the executive in Article II and the judiciary in Article III. Although the provision for veto power for the president and the assumed (let us assume that it was assumed) provision for judicial review as a power for the judiciary were intended as limitations on the legislative branch, there is nowhere in the Constitution an explicit theory of the separation of powers as a basic principle of limitation on the national government. That is to be found in the writings *about* the Constitution and its virtues. I accept the theory of the separation of powers as something that was in the minds and the intentions of the founders. I am stressing the relative silence about the separation of powers and the relative silence about the existence of the second and third branches as significant limitations on the first branch because I think something else was of greater importance in this argument about the legitimacy of public administration and its basis.

My point is this: It seems to me clear from everything about the structure of the Constitution, in particular about the relationship between Article I and Article II, that the executive branch, including the presidency, was to be *an institution of delegated powers*. It is worth repeating by way of emphasis, first, that *all the powers of the national government*, being in Article I, were granted to Congress. Legislative supremacy was everything, and that means rule of law, rule by law, no government action outside the realm of legal provision, including the provision added in Section 9 that "No money shall be drawn from the Treasury, *but in consequence of appropriations made by law*" (emphasis added). Second, not only is the Constitution a constitution of legislative supremacy, it is a constitution in which the presidency is an office of delegated powers, and delegated powers alone. People can jump through all sorts of hoops, and they can dig conscientiously into the writings of John Locke or anybody else, and they cannot infuse into the concept of "executive power" anything that would support an argument that independent powers of government are inherent in the presidency under our Constitution. The only thing that comes anywhere close to such an inherent power is the role of commander-in-chief, and the only occasion when that can be considered a source of power independent of legislation is during time of war. This is why those who adore the idea of the independent executive with its own independent sources of power take Abraham Lincoln as the greatest of them all. *Constitutionally speaking,* the key to Article II is Sections 8 and 9 of Article I coupled with the clause in Article II, Section 3 which provides that "he shall take care that the Laws be faithfully executed." In sum, the executive is indeed the second branch, and, except for war, is constitutionally an institution of delegated powers, powers delegated to it by the legislature. This would seem to me to indicate that if there is to be a general source for legitimizing public administration in America, and if that source is to be found in and developed from a "logic of a constitution," it must come from the authority delegated to administration—more specifically to specific administrative agencies—and from nowhere else. From this standpoint, public administration as a general institution would have no general legitimacy and need none, except within the context of the status of administrators as public employees. All of the legitimacy within public administration would come from the specific grants of authority in statutes adopted through due legislative process in Congress, explicitly granting authority and jurisdiction to specific agencies to carry out specific tasks. This is the unvarying constitutional position. One can find exceptions. I have written a whole book complaining about the problem of statutes that delegate too much discretion with too little legal definition. Nevertheless, the only source of administrative legitimacy within our Constitution has to come from those very statutes.

Now I turn to Spicer and Terry[1] where I find some genuinely astonishing stuff. First, they make a pretty good rendition of the several possible reasons why "rational individuals will agree to develop a constitution because they wish to limit the discretionary power available to government officials." They make a very bad mistake by their observation that "the notion that actors in the political process pursue their own economic interest is controversial among scholars in political science." The assumption of selfish interests is probably the only thing on which all political scientists agree. As Lasswell put it so eloquently for all of us 50 years ago, "private motives displaced on public objects, rationalized in terms of the public interest." For the same reason, Madison can be called the father of modern political science as well as the father of the Constitution. In any event, Spicer and Terry's outline of the various reasons for having a constitution based upon limitations is a good inventory. They even go so far as to make a good one-sentence critique not only of John Rohr but of that whole school of thought by their observation that "Rohr's argument on the separation of powers reflects his desire to justify the exercise of executive, legislative, and judicial power by administrative agencies rather than a concern with the abuse of power."

However, after an intelligent and useful review of what might be the basis for talking about a constitutional logic, they argue that the purpose of all this constitutional logic, of all the limitations and the reasons for putting limitations in the Constitution, is to "[provide] constitutional legitimacy for public administration." Not to provide legitimacy for *governing* but legitimacy for public administration.

Then they carry this argument still further with the passage that if it is accepted that the logic of the Constitution is about restraining discretionary power, then "administrative discretion may be justified on the constitutional grounds that it sometimes enables public administrators to modify, delay, or resist the directives of political leaders in a lawful manner."

Up to now, the point for virtually every student of administration, regardless of ideology or regime, was the reverse. Discretion in this context is the power to govern. Constitutionally that is in the hands of elected officials, and they necessarily have to rely on public administration, and constitutionally delegate in a lawful manner the power of the elected officials to appointed officials. That delegation necessarily involves a considerable amount of discretion, but the delegators retain, constitutionally speaking, their power to limit the power and the discretion of public administrators.

Now in the real political world, limitations go both ways. But in constitutional principle and logic, the authority to use discretion rests with elected officials, primarily Congress, and the power to grant discretion to others and to limit the discretion of others rests with the legislature. If the legislature uses its discretion improperly, either by enacting abusive laws or simply exacting unconscionable charges on citizens, it is subject to our criticism and to electoral defeat, loss of legitimacy, and perhaps even revolution. The discretion—the power to govern with the Constitution—nevertheless rests with the elected officials, in particular the members of the House of Representatives and the Senate.

All of this seems to me to be quite elementary.

The position of Spicer and Terry in this article is neither ludicrous nor, in its own way, illogical. It is to me frightening. What is frightening is not that it is in disagreement with what they call the Constitutional School as represented by John Rohr. What is frightening is not that they disagree but that they agree. They agree that it is time to establish a new legitimacy for administration. They agree that it will be grounded directly in the Constitution. They agree that the role of Congress ought to be one of very restrained restraint—if any role at all. They agree (although Rohr's school is more explicit on this) that public administration is to be entrusted with government. They agree that most of what Congress and the courts do is interference, based on the narrowness and selfishness of the nature of public officials. They agree that public administration is the only check we have against the vulgar and self-destructive Lockean individualism that drives our Constitution and haunts the corridors of all centers of American democratic politics.

These authors, and a very much larger number of authors of whom they are representative, are, together, providing grounds for a new legitimacy of public administration. Of all the preceding efforts to legitimize public administration as a whole, the current effort most resembles the original Federalist approach—with the expectation that good, nonelected administrators will be a sufficient substitute for "good men." Whatever it turns out to be in all its particulars, it is at bottom a self-conscious departure from the New Deal approach to public administration that the present approach is attempting to displace. The New Deal approach was a variation on its meritocratic predecessor, with a more programmatic tilt. The new approach is farther to the right wing side of American politics than the New Deal was to the the new left. The new approach is pessimistic about democracy—if not downright hostile to it. It is pessimistic about contract and about individualism and about basing any system of collective activity on self-interest and greed—otherwise known as the pursuit of happiness. It is not libertarian but genuinely conservative, although it makes common cause with the libertarian wing of the Republican party (erroneously called conservative by many people) because both libertarians and conservatives can agree that greed is okay in the economic system—where it is called rationality—because the economic system is self-correcting, whereas greed is bad in the political system because politics cannot be self-correcting. Thus, this new approach is above all, pessimistic about the ability of an electorally based politics to govern through a crudely representative system of laws.

The New Deal approach to public administration undermined itself and brought the great New Deal liberal consensus to an end by pushing the original constitutional system beyond its limits. It approached public administration through the rule of law, but so badly constructed the rules and so badly guided administrative discretion that it undermined the legitimacy of positive government itself. This system of decadent liberalism I have entitled the Second Republic of the United States.

Conservatism has emerged and is coalescing around an effort to provide America with a new approach to public administration as the core of a new, more conservative regime. We see elements of this effort in Spicer and Terry and in Rohr, despite some disagreements between them. Taking the whole group together, they are pushing us in theory, and eventually in practice, toward the Third Republic. It is a republic that I would like even less than the second.

Note

1 "Advancing the Dialogue: Legitimacy, the Founders, and the Contractarian Argument," *Public Administration Review* Vol. 53 (May/June 1993): 264–267.

8 Public Administration and Constitutional Theory

Reflections on "the Organ of Experience"

Brian J. Cook

My essay "The Organ of Experience" (Cook, 2010) was my first attempt to work through some ideas as part of a larger enterprise to develop a theory of the political constitution of the administrative state. That Stephanie Newbold and David Rosenbloom have found it a fitting addition to their project to promote a Constitutional School in the study and practice of public administration is a wonderful bonus. Any attempt to connect public administration and the character of the administrative state to constitutional theory and constitutional design will be comfortably at home in this venture to create and sustain a Constitutional School tradition in public administration scholarship and education.

At the heart of my own endeavor is my ongoing quest to fashion a thorough and convincing conception of public administration as a constitutive institution of a liberal democratic regime. In "The Organ of Experience" I tried to bring to bear in a concentrated way what I had learned from my study of Woodrow Wilson's ideas about public administration and its role in a constitutional democracy (Cook, 2007). The insights to be found in Wilson's thinking on such matters, synthetic rather than original though they may have been, remain insufficiently known and appreciated by scholars. I thus attempted to add some provocation to the essay by placing emphasis on Wilson's ideas about the nature of constitutions—that they are as much markers of the emergence of a people as a distinct polity as they are blueprints for a regime—and his contention that public administration, far more than just an instrument for running a constitution, plays a central role in continuing constitutional growth and change. The argument is complex and covers a lot of ground, so in this reflection I will add further emphasis to just a few central points, and comment briefly on where the larger enterprise must go next.

Constitutions as Ends and Beginnings

As the constitutional law scholar Adrian Vermeule (2015a) recently argued, "classical" constitutional theory did not give much if any attention to administration as an institutionally distinctive feature of government.

Although one can argue, as Vermeule does, that constitutional theory changed with the rise of the administrative state, constitutional theorists still have a devil of a time contending with a state whose structure and functions are almost wholly ministrant, in Wilson's sense of supporting the growth and development of the autonomous individual. As Vermeule's own efforts to examine constitutional theory reveal, there is very little effort in this body of scholarship to theorize about the administrative state as a distinctive constitutional form or stage of constitutional development (but see Rubin, 2005), or to think about modern bureaucratic administration as a particular problem of constitutional design. Theorizing remains stuck in several parallel tracks, particularly the application of various economic models such as principal-agent theory, or the theoretical straitjacket of a tripartite separation of powers. Moreover, the central, nearly exclusive, concern in such theorizing is the question of how to keep public bureaucracies subordinate and under "political" control lest they tyrannize the populace (Vermeule, 2015b).

In the United States specifically, far more has been published on the seemingly interminable debate over whether the administrative state is constitutional (e.g., Sunstein & Vermeule, 2015) than about how best to redesign the regime to fully incorporate administration institutionally into it, or better yet, how to transform the regime to fit the reality of public governance that is almost wholly administrative. To undertake the latter endeavor requires a perspective on what constitutions are and how administration best relates to them given their nature. I found that sort of thinking in Wilson's writings, and "The Organ of Experience" is the product of that discovery. Two key points are worth repeating in brief.

First, as already noted, Wilson saw constitutions as both shaped by and shapers of social, economic, and political development. His was an organic perspective, seeing in that peculiar human construct—the state—a particular developmental trajectory, not unlike the concept of phylogenesis in biology. It is not stretching the analogy too far to say that this organic perspective treated each individual state as experiencing its own ontogeny, reflecting the phylogeny of all states, but also the specific conditions of its birth and growth toward the ultimate level of maturity, a "constitutional state." Those conditions included primarily the peculiar norms, customs, and values of a people that, through both purposeful action and fortuitous events, might lead to the emergence of a distinctive polity. The marker for such an occurrence would be the codification of its mores in a constitution. That constitution, with its distinctive characteristics, and flaws, would then further shape and reshape the polity over the course of its continued development. In short, a constitution is the product of dynamic processes, and then it initiates a new trajectory for the vibrant social and political life of which it is a part.

We need not adopt Wilson's organicism to appreciate the essential point that constitutions don't come out of nowhere and they are not fixed for all time. That is true of all public law, of course, but this reality has a special meaning for constitutions beyond their status as supreme law. Constitutions are the expression of and give structure to public life, including any given polity's aspirations to a peculiar conception of justice and the general good. In a liberal democracy like the United States, those aspirations include maintaining a vigorous sphere of private autonomy with a distinctive stress on acquisitive activities. But there are also aspirations to a commonwealth and thus the maintenance of a public sphere that is not just about shared responsibility but also about the ennobling and uplifting effect of communal engagement.

The second point, following from the first, is that like any liberal democracy, there are great tensions at the core of the American regime. They certainly are often manifest in the work of the "constitutional" institutions—legislatures, elected executives, and courts. Yet, on a *daily basis* in a highly advanced, densely organized, and deeply interconnected polity like the United States, those tensions are the central preoccupation of public administration. In this regard, I cannot resist repeating my favorite line from Wilson's writings, that administration "rests its whole front along the line which is drawn in each State between *Interference* and *Laissez faire*" (Link et al., 1966–1994, 7, p. 116, emphasis in original). No theoretical or practical thinking about public administration, constitutions and law, and the relationship between the two that ignores this inescapable reality can help advance our thinking about public administration and constitutions. This is so because it is the activity on that line that makes public administration a constitutive institution of a liberal-democratic regime. Why? My attempt to provide an answer constituted the core of the essay.

Public Administration as a Constitutive Institution

The point of departure is to recognize that prominent in the life of a liberal democracy is the frequent reconstitution of the regime, albeit in mostly small ways, with respect to questions of where the line between public and private belongs. That line is under constant pressure and shifts recurrently, reflecting decisions by the state about what conditions justify interventions into the private sphere. The "state" in this case is almost always administration, and the essentially perpetual bargaining over what properly belongs in the public versus the private sphere thus takes place largely in the administrative realm.

Reflecting this unique place administration holds in a liberal democratic regime as its "organ of experience" are at least three facets of its special character as a constitutive institution of the regime. First, in addition to its constant probing of the core liberal democratic question of what is public and what is private, administrative agencies are frequently engaged in probing questions about other principles at the heart of the constitutions to which public administrators pledge their loyalty through their oaths of office. Second, public administrators are constantly navigating the sometimes severe cross-currents of having to think both instrumentally and constitutively. Administrators may be principally concerned with realizing the predetermined and narrowly focused public aims conferred on their agencies. Nevertheless, in the process of using the discretion they have been granted and the adaptive qualities their organizations may possess, they wrestle with core regime principles often enough that across the many agencies in operation and the governing functions they perform, public agencies redefine public purposes in myriad ways. They thus alter public life—the life of society as a collective, political community—in the process. This experience does not remain isolated or self-contained, however. Third, administrative experience in observing and testing the dynamic processes of society, of probing questions thus raised about public versus private and other central regime principles, is almost always the foundation for the much rarer decisions by courts and legislatures to clarify where the line should be drawn between public and private, what constitutes justice, and what more generally is in the public interest. This influence of administrative experience occurs irrespective of whether administrative agencies win or lose on the questions brought before those other institutions by administrative action.

All of this may seem like so much abstract normativity, completely divorced from the reality of public administrators and public agencies having to deliver services, meet performance objectives, and scramble for resources. On top of all that, they must operate in a vastly more complex environment of multiple networks with a dizzying array of public and private organizational forms that, although all essentially bureaucratic, intermingle in myriad ways such that the public–private boundary line is more like an estuary, with its subtly varying levels of fresh and salt water dependent on time, tide, and weather. In governance, however, the intermingling is driven by public aims and aspirations. My contention, therefore, is that this complex developmental stage to which the administrative state has advanced demands more than ever fundamental thinking, or rethinking, about constitutional–administrative relations.

A good place to turn for guidance on where this thinking should go is Stephen Elkin's treatise on the Madisonian commercial republic and its need for reconstruction. Among the elements in Elkin's extensive analysis of the Madisonian system and its flaws, leading to his "republican reform program" (Elkin, 2006, pp. 279–305), four facets stand out as critically in need of attention in any constitutional theory that takes administration seriously. First, the major constitutive institutions—legislatures, elected executives, and courts—are in need of repair, and the whole separation of powers scheme requires reconsideration. Second, the nature of political leadership requires rethinking, especially with respect to concentrated executive power. Third, the American system's design for controlling factions is terribly out of whack, with minority factions, or special interests, now a greater threat than majority faction, especially with respect to the corrosive influence of the owners of capital. Finally, the nature of citizenship and the relationship of the citizenry to government and governing is in considerable disarray, especially given that governance is almost exclusively a matter of administration. These are all matters toward which Woodrow Wilson directed his attention. It is time to do so again, and new or renewed thinking about public administration as a problem of constitutional design or redesign will reveal ways to address these challenges. Central to this thinking is understanding how public administration is and can be a constitutive institution of the regime distinct from the others. In short, thinking about administration with respect to the separation of powers, political leadership, the control of faction, and the nature and health of the citizenry can make a valuable contribution to constitutional theory and the practice of constitutional governance. Not surprisingly, these are concerns of long standing in public administration scholarship. Thinking of them at the level of constitutions will contribute to making the difference in public administration scholarship, education, and practice that the promoters of a Constitutional School seek. Perhaps the difference will eventually be realized in the broader art and practice of republican governance as well.

References

Cook, B. 2007. *Democracy and administration: Woodrow Wilson's ideas and the challenges of public management.* Johns Hopkins Studies in Governance and Public Management. Baltimore, MD: Johns Hopkins University Press.

Cook, B.J. 2010. The organ of experience: A defense of the primacy of public administrators in the design and reform of policy and law. *Administration & society* 42(3): 263–286.

Elkin, S. 2006. *Reconstructing the commercial republic: Constitutional design after Madison.* Chicago, IL: University of Chicago Press.

Link, A.S., Hirst, D.W. & Little, J.E. (eds) 1966–1994. *The papers of Woodrow Wilson.* Princeton, NJ: Princeton University Press.

Rubin, E. 2005. *Beyond Camelot: Rethinking politics and law for the modern state.* Princeton, NJ: Princeton University Press.

Sunstein, C. & Vermeule, A. 2015. Libertarian administrative law. *The University of Chicago Law Review* 82(1): 393–473.

Vermeule, A. 2015a. The administrative state: Law, democracy, and knowledge. In Tushnet, Mark V., Mark A. Graber & Sanford Levinson (eds), *The Oxford handbook of the U.S. Constitution.* New York: Oxford University Press, pp. 259–282.

Vermeule, A. 2015b. Optimal abuse of power. *Northwestern university law review* 109(3): 673–694.

The Organ of Experience

A Defense of the Primacy of Public Administrators in the Design and Reform of Policy and Law

Brian J. Cook

From: *Administration and Society* 43:3: (2010): 263–286. Abridged.

In his most expansive thinking about public administration in a liberal democracy, Woodrow Wilson characterized public administration as testing the "suitability" of law, and actively monitoring social and economic life through its constant "contact with the present" (Link et al., 1969, Vol. 7, pp. 116, 138). Because he regarded law as the codification of social processes, and constitutions as the product of the long historical development of particular regimes, he thus envisioned a critical role for public administrators. They provide the essential observation of and experience with society necessary to guide the formalization of evolving habits, patterns of behavior, and individual and group interactions into new statutes and, ultimately, constitutional reforms.

Wilson's thinking along these lines was grounded in his acceptance of a distinct public sphere, and more particularly a relatively autonomous, organic State. Despite the resurrection of the concept of the state in sociology and political science several decades ago, there is again great skepticism about the continued relevance or even survival of the nation-state (e.g., Van Creveld, 1999). Further challenges come from the increasingly porous boundary between government and society, as reflected in the complex interactions between administrative agencies and an extensive array of public, quasi-public, and private entities. These organizations seem to be engaged in an almost infinite variety of partnerships for both formulating and realizing public aims. In this starkly new context, does the idea of a special, central role for public servants in the design of public law retain any validity? I argue that it does. This article is an attempt to articulate the normative case for that role.

First, I offer a brief defense for grounding my argument in ideas contained in the writings of Woodrow Wilson. Second, I develop my conception of a distinctive institutional role for public administration out of Wilson's ideas about the role of public administration in a liberal democratic regime, with special reference to the United States. I focus on his characterization of public administration as "the State's experiencing organ" (Link et al., 1969, Vol. 7, p. 138). Following this primary articulation of a distinctive role for public administrators in policy design, I consider and respond to three general objections to, and probable constraints on, public servants fulfilling this role. I conclude the article with a defense of this role conception for public administration, including the obligations future scholars and public servants must accept if they are to ensure that public administration as an institution of liberal democratic governance fulfills this vital role.

Why Wilson?

Some scholars and practitioners may doubt the legitimacy of anchoring in Wilsonian thinking a normative claim to a special governing role for public administration. Many references to Wilson in the scholarly and practitioner literature merely cite his famous essay as the anchoring reference for invoking the politics–administration dichotomy, hiding a much broader and deeper body of thought behind a scholarly synecdoche. Sometimes Wilson is referenced as a sort of talisman showing that the writer remembers to acknowledge American public administration's ancestors. For those somewhat more informed of the extent of his thought and practice with respect to administration, Wilson poses a real problem because of perceived defects in his ideas and his practices. These perceived defects give rise to numerous objections to using Wilson as any kind of guide for new thinking about public administration. I briefly respond to three such objections.

First, some critics find Wilson's thinking muddled, inconsistent, and even contradictory. Wilson was hardly a great thinker to begin with, and he admitted as much. His great intellectual strength was synthesis. Moreover, Wilson was hardly the first to have changed course in some way during the evolution of his thought and practice. Practice, after all, has a constitutive effect on ideas. Indeed, relying as much as he did on Edmund Burke, Wilson regarded a careful and deliberate adjustment of ideas in response to changing reality as paradigmatic of good leadership in thought and practice. What is especially fascinating about Wilson, however, is how consistent over the long term he was in his thinking and his governing practice reflecting that thinking. His departures from this "uncanny consistency" (Skowronek, 2006, p. 396) mark the principal episodes of failure in his life and work. What may be at the heart of the verdict by some scholars that Wilson's thinking was fuzzy or contradictory is that he spoke in the language of high principle, against which both he and others often fell short in word and deed. Moreover, he conveyed his ideas and ideals in a number of distinct vehicles, including political speeches, essays for a general readership, and least so scholarly publications. The medium can obscure the real meaning behind the author's words. None of this, however, justifies ignoring whatever insights about public administration scholars may find in his work.

Second, some may object to relying on Wilson as a primary source for thinking anew about public administration's role in a liberal democratic regime because Wilson would seem to have little to say to us today, and there are other sources of sound and more coherent thinking about public administration's role. But why abandon potentially good ideas even though they may have been superseded by more recent voices, which, although appealing, may not have captured a particular perspective present in older thinking? Elsewhere, I have presented an extended case for the current relevance of Wilsonian ideas to public administration theory (Cook, 2007). Simply stated, Wilson was prescient about a number of ideas and practices that became prominent in public administration scholarship in the two generations after his death. Wilson's ideas deserve a place in today's dialogue about public administration's proper governing role.

Perhaps the most powerful argument against the legitimacy of using Wilson's ideas as the principal source to make a normative case for a distinct public administration role in liberal democratic governance is that Wilson's ideas and practices bear the stigma of his racism and ethnocentrism. Indeed, his ideas about governing were extensively shaped by his racialist and southern roots. As both public intellectual and president, he wrote, spoke, and acted in many ways that divided people along racial and ethnic lines. Yet one problem with this objection is that it confuses a normative argument with a moral argument. Wilson himself recognized this distinction in "The Study of Administration":

> If I see a murderous fellow sharpening a knife cleverly, I can borrow his way of sharpening the knife without borrowing his probable intention to commit murder with it; and so, if I see a monarchist dyed in the wool managing a public bureau well, I can learn his business methods without changing one of my republican spots.
>
> (1887, p. 220)

We can learn from Wilson's ideas without having to adopt the immorality of his racism as well.

The more serious problem with rejecting Wilson's ideas as a source of normative argument about public administration is that Wilson's racism formed the foundation of a conception of liberalism and democracy that is still prominent today. Wilson the "thinker-statesman ... was led by his racism to rework received ideals and promulgate principles now associated with liberal democracy in America. A reactionary Wilson did not turn liberal, American liberalism turned Wilsonian" (Skowronek, 2006, p. 387). By basing an argument for a distinctive public administration role on Wilsonian ideas, then, I am implicitly tying the argument to a set of ideals and principles that friends of liberal democracy and the American regime still embrace today. I do not claim that the argument I advance here, grounded in Wilsonian ideas, is a definitive case for the governing legitimacy of public administrators. I merely insist that the thesis is worthy of public debate because of its lineage.

Public Administration as the State's Organ of Experience

There is nothing particularly new, surprising, or objectionable in the claim that public administration as an institution, and public administrators as autonomous political actors, do and should play a significant role in the public policy design process. Beyond this relatively unexceptional validation of a role for the public manager and technically expert public servant in policy making, however, I aim to advance a more vigorous specific argument. First, I contend that what one may call the "experiencing function" is a *central* and *distinct* role that must be fully acknowledged in both the study and practice of public administration. Second, I contend that this distinctive contribution is *qualitatively distinguishable* from and of *greater extent* and *higher quality* than any similar policy-making role of any other political actor. It is thus a signal contribution of public administration to governance in a liberal democratic regime. To elaborate, I begin with key components of Woodrow Wilson's thinking in this regard.

The Line between Interference and Laissez Faire

During the 1890s, Wilson devoted a considerable share of his most advanced cycle of lectures on administration to defining the sphere of public administration's reach in a democratic regime. Four interconnected components of that definition are evident in Wilson's notes. Together, they delineated a remarkably wide scope of action and influence for administration that required a separate, subtle, and careful *political* case for its legitimacy.

First, Wilson made clear his view that administration did not consist of the mere instrumental function of carrying formal, written law into effect. It went beyond "mere executive management" and a concern only with "the mechanism of government" (Link et al., 1969, Vol. 7, pp. 114–115). Because, Wilson argued, administration was grounded in fundamental political principles and the historical development of constitutions, it was not merely a matter of applying business principles to government. Far more, administration was a part of what constituted the vitality of the state and the living, breathing commotion of public endeavor. Public administration thus had to embody the peculiarities—the "national habit and national sentiment" (p. 116)—of a given nation-state and its origins, growth, and likely future developmental directions.

In this first component of his conception of administration, Wilson put great weight on what he called administrative integration. As an institution—an organ of the state—and as the premier form of modern power, Wilson did not accept that administration could be casually, or worse, theoretically, divided into federal, state, and local spheres. Administration had to be understood as an organic whole, not subdivided into disconnected and antagonistic parts. To do the latter would undermine the study and practice of administration, which had to be aimed at national development and adaptation to modernity. Connecting administration to such imperative yet practical aims was central to Wilson's effort at legitimation woven through his analysis.

For the second component of his definition, Wilson identified administration as the realm of pragmatism, of what it was possible for the state to do. It concerned the practical and workable, the sphere of action. It "sees government in contact with the people," and "touches, directly or indirectly, the whole practical side of social endeavor" (p. 116). Wilson thus argued that the scope of administrative power was "considerably wider and much more inclusive" than the executive power of classical liberal theory. "Besides the duty of executing positive law, there rest upon the administrative organs of every State those duties of provident protection and wise cooperation and assistance," whether "explicitly enjoined by [legislative] enactment" or not, that enable the government to fulfill its functions of ministering to the welfare of its citizens (p. 130).

For the third component of his conception of administration's role, Wilson articulated a particular notion about the relationship between law and administration. The source of Wilson's conception was Burke's pronouncement that "the laws reach but a very little way." Burke contended that "all the use and potency of the laws" depended on "the prudence and uprightness of ministers of state." Without such men, "your commonwealth is no better than a scheme upon paper; and not a living, active, effective organization" (see Link et al., 1969, Vol. 7, p. 122, note 1). Wilson quoted from Burke on this score in nearly every classroom and public lecture he delivered on administration, on public and constitutional law, and on democratic theory. It is also one of the epigraphs heading chapter 1 of *Congressional Government* (Wilson, 1981). On its basis, he portrayed administration as tethered to law but not encircled by it.

Both administrative study and administration itself, as an appendage of the state, by necessity had to confront "that great question" concerning the proper functions of government, because "the functions of government are in a very real sense independent of legislation, and even of constitutions." They are "as old as government and inherent in its very nature." Furthermore, the volume and detail of positive law masked the reality that "administration cannot wait upon legislation, but must be given leave, or take it, to proceed without specific warrant in giving effect to the characteristic life of the State" (Link et al., 1969, Vol. 7, p. 121). By doing so, administration was "indirectly a constant source of public law. It is through Administration that the State makes a test of its own powers and of the public needs,—makes [a] test also of law, its efficiency, suitability, etc." (p. 138). Law placed boundaries on administrative action that defined a "sphere of administrative authority ... as wide as the sphere in which it may move without infringing the laws, statutory or customary, either in their letter or in their reasonable inferential meaning" (p. 150).

Given these first three components of Wilson's conception of public administration's role in a democratic polity, one may infer that he saw administration as occupying the social and temporal space where dynamic social life was translated into knowledge—sometimes incomplete, sometimes inaccurate—and in turn into the raw material for the deliberative and often wrenching process of formalizing and codifying social habits and experience in written laws. Public administration does not just carry out such formal law, nor does it just fill in many of the gaps left by law. It also seeks to learn what it is practical for the state to do in the face of continuing change in habits and forms of social interchange growing out of such forces as economic growth and expanding racial, ethnic, and cultural interaction. Because of its special position in the polity, administration can more systematically assemble abundant material on which to base the reform of existing law, the shaping of new law, and even the reform or reconstruction of constitutions.

The fourth component in Wilson's analysis was the most extensive, complex, and remarkable aspect of his conception of the place of administration in a democratic regime. Wilson portrayed administration as playing the vital role in a liberal democracy of balancing public and private on a daily basis. Through its actions, administration defines in continuously recurring fashion what does and does not constitute governmental interference in private life, particularly private economic activity. Administration "rests its whole front along the line which is drawn in each State between *Interference* and *Laissez faire*" (p. 116). As a result of this aspect of its role, added to its more general station as continuing observer of and participant in governmental contact with social life, administration is "the State's experiencing organ" (p. 138). By testing laws already on the books, by taking action on cases for which no law directly and obviously applies, and by repeatedly probing for what is practical (appropriate and acceptable, at the very least) in terms of the state's involvement in the private sphere, the "Real Functions of the Administration are not merely ministerial: they are also adaptive, guiding, discretionary" (Link et al., 1970, Vol. 9, p. 31).

Although Wilson accepted that the bulk of public administration's work and obligations lie with policy management, he regarded public administration's engagement in policy development—the making or remaking of laws, and even constitutions—as its most far-reaching and vital task. It is, however, also the work of public administration most difficult to legitimate in regimes of popular sovereignty. Wilson clearly signaled, particularly in his governing rhetoric and practices (e.g., Cook, 2007, p. 190), that he expected administrative entities to be continuously and substantially engaged in fulfilling this experiencing, informing, policy-shaping function. Wilson's thinking in this regard overwhelms his rather limited association with the axiomatic division between administration and policy-making politics enshrined in orthodox public administration theory. Wilson did insist that in the more instrumental and mechanistic aspects of policy management and day-to-day governing, the political maneuvering and blatant party biases acceptable in the policy formulation process ought not to interfere. Yet viewing governance in a liberal democratic state more broadly, Wilson saw administration continuously and deeply intertwined with policy making. Indeed, if public administration was to function as Wilson envisioned it in his most expansive thinking, administrative entities and the public servants who staff them could not avoid being engaged in the continuously evolving endeavor to articulate the aims and aspirations of a national polity.

The Primacy of Public Administration's Experiencing, Informing, Guiding Role

Wilson's thinking about public administration's experiencing function is in important respects the precursor of what has become an extensive scholarly literature on policy learning, feedback in implementation, and similar phenomena. A defense of the legitimacy of such a function hardly seems necessary, for the function is, to borrow Wilson's phrasing, "as old as government and inherent in its very nature" (Link et al., 1969, Vol. 7, p. 121). The ancient roots of the legitimacy of government's effort to learn about and adapt to its social environment are found in the very etymology of the word *statistics* (Rose, 1989). The cornerstone of any normative argument that public administrators are the *primary* and *most capable* source of guidance on the reform of law, and even of constitutions, is situated here. Governments have an obligation at least to monitor conditions that bear on the health and safety of citizens. This is clearly an administrative function, ergo public administrators have an obligation to maintain the capacity and devote the resources to monitor social conditions.

Yet Wilson advanced a claim reaching beyond the deeply traditional administrative function of the state to gather evidence of changing conditions in its environment. Wilson's focus was on the very specific and more profound matter of making and remaking public law, including, if appropriate, constitutions. A defense of that more sweeping influence of public administration and public administrators begins with recognition of the nature of administrative power. Wilson considered administration a distinctive form of power that flowed from "coordinations of organizations" and "the irresistible energy and efficiency of harmony and cooperation." Cooperation was, for Wilson, "the law of all action in the modern world" (Link et al., 1974, Vol. 17, pp. 135–136), and inherent in the nature of administrative entities. Therefore, they possessed a special capacity to organize and coordinate their experiences and gather and share information efficiently.

As Wilson recognized, these are characteristics of any hierarchically structured organization, public or private, that takes advantage of division of labor, specialized training, and the development of special expertise characteristic of the bureaucratic form. For *public* organizations, of course, the argument is that this special power of coordination and cooperation is specifically oriented toward monitoring and learning from the application of public law. Public organizations also orient cooperation and coordination toward reading and learning from more general engagements with the environment, through the use of discretion in such administration activities as patrol and enforcement, and from broad, general observation. Yet public organizations go further, by also assessing formally the implications of their monitoring, and communicating the formalized findings with the aim of guiding policy making, whether as the reform of existing law or the formulation of new laws.

Nearly all private organizations will, however, have something of a similar aim for the use of their capacities for monitoring their environments and systematically gathering, assessing, and reporting what they have learned because nearly all private organizations are directly affected by public law. They may even take special pains to monitor the suitability of public law, at least with respect to their particular interests. To round out this initial normative case for *public* administrative organizations as the *primary* and *most capable* source of guidance on the reform of law, and even of constitutions, I offer four distinguishing characteristics of public administration's special experiencing, informing, and guiding role. These characteristics speak to the peculiar character and capacities of public administrators and their organizations that are vital to fulfilling that special role.

First, as Wilson argued, public administration may be understood as the science of choice. Wilson pointed out that as long as the state could do whatever it wanted, at any time, "no science of choice or wisdom" was necessary (Link et al., 1969, Vol. 7, p. 117). But with the advent and growth of the liberal democratic state, with its emphasis on the autonomy and development of the individual and thus the need to define and preserve a sphere of private life relatively free from government interference, decisions by the state about what conditions justified interference, to what extent, and in what form were necessary. Administration, and thus administrative science as well, was put to the task. What public agencies learn from their day-to-day contact with citizens in carrying out laws, and in addressing situations in which no existing law clearly applies, they can then contribute to the process of fashioning new laws and, if necessary, making constitutional changes. All of this is part of the living, growing, adaptive life of state and polity, including the transparency that is essential for public assessment of adaptations to ensure their success.

Thus the monitoring, information gathering, analyzing, and reporting and recommending functions of public organizations are all aimed toward informing and refining public, collective choice, serving the public interest, especially the perpetually ongoing bargaining over what properly belongs in the public and private spheres. Granted, many administrative agencies may be engaged in the experiencing function with primary concern for how the conditions they face affect their budgets, other resources, and the laws they are tasked with implementing. But all that public organizations do ultimately reflects collective choices made by the public through its representative institutions. In contrast, private entities, although they may be concerned with matters that involve public law, will engage in the experiencing function, including the potential reform of public law, only with reference to their own specific interests. They are not responsible for serving the public interest and generally ought not to be if they are to fulfill their missions and commitments to their owners. Furthermore, they do not generally have to meet the level of transparency demanded of public agencies, especially with respect to the rationales underlying their decisions (but see Fung et al., 2007).

Second, not only are public agencies responsible for serving the broader public interest in their areas of specialization, they are publicly held to account for their actions, including those associated specifically with the experiencing function. Unlike private organizations, public agencies are accountable to the public at large, and to collective bodies that are in turn accountable to the collective citizenry. There is, of course, some aspect of public accountability even for all private entities. That is, what charters issued by governments allowing these entities to organize and incorporate are in part meant to convey. Private entities that receive public funds are even more extensively accountable to the public's representatives. But public administrators and their agencies are *wholly and exclusively* accountable publicly and to public authority. Their experiencing function both serves this accountability and expresses it; that is, by monitoring the suitability of the law, learning about changes in society that affect their areas of responsibility, and otherwise gathering information that might guide the refinement of public law, public organizations are being accountable and responsible.

Related to their whole and exclusive public accountability and responsibility, the third characteristic of public administrators and their organizations that distinguishes the degree and quality of their experiencing function is their public service orientation. There is certainly some overlap of this characteristic with the first two, but this public service attribute extends further. It centers on the ethic that permeates public organizations, embraced as it is by the people who staff those organizations. And this ethic is not just a matter of professional indoctrination and acculturation; it is tied to the "stable principles" (Wilson, 1887, p. 210) at the heart of the constitutions to which public servants pledge their loyalty through their oaths of office (Rohr, 1986, pp. 186–194). Furthermore, the experiencing function interwoven into public organizations and the staffs who embody these collective values is about preservation as well as refinement and change. It is about public administrators determining in the face of sometimes rapid and disruptive change how to preserve core, and very public, values expressed in public law and embodied in their organizations. This "administrative conservatorship" (Terry, 2003) encompasses the use of monitoring, learning, and information gathering and sharing to make judgments, or to formulate advice for lawmakers, not only about what to change but also what to sustain and preserve.

Finally, whatever experiencing function private organizations and private managers exercise, they do so with an entirely instrumental orientation. They monitor their environment, learn what adjustments in operations they might make, and even test the suitability of public law with respect to their organizations' largely predetermined ends. Managers and executives of private organizations may consider how they might refine or remake their organizations in light of what they have learned in pursuit of their organizations' ends, but they are rarely if ever concerned with the refining or remaking of *public* life. In contrast, public administrators are constantly negotiating the sometimes severe cross-pressures of having to think both instrumentally and constitutively. Although they may be principally concerned with realizing the predetermined public aims conferred on their agencies, in the process of using the discretion they have been granted and the adaptive qualities their organizations may possess, they are recurringly redefining public purposes. They thus alter public life—the life of society as a collective, political community—in the process. This is the true meaning of Wilson's insight about public administration functioning as the vanguard in the continuous negotiations over where to draw the line between "*Interference* and *Laissez faire*."

Autonomous Legislators, the Transformation of Governance, and Questionable Legitimacy

I now turn to an enumeration of several probable objections to the claims I have advanced about public administration serving a special experiencing function—distinctive in kind, degree, and quality from that of other political actors—to guide the reform and advancement of public law, including constitutions. Space limitations prohibit the exploration of additional possible objections and further elaboration of the critiques I present here. The objections I consider are far reaching because they reflect the peculiar character of the system of separate institutions sharing powers in the United States, the triumph of the public management reforms now well documented by scholars as having occurred across the globe, and questions about the popular legitimacy of the role for public administration I propose.

Institutional Autonomy versus the Policy-Making Imperatives of Ties that Bind

Do legislators as the first-order policy makers in representative democracies rely primarily on administrators for guidance on the reform of existing law and the formulation of new law? Certainly, a great deal of adjustment and adaptation in public law takes place almost wholly within administrative agencies as a result of discretion granted by legislators. Legislators must tacitly accept a substantial share of these adjustments and adaptations because of the limited resources they can devote to oversight and because they have granted considerable administrative discretion precisely to allow public managers to make such adjustments to public law as a substitute for constant legislative scrutiny and excessively frequent, minor, and potentially destabilizing statutory changes.

Yet legislators obviously rely on a wide variety of sources of information to guide their decision making (see, e.g., Schick, 1991). Over time, as legislatures in the United States have struggled to maintain some semblance of equilibrium in policy-making capabilities with presidents and governors (see Krause, 2002), they have cultivated a wider variety of information sources of greater sophistication to guide collective assessments of the suitability of statutes, as well as decision making about statutory changes or formulation of new law, with a bias in favor of the latter (Schick, 1991).

Individual legislators rarely undertake information search, analysis, and decision formulation in synoptic fashion (Schneider & Ingram, 1988). They are political generalists who rely on "ordinary knowledge" (Lindblom & Cohen, 1979; Schick, 1991) rather than the "professional knowledge" (Lowi, 1991) generated by the likes of social science research and formalized policy analysis. Individual legislators thus rely on a relatively fixed set of contacts for reconnaissance and cue taking about issue positions. At the level of the legislative "enterprise" (Whiteman, 1995) that encompasses legislative staff, however, and even more so at the subcommittee and committee levels, the search for information about how statutes are working and what statutory changes or new laws may be necessary is richer and deeper. That search goes beyond both "fire alarms" and "police patrols" (McCubbins & Schwartz, 1984) to include more systematic research, even if prepared by particular groups with their own interests and biases. At the institutional level, legislatures long ago recognized the value of creating their own research and analysis arms—legislative research bureaus of various sorts at the state level, as well as the Congressional Research Service, the Government Accountability Office, and the now defunct Office of Technology Assessment (see Bimber, 1996)—to assist them in the lawmaking process.

Considered from a slightly different perspective, iron triangle and subgovernment models of policy making tell us that legislatures, or at least the U.S. Congress, rely primarily on affected interests and administrative implementers for signals about how laws are functioning and what legal reforms or new laws are needed. The issue network and advocacy coalition models, in contrast, suggest a wider spectrum of information sources feeding into the "problem" and "policy" streams (Kingdon, 1995) of the lawmaking process. Thus the scholarly literature on policy making suggests an evolution or transition from legislative reliance on a relatively narrow information base, as indicated by the iron triangle/subgovernment models, to a broader information base as indicated by the more open and fluid network or advocacy coalition conceptions of policy politics.

No matter what the model, however, administrative agencies are prominent players in the policy process, if not the most prominent after legislators themselves. But *should* administrative agencies be the *primary* source of information about how laws are working and what changes or new laws should be made? And should lawmakers expect administrative agencies to provide the *most valuable* information and guidance in this regard? In the U.S. context, at least, there are several arguments against these propositions.

First, in a separation-of-powers system, legislators certainly ought not to rely exclusively, and perhaps not even primarily, on executive branch agencies for information and guidance on evaluating currently operational statutes as well as for reforming existing statutes or creating new ones. Separate governing institutions with distinct political time horizons and constituent orientations have distinct institutional interests, strengths, and weaknesses. For the theory of separate institutions to work as James Madison envisioned, the two main policy-making institutions must maintain considerable independence from one another. This means developing parallel, if sometimes redundant, mechanisms for policy reconnaissance, policy assessment, and policy formulation or reformulation. In times when the relationship between the executive and legislative branches is particularly adversarial, or when the elected chief executive exercises particularly stringent control over executive agencies and insists on particularly strict subordination of those agencies to his or her specific policy views and dictates, legislators must exercise special care in relying on administrative agencies for guidance on policy performance and policy reform.

Second, in a separation-of-powers system, administrative agencies are able to achieve at least some autonomy from their two major political principals. The developmental foundations of this autonomy (e.g., Carpenter, 2001) and the verification of the considerable variation in extent and character of this autonomy (e.g., Wood & Waterman, 1994) have been reasonably well documented. For information and guidance on how laws are performing and whether they should be changed or replaced, lawmakers thus ought not to rely exclusively, or perhaps even primarily, on public organizations because those organizations have their own particular interests, ideologies, and technical competencies (and consequent biases) that will color their information search and collection, and the analysis and guidance they offer. Agencies are certainly not exclusively, and perhaps not primarily, dedicated to aiding legislators in fulfilling their lawmaking responsibilities, if for no other reason than that legislators are at least some of the time engaged in satisfying their own interests and those of a select few special constituents rather than the agencies' interests, or the public interest generally. On the other hand, although the executive branch is much more hierarchically structured and the subordination of public administrators to elected executives is well established in both law and practice, agencies will not operate wholly and exclusively to serve the aims of elected executives either, thus reducing the risk to lawmakers of using agencies as a major source of guidance about the need for new or revised public law.

It thus may be quite practical for legislators, given their particular strengths and proclivities as political actors, not to rely primarily on the information, analysis, and guidance of administrative agencies regarding the suitability of existing laws, and the need for their refinement or replacement. Legislators would appear to function best when they can take advantage of a rich and varied flow of information about policy performance and about the needs of society for new or revised public law. Yet no less than the U.S. Congress itself has seen no barrier in the theory and practice of the separation-of-powers scheme to treating administrative agencies as instruments of Congress, vital to Congress in fulfilling both its lawmaking and representative functions. This "legislative-centered public administration" (Rosenbloom, 2000) regards the subordination of public administrators to the president as merely a matter of good internal management, and regards the agencies themselves as a valuable source of information and support to lawmakers for constituency service, reelection, and other aspects of their roles as elected representatives. Such legislative-centered public administration thus means that administrative agencies are a central and nearly constant focus of legislators in most of what they do. From the perspective of legislators as well as administrators, then, the core of day-to-day governance, of collective choice and public action at the national level is the legislator–administrator nexus. Individual legislator offices, the "little legislatures" of committees and subcommittees, and public administrators and their agencies are engaged in almost continuous interaction aimed at mutual adjustment of interests and aims and policy refinement.

In addition, the preference of legislators runs strongly in the direction of searching for opportunities to make new law, and claim the credit that goes along with virgin policy, rather than the much more tedious and less political credit-rich task of overseeing the implementation of existing law and considering necessary refinements and adjustments. To the extent that legislators concern themselves with oversight, they tend toward a focus on what has gone wrong with implementation and policy management, and not on what changes in law may be required, the latter implying faulty initial policy design. Some other actors in the policy process must take up the slack and give particular attention to the needs for policy refinement that may arise along with the need for wholly new law. Although the density and reach of policy networks are likely to vary by policy area, for nearly every public issue there is also likely to be a surfeit of organized interests and purveyors of self-proclaimed disinterested analysis willing to fill the gap in legislator attention. Even in a networked governance world, however, public organizations retain special, central status because of the political responsibility and legal accountability they have for the laws entrusted to them. Lawmakers recognize this; indeed they have structured the system of policy management to further heighten and clarify the responsibility and accountability of administrators. Even in an information-rich environment, the avenues for information transfer are likely to be the most varied and numerous between legislators and their administrative agents. Despite a system designed to separate policy making and policy management, therefore, the makers and the managers have a distinct and special relationship.

Governance Transformation, Blurred Boundaries, and the Advantage of Distance

A second set of objections to the argument that public organizations should be the primary source, and regarded as the best source, of information, analysis, and guidance about the law's suitability and need for reformulation or replacement, stems from the "transformation of governance" (Kettl, 2002) that has swept the world in the past three decades. The transformation encompasses reforms associated with the new public management, as well as the multiplication of the "tools of government" (Hood & Margetts, 2007; Salamon, 2002) and the remarkable expansion of networks in the development and implementation of public policy (Goldsmith & Kettl, 2009). When public agencies were the nearly exclusive provider of public services, and thus when their staffs were strongly oriented toward direct contact with clients, with the public at large, and with the rhythms of everyday social life, they may have had extensive, intimate, and exclusive possession of information about the performance of the law, and about what adjustments, adaptations, changes, and new actions were necessary to attend to the ever-changing dynamics of an open society. These conditions still obtain in such prominent public professions as law enforcement and education. With the emergence of a revitalized conservatism, the particular rise of neoliberalism, and the devolution, deregulation, contracting out, and outsourcing those political changes have engendered, however, many of the experiences of the state's engagement with the private sphere that were special to public administrators and public employees are now also the province of private employees in both for-profit contractors and specialized human service delivery nonprofits. Thus robbed of their exclusivity as the leading edge of the state occupying the boundary between state and society, in part because the boundary itself seems to have become so much more blurred, how can public organizations claim any special status in providing guidance to lawmakers on what changes have become acceptable or necessary and thus should be enshrined in statutes?

As I noted in the previous section, one possible response to this question may be found by considering matters of accountability. Yet the governance transformation has been in substantial part a transformation in conceptions of accountability. Public administrators are now public *managers*, and they are principally accountable to their overseers for performance—producing defined program outputs and outcomes. This has placed a premium on devising yardsticks for assessing performance, and the change in terminology, from public administration to public management, has signaled that production is now more than ever to be the primary concern of public officials, and public organizations are now more than ever to be operated like private enterprises. The rise to prominence of a managerial orientation in the public sector, and the narrowing conception of public administrators as managers of a production process, is reinforced by the expansion and multiplication of networking. Although once public administrators were primarily engaged in governing, now governing activity is more broadly diffused across a multiplicity of actors. Where governing authority, and especially responsibility, rest is now much harder to pin down. Public managers are primarily and more narrowly responsible for supervising, or even just participating in, a production process involving a far-flung assortment of public, quasi-public, and private actors.

An emphasis on performance suggests that when public managers fall short of the public production goals set for them, or which they set for themselves, the problem is in their performance, not in the design of policy. With the focus on performance and the imperative to meet production demands, public managers do not have the luxury to contemplate changes in society that may require changes in the underlying statutory authority on which they operate. Indeed, they may not be regarded as the most trustworthy sources of information, analysis, and guidance about refinements in public law or the need for new law, because their interest now lies even more substantially with meeting production benchmarks. The experiencing function thus passes to seemingly more objective, dispassionate third parties—universities, think tanks, and even special interest groups—whose program and policy assessments lawmakers will find easier to tailor to their own political needs and personal policy aims. The performance focus further relieves legislators of the burden of oversight, because they have further rationalized and systematized information gathering and assessment of policy implementation performance; they can simply compare it to program benchmarks and strategic plans.

Nevertheless, the altered architecture of institutional arrangements and governing processes of the much heralded transformation of governance may yet prove to be more a boon than a bane to a special, high-quality role for public organizations in the shaping and reshaping of public law. The more diffuse and far-reaching interconnections characterizing the rise of a networked governing structure give public administrators much greater access to, much more frequent interactions with, and potentially much richer insights into the dynamics of society in the present and into the immediate future of social change than permitted by the more hermetic boundary between public and private defined by mid-20th-century public administration orthodoxy. What many public organizations have sacrificed in terms of direct responsibility for service delivery may be compensated for by the much richer environment of social contact, at least with the organized segment of the private sphere, provided by the new governing reality.

Furthermore, although the greater dispersal and privatization of service delivery tasks and other forms of policy execution present increased complexity and therefore ambiguity about where responsibility lies when troubles arise, the greater diffusion and haziness of public action also afford public administrators some distance from the day-to-day governing fray. The distance may not be much, but just enough, perhaps, to provide them the opportunity for reflection not only about questions concerning where responsibility and accountability might lie in the more tangled governing reality of networks, but also about the most basic questions of public administration. Has the agency chosen the most appropriate enabling actions to carry out this law? Is this law in its current form really suitable for confronting the problem it was designed to address? What new or altered conditions require adjustments to the agency's implementation strategy, or to the law itself? What, overall, can the agency learn from the execution of this law that may guide future policy making? Because of their primary obligation to the public good, no political actors save public administrators can fully bear the responsibility and exercise the capacity for asking and trying to answer such questions.

Constitutional Reform and Tacit Legitimacy

It is one thing to assert that public organizations should play a central role in informing and guiding the refinement and adaptation of public law to changing societal circumstances. But to claim that this role may extend to constitutional reform seems patently absurd. The courts are the province of constitutional examination and change. They should not take their cues from mere bureaucrats. Of course, my argument is not dependent on the claim that public administrators should be the *sole* source of guidance about constitutional adaptation, only that they have a distinctive role in providing critical information and guidance that might lead not just to statutory but also to constitutional change. My claim follows from Woodrow Wilson's conception of the place of public law, including constitutions, in political development.

Reflecting the lessons he drew from the development of the English commonwealth, Wilson regarded public law, especially constitutions, as the culmination of the long development and accumulation of habits and mores of a people. Indeed, it was not until their social and political development were long underway that a people's sense of themselves as a distinctive polity could be codified in a written constitution, or in a recognized body of common law and government acts. Although a constitution may be the culmination of a particular stage of development, no polity can be static. The dynamism and disruptiveness of modernity assured that, Wilson concluded. Hence in any liberal democratic regime, the further development and adaptation of public law, including the constitution, is dependent on what Wilson described as the state seeing "government in contact with the people" and remaining in constant "contact with the present." Again, this is the role that Wilson theorized for public administration. Yet he did acknowledge, long before it was recognized in more recent scholarship (e.g., Skowronek, 1982), that the courts played a central role at a critical stage in American political development, serving as perhaps the principal vehicle for administrative adaptation and integration, linking individual citizen demands to national interests so as to create a true national polity (Wilson, 1908). Hence, in addition to the courts being by far the primary if not exclusive source of constitutional examination, reinterpretation, and change in purely *legal* terms, one may argue that the courts, including especially national constitutional courts like the U.S. Supreme Court, still play a vital role in harmonizing individual and group interests with national interests, continually probing the line between "*Interference* and *Laissez faire*." This greatly diminishes any such claims for public administration.

Continued popular legitimacy of the separation-of-powers design generally and of the role of the courts in particular reinforce this argument. As in the case of their elected representatives, with the public at large there is likely to be tacit acceptance of a substantial level of influence for public administration in policy assessment, adaptation, and reform. The legitimacy of far-reaching bureaucratic influence on the shape of the law is, however, likely at best to be on shaky ground. This stems from the general decline of public trust in government since the 1960s, well documented in the United States. With a few notable exceptions, this decline in trust has extended to a host of both public and private institutions. Among national public institutions, however, citizens express far greater trust and confidence in the U.S. Supreme Court than in the executive and legislative branches (NORC, 2007, pp. 236–238). When more than half of the respondents to the General Social Survey disagree with the statement that "most government administrators can be trusted to do what is best for the country" and another one fifth are indifferent (p. 1526), the normative case for substantial, even central, public administration influence on the shape of public law, and especially the Constitution, is weakened considerably.

That the courts continue to play a significant role in harmonizing individual and group interests with national interests through statutory and constitutional interpretation and adjustments to both common law and constitutional law is not, however, a significant threat to my claim for a special, high-quality role for public organizations in the shaping and reshaping of public law, including constitutions. Administrative agencies frequently appear before the courts as parties to cases and controversies, and the courts have shown a general deference to administrative expertise. Usually, agencies only get into trouble when they fail to meet established standards of procedural justice, such as when their actions are unbalanced or arbitrary, or their decision-making processes are insufficiently transparent. Otherwise, although administrative agencies may be seen as instruments of the courts for furthering the latter's aims to make adjustments among contending interests and further refine common, statutory, or constitutional law, one may also see the matter in just the opposite light. The judicial process is an additional vehicle by which public administration may enlighten lawmakers about changing societal conditions, and through their role as parties to major cases, public administrators may use their experience, knowledge, and expertise to guide the policy process toward policy refinements, new policy, or critical adjustments to the fundamental laws of the land.

This leaves questions of legitimacy and the challenge of the antigovernment strain in the public philosophy of the American polity. Not only was the larger part of the Declaration of Independence a litany of complaints about what the newly proclaimed Americans considered illegitimate administrative actions taken under the Crown's auspices, but the founding act of the constitutional convention and the ratification debates that followed unleashed a fierce struggle over the legitimacy of a particular conception and design for governance, including a defense of a relatively robust administration. The rise of a more definitively administrative state roughly a century later renewed the legitimacy struggle. To some extent, that struggle is ongoing, because all the arguments advanced in the United States in favor of a legitimately far-reaching and powerful role for unelected administrators are partial or inadequate in some way. Some citizens are quite vocal in their contempt for public bureaucracy, and many are ambivalent, to say the least, about the effectiveness of government administration. Yet few scholars and other thinkers, let alone citizens at large, have anything to offer in the way of functional substitutes. One may safely conclude that the tacit legitimacy of administrative power is the default setting in current American political culture, and this extends to acceptance of a central role for public administrators and their organizations in information gathering, assessment, and assertive guidance of the process of reform and renewal of public law including the "working Constitution" (Long, 1952).

Overcoming Bureaucratic Pathologies and the Cult of Performance Management

The central obstacles to the full realization of the special governing role I have put forth lie within public administration itself. These twin obstacles are rooted in the nature of formal organizations, especially public organizations, and in the evolving values of the new governance. With respect to the nature of formal organizations, the challenge to my argument arises in particular from how organizations socially construct knowledge—how they define what constitutes facts, how they organize the search for information, how they formally assemble that information, and how that information becomes instilled in organizational routines. Here I am using the terminology and insights of Lynn Eden's (2004) superb study of the failure of the U.S. defense establishment, and particularly the U.S. Air Force, to take account of the likelihood of devastating mass fire from nuclear attack. Both civilian and military administrators thus failed to guide lawmakers about the proper design of U.S. nuclear weapons policy, especially the size and cost of the nation's nuclear arsenal. As Eden argues, the "organizational frames" that develop out of the professional specialties and value-laden choices that define the founding of a public organization strongly influence what members of the organization are capable of seeing in their immediate environment and the wider society that may be relevant to their organizational goals and the missions lawmakers have given them. As "knowledge-laden" routines evolve based on what organizational members can detect, those routines further shape or reinforce the frames the organization uses to conduct information searches, assess the information gathered, and develop formal recommendations and general guidance to lawmakers regarding revising policy or creating wholly new policy. What one might call "organizational myopia" may be widespread throughout most public organizations and a hindrance to the experiencing function.

The challenge to my argument from the evolving values of the new governance arises from the juggernaut that performance management has become. The extent to which public administrators have inculcated the precepts of the new governance, especially the focus on performance management, is remarkable but not altogether surprising. The precepts of performance management are consistent in many ways with the old public administration orthodoxy that still survives in the culture of many public organizations and in American government more generally. Nor is performance management wrong-headed. Promoting good performance in public management is valuable in itself, and realizing better organizational performance reinforces legitimacy and serves the public interest well. But the embrace of performance management in the public sector may be getting out of hand, becoming an end in itself. This would signal the loss of the critical perspective among public administrators that they are stewards of public law in a larger sense. A wholesale focus on the part of public managers on their own and their organization's performance threatens the loss of their vital role as the most careful critics of the policies for which they are responsible. The nation needs public servants with a sufficiently broad perspective on the policies they carry out so that they consciously and continuously monitor society for changes that may render policies less effective or even obsolete. A broader perspective on their role than merely meeting benchmarks and targets will give public managers the courage, in facing likely criticism of their performance, to assert themselves in offering guidance to policy makers when they are convinced that fine-tuning, more substantial reform, or replacement, is called for. Ultimately, they may even find the courage to call for more sweeping changes to the core constituents of the regime.

It is time for public administrators to lay forceful claim to their primacy in the experiencing, informing, and guiding function, which responds to the demands for adjustments that even carefully crafted public laws inevitably require. This will necessitate clearly delimiting the boundaries of a public management orientation, making it subservient to the core principles of self-government. Those principles stress that law must be made, remade, or replaced only on careful reflection and with due diligence in selecting only those adjustments that serve the common good. By claiming for themselves the indispensable governing role as principal organ of experience, public administrators can more fully satisfy their aspirations to stewardship of public law. This is a challenge the next generation of public administration scholars and practicing public administrators must fully embrace if they are to carry on as a body of citizens with a sustained concern for the health of the whole regime.

References

Bimber, B. (1996). *The politics of expertise in Congress: The rise and fall of the Office of Technology Assessment.* Albany, NY: State University of New York Press.

Carpenter, D.P. (2001). *The forging of bureaucratic autonomy: Reputations, networks, and policy innovation in executive agencies, 1862–1928.* Princeton, NJ: Princeton University Press.

Cook, B.J. (2007). *Democracy and administration: Woodrow Wilson's ideas and the challenges of public management.* Baltimore, MD: Johns Hopkins University Press.

Eden, L. (2004). *Whole world on fire: Organizations, knowledge & nuclear weapons devastation.* Ithaca, NY: Cornell University Press.

Fung, A., Graham, M. & Weil, D. (2007). *Full disclosure: The perils and promise of transparency.* New York: Cambridge University Press.

Goldsmith, S. & Kettl, D.F. (2009). (eds). *Unlocking the power of networks: Keys to high-performance government.* Washington, DC: Brookings Institution.

Hood, C.C. & Margetts, H.Z. (2007). *The tools of government in the digital age* Basingstoke: Palgrave Macmillan.

Kettl, D.F. (2002). *The transformation of governance: Public administration for twenty-first century America.* Baltimore, MD: Johns Hopkins University Press.

Kingdon, J.W. (1995). *Agendas, alternatives, and public policies*, 2nd edn. New York: HarperCollins.

Krause, G.A. (2002). Separated powers and institutional growth in the presidential and congressional branches: Distinguishing between short-run versus long-run dynamics. *Political Research Quarterly* 55: 27–57.

Lindblom, C.E. & Cohen, D.K. (1979). *Usable knowledge: Social science and social problem solving.* New Haven, CT: Yale University Press.

Link, A.S., Hirst, D.W. & Little, J.E. (eds) (1966–1994). *The papers of Woodrow Wilson* (69 vols.). Princeton, NJ: Princeton University Press.

Long, N. E. (1952). Bureaucracy and constitutionalism. *American Political Science Review* 46: 808–818.

Lowi, T.J. (1991). Toward a legislature of the first kind. In W.H. Robinson & W.H. Wellborn (eds), *Knowledge, power, and the Congress.* Washington, DC: Congressional Quarterly, pp. 9–43.

McCubbins, M.D. & Schwartz, T. (1984). Congressional oversight overlooked: Police patrols versus fire alarms. *American Journal of Political Science* 28: 165–179.

NORC. (2007). *General social surveys 1972–2006: Cumulative codebook*. National Opinion Research Center. Chicago, IL: University of Chicago Press.

Rohr, J.A. (1986). *To run a constitution: The legitimacy of the administrative state*. Lawrence: University Press of Kansas.

Rose, R. (1989). Signals for steering government: A symposium of the Wissenschaftszentrum, Berlin. *Journal of Public Policy* 9: 233–240.

Rosenbloom, D.H. (2000). *Building a legislative-centered public administration: Congress and the administrative state, 1946–1999*. Tuscaloosa: University of Alabama Press.

Salamon, L.M. (ed.) (2002). *The tools of government: A guide to the new governance*. New York: Oxford University Press.

Schick, A. (1991). Informed legislation: Policy research versus ordinary knowledge. In W.H. Robinson & W.H. Wellborn (eds), *Knowledge, power, and the Congress*. Washington, DC: Congressional Quarterly, pp. 99–119.

Schneider, A. & Ingram, H. (1988). Systematically pinching ideas: A comparative approach to policy design. *Journal of Public Policy* 8: 61–80.

Skowronek, S. (1982). *Building a new American state: The expansion of national administrative capacities, 1877–1920*. New York: Cambridge University Press.

Skowronek, S. (2006). The reassociation of ideals and purposes: Racism, liberalism, and the American political tradition. *American Political Science Review* 100: 385–401.

Terry, L.D. (2003). *Leadership of public bureaucracies: The administrator as conservator*. Armonk, NY: M.E. Sharpe.

Van Creveld, M. (1999). *The rise and decline of the state*. Cambridge: Cambridge University Press.

Whiteman, D. (1995). *Communication in Congress: Members, staff and the search for information*. Lawrence: University Press of Kansas.

Wilson, W. (1887). The study of administration. *Political Science Quarterly* 2: 197–222.

Wilson, W. (1908). *Constitutional government in the United States*. New York: Columbia University Press.

Wilson, W. (1981). *Congressional government: A study in American politics*. Baltimore, MD: Johns Hopkins University Press. (Original work published 1887.)

Wood, B.D. & Waterman, R.W. (1994). *Bureaucratic dynamics: The role of bureaucracy in a democracy*. Boulder, CO: Westview.

9 Crafting the Intellectual History of U.S. Public Administration Anew

The Constitutional Foundations of the President's Committee on Administrative Management

Stephanie P. Newbold

The High Noon of American public administration orthodoxy resides in President Franklin Roosevelt's masterful effort to shape, define, and craft a vast administrative system of government that allowed the executive branch to play a more direct and central role in the economic, social, and political lives of the American people. The nation's 32nd president took office in 1933 promising a New Deal for the nation. Applying the economic philosophy of John Maynard Keynes, Roosevelt abandoned Adam Smith's invisible hand theory and expanded the size, role, and responsibility of the U.S. federal government in an effort to establish a political and administrative infrastructure designed to tackle the economic devastation caused by the Great Depression.

One of the most interesting and often underappreciated legacies of the Roosevelt administration is the president's reliance on public administration scholars to aid in the creation, development, and maintenance of a growing, more responsive, more demanding, more involved federal government. Louis Brownlow, Arthur Buck, Robert Cushman, James Fesler, Luther Gulick, Joseph Harris, James Hart, Arthur MacMahon, Harvey Mansfield, Sr., Charles Merriam, Floyd Reeves, and Leonard D. White all contributed great knowledge and expertise to the Roosevelt administration. Just as importantly, their individual and collective experiences within the executive branch fundamentally transformed how this distinguished group of scholars was able to contribute and advance the theoretical and practical foundations of public administration, democratic governance, and the intellectual history of the field as their academic careers progressed. The President's Committee on Administrative Management is but one noteworthy example of how this generation of public administration academics contributed to the practice of managing the federal government.

Herbert Kaufman has often addressed the impact of the New Deal period on the fields of public administration and political science. On the 70th Anniversary of the Brownlow Report, Kaufman reviewed the Committee's fourth paper, Problems of Administrative Management, which was co-authored by his dissertation chair and mentor Arthur MacMahon, and observed: "The work endures because the problems with which it grapples are timeless" (2007, p. 1046). The field of U.S. public administration generally agrees with this assessment because we continue to study and engage the works of scholars who contributed to the New Deal era not only because they add to our intellectual history but more importantly because these collective ideas speak to some of the most fundamental issues that continue to affect administrative management in complex public organizations.

Exploring the intellectual significance of Roosevelt's efforts to transform the workings of the federal government into what would become the modern administrative state is a critical piece of the intellectual history of U.S. public administration (Fesler, 1987; Karl, 1963; Newbold and Rosenbloom, 2007; Polenberg, 1966; Rosenbloom et al., 2015; Schlesinger, 1978; Stillman, 1988). From the time President Roosevelt submitted the Final Report of the President's Committee on Administrative Management to Congress in January 1937, formally entitled Administrative Management in the Government of the United States, it became clear that the executive branch of American government was going to become a more prominent actor within the management of the nation's government and within the development and implementation of national policy initiatives. As such, this effort established the Executive Office of the President in 1939 and "fundamentally transformed the presidency from a weak office with a few staff assistants to what we know it as today, that is, one of the most powerful chief executive positions in the world" (Stillman, 1988, p. 135).

Chaired by Louis Brownlow with the support of Charles Merriam and Luther Gulick, the President's Committee on Administrative Management sought to create the type of infrastructure necessary for Roosevelt to implement a vast portion of his New Deal agenda. The public administration and political science academic communities have recognized the Final Report of the President's Committee on Administrative Management as making significant contributions to the development of executive branch dynamics, executive leadership, and executive organization (Denhardt, 1995; Karl, 1963; Rohr, 1986; Rosenbloom et al., 2015). The five central recommendations that scholars rely on most when describing how this study influenced the development of contemporary administrative management include: 1) expanding the White House staff; 2) reorganizing the executive branch; 3) strengthening managerial agencies; 4) expanding the merit system in the federal government; and 5) increasing accountability standards on behalf of the executive to Congress (Brownlow et al., 1937).

From 1937 to 2006, what remained surprisingly overlooked within the intellectual history of American public administration and to a large extent political science were the five accompanying papers that were part of the official record associated with the President's Committee on Administrative Management. As Newbold and Terry (2006) explain, the Final Report of the Committee did not occur in a vacuum and its recommendations were largely a product of a collaborative effort to improve the quality of public management within the executive branch in a way that complemented the constitutional traditions of American government. These five studies focused on (1) personnel management; (2) fiscal management; (3) independent regulatory commissions; (4) administrative management; and (5) rule-making and the preparation of proposed legislative measures by administrative departments.

Taken together, these official government documents constituted nearly 300 pages of text and almost all of the recommendations and analyses found within the Final Report that President Roosevelt submitted to Congress are derived from these five papers. The U.S. Government Printing Office printed copies of each paper and sold them for 15 to 25 cents apiece. Moreover, each of these papers can be found within the government documents section of any major U.S. library. Newbold and Terry's exploration of these overlooked papers, which constitutes the complete story of how the Brownlow Project's Final Report came to its final recommendations, not only enriches the intellectual history of U.S. public administration but also illustrates that this effort of governmental reform encompassed much more than managerial recommendations for how to improve executive branch organization and empower the American president.

On the 70th Anniversary of the Brownlow Project, Peri Arnold reflected on Robert Cushman's analysis of independent regulatory commissions and observed the following: "Today, far from being just an interesting episode in American public administration, its work on regulation, as much as its work on executive organization, heralded and enabled a new era of presidential administration" (2007, p. 1039). This new era of executive administration is also one that transformed U.S. public administration in fundamental ways, working to establish both an increasingly powerful president and administrative state. As David Rosenbloom (2000) has correctly shown, however, this effort also motivated Congress beginning in 1946 to create a more comprehensive, wide-ranging role for the legislative branch in the management and support of the federal government and its administrative agencies. The Brownlow Project ironically was also responsible for establishing a legislatively oriented approach to U.S. public administration.

The unifying theme of the President's Committee on Administrative Management is its collective emphasis on how to improve democratic governance within the American republic. The Committee's effort in this regard relates directly to how and why a Constitutional School is central to U.S. public administration theory and practice. The purpose of a Constitutional School of U.S. public administration is to demonstrate how the constitutional fabric of the nation serves as the bedrock of American government and administration (Newbold, 2010). Throughout the Brownlow Project, the Committee members relied on *Federalist 70* as the constitutional justification to expand executive responsibility and executive function. Alexander Hamilton maintained that unity in the executive created the framework needed for a strong president to lead the nation more effectively. According to the Brownlow Committee, the more powerful the American president becomes, the more likely he is able to address and solve key problems facing the management of government and of the country. The authors of the Brownlow Project, moreover, were emphatic in their understanding that the Constitution and the nation's founding documents serve as the foundation for how to begin solving some of the most critical managerial problems facing the nation. Almost every recommendation the Committee made in its Final Report and in the supplemental research that directed the Committee as a whole was grounded in the ideas espoused by Hamilton in *Federalist 70*.

The most important lesson to ascertain from Newbold and Terry's exploration of the President's Committee on Administrative Management is that the Final Report championed by President Roosevelt was not just about improving executive branch management as almost all of the literature claims was the central contribution of this groundbreaking study. That was certainly key, but the Committee members were even more concerned with improving the constitutional infrastructure of the second branch of government in such a way that would enable the executive to manage the needs of the nation more efficiently and responsively.

The Constitutional School encourages "scholars and practitioners to engage, debate, and write on issues that are significant to the constitutional heritage of the United States, its democratic institutions, and its administrative agencies" (Newbold, 2010, p. 544). Newbold and Terry's article supports this very mission. It highlights the forgotten intellectual history of one of the most important periods in the development of U.S. public administration and in doing so provides the field with a rich, comprehensive example of how and why constitutional tradition and democratic values are the most important elements of public sector governance and of efforts to reform the practice of public management.

References

Arnold, P. 2007. The Brownlow Committee, regulation, and the presidency: Seventy years later. *Public administration review* 67(6): 1030–1040.

Brownlow, L., Merriam, C. & Gulick, L. 1937. *Administrative management in the government of the United States*. Washington, DC: President's Committee on Administrative Management.

Denhardt, R. 1995. *Public administration: An action orientation*, 2nd edn. Fort Worth, TX: Harcourt Brace.

Fesler, J. 1987. The Brownlow Committee fifty years later. *Public administration review* 47(4): 291–295.

Karl, B. 1963. *Executive reorganization and reform in the New Deal: The genesis of administrative management, 1900–1939*. Cambridge, MA: Harvard University Press.

Kaufman, H. 2007. Administrative management: Does its strong executive thesis still merit our attention? *Public administration review* 67(6): 1041–1048.

Newbold, S.P. 2010. Toward a Constitutional School for U.S. public administration. *Public administration review* 70(4): 538–546.

Newbold, S.P. & Rosenbloom, D.H. 2007. Brownlow report retrospective. *Public administration review* 67(6): 1006–1009.

Newbold, S.P. & Terry, L.D. 2006. The president's committee on administrative management: The untold story and the Federalist connection. *Administration and society* 38(5): 522–555.

Polenberg, R. 1966. *Reorganizing Roosevelt's government: The controversy over executive reorganization, 1936–1939*. Cambridge, MA: Harvard University Press.

Rohr, J.A. 1986. *To run a constitution: The legitimacy of the administrative state*. Lawrence: University Press of Kansas.

Rosenbloom, D.H. 2000. *Building a legislative centered public administration*. Tuscaloosa, AL: University of Alabama Press.

Rosenbloom, D.H., Kravchuk, R. & Clerkin, R. 2015. *Public administration: Understanding management, politics, and law in the Public Sector*, 8th edn. Boston, MA: McGraw-Hill.

Schlesinger, A. 1978. Roosevelt as chief administrator. In Francis Rourke, ed. *Bureaucratic power in national politics*, 3rd edn. Boston, MA: Little, Brown, and Company, pp. 257–269.

Stillman, R. 1988. *Creating the American state: The moral reformers and the modern administrative world they made*. Tuscaloosa, AL: University of Alabama Press.

The President's Committee on Administrative Management

The Untold Story and the Federalist Connection

Stephanie P. Newbold and Larry D. Terry

From: *Administration and Society* 37 (November 2006): 523–555. Abridged.

In January 1937, President Franklin D. Roosevelt submitted to Congress a study entitled *Administrative Management in the Government of the United States*, produced by the President's Committee on Administrative Management.[1] This 53-page document, commonly referred to as the Brownlow Report—named in honor of the Committee's Chair, Louis Brownlow—has been widely cited in both the public administration and political science literature as a landmark study specifically designed to improve executive-branch management. President Roosevelt appointed Charles E. Merriam and Luther Gulick as members of the Committee. In addition, the Committee appointed Joseph P. Harris as Director of Research. Although Harris did not serve as a Committee member, he was an integral figure who helped to shape the operational structure of the Brownlow Committee's findings and, according to James Fesler, played a significant role in organizing the Brownlow Project.[2]

The final report that Roosevelt approved was accompanied, as part of the President's Committee on Administrative Management, by five other studies that were not only led by Brownlow, Merriam, and Gulick and supervised by Harris but were also commissioned by the president. These five papers included nearly 300 pages of text. Although the substantive nature of the recommendations made by these authors was highlighted in the final report, in order to develop a more comprehensive understanding of the value-added dimension that these recommendations bring to public administration, generally, and executive-branch management, specifically, the field needs to examine the Brownlow Committee's findings in their entirety.[3]

In his authoritative work, *Executive Reorganization and Reform in the New Deal* (1963), Barry Karl indicated that the report of the President's Committee on Administrative Management "appended nine 'Special Studies,' which Merriam, with a wry mixture of poetry and justice, called the 'non-supporting documents'" (p. 222). In 1937, the U.S. Government Printing Office published the findings of the President's Committee on Administrative Management in three different formats. The first was the 53-page final report President Roosevelt submitted to Congress. The second was entitled,

"The President's Committee on Administrative Management: Report of the Committee with Studies of Administrative Management in the Federal Government." This 382-page document included the final report and each of the accompanying studies that served as the basis for the 53-page document. The table of contents for this publication lists each study by author and not by title, although the titles of each study are mentioned. When Karl analyzed these studies, he followed this format and counted by author and not title, which adds up to nine studies instead of five. This calculation is how he found the "nine Special Studies." Finally, the U.S. Government Printing Office published each of the five accompanying studies individually and sold them for 15 to 25 cents a piece by the Superintendent of Documents in Washington, DC In our analysis of each of these reports, however, we did not find any appendices like those referenced by Karl. If such appendices do exist, they are not listed in the table of contents of any of the three reports produced by the President's Committee on Administrative Management and published by the U.S. Government Printing Office.

We make the case that these authors were guided by their knowledge and understanding of American constitutional heritage and the specific application of *Federalist 27* and *Federalist 70* to the contemporary issues affecting executive-branch dynamics during the early 20th century. Such an examination answers the call of scholars such as Dwight Waldo (1948), Lynton Caldwell (1955), and Leonard D. White (1948, 1951, 1954, 1958), who eloquently reminded us of the importance of administrative history to the study and practice of public administration.[4]

The Brownlow Report: Advancing Democratic Governance

From the moment that President Roosevelt submitted the final report of his Committee on Administrative Management to Congress, the public administration community was—and continues to be—particularly interested in the findings and recommendations of this study.[5] Highly regarded scholars of public administration (Denhardt 1995; Karl 1963; Rohr 1986; Rosenbloom and Kravchuk 2002; Stillman 1988, 1991) have correctly pointed to the fact that the Brownlow Report recognized the president's need for additional help while also emphasizing the importance of expanding the White House staff, reorganizing the executive branch, strengthening managerial agencies, expanding the merit system, and increasing accountability standards on behalf of the executive branch to Congress.

Although this analysis enhances our understanding of what the President's Committee on Administrative Management recommended, the Committee Members, as well as President Roosevelt, also recognized that the most important objective of the report was the *preservation of the nation's democratic institutions*. The Committee clearly saw the symbiotic relationship between democracy and public management. According to the

Committee's authors, administrative efficiency must be built into the machinery of government. The goal of the Brownlow Report, the authors claimed, was:

> to make democracy work today in our National Government; that is, to make our Government an up-to-date, efficient, and effective instrument for carrying out the will of the Nation. It is for this purpose that the Government needs thoroughly modern tools of management ... We know that bad management may spoil good purposes, and that without good management democracy itself cannot achieve its highest goals.
> (1937, p. 4)

The "highest goals" of the American Administrative State are the same today as they were in 1937 as well as in 1787: *Public administration is first and foremost concerned with upholding the democratic values embedded within our constitutional heritage.* For as Alexander Hamilton appropriately reminded us in *Federalist 27:* "I believe it may be laid down as a general rule, that [the people's] confidence in and obedience to a government, will commonly be proportioned to the goodness or badness of its administration" (Cooke 1961, p. 178).

One of the central themes connecting these papers is Hamilton's position on unity, articulated in *Federalist 70.* He capitalized this word in his text and argued that the doctrine of unity is an important and necessary component of energy in the executive. Energy in the executive, according to Hamilton, is essential for good government because a weak executive—the preference of the Anti-Federalists—implies an inability to execute important and necessary responsibilities associated with republican statecraft.[6] The four components that make up energy in the executive include (1) unity; (2) duration; (3) an adequate provision for its support; and (4) competent powers. According to Hamilton, unity of the executive[7] is conducive to energy in the executive because, if unity is not maintained, the form of constitutional democracy advocated in *The Federalist Papers* cannot survive.[8] Hamilton concluded his analysis by observing that "the UNITY [emphasis in original] of the Executive of this state was one of the best of the distinguishing features of our constitution,"[9] and it is precisely this point that served as the philosophical foundation of the five accompanying studies that represent the complete Brownlow Report.

Study I: *Personnel Administration in the Federal Service* by Floyd W. Reeves and Paul T. David

Floyd Reeves and Paul David divided their 75-page study into four sections that focused on (1) the problems associated with effective personnel administration; (2) federal personnel administration of the day; (3) the development of a service of personnel administration; and (4) the extension of the merit system. A central theme of this study—one that was certainly incorporated into the final Brownlow Report—is that personnel administration cannot be examined independent of other aspects of administrative management because effective personnel administration is an important dynamic that affects the president's ability to implement his policy agenda.

Reeves and David argued that the American public regards the president as being primarily responsible for the type and quality of personnel administration implemented throughout the federal service. The structure of the executive branch in 1937, however, did not enable the president to devote an appropriate amount of time and attention to even the most urgent of personnel matters. As a result, the president's ability to balance administrative and political responsibilities, as they relate to personnel management, became increasingly difficult.

The distinction between administrative and political responsibilities draws our attention to Paul Light's (1995) argument that government thickens when presidents place political appointees in positions that are traditionally held by career civil servants. Reeves and David maintained that one way to aid the president in balancing these administrative and political responsibilities is executive discretion. They argued that personnel reform was needed not only to buffer the president against political pressure regarding his administrative responsibilities and appointment powers but also to serve as a preventive measure against the enormous waste that occurs when appointments are open to political consideration. Reeves and David maintained that the president must have the authority to appoint individuals who support his policies and programs to the highest levels of government. They also recommended, however, that increasing the number of higher-level positions in the civil service would lift its entire morale and give an incentive for the recruitment of the best talent in the lower positions (Reeves & David 1937, pp. 9 and 72–75).

In the Committee's final report, Brownlow, Merriam, and Gulick recommended that the Civil Service Commission be reorganized into a Civil Service Administration, led by a single executive officer and a nonsalaried Civil Service Board. This type of reorganization, according to the Committee, would "give the agency a degree of *unity, energy*, and responsibility impossible to obtain in an administrative agency headed by a full-time board of several members" (Brown et al. 1937, p. 10: emphasis added). This recommendation, which originated in Study 1, was arguably one of Reeves and David's most important suggestions for improving executive-branch dynamics and points to the connection with *Federalist 70*. The final report stated, "Personnel management is an essential element of executive management" (p. 10), and that was precisely Reeves and David's argument.

In their analysis for improving personnel administration, Reeves and David outlined specific ways to implement this proposal. First, their study maintained that personnel administration should be represented at the highest levels of administrative management by an adequate central personnel agency responsible to the president; at the departmental level by adequate departmental personnel offices responsible to the heads of departments; and at the bureau level by bureau personnel officers responsible to the bureau chiefs. Next, it pointed to the federal government's responsibility to address inequitable variations in compensation levels, hours of duty, and working conditions throughout the civil service. Third, respective heads of the central personnel agency and budget agencies should be among the principal advisers of the president in connection with major problems of organization and reorganization within the executive branch. Fourth, the administrative and professional staffs of the central personnel agency and the personnel offices of operating establishments should be regarded collectively as a unified career service of personnel administration. Finally, all members of the permanent service of personnel administration should be included within the competitive civil service, and other personnel officers should also be appointed on the basis of merit and efficiency through an appropriate procedure (pp. 6–8).

The final report recommended extending the merit system upward, outward, and downward, and this proposal has been viewed by the Committee's evaluators as an important and thoughtful way that its authors aimed to improve executive-branch dynamics. The recommendation to improve and strengthen the merit system in these three areas originated with Reeves and David's study. To achieve these goals, they proposed nine recommendations: some of the most informative included placing all non-policy forming presidential positions in the field services in the competitive classified service by appropriate legislation as soon as possible; requiring that lower positions in the permanent services, now excepted from the classified competitive service by the legislative or executive action, be surveyed in detail and transferred to the classified service by appropriate action as rapidly as feasible; revising the salary scale for higher nonpolitical positions to improve retention and recruitment of well-qualified administrators; and allowing incumbent emergency employees occupying positions that were made permanent and who do not have an appropriate civil service status to receive it after passing a suitable qualifying examination and upon certification by an approved nonpolitical personnel officer stating they have served with merit for at least one year (pp. 8–9).

The analysis of this study in the context of the four that follow suggests that improving personnel administration was only one aspect of the Committee's evaluation for improving executive-branch management. Recommending ways to enhance the president's managerial capacities laid the foundation for more substantive, constitutionally grounded suggestions for advancing democracy within the confines of the American administrative state.

Study II: *Fiscal Management in the National Government* by Arthur E. Buck and Harvey C. Mansfield, Sr.

Arthur Buck and Mansfield divided their 62-page study into two sections. The first, authored by Buck, focused on financial control and accountability, and the second, authored by Mansfield, critiqued the General Accounting Office.

Financial control and accountability

Buck outlined three important recommendations in this section. First, he advised that the president should be fully responsible for the financial management of the government; second, that suitable and up-to-date machinery and methods were required to aid the president in attaining effective financial management; and finally, that executive responsibility for the management of the government was incomplete without full accountability to Congress (Buck & Mansfield 1937, p. 29).

Buck argued that the Bureau of the Budget should be reorganized internally and integrated with the Treasury Department. In turn, its staff should be broadened and strengthened to handle the functions of budgetary control, administrative research, and investigation. Likewise, Buck maintained that the Treasury Department should be reorganized to eliminate all functions extraneous to financial administration (p. 29). Simply put, the federal government needed to implement a modern system of general accounting and reporting.

Buck also critiqued the absence of an independent and prompt auditing system for the financial transactions of the government and the failure to devise and install a modern system of accounting and record keeping. He maintained that the Bureau of the Budget should be the fulcrum of the Treasury Department: It should prepare the financial plan of the government for the president; it should receive the essential information for the current exercise of budgetary control; and it should establish an administrative division to focus on organization, research, investigation, planning, and coordination. Each of these recommendations was thoughtfully incorporated into the final report. In addition, Buck proposed specific ways to improve accounting methods and procedures, effective budgetary control, and accountability. These recommendations were in keeping with the final report's position that "it is the purpose of the budget system to provide in financial terms for planning, information, and control" (Brown et al. 1937, p. 16).

Hamilton's principle of unity of the executive, outlined in *Federalist 70*, is applicable to Buck's argument about the negative effects of reorganization on the Treasury Department. Buck maintained that the Budget and Accounting Act of 1921, as well as the expansion of the department's administrative functions and financial responsibilities within the federal government, had confused and derailed the need for a Treasurer whose duties involved the receipt, custody, and disbursement of public moneys and the need for an auditor whose decisions were subject to review by a comptroller. Hamilton, during his tenure as Secretary of the Treasury, established this type of managerial system, but such organizational efforts no longer existed in 1937. Under Hamilton's model, a clear sense of unity of the executive existed because the department's functions were divided into separate and distinct areas of responsibility; the applicability of what he wrote as *Publius* carried over into his constitutional responsibilities and organizational preferences as the chief administrator of the nation's finances. Buck's analysis of Hamilton's understanding of the proper managerial functions needed within the Treasury clearly pointed to this connection.

The General Accounting Office

Mansfield's analysis examined how the General Accounting Office exercised control over the executive; the relationship between the comptroller general and the president, Congress, and the courts; and some of the consequences of this system of control as it relates to administrative management. According to Mansfield, the problem that faced the federal government was how to secure effective administration under a managerial system that divided authority between the executive and the comptroller general in order to determine administrative policy and procedure (Buck & Mansfield 1937, p. 33). Specifically, he critiqued the administrative difficulties arising from the failure to distinguish between the concepts of audit and control and maintained that "the Budget and Accounting Act of 1921 took the unusual step of vesting both audit and control powers in the hands of an independent officer" (p. 33). Mansfield provided definitions for these terms: an audit is an investigation and report based on the fidelity and legality of fiscal transactions that is ordinarily made by an independent officer. Control, on the other hand, is an important dynamic of executive management because it involves the power to pass on expenditures and prevent them from being made. Like Buck, Mansfield was highly critical of the Budget and Accounting Act of 1921, believing it had created administrative chaos by taking the unusual step of vesting both powers in the hands of one independent officer, the Comptroller General.

Mansfield argued that the position of the comptroller general was unconstitutional and irresponsible because it was independent of all three branches of government (p. 49). For example, the president did not have the authority to remove the Comptroller General from his position nor could he initiate removal. In 1933, the Comptroller General ceased making annual reports to Congress by enforcing provisions in the Legislative Appropriations Act, which authorized the heads of establishments to discontinue the printing of their reports. He was not responsible to the courts, making this the only field of administrative action in which government officials were denied access to the judiciary for the purpose of testing the limits of their authority or the meaning of the laws under which they operate.

Mansfield recommended that the agency's name be changed to the General Auditing Office and that the comptroller general be referred to as the "auditor general" or the "officer of the auditor general." In keeping with this theme, Mansfield argued that the powers of the auditor general should include auditing and investigations and extend to all governmental agencies, unless exempted by Congress.

Like Buck, Mansfield, in his analysis of the General Accounting Office, sought to provide greater unity in the executive by means of improving fiscal management in the national government. He understood the contributions Hamilton had made to the Treasury Department and maintained that the Budget and Accounting Act of 1921 had undermined those important efforts. Specifically, Mansfield argued that "the power to settle all accounts and claims should be transferred to the Treasury Department in order to restore the *unity of Executive responsibility* that existed from 1817–1921" (p. 61: emphasis added). In addition, the power to prescribe administrative forms and methods of accounting should be transferred back to the Treasury. Under this recommendation, the Treasury would have responsibility for deciding legal questions and for the administrative execution of the budget. Such efforts, according to Mansfield, would provide a centralized system for control accounts and eliminate the present division of authority. It would, furthermore, create an environment in which financial responsibility would be clearly imposed on the president.

Study III: *The Problem of the Independent Regulatory Commissions* by Robert E. Cushman

Robert Cushman's work on independent regulatory commissions was regarded as the most controversial of all the recommendations made by the Brownlow Committee, particularly his position that "the regulatory problem is inherent in the progressive development of a complex economic society" (Cushman, 1937, p. 28). He divided this 37-page report into five sections that focused on (1) the historical background of the problem; (2) the inherent problem of the independent regulatory commissions; (3) legal limitations; (4) a suggested solution; and (5) an appraisal of the suggested plan. The problem that Cushman addressed centered on the following argument:

> There is high respect, based on experience, for the independent commission as a device for federal regulation. There exists a strong inclination to use this method for handling new regulatory jobs as they emerge. At the same time, the multiplication of these independent bodies leads toward a decentralized and chaotic administrative system. (p. 1)

The historical dynamics that highlight the problems Cushman associated with independent regulatory commissions were largely based on the commission movement in the United States, regulatory functions in the executive branch, and the segregation of judicial and appellate aspects of administration.

The representation of independent regulatory commissions as a "headless fourth branch of government" came from Cushman's analysis. This observation laid the theoretical and practical foundation for Cushman's critique of how independent regulatory commissions obstructed executive-branch management—a controversial argument for this time, but one that certainly resonated with Hamilton's position on the unity of the executive in *Federalist 70*. According to Cushman:

> The President is the general manager of the United States. The very purpose of the Executive Department under the Constitution is to center upon a *unified* and powerful Executive responsibility for a coordinated policy of administration and its efficient execution. Congress, by its very nature, is incapable either of doing administrative work or of holding accountable in any effective way the many officers or agencies engaged in administration. The President's duties and responsibilities in this field are not routine in nature, but carry with them broad discretionary powers.
>
> (1937, p. 13, emphasis added)

As a means of correcting this political and administrative deficiency, Cushman proposed a plan that would place independent regulatory commissions into established or "suitable" executive departments. Cushman defined "suitable departments as those that have functions relevant to those of the commission and that are neutral with respect to the regulatory duties of the commission rather than 'promotional' or otherwise biased" (p. 23). If the regulatory functions of a particular commission were not "suitable" for an executive department, they should be left independent. When incorporated into an executive department, Cushman proposed, the commission would be divided into judicial and administrative sections. The judicial section would be responsible for the judicial and quasi-judicial aspects of regulation and would be in the department for organizational purposes but otherwise completely independent of the agency. The president would only be able to remove these administrators from their positions for incompetence or misconduct. Neither the president nor the cabinet secretary could review the decisions of the judicial section, meaning the decisions would be based on the records prepared and presented by the administrative section. The judicial section would have the appellate power to review certain decisions made within the administrative section. The administrative section, on the other hand, would become a division within the department and would be responsible to the president and cabinet secretary. Public servants affiliated with this section would become part of the career civil service.

Cushman recognized the controversial nature of his plan for improving judicial and administrative management within independent regulatory commissions, but he also understood that such a proposal supported Hamilton's argument for the unity doctrine. The principle of unity of the executive creates the type of foundation needed to implement responsibility and other important managerial dynamics associated with governing a constitutional republic at the highest levels of government. Along this same line of reasoning, Cushman concluded, "The advantages of the suggested plan are substantial. It meets squarely the problem of the independent commissions. It creates the clear responsibility for policy-determining and administrative work that is so essential to effective over-all management" (p. 34). The authors of the final report concurred and cautioned their audience, "The independent commission, in short, provides the proper working conditions neither for administration nor for adjudication. It fails to provide responsibility for the first; it does not provide complete independence for the second" (p. 40). This observation not only supported the need for unity of the executive but also illustrated how this type of unity would improve the effectiveness of executive-branch management.

Study IV: *Problems of Administrative Management* by Arthur W. MacMahon, James W. Fesler, and Herbert Emmerich

Arthur MacMahon, James Fesler, and Herbert Emmerich divided their 58-page report into three sections. The first, authored by MacMahon, focused on departmental management; the second, authored by Fesler, highlighted executive management and the federal field service; and the third, authored by Emmerich, centered on government corporations and independent supervisory agencies.

Departmental management

MacMahon structured his section of the report into four parts: (1) objectives of departmental management; (2) the emergent pattern; (3) the allocation of supervisory duties; and (4) recruitment, training, and tenure. The first part, objectives of departmental management, focused on ways to assist the department head of each executive agency to manage policy questions more effectively, particularly as they related to formulation and implementation. It also addressed the promotion of coordination, both within the department and with other executive agencies, and how and why the energies of the operating units must be liberated. Specifically, MacMahon argued that administrators who handle the "mass" must be able to detect items that involve unanswered points of policy and those that require further interdepartmental consideration. The department must be able to elicit information promptly from any of its parts. Finally, the central organization in a department can provide more useful assistance to the operating units by ensuring that bureau heads receive appropriate amounts of attention and an early answer when they have plans for approval (MacMahon et al. 1937, pp. 5–7).

The second part focused on the emergent pattern, which supported the notion that department heads need a flexible corps of aides, free from routine responsibility, as well as management consultants to advise them on issues affecting the implementation of the department's policies. The final report supported this recommendation and maintained, "The secretary of a department, as a chief executive of a large organization, requires the assistance of a small number of aides" (Cushman, 1937, p. 39). MacMahon, however, pointed out that the managerial components of an agency cannot work in isolation from the policy dynamics of that same organization; the two are intrinsically connected to one another. The final area MacMahon highlighted in this section involved "incipient departmental managers" who he argued were often unsure of their position and the responsibilities that accompanied it, resulting in "complimenting rather than complementing his political chief" (MacMahon et al., 1937, p. 10). Furthermore, changes in political leadership within executive departments may lead to *uncertainty*, a harmful administrative outcome that can undermine unity of the executive.

MacMahon relied on the third part of his report to outline arguments that favored small executive departments and those that supported large executive departments. The fourth part allowed him to provide recommendations for improving recruitment, training, and tenure within the federal service. MacMahon was troubled by the finding that the average amount of service for assistant secretaries of executive agencies was considerably less than the duration of an administration. This resulted, unfortunately, in a lack of organizational communication and poor leadership and contributed to MacMahon's analysis that "departments cannot be realities unless they have a permanent managerial focus" (p. 21). This observation complemented MacMahon's final argument about the need for stable management in executive departments and provides interesting and informative parallels to Charles Goodsell's (2004) position on the case for bureaucracy. More importantly, it continues the line of reasoning that unity of the executive, at all levels of administration, is a critical element in American constitutional democracy.

Executive Management and the Federal Field Service

Whereas MacMahon emphasized departmental management at the federal level, Fesler focused on the federal field service. In his opening, Fesler made an important utilitarian argument about the prime objectives of executive management: "to render administration as efficient as serviceable to the public as possible; economy in the sense of giving the greatest amount of public service per dollar expended follows as a corollary" (MacMahon et al., 1937, p. 29). In our analysis of Fesler's section, we found that he was outlining ways to connect the federal government to the citizenry in more efficient and effective ways, and he viewed field offices as one way to accomplish this goal. Fesler made recommendations for improving the institutional services of field organizations, expanding coordination efforts of field administration, abolishing the National Emergency Council (which served as the field reporting service), and upgrading public relations at the local level.

Fesler advocated the creation of an agency within the executive branch that would be solely responsible for the coordination of the federal field service. This agency would compose of 10 to 12 administrators who would settle disputes between officials and offices of different federal agencies; hold annual statewide informational meetings for all federal agencies that coordinate field service efforts; compose administrative studies on a functional or territorial basis that focused on the operation of federal agencies; and act in an advisory capacity to federal business associations in their efforts to work effectively with local businesses and social organizations. Although Fesler's proposed agency was in its infancy as far as the specifics of how it would be structured, he reiterated throughout his analysis that such a proposal was an important attempt to create stronger unity within the executive by means of improving public sector management at the highest levels of government and within the federal field service.

Government Corporations and Independent Supervisory Agencies

In the last section of this study, Emmerich focused on the value-added dimension government corporations and independent supervisory agencies bring to the federal government generally and to executive-branch management specifically. This is the only section of the entire five accompanying studies that was copied verbatim into the final report that President Roosevelt submitted to Congress.[10] Emmerich argued that "the government corporation is a useful and efficient means of carrying out powers granted [to] the Federal Government under the Constitution" (MacMahon et al., 1937, p. 49). This exact point was made in the final report. Emmerich was particularly interested in the emergency purposes and economic services, as well as specific examples such as hydroelectric projects that government corporations provided to the federal and state governments. From a managerial perspective, however, Emmerich was quick to point out that although government corporations provide important and needed services to the state and its citizenry, they must comply with the norms and values embedded within our constitutional republic: "The supervisory techniques must be suitable to the corporate form but must ensure efficient operation, public accountability, responsiveness to popular will, and integration with the whole task of executive responsibility for management" (p. 49).

The authors of the final report supported Emmerich's analysis of the purpose of the corporation. Both reports concluded, "By the use of self-sustaining business corporations, it is frequently possible for the Government to provide an economic service of national importance without entering directly into business itself, thereby obviating additional burdens on the Federal Treasury" (MacMahon et al., 1937, p. 50; Brownlow et al., 1937, p. 44). Emmerich provided several examples in American history to support his analysis of the purposes of the corporation in American government—notably, Alexander Hamilton's establishment of the first Bank of the United States in 1791 and the Supreme Court's landmark decision in *McCulloch v. Maryland*.

Emmerich's study, as well as the final report, argued that federal charters were more advantageous than those administered by the individual states because when the federal government decided to charter a corporation under the laws of the various states, conflicts almost always emerged between the two jurisdictions. Discrepancies in tax policy, jurisdiction, and authority over the conduct of business corporations that had state charters were the primary ways, according to Emmerich, states hindered the implementation of government corporations.

The final report listed the exact recommendations that Emmerich made in Study IV. Emmerich maintained these recommendations provided the necessary safeguards to enable corporations to play a valuable role in the public policy process. These recommendations included (1) placing business corporations under special supervisory agencies within appropriate departments of the federal government; (2) placing each governmental corporation under a supervisory agency in the appropriate department; (3) affording the supervisory agency, whenever possible, semiautonomous status in a department, when it proves desirable to preserve the independence of the agency; (4) refusing to allow the boards of directors of corporations to divide management work among themselves, instead assigning the task of corporate administration to a president or general manager who reports to the board (MacMahon et al., 1937, p. 53).

Emmerich's objective for this study was to enhance the power of the federal government and the power of the president by recommending ways to protect government and business corporations from state regulatory restrictions. Our analysis of these recommendations provides another informative example that illustrates how the principle of unity of the executive was a central theme highlighted within each of these studies.

Study V: *The Exercise of Rule-making Power and the Preparation of Proposed Legislative Measures by Administrative Departments* by James Hart and Edwin E. Witte

James Hart and Edwin Witte divided their 66-page study into two sections. The first, authored by Hart, focused on rule-making, and the second, prepared by Witte, addressed proposed legislation written by administrative officials. Both authors expressed concern about the growing power of administrative agencies and their role in writing and interpreting laws and regulations. Hart and Witte's recommendations were *not* highlighted in the final Brownlow Report. Future research may shed some light on this interesting and important area of scholarly inquiry.

Delegated Rule-Making Power and Executive Unity

Hart began his discussion by arguing that the rule-making power of federal administrative agencies was central to the problems of administrative management. He made the case that such power was a direct result of the delegation doctrine (Aranson, Gellhorn & Robinson, 1982; Gellhorn, 1987; Sargentich, 1987) which he traced back to the administration of President George Washington. Hart astutely acknowledged that the delegation of power from the legislative branch to administrative agencies is a necessary requirement of modern government; the delegation of rule-making power is no exception. He asserted that agency rule-making is a viable mechanism for "introducing the rule of law at the administrative level" (Hart & Witte, 1937, p. 3).[11]

That said, Hart expressed uneasiness about the rapid growth in the number of federal administrative agencies (p. 115 in 1937) and their increasing exercise of delegated rule-making power. Hart was especially critical of Congress for what he described as the "splitting up of the Executive Branch of government through the creation of independent commissions" (p. 7). He warned that if these trends continued unchecked and without adequate oversight, the very foundation of American constitutional democracy would be at risk. Drawing on Hamilton's argument in *Federalist 70*, Hart maintained that executive unity would be undermined if the president was not given the power to control and supervise the rule-making activities of administrative agencies.

To preserve executive unity, how should the president control and supervise the rule-making powers of department heads and, in turn, administrative agencies? Hart answered this question by suggesting that the president should use his "general power of direction" and implement five specific recommendations: (1) regularization of the rule-making process at the departmental level; (2) extension and improvement of the use of prenatal procedural safeguards designed to provide group consultation; (3) insurance of adequate postnatal publicity; (4) coordination of Federal rule-making; and (5) prescription of uniform regulations governing the service of institutional operations of the executive branch (p. 4).

Hart's first recommendation was designed to bring some order to what he described as a chaotic, inefficient, and haphazard rule-making process spinning out of control. He was especially critical of the fact that many rules were carelessly drafted by individuals (usually lawyers) with little or no technical expertise in the area. This resulted in the issuance of poorly drafted rules and regulations that were inconsistent in form and, in many instances, raised troubling questions of legality. Hart viewed the regularization of rule-making at the department level as a suitable remedy for the ailing rule-making process (p. 27). To achieve regularization, Hart recommended that the president issue an executive order prescribing a "systematic procedure for the flow of rules in the course of their preparation" (p. 4).

Hart argued that this systematic procedure should be located in a "single permanent official" assigned responsibility for each major aspect of the rule-making process (p. 4). Here again, we see the application of the executive unity doctrine articulated by Hamilton in *Federalist 70.*

Hart's second recommendation was designed to ensure group consultation during the early—or what he called the *prenatal* stages—of the rule-making process (p. 27). When Hart uses the term *group*, he is referring to *special interest groups*. Hart argued that rule-making power, like most other types of power, is subject to abuse. Though such abuses may take different forms, he was primarily concerned with the power and influence of special interest groups. Hart conceded that special interest groups are a permanent fixture of the American political landscape. Instead of ignoring their existence, he suggested that special interest groups be brought out of the smoke-filled backrooms of the halls of power and given a public arena to voice their opinion. According to Hart, this strategy would provide a safeguard for the American public, because it offered an opportunity for powerful, competing interests to air their concerns and differences in a transparent way, thus minimizing the abuse of power. As a means of operationalizing the transparency strategy, Hart advocated the extensive use of advisory committees, notice and formal hearings, publication of draft regulations, informal contacts with groups affected, and a progression from voluntary to mandatory standards (pp. 29–32).

The third recommendation, "the issuance of postnatal publicity," focused on activities of administrative agencies *after* the issuance of proposed rules and regulations. This recommendation suggested that adequate publicity regarding proposed rules is deemed an important requirement for reforming the rule-making process. Hart stated that the president should use his "general power of direction to insure the postnatal safeguard of adequate publicity, so that the rules and regulations may be brought to the attention of those whom they apply" (p. 35).

Hart concentrated on the structure and organization of the *Federal Register*, a publication created by an act of Congress in 1935 to publicize executive orders and other documents relating to the rule-making activities of federal administrative agencies. He suggested that although the creation of the *Federal Register* was an improvement over what had existed before (the absence of a central publication publicizing the rule-making activities of agencies) it was poorly organized and difficult to read and navigate. Surprisingly, but consistent with Hart's commitment to the doctrine of executive unity as expressed in the president's "general power of direction," he recommended a range of seemingly technical and minute changes such as adding a note to regulations or rules explaining changes and suggesting that the form of the *Federal Register* be changed to a "ring binder for rules and regulations" (p. 36).

Hart's fourth recommendation addressed the need to coordinate the rule-making process across federal agencies. He contended that the lack of coordination was a major problem in the formulation of public policy in general, and rule-making in particular. Hart asserted that poor interagency coordination contributed to inefficiency and unnecessary conflict between agencies. Again, he argued that the president should use his power of direction to issue an executive order mandating procedures intended to improve interagency coordination. These procedures would involve some form of "prenatal" clearance of rules and regulations by the Bureau of the Budget. According to Hart, this would minimize conflict among federal agencies.

The fifth and final recommendation pertained to the president's role in ensuring the uniformity of rules and regulations. Hart characterized the president as the "general manager of Federal administration" (p. 43). In performing this role, he argued that the president has the overall responsibility for ensuring the effective and efficient operation of institutional activities of federal administrative agencies. Drawing on W. F. Willoughby's (1927) conceptualization of institutional activities, Hart suggested that the president establish uniform rules and regulations to manage institutional activities such as budgetary policy and practice, financial administration, personnel administration, administrative research, and planning (Hart & Witte, 1937, p. 43). He recommended that the president use the "rule-making technique in the exercise of his general power of direction" to achieve this end. Hart acknowledged that the scope and complexities of federal administrative agencies made it extremely difficult to ensure total uniformity of all rules and regulations. With this in mind, he recommended that the president use the Bureau of the Budget as a staff agency to clear rules and regulations. According to Hart, the Bureau of the Budget would serve as a clearinghouse, thereby ensuring that specific institutional activities conformed to presidential policy. This, in turn, would allow the president to assume full responsibility as the "general manager of the business aspects of the Federal Government" (p. 43).

Writing law: The quest for coordination and control of administrative agencies

Edwin Witte was a seasoned public service veteran. The extensive experience of this "government man" was clearly reflected in his in-depth understanding of the nuisances and, in turn, the important role of federal administrative agencies in the legislative process. Witte began his discussion by outlining several principles that should govern the legislative activities of administrative agencies. These principles, 16 in total, addressed the constitutionality and day-to-day practices of administrative agencies. Witte was quick to point out that the U.S. Constitution afforded the legislative branch of government the primary responsibility for determining legislative policies; administrative agencies should always be cognizant of this fact.

Witte also focused his sights on the legislative activities of administrative agencies. He specifically addressed the manner in which administrative agencies prepared drafts of proposed legislation. Witte was critical of the overall process because it lacked coordination and systematic oversight. Echoing Hart's concern outlined in the first section, Witte described a chaotic situation in which administrative agencies ran amok in drafting proposed legislation. He asserted that many of those drafting proposed legislation were not technically competent do so. Witte also noted that it was not uncommon for bills initiated within administrative agencies to reach the Congress without the knowledge of the agency head.

To remedy this chaotic situation, Witte offered recommendations similar to those made by Hart. It was clear that he, too, relied on *Federalist 70* as an underlying philosophical framework:

> Efficient administrative management must take account of the legislative activities of administrative departments. In the interest of efficient management and in accord with the provisions of the Constitution creating a single Executive and vesting in him the duty of making recommendations for legislation to Congress, the President must be able at all time to control the legislative activities of the departments.
>
> (Hart & Witte 1937, p. 63)

Like Hart, Witte recommended that a central clearance agency assume responsibility for all bills originating within the executive branch of government. He identified several possibilities including the Department of Justice, the Bureau of the Budget, the White House, and at the departmental level. Witte settled on the Bureau of the Budget because most bills drafted by administrative agencies have financial aspects. The Budget and Accounting Act of 1921 required that such bills be cleared through the Bureau of the Budget. From Witte's perspective, this made the Bureau a logical choice. His proposal required that the Bureau of the Budget assume an active role in examining proposed legislation drafted by administrative agencies. According to Witte, not only should the Bureau examine proposed legislation not only from the standpoint of its financial implications, but also it should take a much broader view and examine the effects of legislation on the entire government.

As Hart had done earlier, Witte called for the development of experts who would be trained in writing legislation. This was of utmost importance because poorly drafted and ill-thought-out legislation had a harmful effect on the American political system.

Conclusion

The five accompanying studies that represent the complete Brownlow Report illustrate the contemporary relevance of the nation's State papers to public administration theory and practice. Within these studies, we find that *Federalist 27* laid the foundation for *Federalist 70*. The people's confidence in government is not only proportionate to the goodness or badness of its administration, but also, as these studies show, provides the necessary framework for the unity doctrine, a point of view these authors illustrate with profound understanding and confidence. They understood the American system of government better than almost anyone of their era. The President's Committee on Administrative Management did not produce a study whose primary objective was simply to improve public management—rather, this was a study about improving democracy within the American constitutional republic. The authors' recommendations and suggestions for improving executive-branch dynamics demonstrate the connection between good management and constitutional tradition. Our analysis reveals that these papers were not written from a managerial perspective but from a constitutional one. Such efforts draw our attention to the practical relevance that *The Federalist Papers* continue to have on contemporary democratic governance. This analysis provides another formative example that the legitimacy of the American Administrative State can be found *only* within its constitutional heritage.

Notes

1 At the time President Roosevelt commissioned his Committee on Administrative Management, highly contested political battles were occurring between the executive, legislative, and judicial branches of American government. We consider the relevance of the political environment Roosevelt was operating in as an important historical and contextual underpinning that affected how he viewed the responsibilities associated with the Committee's findings and recommendations. The focus of this research, however, emphasizes the constitutional themes that link each of these papers together and not the political and practical dynamics affecting the U.S. federal government in 1937. We would like to thank Herbert Kaufman for bringing this point to our attention.

2 Conversation between Herbert Kaufman and James Fesler May 16, 2003. Fesler confirmed Harris' administrative and organizational role in this conversation. Also see Fesler (1987) and Karl (1963).

3 Although the preface of each report notes, "The statements and recommendations contained in these studies are those of the individual authors as submitted to the Committee as a part of the body of facts to be considered in the preparation of its report, and do not necessarily embody the ideas of the Committee," the relevance of these documents is that some recommendations were included in the final report that President Roosevelt submitted to Congress, whereas others were not. Regardless of whether these recommendations were included, they are both important and historically significant for scholars and practitioners interested in the development of executive-branch management in the United States.

4 Guy Adams (1992) and Laurence Lynn (2001) also draw our attention to the importance of administrative history. Adams emphasizes the notion that administrative history produces a genuinely open inquiry in the field whereas Lynn argues that traditional public administration stood for respect for law, politics, and

citizens more so than the customer-oriented managerialism, which barely acknowledges the constitutional nature of the American administrative state.

5 John Rohr, an important scholar in the Constitutional School of public administration, provides a formative analysis of the theoretical and practical significance the Brownlow Committee's findings had on the development of the American Administrative State in his work, *To Run a Constitution* (1986, Kansas). We have benefited from his scholarship.

6 While Publius's argument regarding executive unity was in large part a response to the Anti-Federalist's concern that an energized executive would resemble a monarchial form of government instead of a republican one, the authors of the five accompanying studies of the Brownlow Report applied Hamilton's understanding of the unity doctrine to their critique of boards, commissions, regulatory agencies, and the General Accounting Office. The Committee's authors argued that the creation of these regulatory and policy agencies undermined the principle of unity of the executive the way Hamilton feared it would be compromised if the nation operated under a weak executive. We maintain that the Committee's analysis provides an insightful parallel that illustrates the contemporary relevance of *The Federalist Papers* to current issues affecting democratic governance and to those interested in the Constitutional School of American public administration.

7 In discussing the unity of the executive, Hamilton argues, "decision, activity, secrecy, and dispatch, will generally characterize the proceedings of one man, in a much more eminent degree, than the proceedings of any greater number; and in proportion as the number is increased, these qualities will be diminished" (Cooke 1961, p. 472).

8 In *Federalist 70,* Hamilton argues that unity would be destroyed under the following circumstances:

> Either by vesting the power in two or more magistrates of equal dignity and authority; or by vesting it ostensibly in one man, subject, in whole or in part, to the control and co-operation of others, in the capacity of counsellors to him.
>
> (Cooke, 1961, p. 178)

9 See Cooke (1961).

10 See pp. 49–53 of this study and pp. 43–46 of the final Brownlow Report.

11 Theodore Lowi, a leading critic of the delegation doctrine, also makes this point. See Lowi (1993).

References

Adams, G.B. (1992). Enthralled with modernity: the historical context of knowledge and theory development in public administration. *Public Administration Review* 52: 363–373.

Aranson, P., Gellhorn, E. & Robinson, G.O. (1982). A theory of legislative delegation. *Cornell Law Review* 68: 1–67.

Brownlow, L., Merriam, C. & Gulick, L. (1937). *Administrative management in the government of the United States*. Washington, DC: President's Committee on Administrative Management.

Buck, A.E. & Mansfield, H.C. (1937). *Fiscal management in the national government*. Washington, DC: President's Committee on Administrative Management.

Caldwell, L.K. (1955). The relevance of administrative history. *Revue internationale des sciences administratives* 21: 453–466.

Cooke, J.E. (ed.) (1961). *The Federalist*. Middletown, CT: Wesleyan University Press.

Cushman, R.E. (1937). *The independent regulatory commissions*. Washington, DC: President's Committee on Administrative Management.

Denhardt, R. (1995). *Public administration: an action orientation*, 2nd edn. Fort Worth, TX: Harcourt Brace.

Fesler, J. (1987). The Brownlow Committee fifty years later. *Public Administration Review* 47: 291–296.

Gellhorn, E. (1987). Returning to first principles. *American University Law Review* 60: 495–505.

Goodsell, C.T. (2004). *The case for bureaucracy: a public administration polemic*. Washington, DC: Congressional Quarterly Press.

Hart, J. & Witte, E.E. (1937). *The exercise of rule-making power and the preparation of proposed legislative measures by administrative departments*. Washington, DC: President's Committee on Administrative Management.

Karl, B. (1963). *Executive reorganization and reform in the New Deal: the genesis of administrative management, 1900–1939*. Cambridge, MA: Harvard University Press.

Light, P. (1995). *Thickening government: federal hierarchy and the diffusion of accountability*. Washington, DC: Brookings Institution.

Lowi, T. (1993). Two roads to serfdom: liberalism, conservatism, and administrative power. In S.L. Elkins & K.E. Soltan (eds), *A new constitutionalism: designing political institutions for a good society*. Chicago, IL: University of Chicago Press, pp. 149–173.

Lynn, L.E. (2001). The myth of the bureaucratic paradigm: what traditional public administration really stood for. *Public Administration Review* 61: 144–160.

MacMahon, A., Fesler, J.W. & Emmerich, H. (1937). *Problems of administrative management*. Washington, DC: President's Committee on Administrative Management.

Reeves, F.W. & David, P.T. (1937). *Personnel administration in the federal service*. Washington, DC: President's Committee on Administrative Management.

Rohr, J.A. (1986). *To run a constitution: the legitimacy of the administrative state*. Lawrence: University Press of Kansas.

Rosenbloom, D. & Kravchuk, R.S. (2002). *Public administration: understanding management, politics, and law in the public sector*, 5th edn. Boston, MA: McGraw-Hill.

Sargentich, T. (1987). The delegation debate and compelling ideals of the administrative process. *American University Law Review* 36: 419–442.

Stillman, R. (1988). *Public administration: concepts and cases*, 4th edn. Boston, MA: Houghton Mifflin.

Stillman, R. (1991). *Preface to public administration: a search for themes and directions*. New York: St. Martin's Press.

Waldo, D. (1948). *The administrative state*. New York: Ronald Press.

White, L.D. (1948). *The Federalists: a study in administrative history*. New York: Macmillan.

White, L.D. (1951). *The Jeffersonians: a study in administrative history, 1801–1829*. New York: Macmillan.

White, L.D. (1954). *The Jacksonians: a study in administrative history, 1829–1861.* New York: Macmillan.

White, L.D (1958). *The Republican era: a study in administrative history, 1869–1901.* New York: Macmillan.

Willoughby, W.F. (1927). *Principles of public administration.* Washington, DC: Brookings Institution.

Part IV

Applications of the Constitutional School to Public Administration Theory and Practice

10 Measuring What Matters Most

How Democratic-Constitutional Impact Statements and Scorecards Support the Constitutional School

David H. Rosenbloom

I wrote the manuscript for this article in 2006. The impetus for it was the growing emphasis in academic and applied public administration on "managing for results" and its accompanying tendency to dismiss the importance of accountability for democratic-constitutional values and procedure. The National Performance Review (NPR, 1993–1998), which morphed into the National Partnership for Reinventing Government in 1998, called on government to be results oriented in businesslike fashion. Reinventing was followed by President George W. Bush's President's Management Agenda (PMA). Our "first MBA president" also heavily supported management for results and his administration sometimes gave constitutional procedure short shrift in the service of expansive claims of executive power. Little, if any attention was paid to Supreme Court Justice Felix Frankfurter's nagging admonition to "Remember, there are very precious values of civilization which, ultimately, to a large extent are procedural in their nature" (Rosenbloom, 2000, p. 23).

Let's take a brief moment to reflect on the NPR and the Bush II presidency. The NPR was disdainful of "rules," a theme that runs through its 1995 volume on *Common Sense Government Works Better & Costs Less*. The reinventers told us that among government's greatest shortcomings, "The first priority was the rules; the second was those who checked whether the rules were being followed (such as auditors and inspectors general); the third was those who made the rules in the first place (such as Congress and interest groups)" (Gore, 1995, p. 19). Rules were based on misplaced "distrust" and were unnecessary because "Most people want to do the right thing, so long as the right thing makes sense" (p. 33). In a remarkable passage, now laden with irony in view of the 2000 Bush–Gore presidential election, the NPR told us that government "needs to have more trust in the American people—including its own employees" because "when we are not trusted ... we feel powerless" and "Elections alone do not restore that power. The power that matters in a self-governing democracy is the power we can exercise 'over the counter,' on a daily basis, whenever we interact with our government, whenever we seek to make our needs known" (p. 93). The ideal sounded more like "Gov-Mart" (p. 58) than "constitutional-gov."

President Bush's results-oriented PMA relied on the Office of Management and Budget to centralize supervision of agencies' strategic human capital, competitive sourcing, financial performance, e-gov, and integration of budgets and performance (Rosenbloom, 2010, p. 112). The PMA was related to Bush's adherence to a version of unitary executive branch theory, most specifically articulated in his "signing statements" (Rosenbloom, 2010). In terms of "Reinventing Administrative Prescriptions," its most important features were the claims that: (1) The president's constitutional responsibility to "take care that the laws be faithfully executed" requires, or at least authorizes him to ignore statutory provisions that he considers unconstitutional—even while signing them into law; and (2) the president has constitutional authority to exercise directly congressional delegations of legislative authority to executive branch agencies (Rosenbloom, 2010, p. 120; see also Rosenbloom, 2008).

The first claim circumvents the Constitution's provision for presidential vetoes. It was criticized by the American Bar Association's House of Delegates "as contrary to the rule of law and our constitutional system of separation of powers" and a "misuse of presidential signing statements by claiming the authority or stating the intention to disregard or decline to enforce all or part of a law the President has signed, or to interpret such a law in a manner inconsistent with the clear intent of Congress" (American Bar Association, 2006).

The second claim is contrary to over 170 years of constitutional precedent. As the Supreme Court held in *Kendall v. U.S.* (1838):

> It would be an alarming doctrine that Congress cannot impose upon any executive officer any duty they may think proper which is not repugnant to any rights secured and protected by the Constitution, and in such cases the duty and responsibility grow out of and are subject to the control of the law, and not to the direction of the President.
>
> (37 U.S. 524, 610, capitalization modernized)

For instance, when Congress calls on the Environmental Protection Agency to use its scientific expertise and technical knowledge to establish standards for clean air or water, the legislators hardly intend that their delegated legislative authority be exercised directly by the president or his appointees. One answer to Francis Rourke's 1993 question, "Whose Bureaucracy Is This, Anyway?" is "certainly not the president's alone."

Clearly missing from the NPR and Bush approaches to public administration was an appreciation of Madison's concern in *Federalist 51* that the government is obliged to "control itself" and the need for "auxiliary precautions" to ensure that it does (Madison, 1788, p. 269). Requiring that impact statements and scorecards accompany proposed fundamental administrative reforms is obviously not on the level of Madison's separation of powers and checks and balances. However, impact statements and scorecards would force attention to democratic-constitutional values that might otherwise be neglected in the demand for cost-effective results-oriented government and ultimately lost through default.

From the perspectives of results-oriented management, "mission extrinsic" public values are particularly problematic. As explained elsewhere, these are often constitutional and administrative law values, such as transparency, that are largely extraneous to agencies' core mission values and specialized expertise and technologies, viewed as impeding achievement of mission results by deflecting staff time and other resources, often imposed as "one size fits all" requirements rather than with strategic regard to agencies' specific missions, and sometimes disfavored by agency leadership (Rosenbloom, 2014, p. 18). Perhaps the clearest example is freedom of information, as discussed in "Reinventing Administrative Prescriptions." The transparency it seeks to promote is central to the missions of the National Archives and Records Administration and the Government Printing Office, but largely or wholly extrinsic to the missions of most other agencies other than the Department of Justice, which has important responsibilities with respect to government-wide implementation of the Freedom of Information Act (FOIA). However, compliance with FOIA is only one of several public values that fall outside the overall realm of managing for results. Others mentioned in "Reinventing Administrative Prescriptions" include individual constitutional rights, open meetings, the rule of law, and constitutional integrity generally. Democratic-constitutional impact statements and scorecards are one approach to ensuring that attention is devoted to these important values when developing results oriented administrative reforms. After all, we have environmental impact statements and scorecards, why would those for democratic-constitutional government be less important?

As part of the "Theory to Practice" section of *Public Administration Review*, the original article was accompanied by two sets of comments, one by John Kamensky, the other by David Ammons and Carl Stenberg, along with my response to their observations.[1] Here, I will only add that I found these symptomatic of the problem the article confronts. Narrowly redefining public administration, which traditionally has incorporated a host of democratic-constitutional values and concerns (Lynn, 2001), as results-oriented businesslike management poses a substantial risk to the Constitution's commitments to "establish Justice" and "secure the Blessings of Liberty to ourselves and our Posterity."

Note

1 Kamensky's Commentary is at: http://www.aspanet.org/public/ASPADocs/PAR/T2P/KamenskyCommentary.pdf. Ammons and Stenberg's is at: www.aspanet.org/public/ASPADocs/PAR/T2P/AmmonsStenbergCommentary.pdf. My response is at: http://www.aspanet.org/public/ASPADocs/PAR/T2P/RosenbloomResponse.pdf. All three retrieved on January 25, 2016.

References

American Bar Association. 2006. Recommendation adopted by the House of Delegates, August 7–8: www.americanbar.org/content/dam/aba/migrated/leadership/2006/annual/dailyjournal/20060823144113.authcheckdam.pdf. Retrieved January 25, 2016.

Gore, A. 1995. *Common sense government works better & costs less*. Washington, DC: U.S. Government Printing Office.

Lynn, L. 2001. The myth of the bureaucratic paradigm: What traditional public administration really stood for. *Public administration review* 61(2): 144–160.

Madison, J. 1788. *Federalist No. 51* in *The Federalist*, G. Carey and J. McClellan, eds. Indianapolis, IN: Liberty Fund, 2001, pp. 267–272.

Rosenbloom, D.H. 2000. *Building a legislative-centered public administration: Congress and the administrative state, 1946–1999*. Tuscaloosa, AL: University of Alabama Press.

Rosenbloom, D.H. 2007. Reinventing administrative prescriptions: The case for democratic-constitutional impact statements and score cards. *Public administration review* 67(1): 28–39.

Rosenbloom, D.H. 2008. President George W. Bush's theory of a unitary executive branch and the rule of law in the United States. *Journal of political and parliamentary law* 1(1): 227–254.

Rosenbloom, D.H. 2010. Reevaluating executive centered public administrative theory in *The Oxford handbook of American bureaucracy*, R. Durant, edn. New York: Oxford University Press, pp. 101–127.

Rosenbloom, D.H. 2014. Attending to mission-extrinsic public values in performance-oriented administrative management: A view from the United States in *Public administration and the modern state*, E. Bohne, J. Graham, J. Raadschelders, and J. Lehrke, eds. Hampshire: Palgrave Macmillan, pp. 17–30.

Rourke, F. 1993. Whose bureaucracy is this, anyway? Congress, the president, and public administration. *PS: Political science and politics* 26(4): 687–692.

Reinventing Administrative Prescriptions

The Case for Democratic-Constitutional Impact Statements and Scorecards[1]

David H. Rosenbloom

Originally from: *Public Administration Review* 67 (2007): 28–39.

Policy impact statements and scorecards are common tools for prodding public administrative organizations to pay attention to specific concerns and values. In federal administration, environmental impact statements, which were first broadly mandated by the National Environmental Policy Act of 1969 (Public Law 91–109), are complemented by impact statements and assessments regarding the potential effects of agency rules and policies on family values, federalism, environmental justice, and other matters (see Executive Orders 12606 [1987], 12612 [1987], and 12898 [1994]). The contemporary widespread use of scorecards began following the publication of Robert Kaplan and David Norton's (1992) now-classic article, "The Balanced Scorecard: Measures That Drive Performance." We have scorecards for the war on terrorism, freedom, civil liberties, school breakfasts, legislative performance, and corporate social responsibility, among others (American Civil Liberties Union of Northern California, 2002; Food Research and Action Center, 2005; Fluke & Kump, 2004; Human Rights Campaign, n.d.; Levitt, 2002; Marcus, 2006). During the George W. Bush administration, the U.S. Office of Management and Budget (OMB) used a scorecard to assess agencies' progress toward the goals of the President's Management Agenda (PMA) (U.S. Office of Management and Budget, 2001).

Conspicuously missing from the plethora of impact statements and scorecards available today are those focusing on the protection and promotion of democratic-constitutional values, including individual rights, constitutional integrity, transparency, and the rule of law. This chapter proposes (1) that democratic-constitutional impact statements be required as part of all substantial prescriptions for administrative reform and (2) that evaluations of program and policy implementation routinely include democratic-constitutional scorecards. The term democratic-constitutional refers to those aspects of American government and politics that have democratized the original constitutional design, as amended. Examples include freedom of information, open meetings, the Administrative Procedure Act of 1946 (Public Law 79–404), and the expansion of individual rights through constitutional law. It is understood that the United States is a republic, not a democracy.

The chapter begins by placing the contemporary failure to consider democratic-constitutional values in context as a recurring historical failure of U.S. public administration. Reviewed are reasons practitioners and public administration scholars have, at best, marginalized and, at worst, been contemptuous of democratic-constitutional values as well as reasons such disregard matters. Next, the logic of impact statements and scorecards is discussed, including how these might be developed, administered, and used to inform administrative reforms in the future. Illustrated subsequently are the differences that impact statements and scorecards might make in protecting values that are typically slighted—if not ignored—by administrative reformers in their prescriptions for improving public management. Several likely arguments against impact statements and scorecards are then confronted.

Misplacing the Keys to Better Government?

Off and on since Woodrow Wilson ([1887] 1997, p. 15) famously proclaimed, "It is getting harder to run a constitution than to frame one," public administrative reformers have paid cursory attention to democratic-constitutional concerns in their prescriptions. Most commonly, reformers view variants of cost-effectiveness as the "key to better government" (Savas, 1987). They frequently assume that greater cost-effectiveness will automatically improve democratic constitutionalism. For example, in 1937, the President's Committee on Administrative Management (also known as the Brownlow Committee) argued that an aggrandized presidency, diminished Congress, and, consequently, a less vigorous separation of powers was necessary "to make good our democratic claims" while warning that "if America fails" for want of administrative efficiency, the "hopes and dreams of democracy all over the world go down" (President's Committee on Administrative Management, 1937, p. 2). Today's reformers in the Departments of Defense and Homeland Security have followed suit, claiming that the cost-effective defense of democracy requires curtailing employees' rights (McGlinchey, 2005; Rutzick, 2005a, 2005b, 2005c; Shoop, 2005).

Likewise, proponents of other keys to better government have a tendency to slight democratic-constitutional considerations. Reinventers who advocate a heavy emphasis on results offer no plan for protecting values that are not mission based, such as freedom of information and democratic procedures. The National Performance Review, for example, ultimately devalued elections because they have little to do with the ability of administrative agencies to satisfy customers (Gore, 1995, p. 93). Better government reforms in the New Public Administration tradition could easily promote social equity at the expense of the rule of law (Rosenbloom, 2005).

A benign view of reform prescriptions that potentially weaken democratic-constitutional government assumes that advocates take the stability and durability of the U.S. constitutional system for granted. After all, the "miracle at Philadelphia" in 1787 was said to have produced a "machine that would go of itself" (Bowen, 1966; Kammen, 1986). No need to worry about constitutional government in this view—ambition will counteract ambition, and checks and balances will prevail (Madison, [1788] 2001, pp. 268–269). Of course, there is still reason for concern. When Benjamin Franklin, a member of the 1787 Constitutional Convention, was asked, "Well, Doctor, what have we got—a Republic or a Monarchy?" he replied, "A Republic, if you can keep it" (Platt, 1989, p. 1593). Ambition may not immediately check ambition, and institutional imbalances may take time to recalibrate. President George W. Bush's ability to assert expansive, largely unchecked executive power from September 11, 2001, until the U.S. Supreme Court handed down its decision in *Hamdi v. Rumsfeld* (542 U.S. 507 [2004]) is a recent example. A less sanguine view is that administrative prescriptions for better government are based on disaffection with U.S. constitutional design and democratic values. Dwight Waldo (1984, p. 104) noted that orthodox public administration was "hostile to the tripartite separation of powers." Luther Gulick, a pillar of the administrative orthodoxy, only begrudgingly accepted grassroots democracy:

> We are in the end compelled to mitigate the pure concept of efficiency in the light of the value scale of politics and the social order. There are, for example, highly inefficient arrangements like citizen boards and small local governments which may be necessary in a democracy as educational devices.
>
> (quoted in Waldo, 1984, p. 192)

Whether hostile to the constitutional system or confident in its durability, prescriptions for better government and their administrative impacts are incomplete without an assessment of their potential effects on democratic constitutionalism. As Laurence Lynn (2001, 155) correctly observes:

> Often missing in the literature and discourse is recognition that reformers of institutions and civic philosophies must show how the capacity to effect public purposes and accountability to the polity will be enhanced in a manner that comports with our Constitution and our republican institutions. Basic political and legal issues of responsible management in a postmodern era are inadequately defined and addressed.

Arguably, democratic constitutional impact statements and scorecards would force attention at least to individual rights, constitutional integrity, transparency, and the rule of law.

The Logic of Administrative Prescription Impact Statements

Impact statements are prospective assessments of the probable impact of administrative initiatives on particular concerns. For example, the National

Environmental Policy Act requires federal agencies to develop impact statements whenever a proposed action will have a substantial effect on the environment. These statements address possible adverse impacts, alternatives, long-term consequences, and irreversible and irretrievable commitments. In the absence of impact statements and attendant public discussion, an agency charged with developing nuclear power might not view conservation as an alternative to energy generation (*Vermont Yankee Nuclear Power Corp. v. Natural Resources Defense Council, Inc.*, 435 U.S. 519 [1978]).

Impact statements can address virtually any political, social, economic, or other matter touched by public administration. The Assessment of Federal Regulations and Policies on Families Act of 1998 (Public Law 105–177) currently requires "family policy-making assessments" to evaluate the impact of agency actions on marital commitments, the authority and rights of parents, and the overall performance of family functions. Although impact statements have been criticized for creating layers of additional requirements before agencies can issue rules or take other actions, their utility is obvious. If used to assess the democratic-constitutional impact of administrative reforms, they may highlight values that are typically neglected by reformers. For example, if there is any mention of the impact of outsourcing on democratic-constitutional government in E. S. Savas's (1987) 308-page book on privatization, it is not prominent. Yet anyone with a basic understanding of constitutional government and administrative law would know that privatization almost automatically incurs three consequences.

First, rights are lost because, with the exception of the Thirteenth Amendment's ban on slavery and involuntary servitude, private sector workers have no constitutional rights with regard to their employers. By contrast, public employees have a wide (if currently narrowing) array of constitutional rights within the context of their government employment. These include freedom of speech and association, personal privacy, procedural and substantive due process, and equal protection (DiNome, Yaklin, & Rosenbloom, 1999). In some areas, such as civil rights, there are similar protections in private employment, and there are other areas in which private employees have greater rights, including the broad right to strike. However, public employees generally have greater protection against reprisals for whistle-blowing, workplace searches and drug testing, invasions of personal privacy, and adverse treatment based on sexual orientation (ibid.). Ordinary citizens also have constitutional and administrative law rights when dealing with government that are not pertinent to their interactions with private organizations. If, as the Declaration of Independence states, governments are instituted to secure rights such as these, then it follows that better government requires an assessment of whether rights will be diminished, enhanced, or unaffected by administrative prescriptions.

Second, privatization typically reduces transparency. At the federal level, legal requirements for freedom of information and open meetings do not apply to private organizations that perform outsourced government work.[2]

Under the Freedom of Information Act (FOIA) of 1966 (Public Law 89–487), one can obtain information from government agencies but not from the contractors whose work is paid for with the same taxpayer dollars (Rosenbloom and Piotrowski 2005). Likewise, under the Government in the Sunshine Act of 1976 (Public Law 94–409), commissioners of federal regulatory agencies may have to hold open meetings when they draft rules. However, when the task of writing a draft proposed rule is outsourced, contractors are subject to no such statutory requirement.

Third, privatization diminishes oversight. Federal executives and administrators are routinely summoned to testify before and submit documents to congressional committees. The process of obtaining information becomes arduous when Congress has to subpoena private sector executives and employees in order to obtain basic answers regarding the implementation of federal programs and the use of government funds. Being a tool of adversary legal procedure, subpoenas highlight the involuntary quality of individuals' appearances and their unwillingness to cooperate on their own. Testimony and the provision of documents are likely to be less forthcoming—and personal legal counsel more intrusive—than when federal employees, who are generally deferential to members of Congress, testify before legislative committees. Subpoenas also are subject to challenge in court, related delay, and restriction in scope. The enforcement of subpoenas is by contempt of Congress, which is generally viewed as a drastic last resort involving prosecution by the Department of Justice.

Some might argue that these concerns are overstated because core government functions are not being privatized. However, the differences in legal obligations faced by government agencies and their contractors should not be trivialized on this basis. Contractors today analyze proposed legislation; draft reports to Congress; write testimony that agencies deliver to congressional committees; prepare budget documents, proposed rules, and preambles to final rules; respond to public comments submitted as part of the rulemaking process; and conduct public hearings. Even inspector general functions are sometimes outsourced (Light, 1999, p. 14; U.S. Congress, 1989, p. 63, cited in Guttman, 2000, p. 873).

Box 10.1 presents an example of what a democratic-constitutional impact statement for key National Performance Review prescriptions might look like. Impact statements would consider the specifics of the prescribed administrative reforms, assess their potential implications for key democratic and constitutional values, and suggest means of mitigating or eliminating any threats to democratic-constitutional values that might be present. Ideally, the impact statements would be submitted to the relevant congressional committees, the OMB, the Government Accountability Office, and the Congressional Research Service, as well as published in the *Federal Register* for comment by members of the general public, stakeholders, and experts in public administration and related fields. These impact statements, in turn, might even note greater or lesser threats when applied within the context of specific programs. Regardless, the rebuttable presumption is that the implications noted are threats, and the burden of persuasion rests on reformers, who must demonstrate why the concerns are overstated or how they intend to mitigate them in practice. These can then become grist for broader debate among elected officials, attentive publics, and citizens about administrative reforms.

Box 10.1 Example of a Democratic-Constitutional Impact Statement for the Clinton–Gore National Performance Review

Specific Components and Implications for Democratic-Constitutionalism

Steering, not Rowing (Outsourcing)

- Individual Rights: Reduction of constitutional and administrative law rights for individuals
- Transparency: Freedom of Information Act and Government in the Sunshine Act inapplicable; congressional oversight more difficult

Results Orientation

- Rule of Law: Loss of attention to non-mission-based values may compromise rule of law
- Transparency: Accountability for procedure may be weakened

Biennial Budgeting and Budget Rollovers

- Constitutional Integrity: Weakens congressional power of the purse
- Rule of Law: "No year money" reduces legal controls on agency spending

Internal Deregulation and Employee Empowerment

- Rule of Law: Enhances agency and employee discretion
- Constitutional Integrity: Weakens prospects for effective judicial review

Potential Mitigations

- Tailor overall prescriptions to specific programs
- Include protection of democratic-constitutional values in contracts, such as whistleblower protections, equal employment opportunity, and transparency requirements.

The Logic of Administrative Prescription Scorecards

In contrast to impact statements, scorecards are retrospective. They provide evaluative feedback on how organizations are performing on various dimensions. The balanced scorecard, which is said to be used by 50 percent of Fortune 1000 companies, looks at performance along four dimensions: financial, customer service, internal business process, and learning and growth (Kaplan & Norton, 1992; Niven, 2003, p. x). It prevents organizations from neglecting a critical dimension of their overall business strategy or organizational strategic plan. Unfortunately, reinventers' fixation on results parallels the tunnel vision of Kaplan and Norton's hypothetical pilot who has just one cockpit gauge—for airspeed—and none for altitude or fuel. Getting agencies and contractors up to speed in delivering administrative services and constraints is but one aspect of better government.

Using the OMB's scorecard approach to the Bush administration's PMA, red, yellow, and green lights could be assigned to agency performance on dimensions of importance to democratic-constitutional government (U.S. Office of Management and Budget, 2006a).

The PMA "focuses on five areas of management weakness across the government where improvements and the most progress can be made" (U.S. Office of Management and Budget, 2006b): strategic human capital, competitive sourcing, financial performance, e-government, and budget and performance integration. Following the OMB format on democratic-constitutional scorecards would be a relatively easy step toward improved awareness of the impact of reforms on democratic-constitutional processes and values (see Table 10.1).

Certainly, the Government Accountability Office, the OMB, and the Congressional Research Service would be appropriate scorers, as might be the National Academy of Public Administration. To the extent feasible, inspectors general could periodically include democratic-constitutional scorecards in their semiannual reports. An agency receiving a red light on a democratic-constitutional dimension from one or all of the scorers would be alerted to the need for improvement. An agency receiving a green light might decide that future resources would be better devoted to different functions, either those on the democratic-constitutional scorecard or others more closely connected to achieving mission-based results. Regardless of choice—and using the same logic of impact statements noted previously—elected officials, attentive publics, and citizens would benefit from the enhanced dialogue requirements imposed on agencies. Similar to the PMA and other scorecards, scoring could involve a mix of quantitative and qualitative measures developed in the context of each agency's activities. For example, some agencies receive thousands of FOIA requests, and others receive very few. Some have few direct dealings with the public in which individual constitutional rights are pertinent. Others, such as the Bureau of Prisons, are so highly constrained by constitutional law that they might consider periodic "constitutional

Table 10.1 Example of a Democratic-Constitutional Scorecard Modeled on OMB's PMA Scorecard*

PMA Initiative	*Individual Rights*	*Constitutional Integrity*	*Transparency*	*Rule of Law*
Strategic Human Capital	Yellow Light: Reduction of due process	Yellow Light: Enhances executive authority	Yellow Light: Individualized financial arrangements	Yellow Light: Enhanced agency discretion
Competitive Sourcing	Red Light: Loss of constitutional and administrative law rights	Yellow Light: Legislative oversight more difficult	Red Light: Freedom of information, sunshine laws inapplicable	Yellow Light: Requires effective contract monitoring
Financial Performance	Green Light: No impact	Green Light: Enhanced financial accountability	Green Light: Enhanced financial reporting	Green Light: Enhanced control spending
E-Gov	Green Light: Can inform public of legal rights	Yellow Light: Executive-centered control under OMB	Green Light: Enhances transparency	Green Light: Publicizes legal requirements
Budget and Performance Integration	Green Light: No impact	Yellow Light: Can weaken legislative role in budget decisions	Green Light: Greater information about agency performance	Yellow Light: Potential inattention to non-mission-based legal requirements

* In the PMA Scorecard, red indicates at least one serious flaw; yellow indicates success on some, but not all criteria; and green indicates success on all criteria. Here, red means danger, yellow means caution, and green means positive or no impact.

audits" (Feeley & Hanson, 1990, p. 26). The important point is that the scorecard would keep agencies focused on democratic-constitutional concerns.

From Theory to Practice: Scorecards and Impact Statements in Action

The following examples are offered as illustrations—and illustrations only—of how impact statements and scorecards could work in practice. These are intended for purposes of argument only. The merits of democratic-constitutional impact statements and scorecards should not prevail or fail on the basis of the particulars of the illustrations, which are well-researched and reasonable (if not definitive) interpretations.

Protecting Individual Rights

The free exercise of religion is a fundamental human right protected by the U.S. Constitution's First Amendment. The Constitution mandates that "no religious Test shall ever be required as a Qualification to any Office or public Trust under the United States" (Article VI, Section 3). This clause applies at all levels of the federal government (*Torcaso v. Watkins*, 367 U.S. 488 [1961]). However, it did not protect an employee working for the Kentucky Baptist Homes for Children, a contractor providing at-risk youth services for the state of Kentucky. Although conceding she was an excellent worker, the contractor's president explained that the employee had been fired because to "employ a person who is openly homosexual ... does not represent the Judeo-Christian values which are intrinsic to our mission" of providing "Christian support to every child, staff member and foster parent" (Press, 2003, pp. 187–188).

If this woman had been employed directly by a state agency, her situation would have been radically different as a matter of law. The agency could not have a mission of providing Christian support to anyone without violating the First Amendment's establishment clause. It could not have made adherence to Judeo-Christian values a job requirement without violating religious freedom. At a minimum, the Fourteenth Amendment's equal protection clause would require the governmental employer to have a rational, job-related basis for firing an employee for his or her homosexuality. Substantive due process under that amendment might require a more stringent standard of review if the dismissal were deemed an interference with the fundamental personal liberty to "engage in [homosexual] conduct without intervention of the government" (*Lawrence v. Texas*, 539 U.S. 558, 578 [2003]).

A comprehensive democratic-constitutional impact statement would raise these concerns for individual rights as part of the process of prescribing the faith based delivery of public services. Assuming faithfulness to the Declaration of Independence, the Constitution, and national ideals, potential contractors would be notified that all personnel actions involving outsourced government work must comport with the clearly established constitutional standards that apply to public employment. Kentucky Baptist Homes could forego government contracts and continue its refusal to employ openly homosexual persons. It would not be free to repress them gratuitously while performing government work.

Preserving Constitutional Integrity

Reform prescriptions often seek to alter constitutional checks and balances by enhancing executive power while reducing legislative roles in public administration. Confusing the president as "chief executive officer" with "sole executive officer" (Rohr, 1986, p. 139), the Brownlow Committee asserted that the "responsibility for the administration of the expenditures under [a legislative] appropriation is and should be solely upon the executive" (President's Committee on Administrative Management, 1937, p. 22). It viewed checks on the executive's "final authority to determine the uses of appropriations, conditions of employment, the letting of contracts, and the control over administrative decisions, as well as the prescribing of accounting procedures" (ibid., pp. 49–50), as interferences with the president's constitutional responsibility to "take Care that the Laws be faithfully executed" (Article II, Section 3). This view is so alien to the constitutional design for "joint custody" over federal administration that, in 1937, members of Congress rejected it as dictatorial (Karl, 1963, p. 24; Rourke, 1993). By 1946, Congress had responded to the growth of the executive branch (in size and in power) by designing a substantial and coherent role for itself in federal administration. In much the same vein, the Supreme Court rejected President Bush's blank-check approach to implementing the 2001 congressional Authorization for Use of Military Force (*Hamdi v. Rumsfeld*, 542 U.S. 507 [2004]; *Hamdan v. Rumsfeld*, 548 U.S. 557 [2006]).

Undeterred by history, reinventers in the 1990s echoed the Brownlow Committee in calling for fewer congressional earmarks, line items and other spending directives, reporting requirements, and agency staffing floors (Gore, 1993, pp. 13, 17, 34). They also sought greater presidential rescission power and agency budgetary flexibility, including the authority to roll over 50 percent of unspent, unobligated year-end budget balances (ibid., p. 20). Not prone to view its supervision of federal administration as micromanagement, Congress failed to go along with the reinventers' design for a weaker institutional role in the separation of powers.

President Bush's PMA is another example of administrative prescription with potentially significant implications for constitutional integrity (U.S. Office of Management and Budget, 2001). Bush successfully used the tools of executive dominance—appointments, executive orders and agreements, proclamations, and signing statements—to such a degree that it is fair to ask "whether the extensive use of administrative actions for governance has jeopardized the balance of power between the executive and legislative branches" (Warshaw, 2006, p. 23). Less tentatively, an American Bar Association report indicated that "if left unchecked," Bush's practice of issuing signing statements "does grave harm to the separation of powers doctrine and the system of checks and balances that have sustained our democracy for more than two centuries" (CNN, 2006).

Intentionally or not, the PMA also served the interests of expansive executive power. Implementation in each of its five areas provided political appointees with greater flexibility to manage career employees and afforded additional strength to the OMB's already powerful role in federal administration. Briefly, strategic human capital looks toward initiatives at the Departments of Homeland Security and Defense that serve as a model for future personnel reforms that would enhance managerial flexibility while reducing federal employees' collective bargaining rights and protections against unfair or illegal adverse actions (McGlinchey, 2005; Rutzick, 2005a, 2005b, 2005c). Likewise, OMB Circular A-76, "Performance of Commercial Activities," is the instruction manual for organizing competitive sourcing exercises and decisions (U.S. Office of Management and Budget, 2003). At the same time, improving financial performance requires the OMB to play a more vigorous role in designing agencies' financial systems. The OMB also has a major role in overseeing agencies' e-government activities and executive branch efforts to institute performance budgeting.

Whether efforts to improve administrative cost-effectiveness—such as those associated with the Brownlow Committee, the Clinton–Gore reinvention, and the PMA—truly threaten constitutional integrity could be addressed through democratic-constitutional impact statements and scorecards when reforms are first proposed and again after they are implemented. Writes Shirley Anne Warshaw (2006, p. 23), a leading expert and author of seven books on the presidency:

> When the Justice Department argues that the president does not need to adhere to legislative actions that unconstitutionally infringe on his authority, what is the recourse in our political structure? The recourse must emanate from Congress itself, but seems unlikely since both Houses are controlled by Republicans whose leadership remains dominated by conservatives. The issue is problematic through the courts. Matters between the executive and legislative branches often fall under the rubric of a "political question" which the Supreme Court refuses to adjudicate. Thus, unless the public can put substantial pressure on Congress, which is unlikely, the continued use of administrative actions will continue to dominate the policy process. The most likely recourse will be when divided government returns.

Many reasonably consider sacrificing constitutional integrity and then restoring it through divided government a very high price to pay for whatever gains in administrative cost-effectiveness or policy goals may accrue as a result of straying from the Madisonian system. Some trade-offs are obviously tempting and may be necessary. It is important to remember that the definitive guide for making them lies in constitutional law requirements for different degrees of judicial scrutiny rather than the preferences of reformers, officials, or the public. Recall the Supreme Court's words in its ruling on *INS v. Chadha* (462 U.S. 919 [1983]), in which the Court checked what it perceived to be a legislative power grab:

> The choices we discern as having been made in the Constitutional Convention impose burdens on governmental processes that often seem clumsy, inefficient, even unworkable, but those hard choices were consciously made by men who had lived under a form of government that

> permitted arbitrary governmental acts to go unchecked. There is no support in the Constitution or decisions of this Court for the proposition that the cumbersomeness and delays often encountered in complying with explicit constitutional standards may be avoided, either by the Congress or by the President … . With all the obvious flaws of delay, untidiness, and potential for abuse, we have not yet found a better way to preserve freedom than by making the exercise of power subject to the carefully crafted restraints spelled out in the Constitution.

Enhancing Transparency

Two illustrations of recent administrative prescriptions for greater cost-effectiveness that have diminished transparency readily come to mind. First, as noted earlier, although the work may be identical, regulations requiring freedom of information and open meetings typically apply when work is done by government agencies but not when it is outsourced. This lesson was brought home to the media after the space shuttle Columbia disintegrated in 2003. The National Aeronautics and Space Administration (NASA) generally responded well to FOIA requests for e-mails and other sources of pertinent information. However, NASA's chief contractor, United Space Alliance, had no legal responsibility to be as forthcoming and was less so. Much of the information held by United Space Alliance—said to do roughly 90 percent of the launch work (Bonné, 2003)—became widely available only after the Columbia Accident Investigation Board was convened and released its report. Importantly, several states provide models of how freedom of information can be applied to contractors, as does the U.S. Department of Energy Acquisition Regulation (Rosenbloom & Piotrowski, 2005, pp. 116–117). Nevertheless, as a rule, when government work is outsourced, the public loses the right to know how it is being performed. If James Madison is correct, cumulatively, this is no small matter because "a people who mean to be their own Governors, must arm themselves with the power which knowledge gives" (1999, p. 790; see also U.S. Senate 1974, pp. 37–38).

Second, as a practical matter, results-oriented public administration has difficulty accommodating and funding non-mission-based activities. For example, improving performance in meeting FOIA requests received very limited attention in federal agencies' Government Performance and Results Act (Public Law 103–62 [1993]) performance plans for fiscal year 2001 (Piotrowski & Rosenbloom 2002, pp. 650–653). Nevertheless, the fact that four of 24 major agencies included specific goals or targets for FOIA requests in their plans demonstrates that appropriate measures exist. For one of those agencies, the National Archives and Records Administration, freedom of information is mission based. The other three were the Departments of State and Energy and the Office of Personnel Management. Eleven cabinet departments and six agencies made no mention of freedom of information in their performance plans. This group included the Department of Justice, which spent about $69 million on FOIA and related transparency activities, the Department of Defense ($36.5 million), and the Department of Veterans Affairs ($25 million). The remaining agencies mentioned FOIA in their performance plans but without specific goals or targets (ibid., pp. 651–53).

The lack of attention to non-mission-based activities in results-oriented public administration is not surprising. It is axiomatic, as an FOIA expert at the Defense Department explained, that "we all struggle with insufficient funds, insufficient staff, and too many requests to handle in a timely fashion. The people who run the daily mission programs in the agencies find it hard to devote the time to FOIA" (Foerstel, 1999, p. 94). The predictable short-changing of non-mission-based democratic-constitutional values, procedures, and programs is not inevitable. It might have been prevented by subjecting the Government Performance and Results bill to a democratic-constitutional impact analysis and modifying it accordingly. Including democratic-constitutional scorecards in agencies' annual performance reports would almost certainly help protect these values, procedures, and programs by making them more salient in evaluating administrative performance.

Ensuring the Rule of Law

Contemporary administrative prescriptions for greater cost-effectiveness, better customer service, and other objectives emphasize the desirability of increasing managerial flexibility, employee empowerment, deregulation, and client and contractor self-regulation (Gore, 1995, pp. 11–33; Sparrow 1994). The National Performance Review was particularly hostile to rules: "The perverse effect of 'rule by rules' is that instead of reducing arbitrariness it appears to increase it; instead of fostering cooperation it destroys it; instead of solving problems it worsens them" (Gore, 1995, p. 19). Deemphasizing rules and enforcing fewer of them translates into greater reliance on discretionary administration and compliance. Yet, from a legal perspective, discretion is generally viewed as antithetical to the rule of law, potentially fostering tyranny and even evil (Warren, 2004, pp. 345–47; *Delaware v. Prouse*, 440 U.S. 648 [1979]). Two examples, one routine and the other extraordinary, should make the point.

The National Performance Review showcased the Cooperative Compliance Program of the Occupational Safety and Health Administration (OSHA) as a model of common sense, collaborative regulation. Under the program, OSHA offered employers a choice: voluntarily complying with the standards developed by OSHA in consultation with employers and employees or incurring a 70 to 90 percent greater chance of being inspected, perhaps wall to wall (Gore, 1995, pp. 25–27, 32–33; Graves, n.d.; LaBombard, 1998). Viewed and sued by industry for being a "shakedown," "more like coercion than cooperation," and "ambush rulemaking" in violation of the Administrative Procedure Act of 1946, a federal court declared it illegal and the program was terminated (Harris, 1999; LaBombard, 1998; *Chamber of Commerce v. Occupational Safety and Health Administration*, 174 F.3d 206

[DC Cir 1999]). Ironically, OSHA's "Maine 200" initiative, on which the Cooperative Compliance Program was based, received the Innovation in American Government Award from the Ford Foundation and was celebrated with a coveted Hammer Award from the National Performance Review. A democratic-constitutional impact statement addressing the core issue of whether the prototype or the national program circumvented Administrative Procedure Act's rulemaking requirements could have obviated OSHA's misguided peremptory steps, litigation, and the embarrassment of showcasing a program that so obviously flouted the rule of law.

A second example—outsourcing a part of the Iraq War—resulted in a much more disturbing breach of the rule of law. In spring 2006, President Bush said, "The biggest mistake that's happened so far, at least from our country's involvement, is Abu Ghraib" (Elliott, 2006; Thomas, 2006). Were those who issue administrative prescriptions held to the same liability standards as medical doctors who prescribe drugs, the mistake might have been avoided. A doctor who prescribes a dangerous or addictive drug without taking predictable patient behavior into account engages in some level of malpractice.[3] The same is true of administrative reformers who prescribe outsourcing, administrative entrepreneurship, and partnering with contractors in an environment in which violation of the rule of law is all but inevitable. These are the pertinent administrative facts regarding Abu Ghraib: The U.S. Army needed interrogators to obtain information from some of the prisoners held at Abu Ghraib. It turned to the Department of Interior's National Business Center to find a private contractor who could supply interrogators. Using a professional engineering services schedule to procure interrogators, the National Business Center issued a contract to CACI International, despite prior federal government experience that had led the General Services Administration to conclude that it is "inappropriate to use [a] technology contract for interrogation work" (Harris, 2004a). On the ground at Abu Ghraib, a CACI employee "supervised" military personnel, which is illegal but far from the greatest abuse that occurred (Crawley & Adelsberger, 2004). Further breakdown of the rule of law was abetted by the Army's failure to send the military officer responsible for overseeing the contract interrogators' performance to Iraq. Investigators concluded that "it is very difficult, if not impossible, to effectively administer a contract when the [contracting officer's representative] is not on-site" (Harris, 2004b; see also Crawley & Adelsberger, 2004).

The Army broadly followed administrative prescription in outsourcing interrogation through the entrepreneurial National Business Center. However, this attenuated approach to getting its work done and its failure to supervise CACI personnel all but ensured inadequate accountability for the abusive interrogations. Could a democratic-constitutional impact statement for contracting out work in prisons have stopped the depravity at Abu Ghraib? Perhaps. Domestic experience with contracting out prison health services has established that exceptional measures are necessary to protect the rule of law in penal environments (von Zielbauer, 2005).

Conclusion: "You Get What You Measure"

The rationale for impact statements and scorecards is clear. In today's performance oriented world, what is not assessed or measured is apt to be ignored (Radin 2006). Democratic-constitutional values are weakened by default when not addressed in administrative prescriptions. Although trade-offs may be necessary, democratic constitutional impact statements and scorecards could help institutionalize Radin's call on the political system, not administrative reformers, to make them. Requiring impact statements and scorecards also could help to recover the "impressively deep insight into public administration in a representative democracy" that public administrative professionals "once owned" (Lynn, 2001, p. 155).

Historically, administrative reforms were often presented as a means of perfecting or democratizing constitutional government. Thomas Jefferson, Andrew Jackson, the civil reformers of the late nineteenth century, and the Progressives of the early twentieth century viewed their reforms in this way (Goodnow, 1900; Rosenbloom, 1971, pp. 39–41, 47–50, 70–80; Skowronek 1982). In retrospect, some of these reforms were misguided despite ultimately being thoughtfully presented in terms of democratic constitutionalism.

Regardless of what drives today's administrative reformers—cost-effectiveness, business-like models, faith in executive power, social equity, accountability for results, or other concerns—they infrequently focus on whether their prescriptions will promote or diminish individual rights, constitutional integrity, transparency, and the rule of law. In some cases, such concerns are an afterthought at best. Without further explanation—much less analysis of the foreseeable impact of its strategies on democratic constitutionalism—the National Performance Review declared that it sought to "transform bureaucracies precisely because they have failed to nurture" the values of "democratic governance—values such as equal opportunity, justice, diversity, and democracy" (Gore, 1993, p. 8).

Given the tenor of contemporary administrative reforms, the need for democratic-constitutional impact statements and scorecards is probably greater now than ever. Are there obstacles to requiring them? Three objections are predictable. First, some may argue that democratic-constitutional impact statements and scorecards are a solution in search of a problem. The examples presented in this chapter should caution otherwise. Despite some prescient warnings (Moe & Gilmour, 1995), the field of public administration lags the courts and legal scholars to address the problems illustrated (Rosenbloom & Piotrowski, 2005).

Second, adding costs and impediments to administrative action is always a concern. However, in terms of democratic-constitutional impact statements and scorecards, the underlying question is not one of additional cost per se. It is one of priorities, and a key question is whether the money spent could be better used in some other fashion—or, put differently, whether public funds spent for other purposes might be better used to ensure that administrative prescriptions do not detract from U.S. democratic constitutionalism. As for encumbrances, Supreme Court Justice Felix Frankfurter may have said it best: "Remember, there are very precious values of civilization which ultimately, to a large extent, are procedural in their nature" (U.S. Congress, 1940, p. 13664). Although the National Performance Review claimed that "process sometimes cost[s] more than what [is] protected" (Gore, 1995, p. 33), procedure also significantly reduces litigation. Moreover, impact statements and scorecards also can help attenuate a more intangible but nonetheless costly dimension of failing persistently to consider the democratic-constitutional impacts of reforms: an increase in citizen cynicism, the diminution of public trust in government, and bureaucracy bashing. These are, after all, outcomes that administrative reformers typically claim their prescriptions are designed to combat.

Third, developing best practices for implementation may take time and involve a moderate learning curve, especially at a time when a great deal of results-oriented activity is devoted to the war on terror. Initial difficulties can be expected, but democratic-constitutional impact statements should be no more difficult than environmental impact statements or impact assessments regarding families and other matters. "Enacting democracy" through them might even help strengthen public administration's "moral and intellectual authority" in the polity (Lynn, 2001, p. 155). There is already substantial guidance for adapting, developing, and implementing scorecards in the public sector (Kerr, 2002; Niven, 2003).

The particular challenge posed by democratic-constitutional scorecards is to develop appropriate measures for different programs and agencies. The risk is twofold: Measures must be appropriate because "you get what you measure" (Niven, 2003, p. 185); not measuring may be tantamount to neglect. This challenge should not prove insuperable to practitioners who are well versed in the use of scorecards and performance measurement. In this area, as in others, public administration depends on them to be at the forefront of implementation.

Will Franklin's republic be preserved or lost based on the use of democratic constitutional impact statements and scorecards? Neither is likely to be the case. However, they can contribute to its strength by guarding against the weakening of individual rights, constitutional integrity, transparency, and the rule of law by default. Reinventing administrative prescriptions in light of the importance of these values in our constitutional republic is important, long past due, and within the grasp of administrators and scholars in the years to come.

Notes

1 From Robert F. Durant and Jennifer R.S. Durant, eds, *Debating Public Administration: Management Challenges, Choices, and Opportunities* (Boca Raton, FL: CRC/Taylor & Francis, 2013), pp. 111–127.

2 The Openness Promotes Effectiveness in our National Government Act of 2007 (OPEN Government Act) expands the Freedom of Information Act's reach to include as a "record" information "maintained for an agency by an entity under Government contract, for the purposes of record management" (PL 110–175, December 31, 2007, Section 9). This provision establishes that the records produced by outsourced records management are agency records potentially subject to release under FOIA.

3 Note the conviction of Dr. Conrad Murray for his alleged role in the death of Michael Jackson.

References

American Civil Liberties Union of Northern California. 2002. *Bush Administration vs. the Constitution: A Civil Liberties Scorecard*, September. www.aclunc.org/911/scorecard.html [accessed September 27, 2006].

Bonné, Jon. 2003. Ambition and Frustration at NASA. http://msnbc.msn.com/id/3077640 [accessed September 27, 2006].

Bowen, Catherine Drinker. 1966. *Miracle at Philadelphia: The Story of the Constitutional Convention, May to September 1787*. Boston, MA: Little, Brown.

CNN. 2006. ABA: Bush Violating Constitution. July 24.

Crawley, Vince & Bernard Adelsberger. 2004. Abu Ghraib Reports Fault Contracting, Leadership. *Federal Times*, August 30, 12.

DiNome, John, Saundra Yaklin & David H. Rosenbloom. 1999. Employee Rights: Avoiding Legal Liability. In *Human Resource Management in Local Government: An Essential Guide*, edited by Siegrun Fox Freyss. Washington, DC: International City/County Management Association, pp. 93–131.

Elliott, Geoff. 2006. Bush and Blair Reflect on Failures. *The Australian*, May 26.

Feeley, Malcolm & Roger Hanson. 1990. The Impact of Judicial Intervention on Prisons and Jails. In *Courts, Corrections, and the Constitution: The Impact of Judicial Intervention on Prisons and Jails*, edited by John J. DiIulio, Jr.. New York: Oxford University Press, pp. 12–46.

Fluke, Cecily & Lesley Kump. 2004. Beyond the Balance Sheet: Social Scorecard. *Forbes*, December 14. www.forbes.com/free_forbes/2004/1213/171tab.html [accessed September 27, 2006].

Foerstel, Herbert N. 1999. *Freedom of Information and the Right to Know: The Origins and Applications of the Freedom of Information Act*. Westport, CT: Greenwood Press.

Food Research and Action Center. 2005. School Breakfast Scorecard: 2005. www.frac.org/pdf/2005_SBP.pdf [accessed September 27, 2006].

Goodnow, Frank J. 1900. *Politics and Administration: A Study in Government*. New York: Macmillan.

Gore, Al. 1993. *Creating a Government That Works Better and Costs Less: The Report of the National Performance Review*. Washington, DC: Government Printing Office.

Gore, Al. 1995. *Common Sense Government: Works Better and Costs Less*. Washington, DC: Government Printing Office.

Graves, Bev. n.d. OSHA's "Cooperative" Compliance Program. *PF Online*. www.pfonline.com/columns/0798edit.html [accessed September 27, 2006].

Guttman, Daniel. 2000. Public Purpose and Private Service. *Administrative Law Review* 52(3): 859–926.

Harris, Christy. 1999. Lack of Procedure Kills OSHA Reinvention Program. *Federal Times*, April 26, 3.

Harris, Shane. 2004a. GSA Canceled Guantánamo Interrogator Contract. *GovExec.com*, July 16. www.govexec.com/dailyfed/0704/071604h1.htm [accessed September 27, 2006].

Harris, Shane. 2004b. Bad to Worse. *GovExec.com*, September 15. www.govexec.com/features/0904-15/0904-15newsanalysis2.htm [accessed September 27, 2006].

Human Rights Campaign. n.d. U.S. Congress and Scorecards. www.hrc.org/content/navigationmenu/hrc/get_informed/congress_and_scorecard/index.htm [accessed September 27, 2006].

Kammen, Michael G. 1986. *A Machine That Would Go of Itself: The Constitution in American Culture*. New York: Alfred A. Knopf.

Kaplan, Robert S. & David P. Norton. 1992. The Balanced Scorecard: Measures That Drive Performance. *Harvard Business Review* 70(1): 71–79.

Karl, Barry. 1963. *Executive Reorganization and Reform in the New Deal: The Genesis of Administrative Management, 1900–1939*. Cambridge, MA: Harvard University Press.

Kerr, Deborah. 2002. The Balanced Scorecard in the Public Sector. *Performance Magazine* 1(8): 4–9.

LaBombard, Robert. 1998. OSHA's "Cooperative" Compliance Program Faces Uncertain Future. www.bcnys.org/capital/osha0319.htm [accessed September 27, 2006].

Levitt, Matthew A. 2002. War on Terrorism Scorecard. *Middle East Quarterly*, Summer. www.meforum.org/article/494 [accessed September 27, 2006].

Light, Paul. 1999. *The True Size of Government*. Washington, DC: Brookings Institution Press.

Lynn, Laurence E., Jr. 2001. The Myth of the Bureaucratic Paradigm: What Traditional Public Administration Really Stood For. *Public Administration Review* 61(2): 144–160.

Madison, James. 1999. To William T. Barry, August 4, 1822. In *James Madison: Writings*, edited by Jack Rakove. New York: Library of America, pp. 790–794.

Madison, James. [1788] 2001. Federalist No. 51. In *The Federalist*, edited by George W. Carey & James McClellan. Indianapolis, IN: Liberty Fund.

Marcus, Robert. 2006. U.S. Allies among Worst on Freedom Scorecard. *Christian Century*, May 30.

McGlinchey, David. 2005. DHS Management Directives Spark Union Outrage. *GovExec.com*, June 23. www.govexec.com/dailyfed/0605/062305d1.htm [accessed September 28, 2006].

Moe, Ronald & Robert Gilmour. 1995. Rediscovering Principles of Public Administration: The Neglected Foundation of Public Law. *Public Administration Review* 55(2): 135–146.

Niven, Paul. 2003. *Balanced Scorecard Step-By-Step for Government and Nonprofit Agencies*. Hoboken, NJ: Wiley.

Piotrowski, Suzanne J. & David H. Rosenbloom. 2002. Non-Mission-Based Values in Results-Oriented Public Management: The Case of Freedom of Information. *Public Administration Review* 62(6): 643–657.

Platt, Suzy. 1989. Respectfully Quoted: A Dictionary of Quotations. http://209.10.134.179/73/1593.html [accessed September 29, 2006].

President's Committee on Administrative Management. 1937. *Report of the Committee*. Washington, DC: Government Printing Office.

Press, Eyal. 2003. Faith Based Furor. In *Representative Bureaucracy*, edited by Julie Dolan & David H. Rosenbloom. Armonk, NY: M. E. Sharpe, pp. 185–188.

Radin, Beryl. 2006. *Challenging the Performance Movement: Accountability, Complexity, and Democratic Values*. Washington, DC: Georgetown University Press.

Rohr, John A. 1986. *To Run a Constitution: The Legitimacy of the Administrative State*. Lawrence: University Press of Kansas.

Rosenbloom, David H. 1971. *Federal Service and the Constitution: The Development of the Public Employment Relationship*. Ithaca, NY: Cornell University Press.

Rosenbloom, David H. 2005. Taking Social Equity Seriously in MPA Education. *Journal of Public Affairs Education* 11(3): 247–252.

Rosenbloom, David H. & Suzanne J. Piotrowski. 2005. Outsourcing the Constitution and Administrative Law Norms. *American Review of Public Administration* 35(2): 103–121.

Rourke, Francis. 1993. Whose Bureaucracy Is This Anyway? *PS: Political Science and Politics* 26(4): 687–692.

Rutzick, Karen. 2005a. Pentagon Fine-Tunes Personnel Reforms. *GovExec.com*, October 26. www.govexec.com/dailyfed/1005/102605r1.htm [accessed September 28, 2006].

Rutzick, Karen. 2005b. Homeland Security Appeals Decision Blocking Personnel Reforms. *GovExec.com*, November 14. www.govexec.com/dailyfed/1105/111405r1.htm [accessed September 28, 2006].

Rutzick, Karen. 2005c. Pentagon Releases Long-Awaited Details on Personnel Reforms. *GovExec.com*, November 29. www.govexec.com/dailyfed/1105/112905r1.htm [accessed September 28, 2006].

Savas, E. S. 1987. *Privatization: The Key to Better Government*. Chatham, NJ: Chatham House.

Shoop, Tom. 2005. Unions File Suit Challenging Defense Personnel System. *GovExec.com*, November 7. www.govexec.com/dailyfed/1105/110705ts1.htm [accessed September 28, 2006].

Skowronek, Stephen. 1982. *Building a New American State: The Expansion of National Administrative Capacities, 1877–1920*. New York: Cambridge University Press.

Sparrow, Malcolm K. 1994. *Imposing Duties: Government's Changing Approach to Compliance*. Westport, CT: Praeger.

Thomas, Helen. 2006. Bush Admits Mistakes, But Not the Big Ones. http://thebostonchannel.com/print/9336547/detail.html [accessed September 28, 2006].

U.S. Congress. 1940. Congressional Record 86, 76th Cong., 3rd sess. Washington, DC: Government Printing Office.

U.S. Congress. 1989. *Examination of the Use of Consultants and Contractors by the Environmental Protection Agency and the Department of Energy*. Hearings before the Senate Committee on Governmental Affairs, Subcommittee on Federal Services, Post Office, and Civil Service. 101st Cong., 1st sess., February 3.

U.S. Office of Management and Budget (OMB). 2001. President's Management Agenda. Washington, DC: Government Printing Office. www.whitehouse.gov/omb/budget/fy2002/mgmt.pdf [accessed September 28, 2006].

U.S. Office of Management and Budget (OMB). 2003. Circular No A-76 (Revised), Performance of Commercial Activities. www.whitehouse.gov/omb/circulars/ [accessed September 28, 2006].

U.S. Office of Management and Budget (OMB). 2006a. Agency Scorecards. www.whitehouse.gov/omb/budintegration/scorecards/agency_scorecards.html [accessed September 28, 2006].

U.S. Office of Management and Budget (OMB). 2006b. President's Management Agenda. www.whitehouse.gov/omb/budintegration/pma_index.html [accessed September 29, 2006].

U.S. Senate. 1974. Committee on the Judiciary, Subcommittee on Administrative Practice and Procedure. *Freedom of Information Act Source Book: Legislative Materials, Cases, Articles*. 93rd Cong., 2nd sess., S. Doc. 93–82.

Von Zielbauer, Paul. 2005. As Health Care in Jails Goes Private, 10 Days Can Be a Death Sentence. *New York Times*, February 27.

Waldo, Dwight. 1984. *The Administrative State: A Study of the Political Theory of American Public Administration*. 2nd edn. New York: Holmes & Meier.

Warren, Kenneth. 2004. *Administrative Law in the American Political System*. 4th edn. Boulder, CO: Westview.

Warshaw, Shirley Anne. 2006. The Administrative Strategies of President George W. Bush. *Extensions*, Spring, 19–23.

Wilson, Woodrow. [1887] 1997. The Study of Administration. In *Classics of Public Administration*, 4th edn, edited by Jay Shafritz & Albert Hyde. Fort Worth, TX: Harcourt Brace, pp. 14–26.

11 The Significance of the New Federalism to the Constitutional School of U.S. Public Administration

Norma M. Riccucci

Stephanie Newbold, in an insightful 2010 article published in *Public Administration Review*, explains the importance of the establishment of a Constitutional School of Public Administration. Coined by Michael Spicer and Larry Terry (1993a; 1993b), the movement seeks to improve scholarship as well as practice in public administration by exploring the significance of the Constitution to the administrative state. One avenue, she notes, is demonstrating the value of the Constitution in defining the parameters of public administration as practiced as in, for example, the rights of state government employees to seek justice from discriminatory practices. The following article illustrates the need for a Constitutional School in that it clearly demonstrates how the rule of constitutional law characterizes public administration. That is to say, it shows how the U.S. Supreme Court's interpretation of the U.S. Constitution determines the legality of frameworks to protect the rights of public employees.

Background

David Rosenbloom (1971; 1983; 1987; 2003) has written extensively on the vital role the Constitution plays in America's civil service. Indeed, his pioneering treatise, *Federal Service and the Constitution* (1971), was a defining moment in the history of American public administration in that for the first time, the "rights of civil servants and the conception of those rights in both theory and practice" from a constitutional perspective were delineated (Newbold, 2010, p. 539). Indicative of its popularity, *Federal Service* was reissued in 2014 with new insights into the impact of constitutional law on public employment, such as the evolving conception of the federal employee in conjunction with changes in constitutional law. He also examines the effects of the "reinventing government" movement. Rosenbloom (2014, p. 269) states that:

> [Reinvention's] effort to make the public sector more businesslike and the emphasis on outsourcing have produced 'blended workforces' in which federal employees and private employees are colocated and

> working side by side, often doing the same thing. Under these circumstances the distinctiveness of the 'post-doctrine of privilege' public employment relationship may lose some of its rationale and justification, thereby prompting adjustment.

A number of others have also helped to advance the Constitutional School of Public Administration particularly as it pertains to civil servants or bureaucrats (see, for example, Lee & Rosenbloom, 2005; Terry, 2003; O'Leary & Wise, 1991; Levine & Nigro, 1975). John Rohr, an avatar of the Constitutional School, has argued that the cornerstone of American public administration is the Constitution; he has contributed greatly to the school as it relates to, among other realms, public employment (see, for example, Rohr, 1986; 1998; 2002; also see Newbold, 2008). In *Civil Servants and Their Constitutions*, for example, Rohr (2002, p. 141) succinctly makes the point that "civil servants 'run the Constitution,' i.e., they reduce its grand principles to practice by their actions both routine and extraordinary." In essence, bureaucrats, as he maintains, manage the separated powers of government. The Constitution, in effect, is the ultimate source of power for bureaucrats. This being the case, the primary focus of studies on the bureaucracy or civil service, must engage constitutional questions, values and interests. As Newbold (2010, p. 538) aptly sums it up, the Constitution must inexorably be "the normative base for our scholarship."

The Supreme Court and the New Federalism

There has been a growing movement in public administration, political science, and law that explores the new federalism of the courts, which identifies the distribution of power between federal and state courts. This body of literature is a critical component for the Constitutional School of Public Administration in that the Supreme Court determines whether the federal government can exercise sovereignty over the citizenry and the states. Judicial behavior, just as that of the executive and legislative branches, is decidedly political, and the composition of the Court will impact its disposition on state powers. As Althouse (2005, p. 245) points out, for example, a conservative Court will pay great deference to the states, which "connotes a wildly outmoded form of deference, a throwback to pre-Civil War days." To be sure, it is also a sign of increased judicial activism.

Interestingly, between 1937 and 1995, the Supreme Court did not strike down a single piece of legislation passed by the U.S. Congress under the Commerce Clause of the Constitution. In 1995, the Rehnquist Court broke that track record in *United States v. Lopez* (514 U.S. 549) where it invalidated, as discussed in the article to follow, the Gun-Free School Zones Act of 1990, which banned the possession of firearms within 1,000 feet of school zones. As Levinson (2006, p. 590) explains:

> It cannot be denied that Chief Justice Rehnquist presided over a major shift in U.S. law from the liberal Warren Court, and much of the conservative agenda was accomplished in the name of one overriding doctrine—federalism. It is fair to say that the Rehnquist Court's most contentious legacy is a series of decisions handed down in the name of federalism. Although the term refers to maintaining a proper balance between state and federal power, to the Rehnquist Court it has meant reigning in Congress and restoring power to the states.

As discussed in the article below, the Rehnquist Court further expanded its new federalism policy by nullifying the applicability of federal anti-discrimination statutes to state government employees.[1] In *Kimel v. Florida Board of Regents* (528 U.S. 62 [2000]) and *Garrett v. the University of Alabama* (531 U.S. 356 [2001]), the Court greatly reduced the scope of both the Age Discrimination in Employment Act (ADEA) of 1967 and the Americans with Disabilities Act (ADA) of 1990, respectively.[2] In effect, millions of state government employees no longer have the backing of federal law in age or disability discrimination suits.

Martha Neil (2005: online) reports that the Rehnquist Court "overturned more acts of Congress than all previous Supreme Courts combined."[3] But, as Banks and Blakeman (2012) argue, while the new federalism was reinvigorated by the Rehnquist Court, it is now flourishing under the Roberts Court. Based on decisional patterns and projected time lines, they illustrate that the Roberts Court is on pace to promote a new federalism agenda to a capacity greater than previous Courts, including the Rehnquist Court. In fact in March of 2012, the Supreme Court ruled in *Coleman v. Court of Appeals of Maryland* (132 S. Ct. 1327) that states cannot be sued under the federal Family and Medical Leave Act (FMLA) as it pertains to "self-care." The Act allows for up to 12 weeks of unpaid leave for sickness or to care for a newborn or an ill family member. An employee of the Maryland state Court of Appeals was fired after he asked for time off to address problems associated with hypertension and diabetes. In her dissenting opinion, joined by Justices Breyer, Sotomayor, and Kagan, Justice Ginsburg wrote that the "plurality offers no legitimate ground to dilute the force of the Act" (*Coleman v. Court of Appeals of Maryland*, 132 S. Ct. 1327, 1349 [2012]). The dissent was particularly concerned with the effects of the ruling on women, given that the FMLA "in its entirety, is directed at sex discrimination" (*Coleman v. Court of Appeals of Maryland* 132 S. Ct. 1327, 1340 [2012]).

Conclusion

The Roberts Court is still relatively young, but its new federalism judicial policymaking warrants close scrutiny. If it continues to expand that agenda, we will witness the further erosion of state employees' protections from discriminatory practices. Certainly, public administrationists are encouraged to examine the nature of this agenda in years to come.

Notes

1 See, Levinson (2006) for the discussion of additional federalism decisions of the Rehnquist Court.

2 It should be noted that in 2004, after the publication of an article reprinted from the *Review of Public Personnel Administration*, the U.S. Supreme Court issued a ruling in *Tennessee v. Lane* where it upheld the applicability of Title II of the Americans with Disabilities Act to the states, insofar as disabled Tennesseans were denied access to the upper levels of the state's court house which lacked an elevator.

3 The Rehnquist Court did reject the new federalism framework in three key cases. One is *Tennessee v. Lane* (2004), discussed in *supra* note 2. In another case, *Nevada Department of Human Resources v. Hibbs* (2003), the Court ruled that state government employers were subject to damages under the federal Family and Medical Leave Act in an effort to eliminate gender discrimination, which is subject to "heightened scrutiny." The Court ruled that the Act was a "valid exercise of [Congressional] power under Section 5 of the Fourteenth Amendment" (*Nevada Department*, 2003, pp. 1974). But see *Coleman v. Court of Appeals of Maryland* (2012), discussed in the text. In the third case, *Gonzales v. Raich* (2005), the Court not surprisingly backed off its new federalism agenda, given the subject matter of the case: the use of marijuana. The Court ruled that Congress has the constitutional authority to ban the cultivation or possession of marijuana in states even in those which permit its use for medical purposes. While marijuana is still illegal under federal law, a number of states more recently have decriminalized its use. In May of 2013, Colorado became the first state with a legally regulated market for adult use of marijuana. Voters in cities in Michigan and Maine approved similar measures in November of 2013. Also, under Attorney General Eric Holder, the U.S. Department of Justice in 2009 issued new guidelines which deprioritize the use of federal resources to prosecute the use of medical marijuana.

References

Althouse, A. 2005. On dignity and deference: The Supreme Court's New Federalism. *University of Cincinnati Law Review* 68 (Winter): 245–263.

Banks, C. & Blakeman, C. 2012. *The U.S. Supreme Court and New Federalism: From the Rehnquist to the Roberts Court*. Lanham, MD: Rowman & Littlefield.

Lee, Y.S. & Rosenbloom, D.H. 2005. *A Reasonable Public Servant: Constitutional Foundations of Administrative Conduct in the United States*. Armonk, NY: M. E. Sharpe.

Levine, C. & Nigro, L. 1975. The public personnel system: Can judicial administration and manpower [sic] management coexist? *Public Administration Review* 35(1): 98–107.

Levinson, R. 2006. Will the New Federalism be the legacy of the Rehnquist Court? *Valparaiso University Law Review* 40(3): 589–598.

Neil, M. 2005. Cases & controversies. *American Bar Association Journal*, 91 (October), www.abajournal.com/magazine/article/cases_controversies/, accessed October 8, 2013.

Newbold, S. 2008. Teaching organization theory from a constitutional perspective: A new twist on an old flame. *Journal of Public Affairs Education* 14(2): 335–351.

Newbold, S. 2010. Toward a Constitutional School for American public administration. *Public Administration Review* 70(4): 538–546.

O'Leary, R. & Wise, C. 1991. Public managers, judges, and legislatures: Redefining the "new partnership." *Public Administration Review* 51(4): 316–327.

Rohr, J.A. 1986. *To Run a Constitution: The Legitimacy of the Administrative State*. Lawrence: University Press of Kansas.

Rohr, J. 1998. *Public Service, Ethics, and Constitutional Practice*. Lawrence: University Press of Kansas.

Rohr, J. 2002. *Civil Servants and their Constitutions*. Lawrence: University Press of Kansas.

Rosenbloom, D.H. 1971. *Federal Service and the Constitution: The Development of the Public Employment Relationship*. Ithaca, NY: Cornell University Press.

Rosenbloom, D.H. 1983. Public administrative theory and the separation of powers. *Public Administration Review* 43(3): 219–227.

Rosenbloom, D.H. 1987. Public administrators and the judiciary: The "new partnership." *Public Administration Review* 47(1): 75–83.

Rosenbloom, D.H. 2003. *Administrative Law for Public Managers*. Boulder, CO: Westview Press.

Rosenbloom, D.H. 2014. *Federal Service and the Constitution: The Development of the Public Employment Relationship*, 2nd edition. Washington, D.C.: Georgetown University Press.

Spicer, M. & Terry, L.D. 1993a. Advancing the dialogue: Legitimacy, the founders, and the contrarian argument. *Public Administration Review* 53(3): 264–267.

Spicer, M. & Terry, L.D. 1993b. Legitimacy, history, and logic: Public administration and the constitution. *Public Administration Review* 53(3): 239–246.

Terry, L.D. 2003. *Leadership of Public Bureaucracies: The Administrator as Conservator*. Armonk, NY: M. E. Sharpe.

The U.S. Supreme Court's New Federalism and its Impact on Antidiscrimination Legislation

Norma M. Riccucci

From: *Review of Public Personnel Administration* 23:1 (March 2003): 3–22. Abridged.

In the past few decades, we have witnessed an accelerated devolution of powers from the federal government to the states, not only by the executive branch but by the judicial branch of government as well. The issue of federalism—or more appropriately, the new federalism—as it pertains to the courts refers to the distribution of power between state and federal courts. At its core is the concept of "state sovereignty," which, through a number of constitutional provisions, seeks to preserve the "immunity"[1] rights of states, protecting them from unnecessary or unwarranted intrusion by the federal government. Recently, the U.S. Supreme Court has brought the new federalism to the forefront of constitutional law. This article examines the U.S. Supreme Court's role in the new federalism, particularly around two pieces of antidiscrimination legislation: The Americans with Disabilities Act (ADA) of 1990 and the Age Discrimination in Employment Act (ADEA) of 1967 as amended. It begins with a brief examination of the legal framework under which the Supreme Court has been applying and justifying its federalism policy. It then examines the Supreme Court's decisions in two cases involving antidiscrimination laws: *Kimel v. Florida Board of Regents* (2000) and *Garrett v. the University of Alabama* (2001). The implications of these decisions and viable legal responses to them are also addressed.

It should be noted at the outset that the analysis presented here does not address the official or personal immunity doctrines as they pertain to individual government employees (see Rosenbloom, 1994, 1997). These immunity doctrines address whether federal, state, and local government officials or employees who violate an individual's statutory or constitutional rights can be sued and held liable for their actions. However, as will be discussed later in the text, reliance on these doctrines may provide alternative relief to state employees alleging they have been discriminated against based on age or disability.

The New Federalism and the U.S. Supreme Court

In the past two decades or so, as the U.S. Supreme Court has been faced with opportunities to strike a balance between state and federal power, it has sided almost exclusively with the states. The U.S. Supreme Court's policy of federalism has, in effect, resulted in severe restrictions to an individual's ability to sue a state in federal court for federal rights' violations (Braveman, 2000; Wise, 2001). In two landmark cases, *Seminole Tribe of Florida v. Florida* (1996) and *Alden v. Maine* (1999),[2] the U.S. Supreme Court expanded the boundaries of the new federalism to extraordinary dimensions.[3] In *Seminole* and *Alden*, a Court majority held that Congress is barred from authorizing individuals to pursue private suits for damages in the federal courts against the states when it does so pursuant to its commerce clause powers.[4] The Court opined that Congress cannot subject an unconsenting state to suit in either federal or (its own) state court, whether the suit is brought by a citizen or noncitizen of that state and whether it is based on federal law or state law. The rulings limit congressional legislation in favor of states' rights, restrict the role of the federal courts in adjudicating claims alleging state violations of federal rights, and ultimately impede an individual's ability to seek court enforcement of their federal and perhaps even state rights against a state (Goodman, 2001; Wise, 2001).

It is important to enunciate the constitutional provisions invoked by the Supreme Court in its new federalism rulings. When we think of state sovereignty, we typically think of the 10th and 11th Amendments to the U.S. Constitution. The 10th Amendment, ratified in 1791 as part of the Bill of Rights, reserves all powers not specifically granted to the United States to the states and to the people, respectively. It seeks to protect state governments from being "commandeered" by the federal government or from being eviscerated as viable political entities (*Printz v. United States*, 1997). In short, it limits Congress's powers to regulate state governments. The 11th Amendment, which has been more critical than the 10th to the Supreme Court's new federalism policy, gave concrete and specific expression to the abstract or general guarantee of the 10th Amendment. Ratified in 1795, it originally sought to prevent a resident of one state from suing another state in federal court. It was proposed and ratified in response to the U.S. Supreme Court ruling in *Chisholm v. Georgia* (1793), in which the State of Georgia was being sued in federal court by a citizen of South Carolina. Georgia claimed sovereign immunity and refused to appear in court. By a vote of 4 to 1 the Court issued a judgment against Georgia, stating that a state could be sued by citizens of another state.[5] In an explicit effort to overturn the *Chisholm* decision, the 11th Amendment was proposed and ratified. It was a direct solution that remained unambiguous until Congress enacted the Judiciary Act of 1875, which was part of the post-Civil War civil rights legislation and guaranteed the right of a citizen to sue his or her own state in federal court. As will be seen shortly, it is the 11th Amendment that the U.S. Supreme Court has primarily relied upon in applying its new federalism policy, essentially granting state governments much greater immunity from lawsuits.

Finally, state sovereignty claims also weigh congressional power as defined by the commerce clause of Article I of the U.S. Constitution and § 5 of the 14th Amendment, which grants the U.S. Congress authority to enact legislation enforcing the 14th Amendment.[6] The 14th Amendment essentially applies the Bill of Rights to state governments.[7] The Supreme Court's reliance on the commerce clause in applying its new federalism policy was first seen in its 1995 *United States v. Lopez* ruling. For the first time since the New Deal, the Supreme Court invalidated a federal statute enacted pursuant to the interstate commerce clause.[8] In *Lopez*, the Court declared unconstitutional a law[9] banning the possession of guns within 1,000 feet of a school, despite the aggregate impact of the regulated activity on the national economy through its effects on education and crime. Turning heavily on whether the law or the activity being regulated affected "economic activity," the Court ruled that "the possession of a gun in a local school zone is in no sense an economic activity that might, through repetition elsewhere, have such a substantial effect on interstate commerce" (p. 549).[10]

Similarly, in the *United States v. Morrison* (2000), the same narrowly divided Court struck down a provision of the 1994 Violence Against Women Act[11] (VAWA) creating a federal civil remedy against the perpetrators of gender-motivated crimes of violence. Again, the Court stressed the noneconomic nature of the regulated activity, stating that Congress does not have the authority to regulate a criminal offense such as rape because it is not an economic issue. The *Morrison* Court stated that "gender-motivated crimes of violence are not, in any sense, economic activity" (p. 598). It said that:

> [while] the statute *is* supported by numerous findings regarding the serious impact of gender-motivated violence on victims and their families, these findings are substantially weakened by the fact that they rely on reasoning that this Court has rejected, namely a but–for causal chain from the initial occurrence of violent crime to every attenuated effect upon interstate commerce.
>
> (2000, p. 599)

Broadly interpreted, the *Morrison* and *Lopez* rulings suggest, in effect, that Congress, pursuant to the commerce clause, can only regulate an activity if it is economic and has a substantial impact on interstate commerce.[12]

The *Morrison* Court further ruled that § 5 of the 14th Amendment also does not give Congress the authority to enact the provision of the VAWA creating a federal civil remedy for victims of gender-motivated violence. In so doing, the Court referred to its decision in *City of Boerne v. Flores* (1997), in which it ruled that the 14th Amendment places limitations on the manner in which Congress may attack discriminatory conduct. Foremost among them is the principle that the amendment prohibits only state action, not private conduct. The *City of Boerne* Court affirmed that the states should be unencumbered by far-reaching limitations on their authority, particularly in the absence of clear evidence that they have threatened constitutional guarantees. The *City of Boerne* Court ruled that there was "a considerable congressional intrusion into the states' traditional prerogatives and general authority to regulate for the health and welfare of their citizens" (p. 509). Ultimately, the Court's ruling in *Morrison* further tipped the balance of power toward the states and the judiciary.

In sum, the U.S. Supreme Court has placed severe restrictions on the power of Congress to enact legislation enforceable against the states and has attenuated the ability of individuals to sue a state in federal court. The effects of the Court's expansive new federalism policy can be seen in two recent decisions, *Kimel* (2000) and *Garrett* (2001), in which, for the first time, the High Court held antidiscrimination statutes enacted to protect civil rights inapplicable to the states.

The Supreme Court's *Kimel* and *Garrett* Decisions

In 1967 Congress enacted the ADEA, which made it illegal for private businesses to refuse to hire, discharge, or to otherwise discriminate against an individual, in compensation or privileges of employment, between the ages of 40 and 65. The act was amended in 1974 to apply to federal, state, and local governments. A series of amendments to the ADEA banned forced retirement for all employees, except for public safety officers (i.e., law enforcement officers and firefighters at every level of government).[13] Enforcement authority over the ADEA was originally vested in the Department of Labor but was transferred to the Equal Employment Opportunity Commission (EEOC) as part of the federal service reform of 1978.[14]

In 2000 the U.S. Supreme Court issued a decision in *Kimel v. Florida Board of Regents* that widely reduced the scope of the ADEA. In *Kimel*, the Court barred state employees from suing their employers (i.e., state governments) in federal court to redress age discrimination under the ADEA. The Court ruled that the 14th Amendment's § 5 does not permit Congress to abrogate states' 11th Amendment immunity for violations under the ADEA. Unless a state is willing to waive its sovereign immunity, state employees cannot bring a private cause of action in federal court for discrimination under the ADEA. In effect, state employees do not have the same age discrimination protections as private sector and local and federal government employees under the ADEA.[15]

The *Kimel* case served as another opportunity for the Court to advance its policy of new federalism. The Supreme Court in *Kimel* began by taking as a given the interpretation of the state sovereign immunity doctrine offered in the *Seminole Tribe* (1996) line of cases and proceeded to consider whether the ADEA qualified as an exercise of Congress's power under the 14th

Amendment. To do so, the Court applied the "congruence and proportionality test" from its *City of Boerne* (1997) decision. This test asks whether the legislation in question is congruent and proportional with the constitutional problem identified by Congress. In applying the test, the Court focused its attention primarily on the legislative history of the ADEA and determined that Congress did not identify a serious problem in state and local government sufficient to warrant the protections provided by the ADEA. It said that "Congress had virtually no reason to believe that state and local governments were unconstitutionally discriminating against their employees on the basis of age" (*Kimel*, 2000, p. 65).

The Court arrived at this conclusion without even considering the argument that Congress could have relied on statistics showing widespread discrimination in the private sector and assumed that a similar pattern existed for state employees. The Court's insistence on a showing of explicit documentation of unconstitutional conduct by state employers is rather extraordinary because it indicates that the Court will not permit Congress to infer the existence of a problem and may not even permit Congress to anticipate the future emergence of one. As Ray observed:

> The strict limitations the Court appears to place on Congress in *Kimel* begs the question of what sort of constitutional conduct Congress is empowered to reach when it passes legislation to deter or prevent unconstitutional conduct by the states, as well as the nature of the basis that the Court will require in order to permit Congress this flexibility.
> (2000, p. 1767)

The Court went a step further and ruled that the enforcement powers prescribed by § 5 of the 14th Amendment do not permit Congress to determine what constitutes a constitutional violation. It ruled that Congress cannot "decree the substance of the Fourteenth Amendment's restrictions on the States … . It has been given the power 'to enforce,' not the power to determine what constitutes a constitutional violation" (*Kimel*, 2000, p. 81). With the conclusion that there was no constitutional problem respecting age and that Congress, in any event, lacked the power to determine the existence of a constitutional violation, it followed inevitably that the Court would rule that a remedy such as the ADEA was not warranted. The broader implication here is that the High Court is continuing to narrow the nature of the powers it will consider as a valid exercise of congressional authority.

In a second case, *Garrett v. the University of Alabama* (2001), the Supreme Court again accepted an 11th Amendment immunity defense in striking down the applicability of the 1990 ADA to state governments.[16] Title I of the ADA prohibits employment discrimination against qualified disabled persons. It covers nonfederal government employers, employment agencies, labor unions, and joint labor-management committees with 15 or more employees. The federal government, which is excluded from the ADA, continues to be covered by executive orders and the Vocational Rehabilitation Act of 1973 as amended (Lee, 1999; Lee & Greenlaw, 1998–1999).

Interestingly, despite the Supreme Court's rulings in *Seminole Tribe* (1996) and related cases, the U.S. Court of Appeals for the 11th Circuit in *Garrett* (1999) ruled that the ADA is not only valid but also a legitimate use of congressional authority. Thus, the appeals court rejected Alabama's sovereign immunity claim for ADA violations.[17]

In February of 2001, however, the U.S. Supreme Court overturned the appellate court decision in *Garrett*, stating that Congress did not exercise a valid use of power under § 5 of the 14th Amendment in abrogating states' 11th Amendment immunity for violations under the ADA.[18] Consistent with its previous decisions, the Court, in effect, restricted the scope of Title I of the ADA, while at the same time strengthening state sovereignty.

The Court began by examining whether there was "congruence and proportionality" between the injury and the remedy chosen to correct it. Again referring to its *City of Boerne* (1997) decision, the Court argued that this test was appropriate for determining whether remedial legislation such as the ADA is appropriate under § 5 of the 14th Amendment. The Court first ruled that Congress should have made its intentions about the scope of the ADA clear in the record or text of the legislation. The Court majority said that in order to make states liable to private suits for damages, it was inappropriate for Congress to consider general societal discrimination against people with disabilities. Rather, the Court went on to say, Congress must demonstrate a high level of proof that the states themselves had engaged in unconstitutional discrimination.

The *Garrett* Court (2001) thus concluded that the ADA's legislative record failed to show that Congress identified a history and pattern of irrational employment discrimination by the states against the disabled. The Court opined that:

> Although the record includes instances to support ... a finding [that society has tended to isolate and segregate individuals with disabilities], the great majority of these incidents do not deal with state activities in employment. Even if it were to be determined that the half a dozen relevant examples from the record showed unconstitutional action on the part of States, these incidents taken together fall far short of even suggesting the pattern of unconstitutional discrimination on which § 5 legislation must be based.
>
> (2001, p. 959)

The Court went on to say that:

> Although "negative attitudes" and "fear" often accompany irrational biases, their presence alone does not a constitutional violation make. Thus, the Fourteenth Amendment does not require states to make

> special accommodations for the disabled, so long as their actions toward such individuals are rational. They could quite hardheadedly—and perhaps hardheartedly—hold to job-qualification requirements which do not make allowance for the disabled. If special accommodations for the disabled are to be required, they have to come from positive law and not through the Equal Protection Clause.
>
> (2001, p. 959)

The Court concluded that the ADA did not exhibit congruence and proportionality between the injury to be prevented or remedied and the means adopted to that end. By applying the rational basis standard to discrimination, the Court has set a very high hurdle for Congress, which must demonstrate that the state choices (i.e., "discrimination") serve no legitimate governmental purpose or are not rationally related to the achievement of a legitimate government purpose. This very heavy burden of persuasion is ultimately placed on Congress.

Implications of the *Kimel* and *Garrett* rulings

The general effects of the Supreme Court's new federalism on civil rights laws and antidiscrimination legislation are relatively clear. Federal laws are passed to address broad societal issues and problems that the states are either unable or unwilling to address. As many states, particularly those in the South, have historically demonstrated, federal civil rights laws were greatly resisted. And if the states did choose to establish such laws, they differed widely in scope. The question, then, is, Should the states have the power to determine the existence and strength of civil rights laws? If they do, some states will work hard to preserve the civil rights of their citizens, whereas others may be less rigorous in doing so. It is not necessarily the case that state governments would revert to the days of the pre-1960s, wherein pure hate and unmitigated prejudice often governed the actions of policy makers. But rather, state governments today may seek to sidestep employees' civil rights because of the costs that may ultimately be imposed. For example, efforts to achieve pay equity are seen as being very costly to employers, as are efforts to make reasonable accommodations for disabled workers. In seeking to balance the interests of employee's civil rights with economic expenditures, it seems axiomatic that state employers, if given a choice, will decide in favor of cost containment. As a corollary, employees' civil rights could be transgressed.

An analogous situation can be further illustrated in the area of labor relations in the public sector, where there is no national labor law to regulate or oversee collective bargaining in state and local governments.[19] Each state develops its own labor law or policy, resulting in a hodgepodge of regulations or laws in which some states mandate collective bargaining,[20] others permit it,[21] and yet others either have no policy[22] or they prohibit it outright.[23] Moreover, the strength of the state laws varies greatly in terms of scope of bargaining, binding interest arbitration, and striking rights. In the South, several states not only continue to prohibit collective bargaining, but they have developed mechanisms or policies that severely weaken the ability of public employee unions to adequately represent their constituents. In Florida, Georgia, and other southern states, for example, "right-to-work" laws make it extraordinarily difficult to unionize workers, collect union dues, or provide any meaningful protections and benefits to make unionization desirable to public employees (see, e.g., Kearney, 1992; Rosenbloom & Shafritz, 1985).

Another implication of the Supreme Court's devolution of power to state courts is that no national precedents around civil rights will be set. A new body of patchwork case law, expressing the interests of the states, will thus govern the civil rights of the American people. Of course, one might argue the benefits of this, given the conservative majority on the Court. But the issue of the power distribution between federal and state courts, or the federal and state governments, for that matter, goes beyond this concern to the question of which issues should be governed by national interests and, hence, Congress *and* the U.S. Supreme Court and which issues should fall under the jurisdiction of the states. This broader issue surrounding the new federalism goes well beyond the scope of this analysis. So, too, do the numerous other implications of the Supreme Court's burgeoning new federalism. These issues include Congress's concern for individual rights versus the Supreme Court's proclivity toward states' rights, which type of matters the Court sees as the judiciary's exclusive role of constitutional interpretation, and even the less political matter of the workload of the federal courts (see Althouse, 2001).

More specific to *Kimel* (2000) and *Garrett* (2001), the Supreme Court's decisions have resulted in nearly 5 million state employees losing their federal protection from age and disability discrimination. Although the decisions continue to allow state workers to sue state governments, they can do so only in state court, and then only if the state agrees to the suit.[24] Moreover, the suit must be brought under state disability or age discrimination laws,[25] which are often weaker, less effective, and narrower in scope. For example, state disability laws tend to be much less rigorous than the ADA around reasonable accommodations (Levinson, 2000).

Kimel and *Garrett* may also have ramifications for other civil rights statutes. The Equal Pay Act (EPA) of 1963, the Family and Medical Leave Act (FMLA) of 1990, and perhaps even Title VII of the Civil Rights Act of 1964, as amended, may fall prey to the Supreme Court's new federalism crusade. In fact, in accordance with the Supreme Court's new federalism policy, many lower courts have recently determined that the FMLA exceeded Congress's enforcement powers under § 5 of the 14th Amendment.[26]

The implications of *Kimel* and *Garrett* for the EPA, however, are less clear. Prior to these High Court decisions most lower courts ruled that the

EPA meets the "congruence and proportionality" tests, thus rendering it enforceable against state government employers.[27] But since *Kimel* and *Garrett*, there have been conflicting decisions by lower courts around whether the EPA is a valid abrogation of state sovereign immunity. For example, the U.S. Court of Appeals for the First Circuit, in *Jusino Mercado v. Commonwealth of Puerto Rico* (2000), determined that a nonconsenting state cannot be sued in a federal venue by state employees seeking to enforce the EPA. The *Jusino* court justified its ruling here by pointing to post-*Kimel* Supreme Court actions, which vacated appellate court rulings upholding the EPA's applicability to the states[28] (Murdock, Sezer & Hodge, 2000; Ray, 2000).

On the other hand, the Seventh Circuit Court of Appeals in *Varner v. Illinois State University* (2000), *on remand* from the U.S. Supreme Court,[29] upheld its initial decision that the state university was not immune from a wage discrimination suit brought by female faculty members under the EPA. The *Varner* court ruled that "Although the Eleventh Amendment grants unconsenting States immunity from suit in federal court, that immunity is not absolute" (p. 930). It concluded with a finding that "the extension of the Equal Pay Act to the States was a valid exercise of congressional authority under § 5 of the Fourteenth Amendment" (p. 937). Thus, despite the Supreme Court's ruling in *Kimel*, as well as its explicit directions to the Seventh Circuit to reconsider its position on state sovereign immunity, at least one circuit court is unwilling to render the EPA inapplicable to the states.

One of the major unresolved issues as of this writing is whether the U.S. Supreme Court will find Title VII, the cornerstone of civil rights laws in this nation, inapplicable to the states, despite the fact that in its 1976 *Fitzpatrick v. Bitzer* ruling the Court upheld Title VII as a valid exercise of Congress's enforcement powers under § 5 of the 14th Amendment. Since *Fitzpatrick*, lower courts have routinely upheld the applicability of Title VII to state governments.[30] *In re Employment Discrimination Litigation Against the State of Alabama* (1999), for example, the U.S. Court of Appeals for the 11th Circuit ruled that "in enacting the disparate impact provisions of Title VII, Congress has unequivocally expressed its intent to abrogate the states' Eleventh Amendment sovereign immunity, and that Congress has acted pursuant to a valid exercise of its Fourteenth Amendment enforcement power" (p. 1324).

However, in recent years some states have argued that the Civil Rights Act of 1991, which amends Title VII to create a remedy of compensatory damages for plaintiffs who proved intentional discrimination, constitutes a separate intrusion on sovereign immunity and therefore requires a separate, independent expression of congressional intent to abrogate sovereign immunity. States have also argued that the increased risk of large monetary awards allowed under the 1991 act calls for a reexamination of *Fitzpatrick*, which was decided when the only monetary remedy available was back pay (Murdock, Sezer & Hodge, 2000).

A pivotal decision was issued in 1998 by the Seventh Circuit Court of Appeals in *Varner v. Illinois State University*, discussed earlier in the context of the EPA. The *Varner* case involved a challenge to both the EPA's and Title VII's applicability to states. The *Varner* court (1998) flatly rejected the argument that Title VII, as amended by the Civil Rights Act of 1991, violated the 11th Amendment. It stated that:

> The plain language of [the 1991 act] shows that Congress intended to create an additional remedy for Title VII violations, as opposed to a separate cause of action ... Under Title VII, the abrogation of the States' Eleventh Amendment immunity is settled.
>
> (1998, p. 718)

Because the Supreme Court vacated and remanded *Varner* (Seventh Circuit, 1998) to the circuit court for reconsideration in light of *Kimel* (2000), questions have been raised as to whether the Supreme Court was implicitly suggesting that states are immune from suits brought under Title VII of the Civil Rights Act of 1991. Murdock, Sezer, and Hodge (2000) argued that this is unlikely, and that it is much more probable that the case was remanded for reconsideration of the EPA issue. First, the 1998 *Varner* court wrote most of its decision around the EPA, and not Title VII. Second, in rendering its decision on the applicability of the EPA to state governments, the Seventh Circuit relied on one of its own precedents, in which it had decided that the ADEA was enforceable against state governments (see *Goshtasby v. Board of Trustees of the University of Illinois*, 1998). But because *Kimel* clearly reversed the Seventh Circuit's ADEA precedent, the Supreme Court had, in effect, eviscerated the Seventh Circuit's rationale for upholding the power of Congress to abrogate state sovereignty rights under the EPA. By remanding the *Varner* case to the Seventh Circuit, the Supreme Court was thus instructing the circuit court to reconsider its decision around the EPA and not necessarily Title VII of the 1991 Civil Rights Act.[31]

It also seems unlikely that the Supreme Court will decide that Title VII is not enforceable against the states, because in its *Kimel* decision, the Court repeatedly relied on race and gender discrimination as examples of the type of discrimination that Congress can appropriately regulate under § 5 of the 14th Amendment. The *Kimel* Court (2000, p. 83) ruled, for example, that "Age classifications, unlike governmental conduct based on race or gender, cannot be characterized as 'so seldom relevant to the achievement of any legitimate state interest that laws grounded in such considerations are deemed to reflect prejudice and antipathy'" (citing its decision in *Cleburne v. Cleburne*, 1985). It further stated that "Older persons, again, unlike those who suffer discrimination on the basis of race or gender, have not been subjected to a history of purposeful unequal treatment" (*Kimel*, 2000, p. 83).

In short, it appears unlikely that the Supreme Court would actually consider rendering Title VII outside of Congress's purview with respect to applicability and enforcement. However, without a substantive ruling from the High Court on the applicability of the FMLA or the EPA to the states, circuit court decisions, conflicting in the case of the EPA, will govern which states are or are not immune from lawsuits by their employees under the FMLA or the ADA.

Alternative Actions for Enforcing Antidiscrimination Laws

Despite the long line of new federalism decisions issued by the Supreme Court, local government employees are still able to file suit against local government employers. Nothing in *Kimel* (2000) or *Garrett* (2001) suggests that Congress did not have the authority to pass the ADEA or the ADA pursuant to its commerce clause power.[32] *Kimel*, for example, held only that Congress did not have the power to pass the 1974 amendment extending the ADEA to state and local government employers pursuant to its power under § 5 of the 14th Amendment (p. 91). In fact, the Supreme Court had already flatly rejected a 10th Amendment state sovereignty defense in *EEOC v. Wyoming* (1983, pp. 236–239), when it ruled that the amendment to the ADEA was a valid exercise of Congress's Article I commerce clause powers.[33]

Moreover, the Supreme Court has never suggested that the 11th Amendment protects local governmental entities.[34] In its recent decision in *Alden v. Maine* (1999, p. 706), the Court reaffirmed that a core principle of the sovereign immunity doctrine is that it bars suit against states, but it "does not bar suits against lesser entities; it does not extend to suits prosecuted against a municipal corporation or other governmental entity which is not an arm of the state." Thus, Congress need not abrogate 11th Amendment immunity when regulating local governments. Ultimately, local government employees can file suit against their employers (Bodensteiner & Levinson, 2001).

In addition, a disability or age discrimination suit brought under 42 U.S. Code § 1983 claim to enforce the equal protection clause of the 14th Amendment would subject government officials, acting in their official capacity, to suit for prospective relief in accordance with the *Ex parte Young* 1908 doctrine. Section 1983 gives individuals a cause of action for damages and injunctive relief against those persons who violate the 14th Amendment under color of state law. Section 1983 amends and codifies the Civil Rights Act of 1871. Thus, local government officials in their official capacity are subject to lawsuits.[35] Furthermore, state officials may be sued in their personal capacity for damages. Both enjoy qualified immunity, but both are also subject to liability for compensatory as well as punitive damages (see Rosenbloom, 1997).

In addition, neither *Kimel* (2000) nor *Garrett* (2001) precludes the EEOC from filing suit on behalf of an alleged victim of age or disability discrimination. The EEOC, which has enforcement authority over the ADEA and the ADA, can file suit against state or local government employers as well as private sector employers. And suits brought by the EEOC are not barred by the 11th Amendment (Bodensteiner & Levinson, 2001).[36] In fact, the decision in *Kimel* suggests that the EEOC should work more aggressively on behalf of state government employees in order to promote the intention of Congress to eliminate age discrimination by state government employers.

Also, state employees may bring suits against states that have consented to have suits brought against them for certain actions. Some states have specified activities for which citizens may file suit against a state (Wise, 2001), but as of this writing there is no evidence that states have included "civil rights" as one such activity. Finally, when employees lose their rights they sometimes turn to collective bargaining and unions for protection. Public employee unions have a legal responsibility to fairly represent their constituents and can pursue a number of actions to protect them from discriminatory practices. Then, notwithstanding the Supreme Court's ardent propagation of the new federalism, there are still avenues for state and local government employees to mount legal challenges in federal courts against states, localities, or government officials for discrimination on the basis of age or disability.

Conclusion

For almost 50 years, Congress has sought to eradicate various forms of discrimination in the U.S. workplace. Laws prohibiting discrimination on the basis of race, gender, color, religion, national origin, age, and disability have worked to protect workers and help create work environments free of biases and hostilities. However, the Supreme Court's new federalism decisions, particularly in *Kimel* (2000) and *Garrett* (2001) impose new and substantial restrictions on Congress's power to enact antidiscrimination legislation under § 5 of the 14th Amendment. The Supreme Court's decisions ultimately undermine civil rights and employment legislation enacted by Congress.

It is worth noting in closing that although the U.S. Supreme Court has consistently applied its policy of new federalism in recent years, there is one glaring exception in which the Court struck down the decision of a state court. In *Bush v. Gore* (2000), the U.S. Supreme Court was asked to review a decision by the Florida Supreme Court (see *Gore v. Harris*, 2000), which ordered a manual recount of the state's results in the 2000 presidential election. The U.S. Supreme Court reversed the decision of the state court, ruling that the judgment of the state supreme court violated the equal protection clause of the Constitution's 14th Amendment with respect to the fundamental nature of the right to vote. The Court stated that regardless of:

> whether the Florida Supreme Court had the authority ... to define what a legal vote is and to mandate a manual recount implementing that definition, the recount mechanisms ... do not satisfy the minimum requirements for the non-arbitrary treatment of voters that are necessary to secure the fundamental right to vote.
>
> (*Bush*, 2000, p. 530)

At the very least, the decision suggests that the U.S. Supreme Court will continue to devolve authority to state courts, but it will also sit in final judgment of the *merits* of state court rulings.

One week after *Kimel* (2000) was handed down, the U.S. Supreme Court vacated a 1998 judgment in *Varner* and remanded it to the Seventh Circuit for reconsideration in light of *Kimel* (see *Illinois State University v. Varner*, 2000). The 1998 *Varner* decision of the Seventh Circuit held that "Congress clearly expressed its intent to abrogate the States' Eleventh Amendment immunity when it enacted the EPA" (Equal Pay Act) (p. 710).

Notes

1 There is a wide body of case law addressing personal and official immunity from lawsuits (see, e.g., Rosenbloom, 1994, 1997, and Rosenbloom, Carroll & Carroll, 2000). In contrast, the research presented here examines the current Supreme Court's decisions around government *employer* immunity.

2 There were two companion cases handed down on the same day of the *Alden v. Maine* (1999) decision. See *College Savings Bank v. Florida Prepaid Postsecondary Education Expense Board* (1999), holding that Congress could not abrogate state sovereign immunity in federal court on a trademark case, even though the federal courts had exclusive jurisdiction, and rejecting the constructive waiver of sovereign immunity via a state's activities in interstate commerce; *Florida Prepaid Postsecondary Education Expense Board v. College Savings Bank* (1999), holding that Congress could not abrogate state sovereign immunity in federal court on a patent case, and congressional power under the due process clause of the 14th Amendment did not give Congress the power to abrogate state sovereign immunity to protect property rights.

3 It may be recalled that in the *National League of Cities v. Usery* (1976), the U.S. Supreme Court ruled that a 1974 amendment to the Fair Labor Standards Act (FLSA) was not applicable to state and local governments. The 1974 amendment extended federal wage and hour requirements to state and local government employees. However, this decision was effectively overturned by the Court's decision in *Garcia v. San Antonio Metropolitan Transit Authority* (1985, p. 546), in which the U.S. Supreme Court found that *Usery* was "unsound in principle and unworkable in practice." See Kearney (1992).

4 The Court held in *Seminole Tribe of Florida v. Florida* (1996) that the Constitution embodies a principle of state sovereign immunity that is not subject to abrogation by Congress. In so doing, the Court majority advanced a two-part test for measuring Congress's ability to abrogate a state's sovereign immunity: (1) "whether Congress has 'unequivocally expressed its intent to abrogate the immunity'" and (2) "whether Congress has acted 'pursuant to a valid exercise of power.'" The *Alden v. Maine* Court (1999) took a significant step beyond *Seminole Tribe* by announcing that this constitutional immunity applies even in state court lawsuits where the 11th Amendment is wholly inapplicable. It should be further noted that in *Alden*, the Supreme Court held that 11th Amendment immunity does not extend to suits brought against municipal corporations or other governmental entities that are not "an arm of the state."

5 The four justices in the majority based their reasoning not on the original intent of the Framers but on the judicial power granted to the Supreme Court under Article III of the Constitution. Section 2 of Article III was revoked by the 11th Amendment.

6 Section 5 essentially permits Congress to enforce, by appropriate legislation, the constitutional guarantee that no state shall deprive any person of life, liberty, or property, without due process or deny any person equal protection of the laws.

7 There is a body of case law, however, addressing whether two of the rights recognized in the Bill of Rights have actually been "incorporated" into the 14th

Amendment. They are the right to keep and bear arms of the 2nd Amendment and the 5th Amendment right, "No person shall be held to answer for a capital, or otherwise infamous crime, unless on a presentment or indictment of a Grand Jury." Although the U.S. Supreme Court has avoided taking any cases that would require it to rule on the right to keep and bear arms under the 14th Amendment, it has ruled on the 5th Amendment right noted above. See, for example, the Supreme Court's decision in *Hurtado v. California* (1884), in which it ruled that an individual could be tried and convicted by a jury in the California County Court, because a state is not required to indict by grand jury. The plaintiff contended that under the due process clause of the 14th Amendment, he was entitled to a proper indictment by a grand jury before trial.

8 In response to a political backlash from both the executive and legislative branches, the post-New Deal U.S. Supreme Court slowly began legitimating congressional power to address the social and economic ills of the time. Beginning with its 1942 *Wickard v. Filburn* decision, the Court no longer asked whether a particular statute infringed on state sovereignty but whether it was enacted within the scope of congressional power. Thus, with *Wickard* the Court largely abandoned any efforts to curtail congressional power under the commerce clause (see Merico-Stephens, 2000).

9 The Gun-Free School Zones Act of 1990 forbids "any individual knowingly to possess a firearm at a place that [she/he] knows … is a school zone."

10 Also see *Solid Waste Agency of Northern Cook County v. U.S. Army Corps of Engineers* (2001), in which the U.S. Supreme Court just barely bypassed a commerce clause challenge to the Clean Water Act. In effect, the Court sidestepped the issue of whether Congress's regulating of the environment reaches economic activities and thus operates within its constitutional powers under the commerce clause.

11 The Violence Against Women Act was amended in 2000 to improve legal tools and programs addressing domestic violence, sexual assault, and stalking. The act reauthorizes critical grant programs created by the Violence Against Women Act of 1994 and subsequent legislation, establishes new programs, and strengthens federal laws.

12 See Note 10.

13 However, recognizing that age is not an accurate predictor of a public safety officers' fitness to serve, Congress also included a provision to the amendments stating that if a state or local public safety officer is able to pass a physical fitness exam, he or she cannot be forced into mandatory retirement.

14 In 1990 the Age Discrimination in Employment Act (ADEA) was once again amended to include the Older Workers Benefit Protection Act (OWBPA), which ensures that older workers are not compelled or pressured into waiving their rights under the ADEA.

15 As of this writing, a bill is being proposed that will counteract the Court's *Kimel* (2000) decision, thereby restoring the rights of state employees to sue in age discrimination cases.

16 The state also claimed immunity under the Rehabilitation Act of 1973 and the Family Medical Leave Act of 1993.

17 The *Garrett* Appellate Court also ruled that the State of Alabama was not immune from suits under the Rehabilitation Act, but that under the circumstances before the court in this particular case it was immune from suit under the Family Medical Leave Act. See *Garrett* (1999), p. 1214.

18 The Supreme Court in *Garrett* ruled only on the Americans with Disabilities Act (ADA) aspects of the case and not the Rehabilitation Act or the Family and Medical Leave Act.

19 Of course, some might argue that public sector labor relations is not a matter of great national concern and therefore does not need a uniform national response. It should further be noted that all federal employees, regardless of the

jurisdiction or state in which their agencies are located, are covered by Title VII of the Civil Service Reform Act of 1978.

20 New York, Wisconsin, and New Jersey, for example.

21 For example, Louisiana.

22 Mississippi and South Carolina, for example.

23 For example, North Carolina and Virginia.

24 See *Alden v. Maine* (1999), as discussed earlier in the text. It should further be noted that the *Kimel* (2000) and *Garrett* (2001) decisions do not affect private sector employees nor, as will be argued later in the text, local government employees.

25 Although some have argued that litigants will have to research state waiver laws to determine whether they can rely on the ADA or the ADEA to sue their employers in state courts (see Levinson, 2000).

26 See, for example, *Garrett* (1999) addressed earlier in the text and in Note 15. Also see *Sims v. University of Cincinnati* (6th Cir. 2000); *Kilvitis v. County of Luzerne* (M.D. Pa. 1999); *Driesse v. Florida Board of Regents* (M.D. Fla. 1998).

27 See, for example, *Hundertmark v. State of Florida Department of Transportation* (11th Cir. 2000).

28 See *State University of New York, College at New Paltz v. Anderson* (2000) and *Illinois State University v. Varner* (2000).

29 One week after *Kimel* (2000) was handed down, the U.S. Supreme Court vacated a 1998 judgment in *Varner* and remanded it to the Seventh Circuit for reconsideration in light of *Kimel* (see *Illinois State University v. Varner*, 2000). The 1998 *Varner* decision of the Seventh Circuit held that "Congress clearly expressed its intent to abrogate the States' Eleventh Amendment immunity when it enacted the EPA" (Equal Pay Act) (p. 710).

30 See, for example, *In re Employment Discrimination Litigation Against the State of Alabama* (11th Cir. 1999).

31 On remand, the Title VII claim had been waived, and so the *Varner* circuit court did not ultimately reconsider its earlier decision upholding the applicability of Title VII to the states.

32 It may be recalled, however, that the *Seminole* Court (1996, pp. 72–73) interpreted Congress's Article I commerce clause powers *not* to include the power to subject states to suit at the hands of private individuals. Rather, as it made clear in its *Fitzpatrick v. Bitzer* (1976, p. 456) decision and reaffirmed in *Kimel* (2000), it is § 5 of the 14th Amendment that grants Congress the authority to abrogate the states' sovereign immunity. The *Kimel* Court further ruled that the ultimate interpretation and determination of the 14th Amendment's substantive meaning remains the province of the judicial branch.

33 Also see Bodensteiner and Levinson (2001).

34 See *Will v. Michigan Department of State Police* (1989, p. 70). Also see Bodensteiner and Levinson (2001).

35 In *Ex parte Young*, the Supreme Court ruled that 11th Amendment sovereign immunity does not bar federal suits against state government officials for violations of federal rights. It should further be noted, however, that a number of recent U.S. circuit court decisions have limited liability claims under certain statutes, including the ADEA, the ADA, and Title VII to employers only, thus eliminating the possibility of naming state governmental officials in their official capacity. See, for example, *Silk v. City of Chicago* (7th Cir. 1999), holding that the ADA provides only for employer, not individual liability; *Wathen v. General Electric Company* (6th Cir. 1997), holding that individual liability is prohibited under Title VII; *Mason v. Stallings* (11th Cir. 1996), holding that Title I of ADA does not provide for individual liability, only for employer liability. Also see Bodensteiner and Levinson (2001).

36 Also see *Alden v. Maine* (1999), in which the Supreme Court recognized that the FLSA remains enforceable against state governments in actions brought by the U.S. Department of Labor.

References

Alden v. Maine, 527 U.S. 706 (1999).

Althouse, A. (2001). Inside the federalism cases: Concern about the federal courts. *The Annals of The American Academy of Political and Social Science* 574: 132–145.

Bodensteiner, I. E. & Levinson, R. B. (2001). Litigating age and disability claims against state and local government employers in the new "federalism" era. *Berkeley Journal of Employment and Labor Law* 22: 99–129.

Braveman, D. (2000). Enforcement of federal rights against states: Alden and federalism nonsense. *The American University Law Review* 49: 611–657.

Bush v. Gore, 531 U.S. 98 (2000).

Chisholm v. Georgia, 2 U.S. 419 (1793).

City of Boerne v. Flores, 521 U.S. 507 (1997).

Cleburne v. Cleburne, 473 U.S. 432 (1985).

College Savings Bank v. Florida Prepaid Postsecondary Education Expense Board, 527 U.S. 666 (1999).

Driesse v. Florida Board of Regents, 26 F. Supp. 2d 1328, 1332–1334 (M.D. Fla. 1998).

Equal Employment Opportunity Commission v. Wyoming, 460 U.S. 226 (1983).

Fitzpatrick v. Bitzer, 427 U.S. 445 (1976).

Florida Prepaid Postsecondary Education Expense Board v. College Savings Bank, 527 U.S. 627 (1999).

Garcia v. San Antonio Metropolitan Transit Authority, 469 U.S. 528 (1985).

Garrett v. the University of Alabama, 193 F.3d 1214 (11th Cir. 1999); *University of Alabama at Birmingham Board of Trustees v. Garrett, cert. granted*, 529 U.S. 1065 (2000); *Board of Trustees of the University of Alabama v. Garrett*, 531 U.S. 356 121 S. Ct. 955 (2001).

Goodman, F. (2001). Preface. *The Annals of The American Academy of Political and Social Science* 574: 9–24.

Gore v. Harris, 772 So. 2d 1243 (2000); *Revised and remanded, Bush v. Gore*, 531 U.S. 98 (2000).

Goshtasby v. Board of Trustees of the University of Illinois, 141 F.3d 761, 765–766 (7th Cir. 1998).

Hundertmark v. State of Florida Department of Transportation, 205 F.3d 1272, 1275, n. 2 (11th Cir. 2000).

Hurtado v. California, 110 U.S. 516 (1884).

Illinois State University v. Varner, 528 U.S. 1110 (2000), *vacating Varner v. Illinois State University*, 150 F.3d 706 (7th Cir. 1998); *on remand, Varner v. Illinois State University*, 226 F.3d 927 (2000).

In re Employment Discrimination Litigation Against the State of Alabama, 198 F.3d 1305 (11th Cir. 1999).

Jusino Mercado v. Commonwealth of Puerto Rico, 214 F.3d 34, 36 n.1. (2000).

Kearney, R.C. (1992). *Labor Relations in the Public Sector*, 2nd edn. New York: Marcel Dekker.

Kilvitis v. County of Luzerne, 52 F. Supp. 2d 403, 408–409 (M.D. Pa. 1999).

Kimel v. Florida Board of Regents, 528 U.S. 62 (2000).

Lee, R.D. (1999). The Rehabilitation Act and federal employment. *Review of Public Personnel Administration* 19: 45–64.

Lee, R.D. & Greenlaw, P.S. (1998–1999). Rights and responsibilities of employees and employers under the Americans with Disabilities Act of 1990. *Journal of Individual Employment Rights* 7: 1–13.

Levinson, R.B. (2000). Litigation and administrative practice course handbook series: Discrimination claims. *Practicing Law Institute* 646: 81–102.

Mason v. Stallings, 82 F.3d 1007 (11th Cir. 1996).

Merico-Stephens, A.M. (2000). Of Maine's sovereignty, Alden's federalism, and the myth of absolute principles: The newest oldest questions of constitutional law. *University of California at Davis Law Review* 33: 325–388.

Murdock, G B., Jr., Sezer, K. & Hodge, J.S. (2000). Developments in Title VII and Section 1981: Implications for Title VII. *Practicing Law Institute, 29th Annual Institute on Employment Law* 637: 597–624.

National League of Cities v. Usery, 426 U.S. 833 (1976).

Printz v. United States, 521 U.S. 898 (1997).

Ray, B. (2000). Out the window? Prospects for the EPA and FMLA after *Kimel v. Florida Board of Regents*. *Ohio State Law Journal* 61: 1755–1792.

Rosenbloom, D.H. (1994). Fuzzy law from the high court. *Public Administration Review* 54: 503–506.

Rosenbloom, D.H. (1997). Public employees' liability for "constitutional torts." In C. Ban & N.M. Riccucci (eds), *Public Personnel Management: Current Concerns, Future Challenges*. New York: Longman, pp. 237–252.

Rosenbloom, D.H., Carroll, J. & Carroll, J. (2000). *Constitutional Competence for Public Managers: Cases and Commentary*. Itasca, IL: F.E. Peacock.

Rosenbloom, D.H. & Shafritz, J.M. (1985). *Essentials of Labor Relations*. Reston, VA: Reston Publishing.

Seminole Tribe of Florida v. Florida, 517 U.S. 44 (1996).

Silk v. City of Chicago, 194 F.3d 788 (7th Cir. 1999).

Sims v. University of Cincinnati, 219 F.3d 559, 566 (6th Cir. 2000).

Solid Waste Agency of Northern Cook County v. U.S. Army Corps of Engineers, 531 U.S. 159 (2001).

State University of New York, College at New Paltz v. Anderson, 120 S. Ct. 929 (2000), *vacating* 169 F.3d 117 (2d Cir. 1999).

Stults v. Conoco, Inc., 76 F.3d 651, 655 (5th Cir. 1996).

United States v. Lopez, 514 U.S. 549 (1995).

United States v. Morrison, 529 U.S. 598 (2000).

Varner v. Illinois State University, 150 F.3d 706, (7th Cir. 1998); *vacated and remanded, Illinois State University v. Varner*, 528 U.S. 1110 (2000); *on remand, Varner v. Illinois State University*, 226 F.3d 927 (7th Cir. 2000).

Wathen v. General Electric Company, 115 F.3d 400, 405 (6th Cir. 1997).

Wickard v. Filburn, 317 U.S. 111 (1942).

Will v. Michigan Department of State Police, 491 U.S. 58 (1989).

Wise, C.R. (2001). The Supreme Court's new constitutional federalism: Implications for public administration. *Public Administration Review* 61: 343–358.

12 Third-Party Government and the Constitution

Private Contractors' Liability for Constitutional Violations

Stefanie A. Lindquist

In 2002, Michael Bitzer and I reviewed the status of the law regarding government contractors' liability for constitutional wrongdoing, noting that a full understanding of such liability was critical to inform public managers' decisions whether to privatize governmental functions. Since the publication of that legal note, the growth of "Leviathan by Proxy," to use John DiIulio's phrase, has continued. In many agencies at the federal level, this "shadow government" of private contractors now outnumbers employees in the civilian government workforce (DiIulio, 2014). At the state and local levels as well, outsourcing and privatization of government services has now become pervasive, typically deployed in an effort to generate greater efficiencies and perpetuated and sustained by an ideological preference for the private over the public sector (Bradbury & Waechter, 2009).

Yet the rise of third-party government, supported as it is by the New Public Management or Reinventing Government movements, comes at some cost with respect to the legal framework that protects citizens from arbitrary and unaccountable government action. Indeed, government actors and agencies are subject to certain legal and regulatory constraints that often do not apply to private actors and corporations, or apply only awkwardly or incompletely (Rosenbloom & Piotrowski, 2005; Benesh & Levi-Faur, 2012). For example, the key statute that determines federal agencies' procedural obligations and mandates public participation in agency decision making, the Administrative Procedure Act, applies to "each authority of the Government of the United States" and thus does not directly regulate the activities of private entities acting on the government's behalf through contract. Similarly, the federal Freedom of Information Act does not apply to records maintained by private entities and that are not under the government's control.[1] That private contractors are not always subject to such statutes is, of course, the point: greater efficiency may be obtained when the private sector implements governmental policy precisely because private entities *are not* subject to administrative law norms promoting transparency, accountability, and due process. Nor has this process of privatization and norm avoidance been much hampered through court oversight. The Supreme Court has not invalidated delegation of governmental authority to private entities since 1935, in *A.L.A. Schechter Poultry Corporation v. United States* (295 U.S. 495 [1935]).[2]

Similarly, the U.S. Constitution buffers citizens from abusive and arbitrary government rather than from private action.[3] Thus when private entities and individuals act on behalf of the government, through contract or otherwise, and adversely affect the rights or property of citizens, those citizens may face an uphill battle in enforcing their constitutional rights against such private defendants. In the absence of a claim for damages arising from a constitutional violation, plaintiffs must rely on statutes or state common law for compensation for injuries caused by private parties acting for the government. As a corollary matter, it is also important to note that private contractors themselves face certain legal risks when working for the government, which they might not encounter as immunized government employees. Both sides of this legal coin—the rights of citizens regarding actions taken by private contractors, as well as the official immunity rights of private contractors working on behalf of the government—must be considered in connection with the choice to privatize government services.

As noted in our 2002 piece, the Supreme Court has created a doctrinal framework for evaluating whether private individuals or entities may be found liable for constitutional torts[4] they are alleged to have committed. As we described in 2002, the Ku Klux Klan Act (42 U.S.C. Section 1983) applies in the state context to allow plaintiffs to sue defendants for compensatory damages and other forms of legal relief for injuries sustained by a defendant "acting under color of state law"[5] in violation of the U.S. Constitution or federal law. This statute extends to private defendants who act while clothed with the authority of the state and whose activities thus may be fairly attributable to the state. According to the U.S. Supreme Court, a private defendant may be deemed to have acted under color of state law in several circumstances: where the private defendant has (1) assumed a traditional public function of the state (the public function test), (2) entered into a conspiracy or agreement with government employees to deprive plaintiffs of constitutional rights (the joint action test), (3) engaged in unlawful conduct that was coerced or significantly encouraged by the state (the state compulsion test), or (4) where the state has "so far insinuated itself into a position of interdependence with the [private party] that it was a joint participant in the challenged action" (the nexus test).[6] Only in these instances may a private party's actions be fairly attributable to the state for purposes of Section 1983's "color of state law" requirement.

Although these categories seem broad enough to capture many functions and activities performed by private contractors, in fact the tests above present a fairly high threshold for plaintiffs. First, the "traditional public function test" has been held to apply only to activities that have been the *exclusive* reserve of the state, such as elections, eminent domain, the governance of a "company town," jury selection, and, in some circumstances, the maintenance of prisons. Thus, for example, a private company providing busing services to a public school was found not to be a state actor for purposes of Section 1983 even though it was carrying out a state program related to public education at state expense.[7] The joint action test requires some form of joint participation or conspiracy to commit actions with the goal of violating the plaintiff's constitutional rights. The state compulsion test requires proof that the state's regulation, actions, or custom coerced the defendant into violating the plaintiff's rights. And the nexus test requires the insinuation of government into the activities of the private party sufficient to produce a "symbiotic" relationship between the private and public entities; a key factual inquiry under this test is whether the private entity acts independently of the state in its day-to-day affairs.

The case law is clear, therefore, that neither the receipt of public funds, the extensive state regulation of the defendant's enterprise, nor the existence of a government contract, standing alone, expose a private defendant to liability under Section 1983. Furthermore, even if a suit against the individual employee under Section 1983 is successful, it may be impossible to reach the "deep pockets" of the individual's corporate employer through a theory of "respondeat superior" (employer's vicarious liability for an employee's actions). Instead, the plaintiff must prove that the corporate employer created an official policy or custom that contributed to the constitutional violation. At least one commentator has argued that corporations such as Blackwater, a prominent defense contractor in Iraq, will not create policies to protect potential victims' civil rights in the absence of respondeat superior liability (Frankel, 2009). In short, claims against a private defendant under Section 1983 for violation of constitutional rights face an uphill battle absent strong evidence that the state was responsible for the defendant's actions through conspiracy, operational interdependence, or coercion, or because the state relinquished control over a governmental function that was traditionally exercised *exclusively* by the state.

We also noted in 2002 that, although Section 1983 applies only to the state context, suits for constitutional torts brought against private individuals "acting under color of federal law" are also possible under the "implied" cause of action (i.e. judicially rather than legislatively created) recognized in *Bivens v. Six Unknown Federal Narcotics Agents* (403 U.S. 388 [1971]).[8] We also observed, however, that the *Bivens* action was a narrow one: (1) it applies only to individual employees rather than to their corporate employer,[9] and (2) it has not been systematically extended beyond rights protected by the Fourth, Fifth and Eighth Amendments. Since 2002, the Supreme Court has continued to narrow the scope of *Bivens*.

In *Minneci v. Pollard* (132 S. Ct. 617 [2012]), a federal prisoner (Pollard) at a private prison sued prison employees for violations of his Eighth Amendment rights by depriving him of adequate medical care. His claim rested on what seemed to be firm legal grounds: in *Carlson v. Green* (446 U.S. 14 [1980]), the Court had authorized a *Bivens* claim for damages against a federal prison for violations of the Eighth Amendment. Nevertheless, the

Minneci Court required dismissal of Pollard's suit, holding that when a prisoner seeks damages against personnel working at a privately operated prison, and when suit under existing state tort law would be sufficient to compensate for the plaintiff's injuries, no constitutional remedy existed under *Bivens*. *Minecci* is the most recent in a line of cases in which the Court denied *Bivens*' claim because alternative remedies existed under state law that would compensate the victim of a constitutional tort. In context, then, the *Minneci* case represents a strong signal from the Court that claims against federal contractors for constitutional violations under the implied *Bivens* action may proceed only under narrow circumstances where no state law claim for damages provides an adequate remedy. Indeed, to the extent *Minneci* forces plaintiffs in federal prisons (and perhaps in other contexts) into suits for state tort damages and out of the realm of a constitutional claim, it constitutes the *legal* privatization of *government service* privatization.

Claims against private contractors for constitutional violations thus face serious obstacles: the state/federal action requirement, the limitation on respondeat superior, and, in the federal context, the Court's contraction of suits available under *Bivens*. But what if a claim is properly brought against a private contractor under Section 1983 or *Bivens* for a constitutional violation? As we pointed out in 2002, under certain circumstances, private individuals may claim immunity from suit under legal theories developed to protect government employees from suit when certain qualifications are met (hence the term "qualified immunity").[10] Immunity for official acts is intended to "protect government's ability to perform official acts" by helping officials avoid excessive timidity in the performance of those acts.[11]

In a constitutional tort suit against a private attorney hired to assist the city with a corruption investigation, *Filarsky v. Delia* (132 S. Ct. 1657 [2012]), the Court clarified (to some degree) when qualified immunity protections would be extended to private individuals working on behalf of the government. Although previously in *Richardson v. McKnight* (521 U.S. 399 [1997]) the Court declined to recognize the qualified immunity defense for prison guards working for a private company that had conceded state action under the public function test, the *Filarsky* Court nevertheless held that defendant Filarsky could seek qualified immunity protections from suit. According to *Filarsky, Richardson* involved "a private firm, systematically organized to assume a major lengthy administrative task (managing an institution) with limited direct supervision by the government, undertak[ing] that task for profit and potentially in competition with other firms."[12] In contrast, Filarsky was hired as a temporary "adjunct" to assist the government in the operations of a specific investigation. The territory between *Filarsky* and *Richardson* remains to be fully explored and mapped. On the one hand, qualified immunity may be recognized for a private individual "briefly" associated with government serving as an adjunct to government employees (as in *Filarsky*). On the other hand, the defense may not be extended to employees who work for a government contractor engaged to manage an independent institution for the government operated for profit in a competitive market. In the latter situation, the Court appeared to be convinced that competitive market forces would act to constrain wrongdoing on the part of the private contracting parties. Mapping the legal terrain between *Filarsky* and *Richardson* will take place only incrementally through adjudication of individual cases over time.

In conclusion, since 2002, the scope of constitutional tort liability for private contractors working on behalf of the government remains fairly limited, especially in the federal context as the Court whittles away at *Bivens*. On the flip side of the coin, private employees performing government functions remain vulnerable to suit for damages depending on the nature of their employers' operations for the government.

Notes

1 *United States Department of Justice v. Tax Analysts*, 492 US 136 (1989); *Forsham v. Harris*, 445 U.S. 169 (1980).
2 See also *Carter v. Carter Coal Co.* 298 US. 238 (1936).
3 The one exception to this general principle is the Thirteenth Amendment, which abolished indentured servitude and slavery within the United States and which applies to both public and private actors.
4 "Constitutional tort" is a short-hand expression to refer to a claim for damages based on the violation of one's constitutional rights by a government official.
5 This statute was critical to enable civil rights plaintiffs to sue government employees and private parties for damages to obtain compensation for injuries that might otherwise be limited by sovereign immunity for the state itself.
6 *Estades-Negroni v. CPC Hosp. San Juan Capestrano*, 412 F.3d 1, 5 (1st Cir. 2005).
7 *Black ex rel. Black v. Ind. Area School District*, 985 F.2d 707 (3rd Cir. 1993).
8 The Federal Tort Claims Act provides a statutory remedy for torts committed by federal officers and employees, but it does not encompass constitutional torts. The FTCA does not apply to private government contractors, however, although they may be sued under state tort law. Whether they can claim immunity, however, is a separate question, discussed in the text above.
9 *Correctional Services Corporation v. Malesko*, 534 U.S. 61 (2001); see also *FDIC v. Meyer*, 410 U.S. 471 (1994).
10 Some government officials enjoy *absolute* rather than *qualified* immunity, including prosecutors, judges and legislators. Otherwise, most executive branch employees enjoy qualified immunity only.
11 *Wyatt v. Cole*, 504 U.S. 158, 167 (1992).
12 In *Richardson,* the defendants conceded that they were acting under color of state law when they transported and guarded prisoners. For that reason, the Supreme Court focused only on the immunity defenses raised by the defendants.

References

Benesh, A. & Levi-Faur, D. 2012. New forms of administrative law in the age of third-party government. *Public administration* 90(4): 886–900.

Bradbury, M. & Waechter, G. 2009. Extreme outsourcing in local government: At the top and all but the top. *Review of public personnel administration* 29(3): 230–248.

DiIulio, J. 2014. *Bring back the bureaucrats.* West Conshohoken, PA: Templeton Press.

Frankel, R. 2009. Regulating privatized government through Section 1983. *University of Chicago law review* 76(4): 1449–1515.

Rosenbloom, D.H. & Piotrowski, S. 2005. Outsourcing the Constitution and administrative law norms. *American review of public administration* 35(2): 103–121.

Government Contractors' Liability for Constitutional Torts

The Legal Implications of Privatization

Stefanie A. Linquist and Michael Bitzer

From: *Review of Public Personnel Administration* 22:3 (2002): 241–245.

In recent decades, public administrators have witnessed a burgeoning trend toward privatization of government services. At the same time, however, existing legal doctrines and principles enunciated in precedent and statutes have sometimes failed to accommodate the privatization movement. In this brief, we address several legal issues raised by privatization concerning the scope of private contractors' constitutional tort liability. Understanding the differences in public and private service providers' liability may assist public managers faced with the decision to privatize.

In recent years, governments have come to rely extensively on the private sector to perform traditional public functions. For example, governments have contracted with private entities to provide public school education, mental health care facilities, detention and correctional facilities, janitorial services and refuse collection, wastewater treatment, and social services. Although viewed in light of potential cost-saving opportunities, the privatization decision has blurred the line between the public and private spheres and raises important philosophical issues related to private contractors performing public functions (Donahue, 1989). At the same time, existing legal doctrines and principles enunciated in precedent and statutes often fail to accommodate the trend toward privatization of governmental services. How should courts respond to such innovations in public management? One area where this question has been raised involves the constitutional tort liability of private firms and individuals who contract with federal, state, and local governments to deliver essential public services.

In this note, we discuss several related questions concerning the scope of a private party's constitutional tort liability, including whether private individuals and corporations are subject to suits for monetary damages for constitutional violations and whether such private defendants may enjoy qualified immunity protections from constitutional torts. Understanding the differences in public and private service providers' liability may assist public managers faced with the decision to privatize. Indeed, private contractors and their employees may not enjoy the same protections from constitutional tort actions as traditional governmental employees.

Private Defendants' Constitutional Tort Liability

For governmental agents at the state level, liability for constitutional torts is derived from the Civil Rights Act of 1871, codified at 42 U.S.C. § 1983. Originally designed to address the Klan's activities in the South during the Reconstruction era, section 1983 provides a civil cause of action for plaintiffs alleging violation of their federal constitutional or statutory rights by persons acting under color of state law. The section was intended to protect persons against misuse of power made possible because the defendant acted while clothed with the authority of the state. State employees whose official actions violate citizens' constitutional rights may be sued personally under section 1983.[1] On the other hand, private parties are not subject to liability unless the plaintiff can prove that a private defendant's actions were undertaken "under color of state law." To so qualify, private parties' actions must be "fairly attributable to the state." Courts have held that where private parties perform traditional state functions or participate with a state to engage in concerted activity, they act under color of state law for purposes of section 1983. As a result, a wide range of constitutional rights may be enforced against private defendants with whom state government has contracted to perform public functions. Moreover, the Supreme Court has authorized suits against both individuals and corporations as proper defendants under section 1983.

Where the focus is on federal action rather than state action, plaintiffs alleging violation of constitutional rights may rely on the judicially created *Bivens* (1971) action. This remedy for violations by federal officials is similar to section 1983 except that it provides for the enforcement of a narrower range of constitutional rights against fewer potential defendants. The narrower scope of the *Bivens* action stems from its source; as a judicially created remedy, the Supreme Court has been reluctant to expand *Bivens* beyond a limited number of claims. According to the Court, a *Bivens* action may be implied only in those situations in which Congress has not provided an alternative remedy or where the Court has not discerned "special factors counseling hesitation in the absence of affirmative action by Congress" (*Schweiker v. Chilicky*, 1988, p. 421, citing *Bivens*). At this time, it is well settled that a *Bivens* action exists for violations of Fourth, Fifth, and Eighth Amendment rights, but the Supreme Court has not extended *Bivens* to other constitutional torts. Thus, in contrast with the wide range of liability under section 1983, private contractors with the federal government may clearly be subject to suit under *Bivens* for unreasonable searches and seizures, for violations of due process, and for cruel and unusual punishment, but suits for other constitutional violations may be limited. Moreover, although lower courts and commentators have indicated that private individuals may be sued under *Bivens*, the Supreme Court recently held that plaintiffs may not seek redress from a corporate defendant in a *Bivens* action. In *Correctional Services Corporation v. Malesko* (2001), a five-member majority held that the corporate operator of a halfway house for federal inmates could not be sued for Eighth Amendment violations. Although the Court did not address the question whether individual corporate employees could be sued in a *Bivens* action, the opinions in the case seem to reflect the emerging consensus that such individual liability does exist (see *Correctional Services Corporation*, 2001, p. 526, n. 6).

Qualified Immunity for Private Defendants

Qualified immunity protects government officials who perform discretionary functions from liability "insofar as their conduct does not violate clearly established statutory or constitutional rights of which a reasonable person would have known" (*Harlow v. Fitzgerald*, 1982, p. 818). If a defendant is able to assert a valid claim for qualified immunity, the plaintiff's suit will not survive a motion for summary judgment, which allows the defendant to avoid the cost and stress of trial. Both federal and state employees enjoy qualified immunity, and the parameters of the defense are essentially the same in both contexts. Yet privatization of governmental services has raised important legal questions regarding the scope of the qualified immunity doctrine. In recent years, courts have struggled with the question of whether qualified immunity protections extend to private defendants who perform public functions or who otherwise participate in governmental activities.

The issue remains largely in flux because the Supreme Court has failed to render a bright line standard concerning the applicability of qualified immunity to private defendants carrying out governmental services. Instead, the Court has developed a standard that requires evaluation of the defendant's role, institutional characteristics, and functional relation to government. The Court has held that this inquiry must begin first with an evaluation of whether history reveals that a "firmly rooted tradition" of immunity exists for the class of private actors involved and, second, whether the policy objectives underlying qualified immunity warrant the doctrine's application in the particular case. For example, in *Mejia v. City of New York* (2000), a federal judge in the eastern district of New York struggled to determine whether qualified immunity extends to private citizens who assist law enforcement in making an arrest. Although an extensive historical analysis did not reveal any firmly rooted tradition of immunity for such private parties, the court held that substantial policy reasons—including preventing unwarranted reluctance on the part of private citizens to assist police—warranted extension of the doctrine under the circumstances. In contrast, the Supreme Court has held that qualified immunity does not apply in the case of a privately run, for-profit prison because "marketplace pressures provide the private firm with strong incentives to avoid overly timid, insufficiently vigorous, unduly fearful, or 'nonarduous' employee job performance" (*Richardson v. McKnight*, 1997, p. 410). More recently, in a case involving hospital security guards, a district court refused to extend qualified immunity even to employees of nonprofit corporations, on grounds that "the behavior of a not-for-profit hospital is similar to that of for-profits" (*Payton v. Rush-Presbyterian-St. Luke's Medical Center*, 2000; but see *Raby v. Baptist Medical Center*, 1998).

Implications

Legal ramifications attach to the privatization decision, both for the private agent and the agent's employees. In the case of constitutional torts, public managers may assume that government employees are shielded from liability by qualified immunity, but the same assumption may not be warranted with respect to private individuals who carry out public functions. Indeed, the Court has held that the presumption is against immunity for private actors "unless tradition and strong policy reasons dictate conferring immunity" (*Wyatt v. Cole*, 1992, pp. 163–164). Moreover, with so few cases decided, it is almost impossible to predict whether a court will confer immunity in individual cases. In addition, at the federal level, citizens' ability to recover damages from corporate defendants for constitutional torts has been strictly circumscribed, a result that will sharply limit recovery for many potential plaintiffs.

Note

1 Suits against state employees named in their official capacity are treated as suits against the state (*Hafer v. Melo*, 1991).

References

Bivens v. Six Unknown Named Agents of Federal Bureau of Narcotics, 403 U.S. 388 (1971).

Correctional Services Corporation v. Malesko, 122 S. Ct. 515 (2001).

Donahue, J. D. (1989). *The privatization decision: Public ends, private means.* New York: Basic Books.

Hafer v. Melo, 502 U.S. 21 (1991).

Harlow v. Fitzgerald, 457 U.S. 800 (1982).

Mejia v. City of New York, 119 F. Supp. 2d 232 (E.D.NY 2000).

Payton v. Rush-Presbyterian-St. Luke's Medical Center, 82 F. Supp.2d 901 (N.D.Ill. 2000).

Raby v. Baptist Medical Center, 21 F. Supp. 2d 1341 (M.D. Ala. 1998).

Richardson v. McKnight, 521 U.S. 399 (1997).

Schweiker v. Chilicky, 487 U.S. 412 (1988).

Wyatt v. Cole, 504 U.S. 158 (1992)

13 After *Garcetti v. Ceballos*

A Chill in the Air—Freedom of Speech and the Public Workplace

Robert N. Roberts

In *Pickering v. Board of Education*, (391 U.S. 563 [1968]), the U.S. Supreme Court sharply limited the authority of public employers to punish their employees for externally speaking out on matters of public concern. The *Pickering* decision held that all public employees have a First Amendment freedom of speech right to speak on matters of public concern unless their speech unduly disrupts the operation of their organization (Rosenbloom, 1975). The *Pickering* two-part balancing test almost immediately transformed the relationship between public employees and management. Instead of being able to enforce sweeping gag rules on their employees, *Pickering* forced public employers to carefully evaluate the external speech of their employees on a case-by-case basis. Yet, *Pickering* did not provide public employees any protection from retaliation for internal complaints involving arguably matters of public concern.

With little fanfare, in *Givhan v. Western Line Consolidated School District* (439 U.S. 410 [1979]), the U.S. Supreme Court handed public employees a major victory by extending the *Pickering* balancing test to the workplace speech of public employees. *Givhan* gave public employees a certain level of protection when they internally complained about the practices of their organizations as long as their complaint dealt with a matter of public concern. After *Givhan*, it appeared that the U.S. Supreme Court had firmly come down on the side of giving public employees broad discretion to speak out externally or internally on matters of public concern without fear of retaliation by their government employers. This conclusion proved highly premature.

In *Connick v. Myers* (461 U.S. 138 [1983]), the U.S. Supreme Court sharply limited the types of internal criticisms of public employees that fell within the protection of the public concern doctrine. In most instances, criticism by a public employee of internal management practices did not constitute a matter of public concern. The *Connick* decision clearly had a chilling impact on the ability of public employees to openly criticize the internal management practices of their employers without facing the prospect of retaliation. By the early 1990s the so-called *Pickering-Connick* two-part balancing had become a fixture of public workplace freedom of speech jurisprudence (O'Neil, 1993, pp. 34–46).

The implications of the recognition of the First Amendment freedom of speech rights of public employees went far beyond protecting public employees from retaliation for speaking out on matters of public concern. The adoption of the *Pickering-Connick* balancing test significantly weakened the public policy justification for the so-called ethic of neutrality doctrine. Through the early 1960s, the doctrine held that public administrators "should carry out the orders of their superiors and the policies of the agency and the government they serve" without criticism (Thompson, 1985, pp. 555–556). In other words, with some First Amendment protection, one could argue that public employees now had a moral obligation to externally and internally speak out when their agencies engaged in conduct that ran counter to the public interest.

A little more than a decade after the *Connick* decision, the U.S. Supreme Court in *Waters v. Churchill* (511 U.S. 666 [1994]), demonstrated confusion on the high court regarding the procedures public employers must apply when implementing the requirements of *Pickering/Connick*. A four Justice plurality held federal courts must grant public employers broad discretion on how to conduct fact-finding investigations into the subject matter of an employee's speech or communications. Even more important, the *Waters* plurality found that if the court found that the public employer had conducted a good faith inquiry into the content of an employee's speech and reasonably found that the speech did not involve a matter of public concern, that reviewing court must accept as fact the finding of the employer regarding the content of the employee's speech or communication (Rosenbloom, 1994, p. 505). Not surprisingly, the decision left public employee freedom of speech advocates stunned. Even though *Waters* arguably required public employers to conduct good faith investigations, to bar federal courts from conducting independent fact-finding inquiries into the content of the public employee's speech made little sense besides conserving judicial resources.

A little more than a decade after the *Waters v. Churchill* decision raised questions about the commitment of the U.S. Supreme Court to the freedom of speech rights of public employees, the High Court in *Garcetti v. Ceballos* (547 U.S. 410 [2006]) sharply limited the freedom of speech rights of public employees by holding that the First Amendment does not protect the internal or external communications of public employees made in the course of performing their official duties (Kleinbrodt, 2013, p. 115). It took time for the significance of the decision to the freedom of speech rights of public employees to become clear.

The *Garcetti v. Ceballos* decision required federal courts to first determine whether the employee's speech or communication took place in the performance of the employee's official duties. If the Court found that the public employee spoke out in the course of the performance of his/her official duties that employee would have no First Amendment claim for a violation against his/her free speech rights (Kleinbrodt, 2013, p. 115), because the federal courts no longer apply the *Pickering/Connick* two-part balancing test: first, whether the subject of the speech or communication constituted a matter of public concern and second, whether the speech or communication unduly disrupted the operation of the employee's organization.

Not surprisingly, lower federal courts have experienced considerable confusion implementing *Garcetti's* scope of official duties test (Kleinbrodt, 2013, p. 115). Specifically, federal courts of appeals have struggled to reach a consensus on the test or tests to apply in determining whether an employee's speech or communications fell within or outside the scope of official duties (Wise, 2010). On the one hand, a number of Circuits have applied a so-called "chain-of-command" approach to resolving the official duties issue. If the employee sent communications up the chain of command and those complaints or communications arguably led to the retaliation against the employee, the First Amendment did not protect the employee from retaliation (Wise, 2010). A 2010 study of federal circuit court decisions found that the Fifth, Sixth, Seventh and Tenth Circuits relied upon the chain of command test to resolve *Garcetti* disputes (Wise, 2010).

On the other hand, other federal circuit courts have "focused on the assigned responsibilities associated with the employee's position" to resolve *Garcetti* disputes rather than whether employees sent communications up the chain of command (Wise, 2010). In *Marable v. Nitchman* (511 F3d 924 [9th Cir. 2007]), for instance, Ken Marable, an engineer for the Washington State Ferries (WSF) reported possible instances of "corrupt" conduct by two of his supervisors to the Chief Executive Officer of the WSF, an auditor with the Washington Department of Transportation and to the Washington State Executive Ethics Board (Wise, 2010).

Marable subsequently alleged that he faced retaliation from his supervisors whom he had blown the whistle on including being suspended without pay for a week. Finding that his complaints regarding possible corrupt activities by his supervisors served a reasonable purpose, the Ninth Circuit found that Marable "was responsible for ensuring that his ferry's physical machinery functioned properly and safely. He was not responsible for attempting to ensure that his superiors abstained from allegedly corrupt financial schemes" (*Marable v. Nitchman* (511 F3d 924, 933 [9th Cir. 2007]).

Federal circuit courts have also found themselves forced to apply *Garcetti* to so-called whistleblower cases where public employees have alleged illegal activities by other government employees. In *Bowie v. Maddox* (642 F.3d 1122 [DC Cir. 2011]), David Bowie, an employee of the District of Columbia's Office of the Inspector General (OIG), refused to sign an affidavit supporting the position of the OIG with respect to an employment discrimination lawsuit brought by a former employee of the OIG. Citing "misstatements of facts," Bowie "refused to sign an affidavit in support of the OIG's defense" (Kleinbrodt, 2013, p. 120). Within two years of his refusal to sign the affidavit Bowie found himself without a job, dismissed due to poor performance. He alleged that he lost his job due to his refusal to earlier sign the affidavit in the employment discrimination case. The DC Circuit subsequently affirmed the district court's dismissal of Bowie's freedom of speech retaliation claim on the grounds that Bowie's refusal to sign the affidavit was within the scope of his employment (Kleinbrodt, 2013, p. 121).

Faced with a similar fact pattern, the Second Circuit rejected the reasoning of the DC Circuit. In *Jackler v. Byrne* (658 F.3d 225 [2d Cir. 2011]), a police officer filed a one-page report corroborating an allegation by a private citizen of police brutality against another police officer. Jackler claimed he had observed the police misconduct. Jackler subsequently alleged that police supervisors pressured him to withdraw his report. Jackler subsequently alleged that the Board of Police Commissioners dismissed him for implicating his fellow police officers in illegal conduct. The United States District Court for the Southern District of New York dismissed Jackler's First Amendment complaint (*Jackler v. Byrne*, 708 F. Supp. 2d 225 [2010]) on the grounds that the First Amendment did not protect public employees from facing retaliation for refusing to make false statements since Jackler's refusal took place in the course of performing his official duties as a police officer. Refusing to apply *Garcetti* to the facts of the case, the Second Circuit found that "Jackler had a strong First Amendment interest in refusing to make a report that was dishonest" (*Jackler v. Byrne*, 708 F. Supp. 2d 225, 240 [2010]). The Second Circuit also held that Jackler's reasons for refusing "to change his statement as to what he witnessed when Metakes struck Jones were directed at a matter of public concern, rather than an effort to further some private interest of Jackler personally" (708 F. Supp. 2d 225, 240 [2010]).

Finally, *Garcetti* left unclear whether it recognized an academic freedom exception for public school faculty including the faculty of public universities and colleges (Roberts, 2012, pp. 45–61). Within a short time of the *Garcetti* decision federal circuit courts made clear that K-12 public school faculty had absolutely no First Amendment freedom of speech protection with respect to speaking out on matters of public concern in the performance of their instructional duties (*Mayer v. Monroe Community Sch. Corp* (474 F.3d 477 [7th Cir. 2007]) outside or inside the classroom. On the other hand, federal circuit courts have split on whether the First Amendment includes an academic freedom exception for college faculty employed by public colleges and universities. In *Renken v. Gregory* (541 F.3d 769 [7th Cir. 2007]) and *Gorum v. Sessions* (561 F.3d 179 [3rd Cir. 2009]), federal circuit courts held that *Garcetti's* official duties rule applied to so-called "intramural speech" (speech outside the classroom) by faculty employed by public colleges and universities. Simply, "intramural speech" of public college and university faculty made in the course of performing their official duties received no First Amendment protection. On the other hand, in *Demers v. Austin* (729 F.3d 1011 [2d Cir. 2013]), the Second Circuit held that *Garcetti* did not apply to writing on academic matters by faculty members employed by public colleges and universities and that the federal district court must apply the *Pickering/Connick* two-part balancing test in order to determine whether the First Amendment protected faculty members from retaliation by university or college officials for their writings.

The Future of *Garcetti v. Ceballos*

Due largely to *Garcetti v. Ceballos*, public employees who make internal complaints about the management of their organizations will face an uphill battle persuading federal courts to ignore *Garcetti*. In *Aves v. Bd. of Regents of Univ. Sys. of Georgia* (2015 U.S. App. LEXIS 18802 [11th Cir. 2015]), for instance, the Eleventh Circuit held that *Garcetti* barred five Georgia State employees employed by the university's Counseling and Testing Center [the Center] from raising a First Amendment freedom of speech retaliation claim after Georgia State University terminated their employment as part of a reorganization. Prior to the reorganization, five Center employees had sent a memorandum to university officials complaining about perceived poor leadership and management of the counseling center. Making use of the "duties and responsibilities" test, the Eleventh Circuit found that the five clinical psychologists had prepared and forwarded the memorandum in the course of performing their official duties.

Yet, some Circuit Courts continue to work to limit the scope of *Garcetti*. In *Hunter v. Town of Mocksville* (789 F.3d 389 [4th Cir. 2015]), for instance, the Court of Appeals for the 4th Circuit allowed a First Amendment freedom of speech complaint to proceed by police officers who were terminated after they forwarded to state officials allegations of corruption and official misconduct. A year earlier, in *Lane v. Franks* (134 S. Ct. 2369 [2014]), the U.S. Supreme Court held that public organizations could not retaliate against a public employee's sworn testimony in a judicial testimony even when the testimony involved matters within the scope of their official duties. Relying upon the reasoning in *Lane v. Franks*, the Fourth Circuit held that the police officers had spoken out as citizens and not within the scope of their duties and responsibilities.

Conclusion

Without debate, *Garcetti v. Ceballos* has had a profound impact on First Amendment freedom of speech rights of public employees. Yet, sharp divisions among federal circuit courts over the application of *Garcetti* means that it may take years for the U.S. Supreme Court to resolve emerging conflicts over the application of *Garcetti* to the public workplace.

References

Kleinbrodt, J. 2013. Pro-whistleblower reform in the post-*Garcetti* era. *Michigan law review* 112(1): 111–138.

O'Neil, R. 1993. *The rights of public employees: The basic ACLU guide to the rights of public employees*. Carbondale, IL: Southern Illinois University Press.

Roberts, R. 2012. The deconstitutionalization of academic freedom After *Garcetti v. Ceballos*? *Review of public personnel administration* 32(1): 45–61.

Rosenbloom, D.H. 1975. Public personnel administration and the constitution: An emergent approach. *Public administration review* 35(1): 52–59.

Rosenbloom, D.H. 1994. Editorial: Fuzzy law from the high court. *Public administration review* 54(6): 503–506.

Thompson, D.F. 1985. The possibility of administrative ethics. *Public administration review* 45(5): 555–561.

Wise, T. 2010. Seeing through the smoke: "Official duties" in the wake of *Garcetti v. Ceballos*. *ABA journal of labor & employment law* 25(3): 509–529.

Developments in the Law

Garcetti v. Ceballos and the Workplace Freedom of Speech Rights of Public Employees

Robert N. Roberts

From: *Public Administration Review* 67(2007): 662–72. Abridged.

On May 30, 2006, the U.S. Supreme Court held in *Garcetti v. Ceballos* [126 S.Ct. 1951; 547 U.S. 410] that the First Amendment does not prohibit public employers from disciplining employees for the content of written communications made in the performance of the employee's official duties, even though that content might qualify for First Amendment protection under the so-called public concern doctrine. The decision prohibits federal courts from considering complaints brought by public employees alleging that they faced discipline for the content of statements made in official communications. Speaking for the five-vote majority, Justice Anthony Kennedy held that "the First Amendment does not prohibit managerial discipline based on an employee's expressions made pursuant to official responsibilities" (*Garcetti v. Ceballos*, 1961). Justice Kennedy went on to explain that "when public employees make statements pursuant to their official duties, the employees are not speaking as citizens for First Amendment purposes, and the Constitution does not insulate their written communications from employer discipline" (*Garcetti v. Ceballos*, 1960).

Despite the limited scope of the *Garcetti* decision, it provides public employers much greater discretion to regulate the internal job-related statements and communications of their employees without fear of triggering a First Amendment lawsuit. Although the *Garcetti* majority argued that the decision would not have a chilling effect on the willingness of public employees to report misconduct and governmental inefficiency, this article maintains that the decision is likely to discourage public employees from making use of the chain of command to report instances of misconduct and government inefficiency or to express dissenting views regarding matters of public concern for fear that they may face retaliation for such communications made in the course of performing their official duties (Rutzick, 2006). This article also argues that although many public agencies may view the *Garcetti* decision as an important first step toward limiting the judicial oversight of routine public personnel disciplinary decisions, in fact, the decision may make it more difficult for public agencies to obtain vital information that is necessary to improve the efficiency and effectiveness of public agencies. Finally, the article argues that it is far too early to tell whether the Supreme Court will extend the reasoning in *Garcetti* to informal workplace communications as well.

Official Workplace Statements and the Freedom of Speech Rights of Public Employees

The case of *Garcetti v. Ceballos* grew out of a controversy between Los Angeles County deputy district attorney Richard Ceballos and his supervisors regarding whether to proceed with a criminal prosecution. After receiving a complaint from a defense attorney alleging inaccuracies "in an affidavit used to obtain a critical search warrant" as part of his duties as calendar deputy in a branch of the Los Angeles County District Attorney's Office, Ceballos conducted an internal investigation to determine whether a county deputy sheriff had misrepresented facts in the search warrant affidavit. Ceballos subsequently concluded that "the affidavit contained serious misrepresentations" (*Garcetti v. Ceballos*, 1955).

In a memo to his superiors, Ceballos expressed his concerns about the affidavit and recommended that the charges be dismissed. A short time later, Ceballos met with his supervisors, the deputy sheriff who had prepared the affidavit, and other sheriff's department employees. The deputy sheriff strongly denied any misrepresentation of facts presented in the warrant affidavit. Afterward, Ceballos's supervisors decided to proceed with the prosecution and leave it up to the court to determine the validity of the search warrant. At a subsequent suppression hearing, the defense called Ceballos to testify regarding his concerns. Despite the testimony of Ceballos, the judge upheld the validity of the search warrant.

In the aftermath of these events, Ceballos claimed that his superiors had taken a series of employment-related retaliatory actions against him, moving him from the position of calendar attorney to trial deputy, transferring him to another courthouse, and denying him a promotion. Even though the District Attorney's Office denied taking any retaliatory actions against Ceballos, it argued that even if it had retaliated against Ceballos for his memorandum, the federal district court must dismiss Ceballos's First and Fourteenth Amendment claims on the grounds that the First Amendment does not treat as protected speech the memo circulated by Ceballos because Ceballos had prepared it "pursuant to his employment duties."

Reversing a district court decision granting the Los Angeles district attorney summary judgment, the U.S. Court of Appeals for the Ninth Circuit found that "allegations of wrongdoing in the memorandum constitut[ed] protected speech under the First Amendment." The Supreme Court then granted certiorari to consider whether the First Amendment protects communications made by public employees in the course of the performance of their official duties. The sharp division between members of the *Garcetti* majority and the four dissenters centered on a disagreement over the authority of public employers to regulate formal workplace communications. From the perspective of the majority, public employers need absolute discretion to regulate workplace communication in order to maintain organizational discipline and to avoid public confusion over the policies of a government agency. From the perspective of the dissenters, the *Pickering* two-part balancing test provided public employers with sufficient authority to discipline disruptive employees, making it unnecessary for the Court to adopt a per se rule placing all formal workplace communications outside the scope of First Amendment protection.

The Evolution of the Two-Step *Pickering* Balancing Test

Nearly 40 years before the Court issued its decision in *Garcetti v. Ceballos*, Justice Thurgood Marshall, speaking for the majority in the case of *Pickering v. Board of Education* (391 U.S. 563 [1968]), held that public employees have a First Amendment right to speak out on matters of public concern. [O]ut of the *Pickering* decision grew the two-part balancing freedom of speech test. Issued one year before Chief Justice Earl Warren retired from the Court, the *Pickering* decision symbolized the ongoing efforts of the Warren Court to dismantle the public employment "privilege doctrine," which held that within the public workplace, employees do not have the right to exercise fundamental constitutional rights they can exercise as private citizens.

The first part of the *Pickering* test required that the federal court determine whether the employee had spoken out on a matter of public concern. In other words, if the reviewing court found that the public employee had not spoken out on a matter of public concern, the *Pickering* decision required the court to grant the public employer summary judgment and dismiss the case. The second part of the *Pickering* test required the federal court to determine whether the disruptive nature of the employee's speech justified the public employer in taking an adverse personnel action. Interestingly, the *Pickering* decision left undecided whether the right of public employees to speak out on matters of public concern extended to internal organizational communications.

However, in the 1979 case of *Givhan v. Western Line Consol. School Dist.* (439 U.S. 410) the Court held that under certain circumstances, communications of public employees made inside their respective workplaces may be classified as protected speech within the scope of the *Pickering* public concern doctrine. The decision had a major impact on First Amendment freedom of speech litigation by public employees. The decision made clear that public employers did not have an absolute right to discipline their employees for statements made within the public workplace. But from the perspective of public employers, the *Givhan* decision opened a Pandora's box. Public employers had traditionally exercised broad discretion to regulate the workplace speech of their employees. This included prohibiting employees from talking to the press without the approval of their superiors.

Although the *Pickering* and *Givhan* decisions did not strip public employers of the right to discipline disruptive employees, they made clear that some workplace communications made in the course of performing official duties might receive First Amendment freedom of speech protection, depending on the content of the communications and the degree of disruption they caused. By adopting the two-part balancing test, the *Pickering* majority sought to balance the freedom of speech rights of public employees with the legitimate interest of public employers to maintain order and discipline within the workplace. Yet the adoption of the *Pickering* two-part test forced the federal courts to assume an unprecedented role in the oversight of arguably routine disciplinary decisions by public employers. The *Pickering* decision and a long line of other Supreme Court decisions that expanded the constitutional rights of public employees significantly increased the ability of public employees to seek judicial review of routine personnel decisions on the grounds that they had violated clearly established constitutional rights.

Throughout the late 1970s and early 1980s, the Supreme Court struggled to provide lower federal courts with clearer guidance on what constitutes a matter of public concern (Hoppmann, 1997, p. 1003). Seeking to reduce the high level of confusion, the Court rook steps to narrow the scope of the public concern doctrine in its 1983 *Connick v. Myers* decision (461 U.S. 138). The *Connick* case involved a decision by the New Orleans district attorney to fire an assistant district attorney for distributing a questionnaire to fellow employees soliciting their views about the management practices of the district attorney. The questionnaire asked her fellow employees about the "office transfer policy, office morale, the need for a grievance committee, the level of confidence in supervisors, and whether employees felt pressured to work in political campaigns" (*Connick v. Myers*, 138). In addition, the questionnaire asked employees whether the district attorney had pressured them to work on political campaigns—a violation of their constitutional rights.

Speaking for the *Connick* majority, Justice Byron White first attempted to clarify which types of communications by public employees constituted a matter of public concern: "When employee expression cannot be fairly considered as relating to any matter of political, social, or other concern to the community, government officials should enjoy wide latitude in managing their offices, without intrusive oversight by the judiciary in the name of the First Amendment" (*Connick v. Myers*, 147).

Disagreeing with the findings of a federal district court and the U.S. Court of Appeals for the Fifth Circuit, the *Connick* majority found that, taken as a whole, the contents of Myers's questionnaire did not involve matters of public concern because it primarily sought information about the management practices of the district attorney. "Indeed, the questionnaire, if released to the public," stressed White, "would convey no information at all other than the fact that a single employee is upset with the status quo" (*Connick v. Myers*, 148). Furthermore, Justice White maintained:

> To presume that all matters which transpire within a government office are of public concern would mean that virtually every remark—and certainly every criticism directed at a public official—would plant the seed of a constitutional case. While as a matter of good judgment, public officials should be receptive to constructive criticism offered by their employees, the First Amendment does not require a public office to run as a roundtable for employee complaints over internal office affairs. (*Connick v. Myers*, 149)

Not surprisingly, a number of commentators saw the *Connick* decision as a major setback for the freedom of speech rights of public employees and a major victory for public employers. Critics of the decision argued that it would discourage public employees from criticizing the internal management practices of their organizations. Critics also argued that with fewer public employees willing to put their jobs on the line to disclose possible mismanagement in public agencies, it would become much more difficult for the public to acquire vital information regarding the operation of public agencies (Allred, 1984).

It is important to stress that the *Connick* decision did not involve official communications between Myers and her superiors. However, it did provide considerable guidance to federal courts with regard to how to apply the *Pickering* two-part test to workplace complaints dealing with internal office affairs. In contrast to the *Garcetti* case, in which Ceballos alleged official misconduct by a deputy sheriff, Myers had sought to gather information—including information on possible official misconduct by the New Orleans district attorney.

The Ninth Circuit and the Freedom of Speech Rights of Whistle-Blowers

The *Connick* decision did not end the debate over what constitutes a matter of public concern. In *Ceballos v. Garcetti*, the U.S. Court of Appeals for the Ninth Circuit broadly construed what constitutes a matter of public concern. Specifically, the Ninth Circuit held that "when government employees speak about corruption, wrongdoing, misconduct, wastefulness, or inefficiency by other government employees, including law enforcement officers, their speech is inherently a matter of public concern" (*Ceballos v. Garcetti*, 1174). The Ninth Circuit based its ruling on a series of earlier decisions in which it had held that the *Pickering/Connick* public concern doctrine prohibited public employers from punishing whistle-blowers who disclosed evidence of corruption, wrongdoing, misconduct, wastefulness, or inefficiency (*Blair v. City of Pomona* 223 F.3d 1079 [2000]). In other words, the contents of the memorandum distributed by Ceballos satisfied the first part of the *Pickering/Connick* two-part test, which required the employee to prove that the statement involved a matter of public concern.

The Ninth Circuit then turned to the second part of the *Pickering/Connick* two-part test. Significantly, the Ninth Circuit found that the memorandum distributed by Ceballos had not unduly disrupted the operations of the District Attorney's Office. Specifically the Ninth Circuit found:

> [T]here is no evidence here that Ceballos spoke recklessly, or that he acted in bad faith. At most, the evidence suggests that his statements proved to be erroneous. As the individual defendants concede, prosecutors have a duty to disclose information favorable to an accused, including information relating to a witness's veracity and integrity. Good-faith statements made in pursuit of this obligation, even if they may ultimately turn out to be incorrect, do not warrant retaliatory action.
>
> (*Ceballos v. Garcetti*, 1179)

Throughout the litigation, the Los Angeles District Attorney's Office argued that the *Pickering/Connick* public concern doctrine did not apply to the speech of public employees "when their speech is uttered in the course of carrying out their employment responsibilities and duties" (*Ceballos v. Garcetti*, 1175). In other words, the Los Angeles district attorney argued that a per se exception to the *Pickering/Connick* public concern doctrine exempted from judicial review disciplinary actions taken by public employers against employees as the direct result of communications made in the course of the performance of official duties. Not unexpectedly, the Ninth Circuit wasted little time in rejecting this reinterpretation of the *Pickering/Connick* public concern doctrine:

> The mere fact that a public employee exposes individual wrongdoing or government misdeeds when making a regular as opposed to a special report does not, by itself, result in the denial of First Amendment protection. Whether a job duty is routine or non-routine is a far less important factor for purposes of First Amendment analysis than the content of the public employee's speech. Regardless of the form in which a government worker makes charges of corruption, criminal misconduct, or public waste, such charges raise serious public concerns that merit careful assessment and justify full application of the *Connick* principles.
>
> (*Ceballos v. Garcetti*, 1177)

Rejecting the argument of the Los Angeles district attorney, the Ninth Circuit left little doubt that it had no intention of granting public employers constitutional immunity for disciplinary actions taken against their employees for communications found to involve matters of public concern made in the course of the performance of official duties. Equally important, the Ninth Circuit broadly construed the public concern doctrine to include communications by employees alleging official misconduct, public corruption, and threats to public health and safety.

Implementation of the New *Pickering/Connick/Garcetti* Three-Part Test

It was not surprising that a majority of the Roberts Court rejected the reasoning applied by the Ninth Circuit. Yet it was somewhat unexpected that a Supreme Court majority decided to make use of a new per se rule to limit the judicial oversight of workplace official communications for possible First Amendment freedom of speech violations. Much like the *Connick* decision, the *Garcetti* decision represented an attempt by a majority of the Supreme Court to further restrict public employee freedom of speech lawsuits directly involving workplace-related communications. Unlike *Connick*, the *Garcetti* case did not involve a disagreement over the application of the *Pickering/Connick* two-part test. The decision effectively prevented federal courts from applying the two-part test to situations in which "public employees make statements pursuant to their official duties" and then allege they became the subject of retaliation for arguably speaking out on a matter of public concern. For understandable reasons, this is the most difficult aspect of the *Garcetti* case to understand.

Interestingly, the *Garcetti* majority provided a clear explanation of why it was necessary to exclude official workplace communications from possible protection under the *Pickering/Connick* two-part balancing test. Simply, the new per se rule would protect public employers from judicial "intervention in the conduct of government operations to a degree inconsistent with sound principles of federalism and separation of powers" (*Garcetti v. Ceballos*, 1961). Speaking for the *Garcetti* majority, Justice Kennedy stressed:

> Our holding likewise is supported by the emphasis of our precedents on affording employers sufficient discretion to manage their operations. Employers have heightened interests in controlling speech made by an employee in his or her professional capacity. Official communications have official consequences, creating a need for substantive consistency and clarity. Supervisors must ensure that their employees' official communications are accurate, demonstrate sound judgment, and promote the employer's mission. Ceballos' memo is illustrative. It demanded the attention of his superiors and led to a heated meeting with employees from the sheriff's department. If Ceballos' superiors thought his memo was inflammatory or misguided, they had the authority to take proper corrective action.
>
> (*Garcetti v. Ceballos*, 1960–61)

There is little doubt that the *Garcetti* majority believed that the decision would help limit "judicial intervention in the conduct of government operations" and prevent judicial interference with routine public personnel decisions "inconsistent with sound principles of federalism and the separation of powers" (*Garcetti v. Ceballos*, 1961). However, a closer examination of the opinion provides strong evidence that instead of reducing litigation, the adoption of a per se exception to the *Pickering/Connick* public concern doctrine will further complicate First Amendment freedom of speech litigation.

First, the *Garcetti* decision requires federal courts to undertake a three-step process to determine whether a public employer has violated the First Amendment freedom of speech rights of a public employee. The *Garcetti* decision requires federal courts to first make a threshold determination of whether the public employee engaged in speech as part of the performance of official duties. This is no easy task. Speaking for the *Garcetti* majority, Justice Kennedy admitted that the majority opinion decision did not "articulate a comprehensive framework for defining the scope of an employee's duties in cases where there is serious debate" (*Garcetti v. Ceballos*, 1961). Anticipating that some public employers might attempt to make use of "excessively broad job descriptions" to limit the freedom of speech rights of public employees, Justice Kennedy stressed that the *Garcetti* majority would not permit public employers to use this type of strategy:

> The proper inquiry is a practical one. Formal job descriptions often bear little resemblance to the duties an employee actually is expected to perform, and the listing of a given task in an employee's written job description is neither necessary nor sufficient to demonstrate that conducting the task is within the scope of the employee's professional duties for First Amendment purposes.
>
> (*Garcetti v. Ceballos*, 1962)

This vague language will inevitably force the federal courts into the difficult position of making determinations of the scope of public employees' official responsibilities. In his dissent, Justice Souter argued that the language of the majority opinion "will not discourage government employers from setting duties expansively" (*Garcetti v. Ceballos*, 1965, n. 2). Equally important, argued Souter, the language of the decision "will engender litigation to decide which stated duties were actual and which were merely formal" (*Garcetti v. Ceballos*, 1965 n. 2).

If a federal court finds that the public employee made the communications in the course of the performance of official duties, the *Garcetti* decision requires the court to dismiss the case. If the court finds that the public employee did not make the statements in the course of the performance of official duties, the *Garcetti* decision requires the court to proceed to a determination of whether the statement involved a matter of public concern. And, if the court finds that the statement involved a matter of public concern, the *Garcetti* decision requires courts to determine whether the statement by the public employee unduly disrupted the operation of the public agency. The *Garcetti* decision has effectively transformed the *Pickering/Connick* two-part test into the *Pickering/Connick/Garcetti* three-part test.

Second, the *Garcetti* decision leaves unresolved a number of important questions that the Court will ultimately be forced to answer as the lower federal courts attempt to apply the *Garcetti* decision to the public workplace. It is important to take note that in his majority opinion, Justice Kennedy carefully limited himself to the issue of whether the First Amendment protected the memorandum prepared and distributed by Ceballos. As a result, the Supreme Court returned the *Garcetti* case to the Ninth Circuit to resolve a number of undecided questions. Specifically, did Ceballos's supervisors retaliate against him for what he had said at the meeting during which his supervisors reviewed the contents of his memorandum, for his testimony at the evidentiary suppression hearing, or for speaking "about the alleged misconduct at a public meeting"? (Lane, 2006b). The decision to limit the scope of the *Garcetti* decision to the written memorandum prepared in the performance of official duties might mean that the Roberts Court will limit the scope of the ruling to a fairly narrow classification of workplace communications. On the other hand, if the Ninth Circuit concludes that Ceballos's supervisors retaliated against him for his oral statements at the meeting or for his testimony on behalf of the defense at the suppression hearing, a majority of the Roberts Court may very well apply the *Garcetti* per se rule to all communications—oral or written—made by a public employee in the performance of official duties. In other words, the Supreme Court will ultimately have to provide public employers and employees with a clearer definition of what constitutes an official communication within the context of the performance of official duties.

Managerial Discretion and the *Garcetti* Nuclear Option

In a forcefully worded dissent, Justice Souter strongly disagreed with the *Garcetti* majority's adoption of a new per se rule. Specifically, Souter argued that:

> private and public interests in addressing official wrongdoing and threats to health and safety can outweigh the government's stake in the efficient implementation of policy, and when they do, employees who speak on these matters in the course of their duties should be eligible to claim First Amendment protection.
>
> (*Garcetti v. Ceballos*, 1963)

By adopting a per se rule barring public employee freedom of speech suits involving statements made pursuant to the performance of official duties, the *Garcetti* decision puts in place a serious disincentive for public employees to disclose to organizational leadership serious problems within their organizations.

Referring to the Supreme Court's 1979 decision in *Givhan v. Western Line Consol. School District*, Justice John Paul Stevens argued that it made no sense to impose a per se exception to public employee freedom of speech cases: "We had no difficulty recognizing that the First Amendment applied when Bessie Givhan, an English teacher, raised concerns about the school's racist employment practices to the principal" (*Garcetti v. Ceballos*, 1963). Consequently, argued Stevens, "Our silence as to whether or not her speech was made pursuant to her job duties demonstrates that the point was immaterial. This is equally true today, for it is senseless to let constitutional protection for exactly the same words hinge on whether they fall within a job description. Moreover, it seems perverse to fashion a new rule that provides employees with an incentive to voice their concerns publicly before talking frankly to their superiors" (*Garcetti v. Ceballos*, 1963).

Also reflecting the view of the *Garcetti* dissenters that the *Pickering/Connick* two-part test provided public employers adequate protection against disruptive statements made by public employees in the course of the performance of official duties, Justice Breyer criticized the majority for failing to recognize that under certain limited circumstances, the Constitution may impose "speech obligations upon the government's professional employee" (*Garcetti v. Ceballos*, 1974). As explained by Justice Breyer, for instance, "A prosecutor has a constitutional obligation to learn of, to preserve, and to communicate with the defense about exculpatory and impeachment evidence in the government's possession" (*Garcetti v. Ceballos*, 1974).

The dissents of Justices Souter, Stevens, and Breyer indicate a general rejection of the *Garcetti* majority's argument that providing public employees with the opportunity to raise First Amendment challenges to disciplinary actions taken as a direct result of statements related to the performance of official duties constitutes unreasonable interference in the affairs of public agencies. Unlike the *Garcetti* majority, the dissenters expressed strong support for the continued use of the *Pickering/Connick* two-part balancing test as a reasonable method of resolving disputes involving the workplace freedom of speech rights of public employees. From the perspective of the *Garcetti* dissenters, the legitimate concerns of public employers could be addressed by fine-tuning the *Pickering/Connick* balancing test. As Justice Souter explained:

> It is thus no adequate justification for the suppression of potentially valuable information simply to recognize that the government has a huge interest in managing its employees and preventing the occasionally irresponsible one from turning his job into a bully pulpit. Even there, the lesson of *Pickering* (and the object of constitutional adjudication) is still to the point: when constitutionally significant interests clash, resist the demand for winner-take-all; try to make adjustments that serve all of the values at stake.
>
> (*Garcetti v. Ceballos*, 1967)

The dissents of Justices Souter, Stevens, and Breyer indicate a general rejection of the argument of the *Garcetti* majority's argument that providing public employees with the opportunity to raise First Amendment challenges to disciplinary actions taken as a direct result of statements related to the performance of official duties constitutes unreasonable interference in the affairs of public agencies.

To limit judicial interference with the legitimate authority of public employers to regulate the speech of public employees made in course of the performance of official duties, Souter proposed that before a federal court hears a case involving job-related communications, the courts should require a public employee to meet the threshold burden of demonstrating that he or she was speaking out "on a matter of unusual importance" (*Ceballos v. Garcetti*, 1967). Finally, Souter suggested that comments related to alleged "official dishonesty, deliberately unconstitutional action, other serious wrongdoing, or threats to health and safety" might qualify as matters of unusual importance (*Ceballos v. Garcetti*, 1967). Even though Justice Breyer questioned whether it was practicable to apply an "unusual importance" threshold test, he expressed absolutely no reservations about applying the *Pickering* balancing test to the facts of the case.

To counter the argument that the decision might deter public employees from exposing government inefficiency or misconduct, Justice Kennedy stressed the existence of a "powerful network of legislative enactments" designed to encourage public employees to report governmental inefficiency and misconduct:

> The dictates of sound judgment are reinforced by the powerful network of legislative enactments—such as whistle-blower protection laws and labor codes—available to those who seek to expose wrongdoing. See, e.g., 5 U.S.C. & 2302 (b)(8); Cal. Govt. Code Ann. & 8547.8 (West 2005); Cal. Lab. Code Ann & 1102.5 (West Supp. 2006). Cases involving government attorneys implicate additional safeguards in the form of, for example, rules of conduct and constitutional obligations apart from the First Amendment. See, e.g., Cal. Rule Prof. Conduct 5–110 (2005) ("A member in government service shall not institute or cause to be instituted criminal charges when the member knows or should know that the charges are not supported by probable cause"); *Brady v. Maryland*, 373 U.S. 83 (1963). These imperatives, as well as obligations arising from any other applicable constitutional provisions and mandates of the criminal and civil laws, protect employees and provide checks on supervisors who would order unlawful or otherwise inappropriate actions.
>
> (*Garcetti v. Ceballos*, 1962)

In other words, Justice Kennedy strongly disagreed with the dissenters' argument that the decision would have a chilling impact on the willingness of government employees to report instances of governmental inefficiency and official misconduct. Equally important, Justice Kennedy argued that nothing in the decision prevented "[a] public employer that wishes to encourage its employees to voice concerns privately retains the option of instituting internal policies and procedures that are receptive to employee criticism" (*Garcetti v. Ceballos*, 1961).

The Freedom of Speech Rights of Public Employees after *Garcetti*

In a 1985 *Public Administration Review* article, Dennis Thompson argued that the "conventional theory and practice of administrative ethics holds that administrators should carry out the orders of their superiors and the policies of the agency and the government they serve" (pp. 555–56) as long as they are lawful. Highly critical of the blind allegiance of many public servants to the "ethic of neutrality," Thompson argued "that the more directly a policy seems to violate an important moral principle (such as not harming innocent persons), the more justifiable dissent becomes" (p. 557). More than a decade earlier, at the height of the Watergate scandal, George A. Graham provided guidance to public administrators facing a conflict between their own personal values and the goals of their organization:

> Recognize that the rules of the game permit him to contest a decision made by his own organization, but not yet final, by going over his superior's head, or by going to other organizations within the government (including the legislative branch) only when he can honestly assure himself (1) that a mistake is being made on an issue of major public importance, (2) that his judgment is unbiased by personal or partisan, as opposed to public interest considerations, (3) that the risk he runs of being forced out of government is justified by the importance of the issue, and (4) that what will be lost by the decisions outweighs the value of his probable future usefulness to the government if he continues in the government.
>
> (1974, p. 92)

The most immediate impact of the *Garcetti* decision is that public employees will no longer be able to attempt to make the First Amendment argument that their employer punished them for speaking out on a matter of public concern if the employee made the statements in the course of the performance of official duties. This is the case even if the employee believed that he or she had a constitutional or professional obligation to make such a disclosure. In the 1963 case of *Brady v. Maryland* (373 U.S. 83), for example, the Supreme Court held that the Constitution required prosecutors to provide defense counsel with evidence that might prove the innocence of a criminal defendant.

During the October 2005 Supreme Court oral arguments in the *Garcetti* case, Justice Souter asked the attorney representing the Los Angeles District

Attorney's Office whether an employee of the office would have a First Amendment claim against the District Attorney's Office if it retaliated against the employee for making a Brady disclosure without the permission of his or her superiors. The attorney representing the District Attorney's Office responded that even if the employee believed that the ruling required Ceballos to make a Brady disclosure to defense counsel, this attempt to comply with Brady still would not create a First Amendment cause of action against the District Attorney's Office. The *Garcetti* majority accepted the position of the District Attorney's Office.

A much more difficult question to answer is whether, at some future point in time, a majority of the Roberts Court will vote to extend the *Garcetti* per se rule to workplace statements made outside the scope of an employee's official duties. In the 1994 case of *Waters v. Churchill* (511 U.S. 661 [1994]), the Rehnquist Court struggled with how federal courts might resolve disputes regarding whether alleged statements made by one employee to another qualified for protection under the *Pickering/Connick* public concern doctrine (Kandel, 1994, p. 283). The *Waters* case involved a statement by one nurse to another that was allegedly highly critical of her supervisor. The nurse who had allegedly made the disruptive comments was subsequently fired by her employer, a public hospital. Reflecting growing concern on the part of the Supreme Court that the federal courts had become too involved in determining the content of the speech of public employees, Justice O'Connor, speaking for the *Waters* plurality, "reasoned that the government employer should be able to act on what it reasonably thought the employee said, rather than only on what a judge or jury, using the rules of legal evidence, might later determine actually to have been said" (Rosenbloom, 1994, p. 505). Instead of engaging in fact-finding over what the employee said, the court should restrict its review to the determination of whether the government employer acted in a reasonable manner in finding the employee had not engaged in protected speech. O'Connor also stressed the need to provide public employers with considerable flexibility in the selection of procedures to determine the content of the employee's speech:

> What works best in a judicial proceeding may not be appropriate in the employment context. If one employee accuses another of misconduct, it is reasonable for a government manager to credit the allegation more if it is consistent with what the manager knows of the characters of the accused. Likewise, a manager may legitimately want to discipline an employee based on the complaints of patrons that the employee has been rude, even though these complaints are hearsay.
>
> (*Waters v. Churchill*, p. 661)

Finally, Justice O'Connor stressed that "[a]n employee who makes an unprotected statement is not immunized from discipline by the fact that this statement is surrounded by protected statements" (*Waters v. Churchill*, 661).

Understandably, it may be quite tempting to a majority of the Roberts Court to make it unnecessary for courts to engage in the type of investigation recommended by the *Waters* plurality opinion by extending the reasoning in *Garcetti* to workplace statements made outside the scope of the performance of an employee's official duties.

With respect to the off-duty statements or conduct of public employees, the *Garcetti* decision has no impact. The courts will continue to apply the *Pickering/Connick* two-part balancing test to the off-duty conduct and statements of public employees. In the 2004 case of *San Diego v. Roe* (543 U.S. 77), for instance, the Supreme Court upheld the dismissal of a San Diego police officer for selling videotapes on the adults-only section of eBay that showed him engaging in sexually explicit acts. Applying the *Pickering/Connick* two-part balancing test, the Court found that the video did not constitute a matter of public concern because it did not constitute a matter of "legitimate news interest" (*San Diego v. Roe*, 83–84). In other words, when a public employee acts as a private citizen in his off-duty activities, he or she is not entitled to First Amendment freedom of speech protection under the public concern doctrine.

Finally, it is unclear how the *Garcetti* decision will affect academic freedom. During the October 2005 oral arguments in the *Garcetti* case, Chief Justice Roberts asked the lawyer representing the Los Angeles District Attorney's Office whether the law permitted a public university to fire a professor solely on the basis of the content of his or her lectures. Not unexpectedly, the lawyer responded, "It would be our view that if the assigned job duties of that university professor [were] to speak on a particular topic or content, and [he was] getting paid for doing that, [it is] job-required speech and ... should not be entitled, presumptively, to first-amendment protection." In other words, it is up to the discretion of public universities to evaluate the effectiveness of their faculty, and the content of a lecture or a statement of a faculty member deserves no special First Amendment protection. Significantly, the National School Boards Association filed an amicus brief in the *Garcetti* case arguing that if the Supreme Court did not overturn the Ninth Circuit's holding, it might cause some teachers to believe that they have a First Amendment right to espouse their own views in class on matters of public concern, thereby hampering "a school's ability to teach students the school's selected curriculum" (LII 2005).

In his dissent, Justice Souter wondered whether the *Garcetti* decision might threaten the "protection of academic freedom in public colleges and universities whose teachers necessarily speak and write" as part of the performance of official duties (*Garcetti v. Ceballos*, 1969). Interestingly, Justice Kennedy declined to discuss the potential impact of the *Garcetti* decision on academic freedom in public schools, colleges, and universities:

> Justice Souter suggests today's decision may have some important ramifications for academic freedom, at least as a constitutional value ...

> . There is some argument that expression related to academic scholarship or classroom instruction implicates additional constitutional interests that are not fully accounted for by this Court's customary employee-speech jurisprudence. We need not, and for that reason do not, decide whether the analysis we conduct today would apply in the same manner to a case involving speech related to scholarship or teaching.
>
> (*Garcetti v. Ceballos*, 1969)

It remains to be seen whether public schools, colleges, and universities will attempt to make use of the *Garcetti* decision to regulate the job-related speech of K-12 public school teachers and faculty members at public universities and colleges.

Conclusion

In an amicus brief submitted in the *Garcetti* case, the International Municipal Lawyers Association warned that if the Supreme Court upheld the reasoning applied by the Ninth Circuit in the *Garcetti* case, public employers would face the prospect of more employee lawsuits, exposing "local governments to the expense, inconvenience, and workplace disruptions of frequent litigation" (LII 2005). On the other hand, amicus briefs filed by the National Treasury Employees Union, the National Association of Criminal Defense Lawyers, and the American Civil Liberties Union of Southern California stressed that if the Supreme Court adopted the per se exception to the *Pickering* balancing test advocated by the Los Angeles district attorney, such an action would deter many public employees from bringing instances of waste, fraud, and abuse in public programs to the attention of their superiors (LII 2005).

It is important to emphasize that the *Garcetti v. Ceballos* decision constitutes a relatively small adjustment to the *Pickering* public employee freedom of speech balancing test. Nonetheless, it has the potential to make it much easier for public employers to sanction public employees for the content of workplace-related communications. Depending on one's perspective, this is either a positive or negative development. Defenders of the freedom of speech rights of public employees argue that rational public servants will respond to the *Garcetti* decision by sharply curtailing their use of official channels to disclose instances of "wrongdoing and incompetence in government" (*Garcetti v. Ceballos*, 1967). From this perspective, the *Garcetti* decision simply reinforces the tendency of employees to go along to get ahead. Equally important, from this perspective, the *Garcetti* decision makes it more difficult for the public to obtain reliable information about what goes on within government agencies. As Justice O'Connor emphasized in her plurality opinion in *Waters v. Churchill*, "Government employees are often in the best position to know what ails the agencies for which they work" (*Waters v. Churchill*, 674).

On the other hand, defenders of the *Garcetti* decision argue that the benefits of the decision far outweigh any impact on the willingness of public employees to disclose wrongdoing and governmental inefficiency to their superiors. From this perspective, the *Garcetti* decision simply makes clear to public employees that they can no longer expect to turn professional disagreements into constitutional lawsuits. Equally important, from this perspective, the *Garcetti* decision makes it easier for public managers to discipline disruptive employees without fear of having to justify their actions before a federal judge. Consequently, the decision will only improve the efficiency and effectiveness of public agencies. As Justice Kennedy argued in his *Garcetti* opinion,

> Employers have heightened interests in controlling speech made by an employee in his or her professional capacity. Official communications have official consequences, creating a need for substantive consistency and clarity. Supervisors must ensure that their employees' official communications are accurate, demonstrate sound judgment, and promote the employee's mission.
>
> (*Garcetti v. Ceballos*, 1960)

Although both critics and supporters of the *Garcetti v. Ceballos* decision make good points, the fact remains that in the long run, the decision is likely to hamper the flow of important information from employees to their superiors. As the dissenters in *Garcetti* pointed out, the majority opinion did not explain how the *Pickering/Connick* two-part balancing test failed to adequately protect the discretion of public managers to discipline unduly disruptive public employees. As the *Pickering/Connick* two-part balancing test was not broken, no rational basis existed to carve out a new per se exception for public employee statements made pursuant to the exercise of their official duties.

References

Allred, Stephen. 1984. Note: *Connick v. Myers*: Narrowing the Freedom of Speech Rights of Public Employees. *Catholic University Law Review* 33: 429–456.

Dotson, Arch. 1955. The Emerging Doctrine of Privilege in Public Employment. *Public Administration Review* 15(2): 77–88.

Goshko, John M. 1976. Justice May Drop LEAA Regulation Hit as "Gag" Rule. *Washington Post*, January 8.

Greenhouse, Linda. 2006. Some Whistle-Blowers Lose Free-Speech Protections. *New York Times*, May 31.

Hayford, Stephen L. 1985. First Amendment Rights of Government Employees: A Primer for Public Officials. *Public Administration Review* 45(1): 241–248.

Hoppmann, Karin B. 1997. Note: Concern with Public Concern: Toward a Better Definition of the *Pickering/Connick* Threshold Test. *Vanderbilt Law Review* 57(4): 993–1028.

Jaegel, Don & N. Joseph Cayer. 1991. Public Personnel Administration by Lawsuit: The Impact of Supreme Court Decisions on Public Employee Litigiousness. *Public Administration Review* 51(3): 211–221.

Kandel, William L. 1994. *Waters v. Churchill*: Judicial Deference to the Reasonable Employer and Workplace Realties—Plus a Plea for ADR? *Employee Relations Law Journal* 20(2): 283–297.

Lane, Charles. 2006a. Alito May Tilt Vote in Reargued Cases. *Washington Post*, May 1.

Lane, Charles. 2006b. High Court's Free-Speech Ruling Favors Government: Public Workers Not Protected. *Washington Post*, May 31.

Lane, Charles. 2006c. Justices to Rehear Speech Case from October; High Court's Announcement Could Indicate that O'Connor Cast the Decisive Voce. *Washington Post*, February 15.

LII (Legal Information Institute). 2005. Supreme Court Oral Argument Previews: *Garcetti v. Ceballos* (Docket No. 04–473). www.law.cornell.edu/supcc/cen/04–473.html [accessed March 11, 2007].

Rosenbloom, David H. 1975. Public Personnel Administration and the Constitution: An Emergent Approach. *Public Administration Review* 35(1): 52–59.

Rutzick, Karen. 2006. High Court: On-the-Job Whistleblowing Not Free Speech. *GovExec.com*, Daily Briefing, May 30. www.governmencexecutive.com/dailyfed/0506/053006r1.htm [accessed March 9, 2007].

Schauer, Frederick. 1979. "Private Speech" and the "Private Forum": *Givhan v. Western Line School District. Supreme Court Review* 1979: 217–249.

Thompson, Dennis F. 1985. The Possibility of Administrative Ethics. *Public Administration Review* 45(1): 555–561.

The Supreme Court and the Continuing Deconstitutionalization of Public Personnel Management

Robert N. Roberts

From: *Review of Public Personnel Administration* 29 (March 2009): 3–19. Abridged.

In *Engquist v. Oregon Department of Agriculture* (2008b), by a six–three vote, the Roberts Court held that public employees may not use the so-called class-of-one equal protection clause doctrine to challenge the constitutionality of arguably arbitrary personnel actions.[1] The case involved a lawsuit brought by an Oregon state public employee who alleged that her agency laid her off as part of a reduction in force "for arbitrary, vindictive, and malicious reasons" (*Engquist v. Oregon Department of Agriculture*, 2008b, p. 2148). In other words, the employee alleged that her agency treated her differently from similarly situated employees.

The 2000 Supreme Court decision, in *Village of Willowbrook v. Olech*, opened the door for public employees to bring class-of-one equal protection claims against public employers. In a per curiam opinion, the high court stated the following:

> The Equal Protection Clause [gave] rise to a cause of action on behalf of a class of one where the plaintiff does not allege membership in a class or group, but alleges that she has been intentionally treated differently from others similarly situated and there is no rational basis for such treatment.
>
> (*Village of Willowbrook v. Olech*, 2000, p. 562)

By recognizing class-of-one equal protection claims, the Rehnquist Court clearly sought to address the perceived problem of citizens having limited remedies against local government officials who treated them differently from citizens with similar situations. Not unexpectedly, the *Village of Willowbrook* decision led to an explosion in class-of-one claims filed against local governments for arguably arbitrary decisions (Gehan, 2002). Yet, when the Rehnquist Court sanctioned the use of class-of-one equal protection claims against local governments, it probably did not anticipate that public employees would make use of the doctrine to challenge arguably arbitrary personnel actions by public employers. Yet, shortly after the issuance of the

Village of Willowbrook decision, public employees began to make use of class-of-one equal protection claims to challenge arguably arbitrary personnel decisions.

This article argues that the *Engquist v. Oregon Department of Agriculture* (2008b) majority took the action to prevent public employees from using class-of-one equal protection claims as part of an ongoing effort by the Roberts Court to deconstitutionalize public personnel administration. To accomplish this goal, the Roberts Court has relied on new per se rules that more narrowly define the constitutional rights of public employees instead of relying on an ad hoc approach for the resolution of disputes between public employees and public employers over the constitutional rights of public employees. Even though it is highly unlikely that a majority of the Roberts Court will strip public employees of a significant number of existing constitutional rights, it is likely that the Roberts Court will undertake an effort to narrow the constitutional rights of public employees and make much greater use of per se rules to limit the access of public employees to the federal courts to challenge arguably arbitrary personnel policies and practices. Finally, the article argues that, if this trend continues, public employees, much like their private sector counterparts, will become dependent on statutory law and collective bargaining agreements to protect themselves from discriminatory personnel policies and practices.

The Equal Protection Clause and the Public Workplace

The period from the mid-1970s through the 2000 *Village of Willowbrook* decision saw a sharp decline in the number of equal protection claims filed by public employees against their employers alleging discriminatory or arbitrary personnel policies and practices. This decline was the direct result of several significant trends in equal employment opportunity (EEO) law, constitutional tort litigation, and equal protection clause jurisprudence. First, the second half of the 1970s saw the Burger Court narrowly construe the scope of the equal protection clause with respect to judicial review of public personnel policies and practices. Second, with the extension of a number of major EEO laws to public employers, many public employees found it easier to pursue EEO complaints by pursuing private causes of action pursuant to the provisions of Title VII of the 1964 Civil Rights Act, the Age Discrimination in Employment Act (ADEA), the Americans with Disabilities Act (ADA), and the Civil Rights Act of 1991 (U.S. Equal Employment Opportunity Commission, 2008). Third, the late 1960s and 1970s saw the Warren and Burger Courts develop a body of law recognizing specific constitutional rights of public employees, including (a) freedom of speech, (b) freedom of association, (c) liberty, (d) procedural due process, and (e) privacy (Rosenbloom & Bailey, 2003).

Historically, federal courts required evidence of a significant impact of some type of governmental classification on a specific group of individuals.

Between 1950 and 1987, the Warren and Burger Courts developed a three-tiered structure for evaluating the constitutionality of governmental classifications (Rosenbloom, 2003). The court subjected race-based classifications to strict scrutiny. In *Brown v. Board of Education* (1954), the Warren Court held that race-based governmental classifications were inherently suspect and subject to "strict scrutiny" (Rosenbloom & Bailey, 2003, p. 38). Consequently, only race-based classifications that serve a compelling governmental interest may survive an equal protection challenge (Rosenbloom & Bailey, 2003). The court subjected gender-based classifications to intermediate scrutiny. The court subjected other types of classifications to rational basis analysis (Rosenbloom, 2003).

Not surprisingly, from the 1950s through the 1970s, the Warren and Burger Courts heard many equal protection challenges to classifications based on race, sex, wealth, citizenship, residency, and age. Yet, the mid-1970s saw the Burger Court make it much more difficult for public employees to make use of the equal protection clause to challenge public personnel policies and practices. In *Washington v. Davis* (1976), the Burger Court held that for a public personnel policy or practice to violate the equal protection clause, it "must manifest a discriminatory purpose of some kind" (Rosenbloom & Bailey, 2003, p. 38). The *Washington v. Davis* decision effectively ended the so-called "disparate impact" equal protection challenges to public personnel policies and practices (Rosenbloom, 1983, pp. 36–37). In other words, the decision blocked public employees from making use of the equal protection clause to challenge personnel policies or practices arguably neutral on their face but disproportionally affecting groups such as minorities or women. The decision, for instance, forced female applicants for law enforcement positions to rely on Title VII of the 1964 Civil Right Act to challenge minimum height requirements (*United States v. Buffalo*, 1978).

In a series of other cases from the mid-1970s through the death of Chief Justice William Rehnquist in 2005, the Burger and Rehnquist Courts rejected equal protection clause challenges to other public personnel policies and practices (Rosenbloom & Bailey, 2003). In *Massachusetts Board of Retirement v. Murgia* (1976), the Burger Court turned away a challenge to a state law that required state police officers to retire at the age of 50 even though some of the officers forced to retire were still "physically and mentally fit to continue their jobs" (Rosenbloom & Bailey, 2003, p. 39). Even though the *Murgia* majority had concerns about the fairness of the policy, the court found a rational relationship between the policy and maintaining physical preparedness of state police officers.

More recently, in *Central State University v. American Association of University Professors* (1999), the Rehnquist Court made clear it had no intention of significantly limiting the discretion of state legislatures to establish personnel policies for state employees. Responding to complaints that public university faculty spent too little time in the classroom, the Ohio legislature passed a state law that required state universities to develop instructional standards for college faculty. Of particular significance, the law exempted from collective bargaining the establishment of the new instructional workload standards. A union representing college faculty affected by the new workload standard brought suit, arguing the law "created a class of public employees not entitled to bargain regarding their workload and thus violated the equal protection clauses of the Ohio and Federal Constitutions" (*Central State University v. American Association of University Professors*, 1999, p. 124). In a per curiam opinion, the high court found the instructional workload law rationally related to the "goal to increase the time spent by faculty in classrooms" (*Central State University v. American Association of University Professors*, 1999, p. 124).

Class-of-One Equal Protection Claims and the Public Workplace: The Lower Federal Courts Respond

In 1992, the Export Service Center (ESC), a laboratory within the Oregon Department of Agriculture (ODA), hired Engquist as an international food specialist. Over time, stormy relationships developed between Engquist, her supervisor, and another ODA employee (*Engquist v. Oregon Department of Agriculture*, 2008b). In 2001, the ODA placed Engquist, her supervisor, and fellow employees under an assistant director of ODA. On January 31, 2001, the assistant director informed Engquist that her position was being eliminated as the result of the reorganization of her agency. Engquist then invoked a provision of her collective bargaining agreement that permitted her to "bump" to "another position at her level, or to take a demotion" (*Engquist v. Oregon Department of Agriculture*, 2008b, p. 2149). Engquist was laid off after her agency found her unqualified for another position at her level and she refused a demotion.

Although an Oregon United States District Court subsequently dismissed a number of Engquist's race, sex, and national origin employment discrimination complaints, the district court did allow Engquist's class-of-one equal protection claim to proceed against the assistant director who eliminated her position and a fellow employee under 42 U.S.C. 1983, which created "a private right of action against individuals who, acting under color of state law, violate federal constitutional or statutory rights" (*Engquist v. Oregon Department of Agriculture*, 2004, p. 18844). In finding that Engquist could proceed with a class-of-one claim, the district court relied on the *Village of Willowbrook v. Olech* (2000) decision. Specifically, the district court found the equal protection clause protects a class of one when a plaintiff can show that he or she has been intentionally treated differently from others similarly situated and there is no rational basis for the different treatment (*Engquist v. Oregon Department of Agriculture*, 2004, p. 18844).[2]

Interestingly, the *Village of Willowbrook v. Olech* (2000) decision had nothing to do with public personnel policies and practices. It involved a lawsuit brought by a landowner challenging a decision by a village to require the landowner to grant the village a 33-ft easement instead of the normal 15-ft easement as a condition of being permitted to hook up to the village water system. The *Willowbrook* decision authorized class-of-one equal protection claims where plaintiffs alleged government officials "intentionally treated differently from others similarly situated and there [was] no rational basis for the difference in treatment" (*Village of Willowbrook v. Olech*, 2000, p. 565). The Rehnquist Court clearly saw the *Willowbrook* decision as helping to deter governments, particularly local governments, from treating citizens in an arbitrary manner.

Relying on the *Village of Willowbrook v. Olech* (2000) decision, the district court ruled that Engquist could prevail on her class-of-one claim if the jury found that the defendants had singled her out as the result of personal animosity and that they engaged in "spiteful efforts to punish her for reasons unrelated to legitimate state objective" (*Engquist v. Oregon Department of Agriculture*, 2004, p. 18844). After receiving these jury instructions, the *Engquist* district court found the defendants "liable for violations of equal protection and substantive due process" (*Engquist v. Oregon Department of Agriculture*, 2007, p. 991). The jury awarded Engquist US$175,000 in compensatory damages and US$175,000 in punitive damages, as well as US $172,740 in attorney's fees (*Engquist v. Oregon Department of Agriculture*, 2007).

The United States Court of Appeals for the Ninth Circuit, on appeal, found little support for allowing public employees to pursue class-of-one equal protection claims against public employers. Instead, the ninth circuit found that the Burger, Rehnquist, and Roberts Courts had sought to limit public employee claims that their employers had violated their constitutional rights. After reviewing a number of other decisions by the Supreme Court from the 1970s through 2006 that limited the workplace constitutional rights of public employees (*Bishop v. Wood*, 1976; *Garcetti v. Ceballos*, 2006; *O'Connor v. Ortega*, 1987; *Waters v. Churchill*, 1994), the ninth circuit concluded that the class-of-one theory of equal protection is another constitutional area where the rights of public employees should not be as expansive as the rights of ordinary citizens (*Engquist v. Oregon Department of Agriculture*, 2007). "The paradigmatic class-of-one case," argued the ninth circuit, "should be one in which a public official, for some improper motive, comes down hard on a hapless private citizen" (*Engquist v. Oregon Department of Agriculture*, 2007, p. 995). The ninth circuit then argued that the application of the class-of-one theory to the public workplace presented a direct threat to the common law employment at-will doctrine:

> A judicially-imposed constitutional proscription of arbitrary public employer actions would also upset long-standing personnel practices. Although arbitrary government acts are unreasonable in the legislative or regulatory context, employers have traditionally possessed broad discretionary authority in the employment context. The power of

employers to discharge employees for reasons that may appear arbitrary, unless constrained by contract or statute, is well established under the common law at-will employment.

(*Engquist v. Oregon Department of Agriculture*, 2007, p. 995)

Equally important, the ninth circuit feared that applying the class-of-one theory to public employment might "generate a flood of new cases, requiring federal courts to decide whether any public employee was fired for an arbitrary reason or a rational one" (*Engquist v. Oregon Department of Agriculture*, 2007, p. 995). Therefore, the ninth circuit reversed the jury's verdict and monetary judgment in favor of Engquist and held that public employees may not file class-of-one equal protection lawsuits against their employers. On January 11, 2008, the Supreme Court granted certiorari to consider whether the ninth circuit correctly dismissed Engquist's class-of-one equal protection claim (*Engquist v. Oregon Department of Agriculture*, 2008a).

The Supreme Court and the Oversight of the Constitutional Rights of Public Employees

During the first half of the 20th century, federal and state courts embraced the reasoning of Justice Oliver Wendell Holmes, in the 1892 *McAuliffe v. Mayor of New Bedford* decision, where the Massachusetts Supreme Judicial Court upheld the authority of a local government to dismiss a police officer "violating a regulation which restricted his political activities" (Van Alstyne, 1968, p. 1439). With typical bluntness, Justice Holmes explained that "the petitioner may have a constitutional right to talk politics, but he has no constitutional right to be a policeman" (Van Alstyne, 1968, p. 1439). The public employment "privilege doctrine" gave public employers almost absolute authority to regulate the exercise of basic constitutional rights by public employees ("Developments," 1984, pp. 1742–1744; Dotson, 1955, p. 77; Rosenbloom, 1981, p. 3).

Beginning in the early 1960s, the Warren Court (1954–1969) began the process of modifying the "privilege" doctrine by prohibiting public employers from arbitrarily denying public employees the opportunity to exercise established constitutional rights without fear of retaliation (Rosenbloom, 1975, p. 52). In *Pickering v. Board of Education* (1968), for instance, the Warren Court held that, as a general rule, public employees have a First Amendment right to speak out on matters of public concern (Rosenbloom, 1983). Somewhat surprisingly, the Burger Court (1969–1986) continued the trend of prohibiting public employers from arbitrarily restricting the exercise of constitutional rights by public employees (Rosenbloom, 1988). Through the mid-1980s, the Burger Court carefully balanced the interests of public employers to maintain an efficient workforce with the interests of public employees to be free to exercise basic constitutional rights without fear of retaliation by their employers. Although the Burger Court found in favor of public employers as often as it found against public employers (Rosenbloom, 1978), the ad hoc approach relied on by the Burger Court forced the federal courts to assume an unprecedented role in the oversight of the personnel policies and practices of public employees.

From the early 1970s through the end of the Rehnquist Court in 2005, the vast majority of so-called constitutional tort lawsuits filed by public employees have involved a relatively small number of constitutional issues. The *Pickering v. Board of Education* (1968) and *Givhan v. Western Line Consolidated School District* (1979) decisions led to an explosion in lawsuits alleging violations of the freedom of speech right for public employees (Hayford, 1985; Wells, 2001). The *Elfbrandt v. Russell* (1966), *Elrod v. Burns* (1976), and *Branti v. Finkel* (1980) decisions opened the door for public employees to seek judicial protection for their freedom of association rights (Roback & Vinzant, 1994; Rosenbloom, 1983). The Burger Court decision in *Board of Regents v. Roth* (1972) held that certain public employees had a Fifth and Fourteenth Amendment property interest in their public jobs and provided public employees the opportunity to seek judicial review of whether their employers violated their right to procedural due process (Cooper, 1982; Goldman, 1981). Finally, in *O'Connor v. Ortega* (1987), the Supreme Court recognized that public employees do have a Fourth Amendment expectation of privacy in their public offices but allowed public employers to conduct warrantless searches of public offices as part of investigations of organizational misconduct (*O'Connor v. Ortega*, 1987).

From the late 1960s through the mid-1980s, the Warren and Burger Courts put in place a minimum floor of constitutional rights for public employees. Yet, both the Warren and Burger Courts took great care to balance the interests of public employers in maintaining an efficient workforce with the need to permit public employees to exercise basic constitutional rights. No case better demonstrates the difficulty the court faced in balancing these competing interests than its 1976 *Bishop v. Wood* decision. Although the court held in *Board of Regents v. Roth* (1972) that public employees with more than an expectation of continued employment had a Fifth and Fourteenth Amendment property interest in their public jobs, the *Bishop* majority found that even though a municipal ordinance defined a police officer as a "permanent employee," the police officer did not have a constitutionally protected property interest in his position (Rosenbloom, 1983, p. 38). Speaking for the *Bishop* majority, Justice Stevens argued:

> The federal court is not the appropriate forum in which to review the multitude of personnel decisions that are made daily by public agencies. We must accept the ... harsh fact that numerous individual mistakes are inevitable in the day-to-day administration of our affairs. The United States Constitution cannot feasibly be construed to require federal judicial review for every such error. In the absence of any claim

> that the public employer was motivated by a desire to curtail or to penalize the exercise of an employee's constitutionally protected rights, we must presume that official action was regular and, if erroneous, can best be corrected in other ways. The Due Process Clause of the Fourteenth Amendment is not a guarantee against incorrect or ill-advised personnel decisions.
>
> (*Bishop v. Wood*, 1976, p. 347)

Not surprisingly, the *Bishop v. Wood* (1976) decision led scholars to question the commitment of the Burger Court to maintaining a minimum floor of constitutional rights for public employees. In a 1983 article, commenting on the *Bishop v. Wood* decision, Rosenbloom concluded that "a majority of the Court seemed determined to limit the constitutional requirement of due process even further" (Rosenbloom, 1983, p. 38).

Yet, by the mid-1980s, it became quite clear that the majority of the Burger Court had no intention of restoring the public employee privilege doctrine. In *Branti v. Finkel* (1980), a majority of the court made it even more difficult for public employers to justify patronage appointments by requiring public hiring authorities to "demonstrate that party affiliation is an appropriate requirement for the effective performance of the public office involved" (*Branti v. Finkel*, 1980, p. 518; Rosenbloom & Bailey, 2003, p. 23). In *Rankin v. McPherson* (1987), a majority of the Rehnquist Court held that a local government had violated the freedom of speech rights of an employee for firing her for commenting to a fellow employee after the 1981 assassination attempt against President Ronald Reagan, "Shoot, if they go for him again, I hope they get him" (*Rankin v. McPherson*, 1987, p. 322; Rosenbloom & Bailey, 2003, p. 31). And in *Cleveland Board of Education v. Loudermill* (1985), a majority of the Burger Court held that public employers must provide public employees with more than an expectation of continued employment for some type of pretermination opportunity to be heard (Rosenbloom & Bailey, 2003). Moreover, equally significant, a majority of the Rehnquist Court refused to abandon the ad hoc approach to resolving constitutional rights disputes involving public employees. In *O'Connor v. Ortega* (1987), a majority of the court held that "individuals do not lose Fourth Amendment Rights merely because they work for the government instead of a private employer" (*O'Connor v. Ortega*, 1987, p. 723; Rosenbloom & Bailey, 2003, p. 35). In *National Treasury Employees Union v. Von Raab* (1989), a majority of the Rehnquist Court upheld the constitutionality of random drug testing for government employees "who carry firearms and/or are engaged in drug interdiction" but did not authorize random drug testing for all government employees (Rosenbloom & Bailey, 2003, p. 36). In *Rutan v. Republican Party of Illinois* (1990), a majority of the court extended the patronage removal prohibitions of *Elrod v. Burns* (1976) and *Branti v. Finkel* (1980) to the hiring and promotion of most public employees (Roback & Vinzant, 1994; Rosenbloom & Bailey, 2003).

In *United States v. National Treasury Employees Union* (1995), a majority of the court found that the First Amendment prohibited Congress from stopping all executive branch employees from accepting honoraria for giving speeches or writing articles or books.

A number of factors help to explain why a majority of the Burger and Rehnquist Courts resisted calls to abandon its ad hoc approach to the resolution of constitutional tort lawsuits brought by public employees. First, reliance on an ad hoc approach helped to protect the court from being criticized for engaging in judicial lawmaking. Incremental adjustments to established constitutional doctrines typically did not touch off intense criticism from either public employees or public employers because the narrowly drafted decisions only affected a relatively small number of public employees or public employers. Second, the uncertainty created by an ad hoc approach placed considerable pressure on public employees and public employers to not take extreme positions regarding their respective interpretations of the scope of the constitutional rights of public employees. In other words, reliance on an ad hoc approach created a strong incentive for both public employees and public employers to attempt to resolve conflicts without resorting to litigation. Remarkably, from the late 1960s through the end of the Rehnquist Court in 2005, a majority of the high court maintained their support for a minimum level of constitutional protections for public employees. More important, a majority of the Burger and Rehnquist Courts sought to become embroiled in ideological disputes over the merits of merit systems v. at-will employment systems.

The Roberts Court and the Deconstitutionalization of Public Personnel Management

One may legitimately view the *Engquist v. Oregon Department of Agriculture* (2008b) decision as consistent with the efforts of the Burger and Rehnquist Courts to carefully balance the interests of public employees and public employers. On the other hand, one may make a more pervasive argument that *Engquist* represents an effort by the majority of the Roberts Court to take much more aggressive steps to protect public employers from court-imposed mandates limiting their discretion over personnel policies and practices. The Roberts Court took the appeal and subsequently established a new per se rule rejecting the application of the class-of-one equal protection doctrine to the public employment relationship. Speaking for the *Engquist* majority, Roberts defended the public employment privilege doctrine given up as dead close to 50 years ago:

> We long ago recognized the "settled principle that ... government employment, in the absence of legislation, can be revoked at the will of the appointing officer." [*Cafeteria Workers v. McElroy*, 367 U.S. at 896] The basic principle of at-will employment is that an employee may be

> terminated for a "good reason, bad reason, or no reason at all." Reply Brief for Petitioner 27 … . ("[T]he very concept of 'wrongful discharge' implies some sort of statutory or contractual standard that modifies the traditional common-law rule that a contract of employment is terminable by either party at will").
>
> (*Engquist v. Oregon Department of Agriculture*, 2008b, p. 2155)

In making the statement, Roberts sought to make clear that the federal courts should, if possible, respect the employment at-will doctrine by limiting the use of the Constitution to restrict the discretion of public employers regarding personnel policies and practices. Although Roberts did not specifically call for the return to the public employment privilege doctrine, Roberts argued that the federal courts should exercise much greater restraint in imposing constitutional mandates on public employers. "Our precedent in the public-employee context therefore establishes two main principles," stated Roberts. "First, although government employees do not lose their constitutional rights when they accept their positions, those rights must be balanced against the realities of the employment context," continued Roberts (*Engquist v. Oregon Department of Agriculture*, 2008b, p. 2152). Second, argued Roberts, "In striking the appropriate balance, we consider whether the asserted employee right implicates the basic concerns of the relevant constitutional provisions, or whether the claimed right can more readily give way to the requirements of the government employer" (*Engquist v. Oregon Department of Agriculture*, 2008b, p. 2152). Interestingly, nothing in the *Engquist* majority opinion indicated any hostility toward legislative modification of the employment at-will doctrine through the enactment of EEO laws or reluctance to protect public or private employees' right to engage in collective bargaining. Although Roberts does not call for the abandonment of the ad hoc approach relied on by the Burger and Rehnquist Courts in resolving disputes regarding the constitutional rights of public employees, he does call for much greater judicial deference to the need for public employers to establish their personnel policies and practices without undue judicial interference.

Chief Justice Roberts largely misstated more than three decades of public employee constitutional rights jurisprudence. From the early 1970s through the end of the Rehnquist Court in 2005, centrists on the Burger and Rehnquist Courts (Stewart, White, Blackmun, Powell, O'Connor & Souter) strongly opposed the use of per se rules to limit the constitutional rights of public employers in an effort to improve the efficiency of public agencies (O'Brien, 1987). Instead, these centrists wanted federal courts to serve as honest brokers between public employees and public employers with respect to defining the constitutional rights of public employees. The public service model required that the court balance the constitutional rights of public employees with the "government's interest as an employer in having an efficient workforce" (Rosenbloom & Bailey, 2003, p. 30):

> It is important to note that the public service model is not weighed either in favor of or against broad constitutional rights for public employees. The courts may side with either the government or the individual. Everything depends on how judges apply the model in varying contexts and circumstances. As Chief Justice William Rehnquist once noted, such jurisprudence places a heavy emphasis on "ad hoc weighing which depends to a great extent on how the Court subjectively views the underlying interests at stake" (*Cleveland Board of Education v. Loudermill*, 1985: 562). This quality of the public service model can be frustrating because it makes it difficult to apply general constitutional principles to specific personnel decisions. However, it is all the [more] reason why public personnelists should carefully follow the case law.
>
> (Rosenbloom & Bailey, 2003, p. 31)

In other words, the public service model did not permit the court to give preference to the interests of either public employees or public employers in resolving disputes over the constitutional right of public employees. The majority opinion of Justice O'Connor, in the 1987 *O'Connor v. Ortega* case, provides one of the better examples of the application of the public service model to a public employee constitutional rights dispute. The case dealt with whether the Fourth Amendment required that public employers first obtain a search warrant before conducting an administrative search of an office of one of its employees for evidence of possible violations of administrative standard of conduct regulations. O'Connor stressed:

> The legitimate privacy interests of public employees in the private objects they bring to the workplace may be substantial. Against these privacy interests, however, must be balanced the realities of the workplace, which strongly suggest that a warrant requirement would be unworkable.
>
> (*O'Connor v. Ortega*, 1987, p. 721)

In fact, the approach adopted by the *Engquist v. Oregon Department of Agriculture* (2008b) majority had few similarities to the public service model. Instead, it was remarkably similar to the approach adopted by the majority of the Roberts Court in the 2006 *Garcetti v. Ceballos* decision. Prior to *Garcetti v. Ceballos*, the high court had required federal courts to apply the so-called Pickering/Connick two-part test to determine whether a public employer unlawfully interfered with the exercise of the freedom of speech rights of one of its employees. The first part of the test required that the trial court determine whether the public employee had spoken out on a matter of public concern. If the speech did not involve a matter of public concern, it was not constitutionally protected (Lee, 1988). On the other hand, if the trial court found the subject matter of the speech or communication did involve a matter of public concern, the second part of the test required the trial court "to balance the public employee's interest in free expression against the interests of the government employer in managing the workplace" (Lee, 1988, p. 1110). As a federal district court judge explained in a 2006 decision, "Even if speech relates to a matter of public concern, it is not constitutionally protected unless the speaker's First Amendment interest outweighs the public employer's interests in providing services efficiently" (*Kodrea v. City of Kokomo*, 2006, p. 870). Instead of leaving intact the Pickering/Connick two-part test, the *Ceballos* majority established a new per se rule that exempted from First Amendment protection communications made by public employees in the course of the performance of their official duties (Drachsler, 2008; Nasuti, 2008). In adopting the new rule, a majority of the Roberts Court sought to reduce the "displacement of managerial discretion by judicial supervision" (*Garcetti v. Ceballos*, 2006, p. 1951). According to at least one commentator, "After *Garcetti*, public employees who would unquestionably have been protected under *Pickering* and *Connick* now enjoy no protection because of the Supreme Court's unnecessarily cramped view of the First Amendment" (Drachsler, 2008, p. 203).

In both the *Garcetti v. Ceballos* (2006) and *Engquist v. Oregon Department of Agriculture* (2008b) decisions, the majority of the Roberts Court demonstrated a clear preoccupation with the alleged impact of constitutional tort lawsuits filed by public employees on the efficiency of public agencies. Roberts emphasized the purpose of the new rule in *Engquist* as follows:

> The practical problem with allowing "class of one" claims to go forward in this context is not that it will be too easy for plaintiffs to prevail, but that governments will be forced to defend a multitude of such claims in the first place, and courts will be obliged to sort through them in a search for the proverbial needle in a haystack.
>
> (*Engquist v. Oregon Department of Agriculture*, 2008b, p. 2157)

Not surprisingly, Justice Stevens, speaking for the *Engquist v. Oregon Department of Agriculture* (2008b) dissenters, sharply criticized the majority for abandoning the ad hoc model for resolving class-of-one equal protection claims brought by public employees. "Today, the Court creates a new substantive rule excepting state employees from the Fourteenth Amendment's protection against unequal and irrational treatment at the hands of the State," explained Stevens. "Even if some surgery were truly necessary to prevent governments from being forced to defend a multitude of equal protection 'class of one' claims," stressed Stevens, "the Court should use a scalpel rather than a meat-axe" (*Engquist v. Oregon Department of Agriculture*, 2008b, p. 2158). Furthermore, argued Stevens, "preserving the remnants of at-will employment provides a feeble justification for creating a broad exception to a well-established category of constitutional protections" (*Engquist v. Oregon Department of Agriculture*, 2008b, p. 2160). Much like Justice Souter's dissent in *Garcetti* (*Garcetti v. Ceballos*, 2006), Justice Stevens argued that the remedy to the perceived danger of class-of-one equal protection claims brought by public employees far exceeded the threat to the efficient operation of public employers.

Even though the *Engquist v. Oregon Department of Agriculture* (2008b) decision will have little or no impact on constitutional tort litigation by public employees, it is significant because it demonstrates the breakdown of the public service model, which succeeded in generally preventing the Burger and Rehnquist Courts from dividing into pro- and antipublic employee rights camps. With the breakdown of the public service model in the *Garcetti v. Ceballos* (2006) and *Engquist* decisions, both Chief Justice Roberts and Justice Stevens reverted back to largely ideological arguments in their respective *Engquist* opinions. On the one hand, Chief Justice Roberts justified stripping public employees of the right to pursue class-of-one equal protection claims on the grounds they could lead to an explosion in new federal lawsuits in federal courts. Roberts failed to mention that the vast majority of class-of-one lawsuits brought prior to the *Engquist* decision involved suits alleging violations of multiple statutes or constitutional rights and not single class-of-one equal protection claims. And Roberts also failed to mention that many courts of appeal easily upheld decisions of federal district courts, making use of summary judgment motions to dismiss class-of-one equal protection claims.[3] Instead of providing an accurate description of the potential impact of class-of-one public employee claims, Roberts decided to greatly exaggerate the potential impact:

> If, as *Engquist* suggests, plaintiffs need not claim discrimination on the basis of membership in some class or group, but rather may argue only that they were treated by their employers worse than other employees similarly situated, any personnel action in which a wronged employee can conjure up a claim of differential treatment will suddenly become the basis for a constitutional claim. Indeed, all allegations of arbitrary differential treatment could be made in nearly every instance of an assertedly wrongful employment action—not only hiring decisions, but any personnel action, such as promotion, salary, or work assignments—on the theory that other employees were treated wrongfully.
>
> (*Engquist v. Oregon Department of Agriculture*, 2008b, p. 2156)

On the other hand, Justice Stevens also attempted to paint a worst-case scenario brought about by stripping public employees of their right to bring class-of-one equal protection clause actions against public employers and the potential burden on public employers of having to defend against this type of employment-related lawsuits in addition to EEO-related complaints. Stevens refused to acknowledge that allowing class-of-one equal protection claims by public employees significantly expanded the role of the federal courts in the oversight of public personnel policies and practices, particularly those involving at-will public employees. Even though prior to the *Engquist v. Oregon Department of Agriculture* (2008b) decision the vast majority of federal district courts dismissed class-of-one equal protection claims brought by public employees in response to summary judgment motions brought by public employers, the fact remained that public employers did have to present some reason for the action challenged by their employees. One may argue that public employers should be required to provide a rational reason for firing any employee, but Stevens attempted to downplay the significance of requiring public employers to provide a rational justification for the removal of at-will employees by arguing that only in the most exceptional circumstances would federal courts intervene. Quoting from Stevens' dissent:

> Experience demonstrates, however, that these claims ... are brought infrequently, that the vast majority of such claims are asserted in complaints advancing other claims as well, and that all but a handful are dismissed well in advance of trial. Experience also demonstrates that there are in fact rare cases in which a petty tyrant has misused governmental power. Proof that such misuse was arbitrary because unsupported by any conceivable rational basis should suffice to establish a violation of the Equal Protection without requiring its victim also to prove that the tyrant was motivated by a particular variety of class-based animus.
>
> (*Engquist v. Oregon Department of Agriculture*, 2008b, pp. 2160–2161)

Simply, to provide the best argument for their relative positions, Roberts overestimated the impact of allowing public employees to pursue case of one equal protection claims, and Stevens underestimated the potential impact on public employers of having to document adverse personnel action, including personnel actions involving at-will employees.

Conclusion

It is difficult to evaluate the long-term impact of the ongoing deconstitutionalization of public personnel management pursued by a majority of the Roberts Court. Because the majority of the Roberts Court has shown much less hostility to the enforcement of EEO laws, the impact of reduced constitutional protections for public employees may be somewhat mitigated. The Roberts Court did receive considerable criticism for its 2007 decision in *Ledbetter v. Goodyear Tire & Rubber Co.* (2007), which held that employees must file Title VII complaints with the Equal Employment Opportunity Commission (EEOC) "within 180 days" of when the discriminatory conduct occurred (Riccucci, 2008, pp. 91–96). On the other hand, in several 2007–2008

EEO decisions, a majority of the Roberts Court broadly construed the scope of EEO laws. In *Federal Express v. Holowecki* (2008), the Roberts Court agreed with the EEOC that under certain circumstances individuals should be allowed to proceed with their discrimination complaints, even if they incorrectly assumed filing an intake questionnaire satisfied Title VII's requirement that a formal complaint must be filed within 180 days of the discriminatory conduct. In *CBOCS W. Inc. v. Humphries* (2008), the Roberts Court held that Congress intended to permit individuals to file job-related retaliation provisions in relation to alleged violation of Section 42 U.S.C. 1983—a civil rights law enacted by Congress long before Congress passed the Title VII of the 1964 Civil Rights Act. Finally, in *Gomez-Perez v. Potter* (2008), the Roberts Court found that Congress had intended to permit federal employees to file retaliation claims under the provisions of the federal-sector provisions of the ADEA of 1967. Historically, the Supreme Court has had little impact on the scope of public sector collective bargaining statutes (American Federation of State, County and Municipal Employees, 2008). In contrast to the 7.5% of private sector employees who belong to unions, by 2007, public sector union membership had climbed to 35.9% for government workers (U.S. Department of Labor Bureau of Labor Statistics, 2008). Yet, there is a tremendous variation between the collective bargaining rights of public employees from state to state. Consequently, in contrast to the constitutional rights of public employees and EEO laws, there is a significant variation in the collective bargaining rights of public employees.

Many public employers will welcome the deconstitutionalization of public personnel management. It is understandable that many public employers had serious problems with the public service model as applied by the majority of the Burger and Rehnquist Courts because it required the court to give equal weight to the interests of public employers in maintaining an efficient workplace and to the interests of public employees in being permitted to exercise basic constitutional rights in the public workplace. In the *Garcetti v. Ceballos* (2006) and *Engquist v. Oregon Department of Agriculture* (2008b) decisions, a majority of the Roberts Court is sending a clear message that it intends to give much greater deference to personnel policies and practices of public organizations. In 1978, Rosenbloom saw the 1976 *Bishop v. Wood* decision as persuasive evidence that the Burger Court had embarked on the deconstitutionalization of the public workplace. Thirty years later, it appears that Chief Justice Roberts has the votes to attempt to level the playing field between public and private employers by limiting the constitutional rights of public employees.

Notes

1 Chief Justice Roberts and Justices Kennedy, Thomas, Scalia, Alito, and Breyer made up the majority, and Justices Stevens, Souter, and Ginsberg dissented.

2 The only citation available for this district court case is the one provided by LexisNexis Academic.

3 For instance, in the following cases, courts of appeals upheld the dismissal of class-of-one claims by federal district courts: *Bartell v. Aurora Public Schools* (2001), *Campagna v. Massachusetts Department of Environmental Protection* (2003), *Eggleston v. Bieluch* (2006), *Hill v. Borough of Kutztown* (2006), *Jackson v. Norman* (2008), *Lauth v. McCollum* (2005), *Marwood v. Elizabeth Forward School Dist.* (2004), *Matsey v. Westmoreland County* (2006), *Mosca v. Cole* (2007), *Sellers v. City of Gary* (2006), *Stotter v. University of Texas* (2007), *Teigen v. Renfrow* (2007), *Vigil v. S. Valley Acad.* (2007), *Whiting v. University of Southern Mississippi* (2006), and *Williams v. Riley* (2008).

References

American Federation of State, County and Municipal Employees. 2008. *Public sector collective bargaining laws*. http://www.afscme.org/members/11075.cfm (accessed August 30, 2008)

Bartell v. Aurora Public Schools, 263 F.3d 1143 (2001).

Bishop v. Wood, 426 U.S. 341 (1976).

Board of Regents v. Roth, 408 U.S. 564 (1972).

Branti v. Finkel, 445 U.S. 507 (1980).

Brown v. Board of Education, 347 U.S. 483 (1954).

Campagna v. Massachusetts Department of Environmental Protection, 334 F.3d 150 (1st Cir. 2003).

CBOCS W. Inc. v. Humphries, 2008 LEXIS 4516 (2008).

Central State University v. American Association of University Professors, 526 U.S. 124 (1999).

Cleveland Board of Education v. Loudermill, 470 U.S. 532 (1985).

Cooper, P.J. (1982). Due process, the Burger court, and public administration. *Southern Review of Public Administration* 6: 43–65.

Developments in the law: Public employment. (1984). *Harvard Law Review* 97: 1611–1800.

Dotson, A. (1955). The emerging doctrine of privilege in public employment. *Public Administration Review* 15: 77–88.

Drachsler, D.A. (2008). Public employee whistleblowers after Garcetti v. Ceballos. *Labor Law Journal* 59: 201–208.

Eggleston v. Bieluch, 203 Fed. Appx. 257 (11th Cir. 2006).

Elfbrandt v. Russell, 384 U.S. 1 (1966).

Elrod v. Burns, 427 U.S. 347 (1976).

Engquist v. Oregon Department of Agriculture, 2004 U.S. Dist. LEXIS 18844 (D. Or. Sept 14, 2004).

Engquist v. Oregon Department of Agriculture, 478 F.3d 985 (2007).

Engquist v. Oregon Department of Agriculture, 128 S. Ct. 977 (2008a).

Engquist v. Oregon Department of Agriculture, 128 S. Ct. 2146 (2008b).

Federal Express v. Holowecki, 128 S. Ct. 1147 (2008).

Garcetti v. Ceballos, 126 S. Ct. 1951 (2006).

Gehan, S.M. (2002). With malice toward one: Malice and substantive law in "class of one" equal protection claims in wake of Village of Willowbrook v. Olech. *Maine Law Review* 54: 329–386.

Givhan v. Western Line Consolidated School District, 439 U.S. 410 (1979).
Goldman, D.D. (1981). Due process and public personnel management. *Review of Public Personnel Administration* 2: 19–28.
Gomez-Perez v. Potter, 128 S. Ct. 1931 (2008).
Hayford, S.L. (1985). First amendment rights of government employees: A primer for public officials. *Public Administration Review* 45: 241–248.
Hill v. Borough of Kutztown, 455 F.3d 225 (3rd Cir. 2006).
Jackson v. Norman, 264 Fed. Appx. 17 (1st Cir. 2008).
Kodrea v. City of Kokomo, 458 F. Supp. 2d 857 (2006).
Lauth v. McCollum, 434 F.3d 631 (7th Cir. 2005).
Ledbetter v. Goodyear Tire & Rubber Co., 550 U.S. 618; 127 S. Ct. 2162 (2007).
Lee, C.K.Y. (1988). Freedom of speech in the public workplace: A comment on the public concern requirement. *California Law Review* 76: 1109–1146.
Marwood v. Elizabeth Forward School Dist., 91 Fed. Appx. 207 (3rd Cir. 2004).
Massachusetts Board of Retirement v. Murgia, 427 U.S. 304 (1976).
Matsey v. Westmoreland County, 185 Fed. Appx. 126 (3rd Cir. 2006).
McAuliffe v. Mayor of New Bedford, 155 Mass. 216, 29 N.E. 517 (1892).
Mosca v. Cole, 217 Fed. Appx. 158 (3rd Cir. 2007).
Nasuti, J.L.Y. (2008). Garcetti et al. v. Ceballos—A reworking of first amendment free speech rights for public employees. *North East Journal of Legal Studies* 20: 55–82.
National Treasury Employees Union v. Von Raab, 489 U.S. 656 (1989).
O'Brien, D.M. (1987). The Supreme Court from Warren to Burger to Rehnquist. *PS: Political Science and Politics* 20: 12–20.
O'Connor v. Ortega, 480 U.S. 709 (1987).
Pickering v. Board of Education, 391 U.S. 563 (1968).
Rankin v. McPherson, 483 U.S. 378 (1987).
Riccucci, N.M. (2008). A major setback for pay equity: The Supreme Court's decision in Ledbetter v. Goodyear Tire & Rubber Company. *Review of Public Personnel Administration* 28: 91–96.
Roback, T.H. & Vinzant, J.C. (1994). The constitution and the patronage–merit debate: Implications for personnel management. *Public Personnel Management* 23: 501–514.
Rosenbloom, D.H. (1975). Public personnel administration and the constitution: An emergent approach. *Public Administration Review* 35: 52–59.
Rosenbloom, D.H. (1978). The Burger court and the public employee. *Southern Review of Public Administration* 2: 239–244.
Rosenbloom, D.H. (1981). The sources of continuing conflict between the constitution and public personnel management. *Review of Public Personnel Administration* 2: 3–19.
Rosenbloom, D.H. (1983). What every public personnel manager should know about the constitution. In S. Hays & R.C. Kearney (eds), *Public personnel administration: Problems and prospects*. Upper Saddle River, NJ: Prentice Hall, pp. 27–42.
Rosenbloom, D.H. (1988). The public employment relationship and the Supreme Court. *Review of Public Personnel Administration* 8: 49–56.
Rosenbloom, D.H. (2003). *Administrative law for public managers*. Boulder, CO: Westview.
Rosenbloom, D.H. & Bailey, M. (2003). What every public personnel manager should know about the constitution. In S. Hays & R.C. Kearney (eds), *Public*

personnel administration: Problems and prospects, 4th edn. Upper Saddle River, NJ: Prentice Hall, pp. 29–45.

Rutan v. Republican Party of Illinois, 497 U.S. 62 (1990).

Sellers v. City of Gary, 453 F.3d 848 (7th Cir. 2006).

Stotter v. University of Texas, 508 F.3d 812 (5th Cir. 2007).

Teigen v. Renfrow, 511 F.3d 1072 (10th Cir. 2007).

United States v. Buffalo, 457 F. Supp. 612 (1978).

United States v. National Treasury Employees Union, 513 U.S. 454 (1995).

U.S. Department of Labor Bureau of Labor Statistics. (2008). *Union membership summary. Union members in 2007*. Retrieved June 14, 2008, from http://www.bls.gov/news.release/union2.nr0.htm

U.S. Equal Employment Opportunity Commission. (2008). *Federal equal employment opportunity (EEO) laws*. Retrieved June 14, 2008, from http://www.eeoc.gov/abouteeo/overview_laws.html

Van Alstyne, W.W. (1968). The demise of the right-privilege distinction in constitutional law. *Harvard Law Review* 81: 1439–1464.

Vigil v. S. Valley Acad., 247 Fed. Appex. 982 (3rd Cir. 2007).

Village of Willowbrook v. Olech, 528 U.S. 562 (2000).

Washington v. Davis, 426 U.S. 229 (1976).

Waters v. Churchill, 511 U.S. 661 (1994).

Wells, M.L. (2001). Section 1983, the first amendment, and public employee speech: Shaping the right to fit the remedy (and vice versa). *Georgia Law Review* 35: 939–1017.

Whiting v. University of Southern Mississippi, 451 F.3d 339 (5th Cir. 2006).

Williams v. Riley, 2008 U.S. App. LEXIS 8990 (5th Cir. 2008).

Part V

Conclusion

14 Connecting U.S. Public Administration to all its Parts

The Maintenance and Preservation of the Constitutional School

Stephanie P. Newbold and David H. Rosenbloom

The establishment of the Constitutional School of U.S. Public Administration is one of the most enduring efforts to shape the priorities and responsibilities of running the Constitution in the 21st century. The selections in this book demonstrate empirically how public administration scholars can ground their multi-faceted research in democratic-constitutionalism and the rule of law, both of which advance American constitutional tradition. When *Public Administration Review* published Stephanie Newbold's 2010 article on the Constitutional School, the editors classified it as a "big idea" in public administration theory. The purpose of this edited volume is to make the Constitutional School's presence within the field's literature even more prominent, vibrant, and useful to scholars and practitioners alike.

With this objective in mind, there is a need to be bold. We have discussed in previous work our growing concerns over the direction the field of U.S. public administration has taken, intellectually and pedagogically (Newbold, 2011, 2014; Newbold & Rosenbloom, 2014). Ever since Herbert Simon published *Administrative Behavior* in 1946, the public administration community has been on a quest to make its research and knowledge base more scientific. That effort has led to an overwhelming emphasis on the application of statistical models and quantitative techniques to answer some of the most central questions affecting public administrative management. Without question quantitative and qualitative methodologies play important roles in public administration scholarship and pedagogy. Equally unquestionably if a comprehensive science of public administration develops, future scholars and practitioners will look back on contemporary research as but a step—perhaps only a very preliminary one—in its evolution. In the spirit of incorporating scientific methods into the field, we have inadvertently undermined the importance of more traditional epistemological and methodological approaches to answering and addressing major issues affecting the administrative state. In Simon's (1991) autobiography even he observed that the pendulum had swung too far in favor of using scientific approaches and quantitative techniques to solve political problems (pp. 56, 285). In contributing to the further development and advancement of the Constitutional School, we seek to provide greater intellectual balance in the field's epistemology, body of knowledge, and literature. We seek to create a space where big theoretical ideas regarding the political and administrative organization, design, and behavior of polities have a place to call home and where normative questions concerning law, constitutional thought, ethics, and democratic-constitutionalism are supported and encouraged.

Reflecting on the great intellectual history of U.S. public administration is both rewarding and disheartening. It is rewarding because it allows for serious, thoughtful reflection into some of the most engaging ideas of the modern era. These include questions about *the purpose of government* (Appleby, 1945; Brownlow, Gulick & Merriam, 1937; Gaus, 1950; Gulick & Urwick, 1937; Mosher, 1968; Pfiffner & Presthus, 1935; Waldo, 1948; Wilson, 1908); *the importance of politics to administration* (Gaus, 1950; Goodnow, 1900; Kaufman, 1969; Storing, 1962; Waldo, 1948); *the value public institutions bring to the citizens they serve* (Selznick, 1957; Waldo, 1948); *the contemporary relevance of political and administrative history to democratic governance and public management* (Mosher, 1976; Storing 1970, 1981a, 1981b; White, 1948, 1951, 1954, 1958); *democracy* (Appleby, 1945; Mosher, 1968; Strauss & Cropsey, 1963; Waldo, 1948); *law and the federal courts* (Hart & Witte, 1937; Pfiffner & Presthus, 1935; Schaeffer, 1953; Willoughby, 1929; Wilson, 1908); *the political, governing, and managerial responsibilities required by public administrative institutions* (Brownlow, 1937; Gulick & Urwick 1937; Pfiffner & Presthus, 1935; Polenberg, 1966; White, 1926; Wilson, 1887); and *bureaucracy* (Downs, 1966; Kaufman, 1977; Merton, 1957; Weber, 1922).

It is disheartening, because we recognize that the work produced by highly influential thinkers and intellectual contributors to the history of American public administration including but not limited to Paul Appleby, Louis Brownlow, John Gaus, Frank Goodnow, Luther Gulick, Herbert Kaufman, Charles Merriam, Frederick Mosher, Herbert Storing, Dwight Waldo, Leonard White, and W.F. Willoughby would likely find their work desk rejected by some of our field's leading academic journals if they were writing today. These scholars all focused on big ideas; ideas that provided extraordinary insight into the affairs of governance. They were not dependent upon big data to create a big idea. They delineated the core concerns and big questions that define public administration and public management and created the theories and theoretical frameworks that continue to guide research and practice even as the contemporary focus on quantitative analysis and the use of big data progresses. Without their ideas the fields of public administration and public management would not have developed as they did; without intellectual space for the introduction and discussion of new ideas of their magnitude, these fields will stagnate. Indeed, it is not unfair to say that today these fields are embraced by narrowness of depth and thinness of breadth that fills journal pages but leaves very little room for big theoretical ideas to take center stage. As Larry Terry often observed, the only numbers you find in Simon's *Administrative Behavior* are for pagination. The qualification of this quantification is insightful and poignant for this conversation.

Constitutions matter. We cannot begin to understand U.S. public administration without first developing a foundation for how natural law and common law underpin the Constitution and the rule of law that govern the American state and its administrative institutions. Although Leonard White (1926) first argued that the study of public administration should begin with a management orientation rather than a legal foundation, after working in the F.D. Roosevelt administration he recognized how unrealistic that recommendation was to both the study and practice of public administrative management. This transformation provides one of the most valuable examples for how practice can inform theory, and exemplifies a very big idea regarding the power to reframe our disciplinary perspectives.

U.S. public administration is oftentimes thought of as operating on a continuum where Dwight Waldo and Herbert Simon anchor each end. Over the past forty years, the field has moved substantially towards Simon's orientation. An important goal of the Constitutional School is to shift the discourse in the direction of Waldo and the intellectual traditions he fully established and brought to the forefront of public administrative theory and research. Waldo emphasizes the need for more focus on what types of norms, values, and behaviors contribute to how the three branches of government shape the modern American administrative state and the processes of democratic governance it engages. As Gary Wamsley (1990) observed more than two decades ago, public administrators make the most influential decisions when they acquire as much information as possible. The same holds true for the intellectual development of our field. The fundamental reason that democratic-constitutionalism and the rule of law form *the* foundational bedrock of public administration is precisely because over time constitutional principles and values become institutionalized in our everyday lives as citizens. This institutionalization is publicly reflected through shared norms, expectations, and values that define rights, create public and private space, and establish multiple forms of mutual accountability (Newbold, 2014). As such, it is not just court cases and laws that we must examine and understand, but it is the institutionalization of broad constitutional tradition that requires us to incorporate and rely on sociology, the arts and humanities, and the natural sciences to help explain how these values reflect and change the public meaning of citizenship, roles, and expectations, all of which govern the relationship between leaders and followers, government and citizens, public agencies and the individuals they serve (Newbold, 2014, p. 17).

The Constitutional School of U.S. Public Administration works to create the space needed for scholars and practitioners to come together and analyze, debate, refute, and create common understandings that are focused on a variety of topics relating to democratic-constitutional traditions. It also helps us to explain how and why our values and preferences for governance might be changing. Not everyone has to agree with the perspectives of scholars associated with the Constitutional School and what they advocate. There are certainly competing ideas and analytical approaches within this school of thought regarding which democratic norms and values should inform practice and how. The field does, however, have to take the Constitutional School seriously. It deserves to be engaged substantively and intellectually. For as James Madison noted more than 200 years ago in *Federalist 51*: "The interest of the man must be connected to the constitutional rights of the place" (Cooke, 1961, p. 349). The Constitutional School anchors public administration precisely where the American framers wanted it to reside—within the rule and philosophy of law.

References

Appleby, P. 1948. *Big democracy*. New York: Knopf.

Brownlow, L., Gulick, L. & Merriam, C. 1937. *The President's Committee on Administrative Management*. Washington, DC: U.S. Government Printing Office.

Cooke, J.E. (ed.) 1961. *The Federalist*. Middletown, CT: Wesleyan University Press.

Downs, A. 1966. *Inside bureaucracy*. Boston, MA: Little, Brown.

Gaus, J.M. 1950. Trends in the theory of public administration. *Public administration review* 31(2): 161–168.

Goodnow, F.J. 1900. *Politics and administration: A study in government*. New York: Russell and Russell.

Gulick, L. & Urwick, L. 1937. *Papers on the science of administration*. New York: Institute of Public Administration.

Hart, J. & Witte, E.E. 1937. *The exercise of rule-making power and the preparation of proposed legislative measures by administrative departments*. Washington, DC: President's Committee on Administrative Management.

Kaufman, H. 1969. Administrative decentralization and political power. *Public administration review* 29(1): 3–15.

Kaufman, H. 1977. *Red tape: Its origins, uses, and abuses*. Washington, DC: Brookings Institution Press.

Merton, R.K. 1957. *Social theory and social structure*. New York: Free Press.

Mosher, F.C. 1968. *Democracy and the public service*. New York: Oxford University Press.

Mosher, F.C. 1976. *Basic documents of American public administration, 1776–1950*. New York: Holms and Meier.

Newbold, S.P. 2010. Toward a Constitutional School for American public administration. *Public administration review* 70: 538–546.

Newbold, S.P. 2011. No time like the present: Making rule of law and constitutional competence the theoretical and practical foundation for public administration graduate education curriculum. *Journal of public affairs education* 17(4): 465–481.

Newbold, S.P. 2014. Why a constitutional approach matters for advancing new democratic governance. In D.F. Morgan & B.J. Cook (eds), *New public governance: A regime centered approach*. Armonk, NY: M.E. Sharpe, pp. 13–22.

Newbold, S.P. & Rosenbloom, D.H. 2014. Rethinking doctoral education in the age of new democratic governance. In D.F. Morgan & B.J. Cook (eds), *New public governance: A regime centered approach*. Armonk, NY: M.E. Sharpe, pp. 284–298.

Pfiffner, J.M. & Presthus, R. 1935. *Public administration.* New York: Ronald Press Company.

Polenberg, R. 1966. *Reorganizing Roosevelt's government 1936–1939: The controversy over executive reorganization.* Cambridge, MA: Harvard University Press.

Schaeffer, W.G. 1953. Management in the judiciary. *Public administration review* 13: 89–96.

Selznick, P. 1957. *Leadership in administration: A sociological interpretation.* Berkeley: University of California Press.

Simon, H.A. 1946. *Administrative behavior: A study of decision-making processes in administrative organizations.* New York: Free Press.

Simon, H.A. 1991. *Models of my life.* Boston, MA: MIT Press.

Storing, H.J. (ed.) 1962. *Essays on the scientific study of politics.* New York: Holt, Rinehart and Winston, Inc.

Storing, H.J. (ed.) 1970. *What country have I? The political writings by Black Americans.* New York: St. Martin's Press.

Storing, H.J. 1981a. *What the Anti-Federalists were for: The political thought of the opponents of the Constitution.* Chicago, IL: University of Chicago Press.

Storing, H.J. 1981b. *The Anti-Federalist: Writings by the opponents of the Constitution.* Chicago, IL: University of Chicago Press.

Strauss, L. & Cropsey, J. 1963. *History of political philosophy.* Chicago, IL: University of Chicago Press.

Waldo, D. 1948. *The administrative state.* New York: Ronald Press.

Wamsley, G.L. (ed.) 1990. *Refounding public administration.* Newbury Park, CA: Sage.

Weber, M. 1922. *Essays in sociology.* New York: Oxford University Press.

White, L.D. 1926. *Introduction to the study of public administration.* New York: MacMillan.

White, L.D. 1948. *The Federalists: A study in administrative history.* New York: MacMillan Company.

White, L.D. 1951. *The Jeffersonians: A study in administrative history 1801–1829.* New York: MacMillan Company.

White, L.D. 1954. *The Jacksonians: A study in administrative history 1829–1961.* New York: MacMillan Company.

White, L.D. 1958. *The Republican Era: A study in administrative history 1869–1901.* New York: MacMillan Company.

Willoughby, W.F. 1929. *Principles of judicial administration.* Washington, DC: Brookings Institution Press.

Wilson, W. 1887. The study of administration. *Political science quarterly*, 2, 197–222.

Wilson, W. 1908. *Constitutional government in the United States.* New York: Columbia University Press.

Index

CPSIA information can be obtained
at www.ICGtesting.com
Printed in the USA
LVHW082158201020
669344LV00003B/12

9 781466 567252